TEAMS
TEAMWORK &
TEAMBUILDING

TEAMS
TEAMWORK & TEAMBUILDING

The Manager's Complete Guide to
TEAMS in Organisations

KENNETH STOTT ● ALLAN WALKER

PRENTICE HALL

New York London Toronto Sydney Tokyo Singapore

First published 1995 by
Prentice Hall
Simon & Schuster (Asia) Pte Ltd
Alexandra Distripark
Block 4, #04-31
Pasir Panjang Road
Singapore 0511

Cover photograph by Kay Chernush and The Image Bank

Permissions are gratefully acknowledged for the use of quoted material from
the following: *Human Resource Management: Concepts and Perspectives,*
edited by V. Anantaraman, L. Chong, S. Richardson and C. Tan, copyright © 1984
by Singapore University Press (Pte) Ltd; *Team Management: Leadership by
Consensus* by Richard Wynn and Charles W. Guditus, reprinted with the
permission of Macmillan College Publishing Company, copyright © 1984 by
Macmillan College Publishing Company, Inc.

Printed in Singapore

3 4 5   99 98 97 96

ISBN 0-13-606005-6

Prentice-Hall International (UK) Limited, *London*
Prentice-Hall of Australia Pty. Limited, *Sydney*
Prentice-Hall Canada Inc., *Toronto*
Prentice-Hall Hispanoamericana, S.A., *Mexico*
Prentice-Hall of India Private Limited, *New Delhi*
Prentice-Hall of Japan, Inc., *Tokyo*
Editora Prentice-Hall do Brasil, Ltda., *Rio de Janeiro*
Prentice-Hall, Inc., *Englewood Cliffs, New Jersey*

CONTENTS

Section 2

THE INDIVIDUAL TEAM MEMBER

<hr>

Section 3

THE TASK

<hr>

Section 4

THE TEAM

━━━━━━━━━━━━━━━━━━━ Section 5 ━━━━━━━━━━━━━━━━━━━

THE ORGANISATION

━━━━━━━━━━━━━━━━━━━ Section 6 ━━━━━━━━━━━━━━━━━━━

TEAM GROWTH AND DEVELOPMENT

PREFACE

THIS IS a book about teams, teamwork and the development of teams. We have tried to provide a comprehensive guide to many issues relating to teams, but the focus of the book is essentially on improvement. The major part of the text is concerned with how managers, team leaders, team members and other interested individuals might engage strategies that facilitate development and improvement.

The central tenets of the book are as follows:

1. Development has more than one dimension. There may be scope for improvement in a wide range of areas, which relate to individuals, the task, the team, and the organisation.
2. Development should take place only in those aspects of operation where it is needed.
3. All the above areas (individuals, task, team and organisation) should be considered. A weakness in one area can critically affect performance in other areas.
4. Teams are unlikely to succeed unless there is real support and commitment from the top of the organisation, and this may require some radical rethinking about the systems and processes used.

Adding something new to what many colleagues said was a saturated field in terms of publications was a daunting thought, but it was apparent when scanning the bookshop shelves that much of the available material in the area of team development is intuitive in its approach and fails to explain the contributory concepts fully. This is where our text enters the scene. We have included detailed explanations of what we consider the more important items of conceptual material and included a number of areas largely ignored in other texts. For example, the chapter on 'Influencing' explains the conceptual foundation of the skill and provides advice on how individuals might increase their competence. While we have drawn extensively on a broad range of literature items, we have exercised caution in accepting without reservation all assertions and claims about the supposedly 'right' way to do things. Despite this, in the absence of rigorous research, it has been necessary to accept many items of common wisdom and expedient to draw on the writings and experiences of respected and scholarly colleagues.

What made the task even more daunting was the fact that this book was always intended for what are normally considered two discrete markets: students of management and busy practitioners. It is generally assumed that one can write in a serious mode for the former, supporting arguments with rigorous evaluation, while the latter demands a lighter 'simply tell them how to do it' approach. This seems somewhat patronising to those practitioners who take their profession seriously and, in the case of this book, want to gain a greater understanding of the whole issue of organisational teams. We believe we have written in such a way as to appeal to all who are interested in the subject of this text. For those who wish to support academic study, we have provided extensive references and a relatively comprehensive bibliography. For the manager seeking sound practical advice, we have suggested effective practice throughout the text, and reinforced this by including a summary of the implications for managers at the end of each major section.

We are indebted to those who have helped us in one way or another to assemble our ideas and write this book. Particular gratitude must be expressed to Jerene Tan of Prentice Hall, Singapore, who encouraged us to take on the project, and her colleague Ang Lee Ming who has worked closely with us throughout the project; to Michael Heng, Managing Director and Principal Consultant of Mikros Management Consultants for sharing his extensive knowledge of human resource management with us; Doug McGuffick for his assistance with the chapter on 'Team Roles'; and Andrea and Kim who have been supportive of our efforts. To all these, we are immensely grateful.

INTRODUCTION

FOR SOME, the topic of teams in organisations is of only peripheral concern. However, it is worth noting Blanchard's (1988: 6) comments: "Most managers spend no less than 50 percent – and possibly as much as 90 percent – of their working time in some type of group activity. Groups or teams are the backbones of organizations. They can produce more and better solutions to problems than individuals can."

Whether the figures are accurate or not is of no real concern. The evidence to date is fairly conclusive: teams are capable of outstanding performance and they must therefore be worth serious consideration. Schutz (1989: 7) claims teamwork "holds all the cachet of a corporate Alladin's Lamp [sic]. With it, anything is possible". As Margerison (1973: 33) notes too, managers need to pay more attention to work groups and their attitudes than to individuals. While these opinions may be slightly overstating the case, many organisations have indeed recognised the immense value of teams and have both expanded their scope of operation and implemented programmes to develop their work. As Chance (1989: 18) notes of the United States: "The traditional, hierarchical structure of corporate America is cracking.

Increasingly, the work of business is being done by semiautonomous teams." He cites several examples. One is the joint venture between General Motors and Toyota, where teams establish their own work and standards, its sequence, the production process, tools and schedules. Another is that of Honeywell, where plant functions, including production, conflict problems, and fund allocation, are all handled by teams.

Other authors (e.g. Teire, 1982: 201) tell of the expanding role of such units as multidisciplinary and project teams. Peterson (1991: 11), former chief executive officer at Ford, supports this expansion and believes that all organisations can make major quality improvements by tapping the power of teamwork: that means, people working together in a positive and nurturing environment.

Even the leaders of those organisations that have not utilised team approaches have tended to acknowledge the benefits of teamwork, and Bradford (1990: 42) suggests that it is only their fears about productivity decreasing or the walls of empires being broken down that has stopped them from proceeding. Wynn and Guditus (1984: 1) claim that interest in the team concept has been one of the most significant developments in management thought and practice. Managers have shown interest in teams, teamwork and teambuilding. Woodcock (1989: 23) indeed explains how teamwork is being increasingly seen as an important subject and how teambuilding is one of the most popular and effective ways of improving organisational health.

Increasing Interest in Teams

How has this upsurge of interest in the use of teams come about? There are many possible answers, but at the root of them is the manager's dilemma, best expressed in two key questions: First, how does the manager mobilise the energy and talent of organisational members to achieve the organisation's goals? Second, how is a climate established in which there is commitment, involvement and high performance? (Ends and Page, 1977: 187.) Solving these problems has inevitably led to a realisation of the considerable benefits of people working together and drawing on their collective capabilities. It has also resulted in a recognition that people are the most important resource, and that using the pool of knowledge and experience in a productive way leads to improvements in products and services quality.

Graham (1991: 31) too notes that attitudes have changed. The autocratic stereotype has been replaced by a notion of the manager as team leader and 'transformer', with a belief that working together to achieve results is a model for modern times.

> The emphasis has moved from getting, by order, the most out of individuals to that of creating the conditions in which they, as parts of the group and of their own volition, will want to give of their best. The new managerial mode requires changes in perception and a subtle understanding of the dynamics involved in group-work.

The importance of effective interaction is nowhere better illustrated than in an account of teamwork amongst hospital staff (Horak *et al.*, 1991: 65). Drawing on a 1986 study, they conclude: "Differences in mortality in intensive care units are directly influenced by the level of involvement and interaction between physicians and nurses." It is easy to accept the link between teamwork and effectiveness in such dramatic situations, but it appears to be less easy to support the linkage in others for some organisations.

Such organisations may actually believe that teamwork is adequate, even when it barely exists. Expressions such as 'we have a good team of people here' may represent a gross distortion of reality. But how does one detect imperfections in teamwork? Woodcock (1989: 11) provides some clues in identifying some symptoms of what he calls bad teamwork. These include frustration, little inspiration, lack of commitment and motivation, grumbling and retaliation, unhealthy competition, back-biting and rivalry between departments, and jockeying for organisational position, influence or perks. This list is not exhaustive, but it indicates just some of the dysfunctional behaviours that can occur. Part of the challenge in development, therefore, is to transform these into positive and supportive behaviours in order that teams might operate effectively.

Innovative Environments

The team approach is probably more important in the environment that requires innovation than any other. That is why high-technology operations strongly promote team approaches. Some organisations have to process complex and confusing information; they may operate in frequently changing technological and market conditions, and they have to adapt to these changes; in order to survive they must become innovative. As Jacobs and Everett (1988: 15) note: "Developing genuine teams is a prerequisite for productive and innovative environments." And Peterson

(1991: 89) claims that companies using the creativity of teamwork to find new ways of doing things will be profitable and the leaders of the future.

Such environments throw up new challenges to organisations. They require teams from a variety of disciplines and functions. They may also involve team members from different organisational units, each with different needs, backgrounds, interests and expertise, and the challenge is to transform this diversity into an integrated whole so that both team and organisational objectives can be pursued (Thamhain, 1990: 7).

Teams at All Levels

It would be a mistake, however, to believe that teamwork is relevant only to such organisational environments. It is becoming increasingly important to a wide range of operations. It also applies to all levels of the organisation. As Maddux (1989: 16) observes, it is just as important for top executives as it is to middle management, supervisors and shop-floor workers. Poor teamwork at any level or between levels can seriously impede organisational effectiveness and may, in some cases, contribute to organisational demise.

Wynn and Guditus (1984: 19) discuss the need to have teamwork throughout the organisation as a way of releasing human energy in constructive ways rather than stemming and controlling it. Having a successful team approach at the top means that there is a focal point for team effort and that decision making, where it counts initially, is of acceptable quality. But the management team needs to look at team management in order to fully utilise resources in the rest of the organisation.

Development

When discussing teams and their role in organisational life, the issue of development becomes preeminent. The dynamic of teams is essentially a simple one: Individuals affect other individuals in the group and are reciprocally affected by them (Graham, 1991: 33). The key question in looking at development then is: How might these dynamics be used to affect team performance positively? The understanding of dynamics, therefore, is crucial to development efforts. Through observation and experiment, it is possible to learn how team members interact, and we can use the knowledge to promote more effective interactions, so that the team's work can be completed successfully. Reciprocal interactions – or the dynamic – is really the creative factor in any team operation (p. 34).

Effective team management is inseparable from development. Since most teams start off as a collection of individuals, each seeking varying levels of power, recognition and autonomy, there is obviously scope for progression. This means that team members have to develop teamwork skills. Indeed, in looking at how teams might develop, we mention skill acquisition frequently in this book. But what do we mean by skill development? Ends and Page (1977: 117) define it as "the dynamic process by which knowledge, experience, and ability are blended and applied in real-world situations to produce some desired result". It is important to note that we are concerned with the scene of real activity, and we therefore emphasise the need for teams to improve in the workplace. While we support many of the various forms of intervention that focus on development by taking teams and individuals away from the workplace, it is the real situation that matters, and many of the efforts at team development can be applied in that situation.

Talk about skill has inevitably resulted in many writers making the sports analogy, comparing teams in the workplace to teams on the field or court. In some ways, this can be useful. In others, it is highly simplistic. It is true that we see attributes in sports teams that are desirable in any form of organisational endeavour, things like cameraderie, commitment to goals, sacrifice, disciplined coordination, and strong cooperation. But there are also differences. The sports team has clear goals and usually directive leadership. To equate modern complex organisations, and their diverse and often ambiguous goals, with teams out to win a game of football would be a misleading parallel to draw. One point to note that is common, however, is the need to grow and develop in order to meet the considerable demands and challenges teams face in their respective spheres.

Organisation of the Book

The book is divided into six sections. The first and last cover general issues, while Sections 2–5 deal with four areas of development . We have called these areas 'dimensions' and suggest that diagnosis and action within these dimensions will set teams on the path to total, rather than partial, development. The concept of dimensions will be explained in detail in a later chapter, but it is worth stating briefly at this stage how we understand team development.

Unlike many writers and consultants, we see little point in improving features that need no improvement, nor in ignoring very real needs for development. For example, while a teambuilding 'expert' may dwell, by preference, on improvements in communication and interpersonal relationships, the team's real need may be for learning how to make full use of individual abilities or how to motivate individual team members. Like the physician, whose diagnostic skills are of critical importance, the team developer too must diagnose where the true needs lie.

This draws attention to the fact that there are different needs. We have chosen to identify four areas or 'dimensions', and these may help in understanding where the focus of development efforts should be directed. We must emphasize, however, that the framework is an aid to understanding and analysis, and the dimensions must not be seen as entirely discrete. Essentially, Sections 2–5 are concerned with how teams might develop their competence and effectiveness by considering one or a combination of these dimensions:

1. The individual team member
2. The team's task
3. The team itself
4. The team in the broader organisation

First, however, **Section 1** looks at some important general issues in relation to teams in organisations, teamwork, and development. In Chapter 1 we look at the environment within which modern organisations must operate and examine the part the organisational environment plays in determining the relevance of the team approach. It is suggested in the literature that changing, unpredictable, turbulent and volatile contexts for organisations lead to the need for involvement and collaboration. These conditions are most likely to emerge from strategies that employ team management. There are many other factors, however, that are seen as giving rise to an increased recognition of the need for teamwork, and the literature is quite conclusive in asserting that team management has a considerable role to play in the present day organisational context.

In the second part of the chapter we attempt to answer the most obvious question: What is a team? While there are many common themes in the literature, there is far from total agreement on how to define a team as compared with a group. Nevertheless, we try to offer a definition that provides a basis for considering development.

Chapter 2 looks at the many types of teams that may exist in an organisation. We examine the typical work of top management teams, mid-management teams, project teams and task forces, and work groups. An interesting development of work groups has been the proliferation of teams at all levels of organisations which are given the opportunity to contribute ideas and expertise for the good of their organisations. We therefore discuss the extended use of the familiar quality control circles, some derivatives of such teams, and probably the most advanced form to date of empowered team management – self-managing teams.

Chapter 3 first considers the characteristics of effective teams and the key ingredients identified in the literature. The purposes that teams might serve are then examined and viewed from two perspectives, namely, the organisation and the individual. An attempt is made to identify the benefits that teams might provide. In this area, the literature provides a comprehensive list of advantages of employing team approaches. Finally, the issue of performance is examined from the perspective of driving forces and blockages. In relation to performance, the notions of quality and synergy are also briefly explored.

Chapter 4 moves on to the topic that is central to this book, that of total team development. As relevant background, we explain the concepts of Organisation Development and Teambuilding, and, in the case of the latter, the various models that are commonly used are described.

We then examine research which has been conducted into team development in an attempt to identify what works and what does not. The research into teambuilding is largely inconclusive. Indeed, comparatively little rigorous inquiry has been conducted in attempting to explain how team development interventions might impact on the workplace. Much of what has been recorded is very much anecdotal or based on supportive participant evaluations immediately following training events. We suggest, therefore, that it may be advisable to improve the quality of research, but, at the same time, to respect the diversity of approach which is characteristic of teambuilding interventions and avoid over-limiting the scope of the development concept.

We continue Chapter 4 by highlighting some problems with team development and look briefly at intra- and inter-team development. We also mention a development strategy that has enjoyed widespread popularity in recent years, that of Outdoor Management Development.

We then come to the central part of the chapter, the introduction and explanation of a multidimensional model of team development. Several propositions associated with the model are stated, and the specific items for consideration which form the basis of this book are identified.

Section 2 considers the important notion of the individual in the team and a range of related issues. It has been suggested that, in an age when the cause of the individualist is pursued vigorously, people need to suppress their tendency to behave as individuals and discipline themselves to abide by the standards of the teams in which they serve. It is true that cooperative effort is more productive than individual effort. At the same time, it has to be recognised that teams which treat their members as individuals are more likely to be successful than those that see their memberships as mere resources without identity. Adair (1986: 57) draws attention to this paradox of modern life. It is "that while the claims of individuality are more frequently and more vociferously voiced than ever before, we are organising ourselves more busily along lines that suppress individuality. In one group after another we are being persuaded, cajoled, trapped or pressured into suppressing our initiative, judgement and responsibility."

The section starts appropriately with a chapter on one of the more critical issues of team management, that of motivation. The concept of motivation is examined, and a framework is advanced that might help in elevating motivational levels amongst team members. It involves developing a rudimentary understanding of motivation theory, accepting that there is mutual responsibility in the team for increasing motivation, identifying individual members' needs and the factors that support motivation for them as individuals, and acting consciously to improve the climate for motivation.

The related issue of commitment is also examined, followed by another prime indicator of motivation, that of attitudes. Having team members with the right attitudes is of obvious importance, and this is particularly true at times of major change. With that in mind, after a brief look at the role of expectations as a complex form of attitudes, the issue of attitude to change is examined, and suggestions are made about how appropriate attitudes might be developed and supported.

Are individuals considered as mere numbers to make up a full team – a form of token participation – or are they used as highly valued resources with potentially useful abilities and worthwhile contributions to make? These obviously represent perspectives that are diametrically opposed. If the team is to be genuinely productive, it is suggested in Chapter 6 that an environment that supports individual ability and talent has to be created, and that developing ability is an integral part of team growth. We also look at the basic tenets of adult learning and how this may affect the development of individual resources. The chapter also covers the issue of participation, and considers its extent and scope.

Section 3 is concerned primarily with two major development strategies for improving task accomplishment. Chapter 7, following a discussion of issues relating to team goals, concentrates on laying out a system of setting targets. Target Management is a useful way of approaching the goal setting process, and ensures a high degree of specificity. Some of the benefits and drawbacks are identified, and advice is given on writing target statements.

Chapter 8 explains a systematic way of dealing with team tasks and goes through a series of seven stages in detail. The scheme focuses predominantly on planning activity and provides specific activities that ensure the process is comprehensive, coherent and systematic. It also covers the stages of implementation and review. In essence, it is argued that adopting a systematic approach facilitates planning and ensures that efforts and skills are appropriately harnessed for task completion.

Section 4 looks at a wide range of issues connected with the team and its operation. One of the topics most widely written about is that of leadership; this forms the subject of discussion in Chapter 9. It is difficult to separate team leadership from leadership in the organisation generally, since many of the issues involved are similar. For that reason, we have provided an overview of leadership theory, including some of the more recent developments, and commented on their relevance to the team leadership role. We also present a comprehensive model that acts as a useful guide to the sorts of actions team leaders can take, and we discuss three important related issues: the leader's role, skills and team leadership style.

Chapter 10 addresses the fascinating topic of behavioural roles and suggests it is not sufficient to consider only the functional expertise individuals bring with them to the team. Of great importance are the sets of preferred behaviours and how these might combine to ensure tasks are processed effectively. For example, a high-performing team may need one or more members to be idea generators, and others to critically evaluate those ideas. These are just two of several roles that can go together to lead to success. The chapter draws on the highly regarded work of Meredith Belbin and outlines nine distinctive roles. It also deals with the notion of an 'ideal' team and offers advice on how an effective unit might be put together. People can learn to develop their preferred roles to support the team, or, in some cases, they can adopt other roles that are considered necessary. With this in mind, we provide guidelines on how each of the nine roles might be developed.

Chapter 11 deals briefly with the broad topics of communication and relationships. Feedback and coaching processes are also covered and, in examining the issue of interpersonal relationships, we discuss the need to establish high levels of trust and openness.

A special case of communication is addressed in detail in Chapter 12, that of influencing. The ability to determine the behaviour of others is a vital skill in teams, because it comprises a set of strategies that have high potential for successful outcomes. Such success can be evaluated through compliance, commitment and the maintenance of healthy relationships. Seven strategies are discussed, and it is suggested that the successful influencer develops skill in at least several of them, knows which one to use at any given time, and has considerable skill in marshalling arguments and reasoning things out. The chapter acts as a challenge to those who believe the application of a single strategy in any situation will guarantee success.

Whether or not it is desired, conflict is an inevitable part of team life, and it can be either destructive or constructive. Chapter 13 looks at the common causes of conflict and a set of strategies for dealing with it. The strategies are avoiding, accommodating, competing, compromising, and collaborating. We suggest the collaborative approach can be a highly productive strategy and we provide an outline for using the strategy to maximum effect. The issue of conflict between teams is also discussed.

Chapter 14 examines in detail the topic of decision making in teams. A typology of decisions is presented, followed by a description of several decision-making models. We then look at the process itself, starting with an explanation of how problems might be identified and analysed. We also examine in detail the significant issues of who should be involved in decisions and the criteria that might be used to determine such involvement. The process of consensus is also addressed in detail, followed by a discussion on dissent and the part it might play in ensuring decision quality. We then move on to the part of the process in which options are generated, and this takes us into a detailed examination of creativity and some of the strategies and techniques that might be used to enhance or support it. We consider how the various alternatives can be evaluated, and finally explain how to make the decision. It is suggested that serious attention needs to be given to each part of the process if the team is to reach decisions characterised by quality.

Team meetings are the focus of attention in Chapter 15. We look at different types of meetings and the purposes for which they are used. In considering developing team meetings into effective events, advice is given on the actions to be taken before, during and after the meeting. We also address the issues of the leader's role and the setting of conducive conditions.

Chapter 16 discusses a range of important issues which may have received only limited attention in previous chapters. Several of these issues are part of the vocabulary associated with teamwork, and we attempt to explain them and their relevance to developing effectiveness. The discussion of the responsibility teams might take collectively is followed by an explanation of four issues, namely, coordination, cooperation, competition, and cohesiveness. The notion of cohesiveness, in particular, has received much attention in the teams literature, and in defining it, we also show how it can be a powerful force for performance and, applied inappropriately, possibly a barrier to true effectiveness. Conformity can be seen in the same light, both a blessing and a curse, and this is part of our discussion of norms and values and how they might be used to support production-oriented behaviour. The final issue, membership, which addresses questions about balance and heterogeneity is preceded by a review of what the literature has to say about the ideal size of teams, a topic of interest to researchers and writers, but one that seems to have been ignored by many practitioners.

Section 5, while comparatively short in relation to the previous section, raises equally important issues. Indeed, the subject of concern, namely support from the organisation for team operation, is arguably of critical importance. Without a commitment from the top of the organisation and an infrastructure for teamwork, all efforts at development are wasted. What is the point in developing the task capabilities of self-managing teams, for instance, if they are not allowed to really manage themselves? The sorts of team involvement that are being talked about at the present day more than ever need full organisational support and commitment. Chapter 17 takes up the issue of support and stresses the need for a supportive structure and climate. The organisation must also decide if it wants to encourage teamwork or individualism, and the reward system is likely to reflect the way it approaches those orientations. If teamwork is the key, reward systems may have to be radically altered. Support is needed not just for teams but also for their development, and this may necessitate organisations ensuring that all development efforts tie in with improvement in the real setting – the workplace.

In Chapter 18, we look at the issue of culture and its impact on teams. We begin by examining briefly the concept of organisational culture and its influence on team functioning. We also look at subcultures which may exist within teams themselves. The focus then changes from organisational to national or ethnic culture. In terms of development, the possibilities may be moderated by the prior experiences and cultural backgrounds of team members. Some, for example, may desire highly directive leadership and react badly to conditions of openness and trust that are so widely promoted. Similarly, some members may not be able to cope with conditions of uncertainty and ambiguity. These problems have become more evident in recent years, as many teams have acquired memberships with a diverse cultural mix, due in part to globalisation strategies. This obviously has implications for team builders and leaders, and some advice is given, therefore, on actions that can be taken to accommodate these different backgrounds.

The final chapter suggests teams may go through a series of stages before they mature into competent outfits. This view is widely supported in the literature. The progression, however, may be an erratic one. It is generally accepted that, in most cases, teams that can reach a stage of maturity in which they show signs of competence are more likely to be effective than immature teams. With that in mind, we suggest strategies for helping teams to progress. At the same time, we warn against the dreaded malady of 'groupthink', which can make a seemingly mature team highly ineffective.

The challenge of developing teams and teamwork is a fascinating one, well expressed by Schutz (1989: 7): "Until now, we have been essentially mystified by the dynamics of how teams can operate without the bugaboos of sabotage, hidden agendas and internal politics. Producing a reliable method for creating teams that are highly effective, mutually supportive, and motivated over time has challenged the best and the brightest." We hope we can make in this text at least a minor contribution to helping work teams and organisations meet that challenge.

Finally, in our book *Making Management Work*, we emphasized time and time again the importance of people in the organisation. The manager manages people, not machines. The leader leads a group of people. And it is people who comprise teams and enable them sometimes to make the most remarkable achievements. Weisbord (1985: 28) makes this very point. He explains that there was a missing link in his thinking: he was managing a team of people, not a set of outcomes. He thought he was managing computer system technology, but in fact there was a set of teamwork issues about which he knew nothing. It is fitting we end this introduction, but begin the book, with a quote from someone who knows just how important it is to cherish the most precious organisational resource:

> If you look at the writings of various religions and of great leaders such as Abraham Lincoln and Martin Luther King, Jr, you'll see a common pattern of deep concern for people – and a desire to give them a chance to live meaningful lives. In business, we seem to lose sight of that, and to forget how much inherent potential each human being has. If given a sense of importance, a reason to take pride in their work, people will accomplish marvellous things. And they'll feel pretty good about themselves (Peterson, 1991: 11).

Section 1

Teams in Organisations

1

THE MODERN SETTING FOR TEAMS

THE FOCUS of this book is teams, and how their effectiveness can be improved through conscious development. In this first chapter we attempt to lay the background to explain why we (and many others) believe correctly formed and utilised teams may be vital for continuing organisational effectiveness, especially in times of substantial change. First, we look at the environment of modern organisations and examine the part the broader organisational environment plays in determining the relevance and necessity of the team approach. Using the literature, we suggest that unpredictable, constantly changing organisational contexts increase the necessity of collaboration, cooperation and involvement, and that these conditions are most likely to emerge from strategies that employ team management and teamwork. We note other factors which seem to indicate an increased need for teamwork and assert that team management has an important role to play in the present day organisational context.

In the second section of the chapter we try to define a team, to answer the question: What is a team? We find little total agreement to answer this question succinctly, but identify a definition that at least provides a basis for considering team development.

Teams and the Changing Environment

Much has been written about the changing face of the environment in which organisations must operate. You will find little argument from any quarter that organisations need to change. As we shall see, many of the important moves for revitalising organisations revolve around people and changing notions of why and how we work, and what we work with.

Harris and Harris (1989: 28) describe the characteristics of emerging 'work' cultures:

> Among the principal ones are the desire for more autonomy and control over their [workers'] work space, for more organisational communication and information, for more participation and involvement in the enterprise, for more meaningful and synergistic organisational relations, for more creative/ high performance norms and standards, for improved productivity ... and for more emphasis on enhanced quality of work life and enterpreneuralism.

They add: "Strategies which employ team management make the achievement of such goals feasible."

The same authors suggest that new corporate cultures should employ a variety of approaches to encourage teamwork and improved performance, believing that "team management offers the most viable format for leverage" (p. 29). These are worth listing here as they provide much of the rationale for teams and will continue to surface throughout the book. Organisations should:

- create supportive and creative environments which motivate workers to energise themselves;
- encourage mutual goal setting with specific performance targets;
- provide positive behaviour reinforcement and constructive feedback;
- provide meaningful work and career development opportunities;
- encourage innovation by capitalising on employee conflicts and differences, instead of seeking conformity.

There is little doubt that the notion of teams and teamwork has generated considerable interest in future-oriented organisations. This interest has been stimulated by several forces significantly changing the face of business and society. Among these are the increasingly recognised dysfunctions in traditional bureaucratic models of organisations, globalisation, recessed economies, the apparent success of participative approaches in Japanese and American industries, and the emerging evidence from research which is showing strong support for employee participation. In 1987, Dyer wrote:

> The role of the manager has changed significantly in many organizations. The strong manager capable of almost single handedly turning around the organization or department, while still a folk hero in the eyes of many, has given way to recent demands of increasingly complex systems for managers who are able to pull together people of diverse backgrounds, personalities, training, and experience and weld them into an effective working group (p. xi).

The most widely proposed reason for the proliferation of teams and the expansion of team management approaches is that changes in the environment within which organisations must operate are dictating innovative approaches. In 1984 John Naisbitt predicted a number of general trends for the 1980s which included moves from centralisation towards decentralisation, from representative democracy towards participatory democracy, and communication and control in hierarchies towards networking. Whereas all Naisbitt's predictions have not transpired to the same extent, the three mentioned have been manifested in most organisations and will almost certainly continue to shape them in the 1990s and beyond. When discussing the future for Australian business, Loton (1991: 30) suggested that managers of the future will need to continue on the track of a less directive management style: "With greater responsibility vested in employees, the manager's task becomes one of providing appropriate training and building confidence rather than direct management of daily tasks." These trends and predictions point towards the greater utilisation of teams for continued success, or even survival.

Robinson (1990: 37), discussing the manager's role in the changing environment of the 1990s comments:

> Leaders in the 1990s will both participate in and encourage teams and teamwork. The information age requires synergy that results when several people, focused on a common goal, work in a collaborative manner. When employees work this way, more is accomplished than could ever be done by them working independently. Leaders must model and coach for this collaborative approach to work.

The changing face of management constantly reflects moves towards collaboration, cooperation and teams. This move was summed up nicely by the chief executive officer of a major Australian-based multinational organisation who stated: "I no longer run a tight ship: I run a tight flotilla"

(Limerick *et al.*, 1985: 32). Walker (1991: 8) further explains the metaphor: "In these words did he typify the collaborative individualism which marks the management of so many private and public organisations." The expression 'a tight flotilla' conjures up images of organisations consisting of collections of collaborative teams.

In a study conducted for the Australian Institute of Management in 1985, Limerick and his colleagues interviewed chief executive officers (CEOs) from fifty key Australian corporations and government departments to seek their views on what made the most successful organisations. The researchers were struck by the number of references to the importance of self-expression by, and collaboration among, individuals. Limerick *et al.* (1985: 32–3) write:

> The more we thought about this the more astonishing it became. We went back over the transcripts and interviews and became uncomfortably aware of the fact that our CEOs had been telling us something important and subtle, but that we had simply not heard it .... While our CEOs had not mentioned the word 'teamwork' throughout the interview, in fact many of them had taken it as a 'prior assumed' in their answers on effectiveness. But in any case many were uncomfortable with the traditional use of the word 'teamwork'. They put this in a number of different ways, but with the same basic thrust ... I want a team of individuals.

They conclude:

> Cooperative individualism has not left behind teamwork: it has built upon it. It does not deny autonomy – it asserts and conditions it. It speaks not of a bias for action, but a bias for proaction, organisationally responsible proaction which asserts independence and accountability, which asserts cooperation while it (also) asserts individual transforming leadership.

Similarly, a major study conducted in the UK and other European countries was bounded by the premise that management and organisations of the future face unprecedented rapid and complex change (Barham *et al.*, 1988: 5). Among the valuable findings of the study were several that relate to the greater utilisation of teams. First, the study concurred with what we mention frequently throughout the book: people are the key. "Many of the firms interviewed are clearly aware of the importance of exploiting new technology and of trying to maintain technological leadership. Some of them, however, also believe that ultimately all firms could have access to similar technology. It is people who will make the difference" (Barham *et al.*, 1988: 5). In line with this, the researchers found that one of the strongest emerging patterns was that companies of the future would need to involve and consult frequently with employees and that one of the best ways to achieve this was through quality circles – a type of team.

Other themes emerging from the research reflected the need for organisational cultures characterised by open dialogue, informal communication, a reappraisal of status and class in organisations, and trust and love. The researchers also predicted continuing moves towards horizontal and away from vertical management structures and that managers need to be capable of dealing with, and in, various project and work teams (p. 38; also see Dunphy and Stace, 1990: 46; and Miller and Longair, 1985: 3) . When describing the changes managers will need to deal with, they include "unprecedented emphasis on people and talent as the organisation's most precious resources, on the need to utilize human resources fully and on the need to draw out people's commitment" (Barham *et al.*, 1988: 37). They suggest that managers need to possess what they label 'doing' skills such as decision making and consensus, communicating, negotiating, motivating, listening, involving people at all levels, counselling and appraisal skill, and delegation (p. 42).

These skills, and indeed the research findings as a whole, point towards greater involvement of all organisational actors – involvement that may best be facilitated through team structures. Research reports and public and private sector policy throughout the globe promote similar contexts. For example, Peters and Waterman (1982) found similar moves towards participatory structures in the US, and governments in Southeast Asian countries, such as Singapore, strongly promote team approaches to management and work.

Anantaraman (1984b: 217), alluding to the need for greater involvement, states that "many organizations are experiencing environmental forces that are rapidly changing and increasingly unpredictable and it appears as if turbulence is now the stable state". Berger (1991: 7) adopts a similar theme in putting a case for inter-departmental team building. He discusses the pressures organisations face to diversify products, respond to competitors and, at the same time, make ever greater economies. He suggests they have to change the way people relate to one another and increase levels of collaboration and planning between organisational subunits.

Rapid change in often unpredictable environmental conditions has forced organisations to reconsider seriously many of the structures and models they have employed traditionally (Maxwell, 1990: 9). Harris

(1986: 28) refers to a set of objectives relevant to the changing organisational context. These include: increased employee autonomy; more communication and information; employee involvement; more meaningful relations with people working together more closely; more creativity and higher performance standards; an increased emphasis on productivity; greater attention to the quality of work life, and an accent on entrepreneurship. "Achievement of these objectives will be most feasible through strategies that employ team management." Concentrating on the productivity theme, Petrock (1990: 9) writes: "Having high quality, high performance natural work teams represents the best way to increase productivity."

Huszczo (1990: 37) focuses on the changing context, but dwells on the need to move away from autocratic styles of management, a stance supported by McLagan (1989: 50) who claims that:

> work structures and design will change dramatically, building on changes that have already begun. Hierarchies will melt into, or be displaced by, flatter and more flexible organisational designs. The boundaries between individual jobs will blur, with more team accountability and flexible, multi-skilled job designs. Autocratic decision structures will give way to more participative modes.

While acknowledging that autocratic styles were successful in past decades, Huszczo (1990: 37) suggests that advanced technology necessitates more employee commitment rather than control and compliance. He also refers to higher levels of competition, and suggests that team approaches are appropriate responses to the situation.

> In encouraging employees to work together, bounce ideas off one another, and come up with solutions to critical problems, organizations are beginning to adopt team strategies to keep up with competition. Competition was and is getting more difficult, and the need for innovation and commitment rather than mere efficiency gains has become apparent.

Massive technological advances have affected and continue increasingly to affect work patterns and structures (Teire, 1982: 201). The work environment is changing considerably through different time scales and shortened product life cycles. These, notes Teire, are putting pressures on organisations to be adaptable and this necessitates new ways of thinking about structures. He suggests that changes in technology increase the potential and usefulness of multi-disciplinary teams and specific project groups. Barry (1991: 31) supports this view, believing that the growth in technology and information has produced large numbers of educated, motivated and self-directed workers who know more in their work area than their managers. He believes that, for these workers to work effectively and efficiently, flexible work structures characterised by high participation are necessary.

It is apparent, then, that organisations are indeed becoming more complex and, as Wynn and Guditus (1984: 8) note, it is not realistic to expect one person to have the wisdom, experience and information to deal confidently with the full range of management tasks. With increased specialisation, "this prompts the need for effective teamwork to coordinate the efforts of those specialists and to facilitate the exchange of information among them". Team approaches, Peterson (1991: 159) suggests, may be particularly appropriate in the present-day service sector environment. Efficiency and quality service may well be the result of a positive atmosphere reflecting processes that allow people to make decisions and offer their experienced input.

Anantaraman (1984b: 218) takes up the organisational context issue and discusses the fact that people themselves have changed. They are better educated and less romantic, and authority has become weakened. Traditional autocratic stances are increasingly being questioned. And like other authors, he sees the use of teams as a logical response to the new environment: "The team approach has become a distinctive style of working, aimed at harnessing the collective talents and energy of people to achieve useful corporate results and, at the same time, respect the needs of the employees." In referring to the formation and extension of senior management teams in particular, Wynn and Guditus (1984: 3) too see it as a rational response, in that senior administrators may see team management as a defence against such challenges to traditional authority, and set up what they consider to be a political alliance which protects their management rights.

As we have seen above, the positive side of change in terms of technological advance and growth is counterbalanced by the less desired effects. Lau (1988: 13), for example, refers to fiscal belt tightening, job insecurity and high stress as characteristics of the era, and emphasizes the importance of imbuing workers with a sense of teamwork and harmony. Barry (1991: 32) perceives the need for teams increasing as companies face an increased level of global and domestic competition and search for ways of rationalising middle-management costs and encouraging more rapid product innovation.

At a practical level, the need to engage cooperative action is fairly obvious. Adair (1986: 96) outlines three task characteristics that demand a group approach. First, the task could be carried out by a single person, but there is insufficient time. Second, the effort required cannot be exerted by one person. Third, several independent operations are required at the same time, but all are needed for the task to be completed. Several of these elements – time, effort, interdependencies – enter our discussion as we look at the broader picture of teams and the reasons for their involvement in organisations.

We are not suggesting that teams are the panacea for all organisational woes. Indeed, not everyone agrees that participation and team approaches provide effective responses. Critics maintain that group activity has a downward levelling effect, that it stunts creativity, and is generally limiting. Others question the claimed consistency between organisational and individual goals and stress the unlikelihood of being able to generate trust and openness in competitive environments, the restrictions on devolving power, the time and effort limitations, and the lack of desire for job enrichment. There also exists considerable literature on the drawbacks of participative decision making, and these have implications for team effectiveness. While these points are worth noting, they tend to represent a view that is not widely shared.

We adhere to the view that the greater utilisation of teams in organisations has always been desirable, but in times of substantial change, they are necessary. This view is not unusual and is strongly supported in the literature. However, there appears to be a tendency to believe that simply putting people together and labelling them as a 'team' is the answer, and we would argue vigorously that this is wrong. To reach the lofty heights commonly demanded of teams, they need to be consciously developed.

Closely tied to the reconsideration of structures during these times of rapid change is the increasingly important role of Human Resource Development. "The accumulated impact of the environmental pressures is an increased demand for all organisations to do more with their Human Resources using less financial and material resources" (Cacioppe et al., 1990: 59). Improvements in both the content and delivery of development opportunities are being called for at all organisational levels. There appears to be a realisation that development programmes need to be more than the traditional 'classroom-based' approaches and that we should concentrate on building collaborative, collegial cultures on an ongoing basis. The underlying message is that all workers must be valued and become committed to the organisation – to feel they are part of a team. If the new

management challenge is seen as a human or
that challenge must be to cater in a more de
development of all organisational actors, both c
collective basis. The book is based on this premise
to this topic later in this section it is necessary to
a team.

Defining a Team

It is difficult to find any two definitions of a team which are identical.
As we saw in the last section, many Australian CEOs sang the praises
of what many people understand as teamwork, without even referring to
the word. If we examine the literature, however, a number of common
elements seem to emerge from various writers. Francis and Young
(1979: 8) describe a team as an "energetic group of people who are
committed to achieving common objectives, who work well together
and enjoy doing so, and who produce high-quality results". Johnson
and Johnson's (1991: 435) definition emphasizes relationships: "A
team is a set of interpersonal relationships structured to achieve
established goals", while Lanza (1985: 47) describes a team as "a group
of individuals working together in which the success of any individual
is dependent on the success of the entire group". The substance of that
definition is supported by Johnson (1986: 48) who sees a team as several
individuals who have to cooperate to fulfil a mission, a definition similar
to that of Adair (1986: vii) who describes a team as "a group in which
the individuals share a common aim and in which the jobs and skills of
each member fit in with those of the others".

Other authors have drawn a parallel with sports teams in their search
for a definition (e.g. Anderson, 1984: 578). Dyer (1977: 4) defines teams
as:

> collections of people who must rely on group collaboration if each member
> is to experience the optimum sense of success and goal achievement. It is
> obvious that in order to score touchdowns (and prevent the opponent from
> scoring) a football team has to play together. It should be just as obvious
> that a work unit or management group must also work together to ensure
> success.

The term used in such contexts may be an arbitrary one and communicate
too simplistic a message. Dyer's definition does, however, through the
terms 'group', 'collection', 'unit' and 'team', introduce some necessary
considerations.

The closely related concepts of 'teams' and 'groups' are often discussed synonymously, although several authors have tried to explain the difference. Hitt (1988: 70), for example, discusses Dyer's definition that teams are "collections of people who must rely on group collaboration if each member is to experience the optimum of success and goal achievement", and points out that not all collections of people meet this requirement. Kezsbom (1990: 51) opines that "a team is a special designation awarded to a group of people who not only share a common goal, but are aware of the very nature of their interdependent roles, and how their respective talents complement their efforts to assure project success". This is similar to Adair's (1986: 95) belief in common task and complementarity amongst contributions as essential elements. Common purpose and interdependencies also feature in Kazemak and Albert's (1988: 108) attempt to show the difference between group and team characteristics: "Groups that function like teams typically have a clear and common purpose. Team members understand where their interdependence on others lies."

Woodcock (1989: 3–4) simply defines a team as a "group of people that share common objectives and who need to work together to achieve them". He attempts to differentiate between teams and groups by suggesting what teams are not:

> A team is not a social gathering where people meet for the purpose of enjoyment, neither is it an 'audience' of people who are assembled to listen and learn. The House of Commons is not a team as its members do not share common objectives. Committees are not usually teams because they comprise people who represent different groups. Often they share concerns but they lack a unified commitment to action (p. 4).

It may be argued, of course, that the search for a distinction is fruitless, since terms such as 'teams' and 'work groups' are used interchangeably anyway. Some writers do not even attempt to distinguish between the two terms. Dunphy (1989), for example, appears to use them interchangeably and refers to team building as a strategy for improving the cohesiveness and effectiveness of various groups. Perhaps he views a team as a group which has gone through an extensive process designed to increase cooperation, participation and effectiveness. Some authors prefer to use 'groups' regardless of the intended function (Mullins, 1985: 188), while Schermerhorn et al. (1991: 235) introduce the word 'teams' only when discussing autonomy and empowerment.

Whilst we accept it is difficult to clearly differentiate in any detailed sense between 'groups' and 'teams', it is worth arriving at a distinction for our purposes here and because of the confusing nature of much of the literature. A satisfactory explanation is that a group comprises two or more people who work together to achieve a goal. A team, therefore, has to go beyond this simple requirement and incorporate features that provide an extension of that simple description.

Anderson's (1984: 578) notion of the team as a specialised unit concerned with specific projects is often shared by those who consider teams primarily in the context of short-term tasks. But this does not explain why terms such as 'senior management team' are widely accepted. Tarkenton (1986: 30) offers a practitioner's definition of the team by focusing on the typical activities of 'teamwork': "Teamwork means that we recognize the value of the members of the team beyond just doing their work, that we want them to become involved in our strategizing. It means pushing the level of creativity and decision making further and further down."

Perhaps the definition that comes closest to our understanding of teams, and one that serves as a basis for development as outlined in this book, is that offered by Harris (1986: 229) who describes a team as

> a workgroup or unit with a common purpose through which members develop mutual relationships for the achievement of goals/tasks. Teamwork, then, implies cooperative and coordinated effort by individuals working together in the interests of their common cause. It requires the sharing of talent and leadership, the playing of multiple roles.

Whatever definition of the team is preferred, and whatever the emphasis, one feature of all such units is that they are all part of an organisational environment in the same way the organisation is part of a wider environment. In the following chapters in this section we examine different types of teams, effective team performance and, central to our main purpose, comprehensive team development.

Summary

In this chapter, we have discussed the difficulty of developing or accepting any single definition of a team. After looking at possible differences between the terms 'group' and 'team', we accepted a definition, but were careful to state that this should not be seen as definitive or restrictive. We have also attempted to highlight the case in favour of the increased use of teams in the present-day environment and we have provided a number of reasons to support this perspective.

2

TYPES OF ORGANISATIONAL TEAMS

IN CHAPTER 1 we attempted to define a 'team' and discussed the growing interest in their use. We uncovered some confusion in the literature about what teams are exactly. Much of this confusion may arise as a result of the numerous types of teams which exist in single and multiple organisational environments. In this chapter we discuss these different types of teams, while maintaining a focus on team development.

Team Types

The importance of team development has become more evident as team usage has expanded and, indeed, there are many types of teams which are now operational. Huszczo (1990: 37), for example, mentions committees, task forces, quality circles, employee-participation groups, joint union-management leadership teams, action committees, project teams, supervisory councils, and autonomous or self-directed work teams. Robbins (1991: 273) adds to the list production teams, investigative commissions, boards of directors, and the highly specialised units of cockpit teams, surgical teams and repair crews. It is easy to see how widely applied the team concept is.

A broad typology is offered by Robbins (p. 274) in referring to command groups, task groups, interest groups and friendship groups. It is the first two with which we are primarily concerned, since they are organisationally determined. The first represents the permanent type of team such as a department or section, while the second is concerned with specific tasks and may cross command relationships. Dunphy (1989: 211) supports this division when categorising teams as either long-term or short-term workgroups.

We have found it useful to divide various types of teams into four categories. Whereas there are other types of teams, or those of similar configuration using different names, we believe the majority of team types can be accommodated under these headings. The categories are:

- top management teams
- mid-management teams
- project teams
- working groups

We shall now look at each of these in more detail.

Top Management Teams

Top management teams serve as the major link between the organisation and the world outside, and as such, the performance of organisations may well hinge on the effectiveness of these teams. Their job is increasingly to account for environmental factors in making important decisions. Top management teams can be regarded as the linchpin bridging the complex, macro external environment with the overarching purpose of the organisation; to accurately identify political and market factors which could influence the organisation. As discussed in Chapter 1, an ignorance, or neglect, of external factors by this team can be disastrous. There seems little doubt that the complex nature of the work in many modern-day organisations demands a team approach. Team development in such teams needs to account for the specialised and complex nature of the work of senior management.

What is the typical work of a senior management team? In some fields (educational institutions are a case in point) there is no such thing as 'typical' work (Walker and Stott, 1992). In fact, in today's often unpredictable environment it would be a brave person who tried to define 'typical'. But in other spheres of operation, there appear to be common themes and practices. Woodcock (1989: 4) suggests that top management teams set the key direction of the organisation and develop overall strategy. Due to the broad task they fulfil they usually have fairly broad membership representing the various aspects of the organisation. They may have temporary members who are attached to the team to add their own expertise at the right time.

Top management teams may meet regularly, say, once each week, and deal with such issues as financial reporting, forecasts, expansion plans, crises and new business. Meetings are also used to raise issues and maintain awareness through dissemination of information. The criteria that might be used by the chief executive in deciding whether to bring matters to the team's attention tend to hinge on the degree of impact, both in functional and corporate terms. Whether it is important for team members to know about certain issues may be another consideration.

It is worth pointing out at this stage that we often assume teams are constantly meeting face-to-face. This may be so in the majority of cases, but physical proximity is not necessarily part of the definition. There are many examples of teams where members are working out of sight of one another, yet they are working towards the same goal and their efforts have to be coordinated. An example of a top management team working together when physically isolated may be a team running a multinational company. Members may be dispersed around the globe but still making decisions together. Modern technology such as computers and video conferencing reduce the need to meet in person. This, in some circumstances, also holds true for other types of teams.

In view of the obvious importance of top management teams to organisational success, member behaviours are a vital consideration. Such teams in today's context require varied membership and innovative lateral thinking. Although we discuss in some detail the roles and behaviours desirable for effective teams in Chapter 10, some points are worth making here.

Hurst et al. (1989: 87) suggest that behaviours typically associated with strategic management and based on rational and analytical thinking are probably too limiting if strategic opportunities are to be exploited. This assertion is based on the premise that environmental determinants are changing. In a dynamic and competitive context, long-term maintenance of the organisation requires re-creation and a review of the logic by which it is managed. Emphases on logic and rationality may be incompatible with the innovative processes needed for change and renewal. Referring to strategic management, they suggest (p. 88) "it cannot deal well with novelty and ambiguity; it cannot bring into being those new activities which lie outside the structure of the managers' current understanding of their existing business, but which may well be required as part of tomorrow's business".

The call in such senior units is for heterogeneity. Hurst *et al.* (1989: 89) advance the notion of a creative management model and assert that "organizations capable of creating tomorrow's businesses while maintaining today's will require a diverse group of senior managers, able to perceive the world differently, yet able to participate in a process that transcends these different views to enact a complex organizational reality". It is easy to see the complexities involved in team development in this context and the emphasis that may need to be given to behavioural roles.

Top management teams, then, are vital if organisations wish to stay in touch with their markets and adjust to changing demands on a macro level. Such teams keep an eye on the 'big picture' and should represent a range of skills and behaviours. In the final analysis, however, regardless of the capacity of the top management team, the organisation is unlikely to reach greater potential unless other 'sub-teams' operate effectively.

Mid-management Teams

Mid-management teams, like their 'top' counterparts, are fairly stable in terms of membership and may include a member of the top management team (we examine the problem of maintaining effectiveness when membership changes later in Chapter 16). They usually involve a manager or supervisor and those who report to him or her, although this person is not necessarily always the 'team leader'. They may carry names such as departments, divisions or units. Team development efforts with such teams can be equally complex, because management teams often carry out a wide range of tasks. They may be difficult to develop for another reason. If people have worked together for some time, but have not derived much satisfaction from their being together, development can be an arduous process. Ends and Page (1977: 170) concur with this view and explain how development is considerably easier with newer and temporary units.

Such teams usually have clearer objectives than the top management team and they control and coordinate the work throughout the organisation, providing the day-to-day leadership. They must be able to relate to both the top management team and other organisational members. They may allocate resources, deal with operational plans, devise strategies for development and attempt to manage the integration of organisational functions.

Mid-management teams must be supported by top management and provided with the flexibility, within organisational parameters, to work towards their own goals. They are usually guided, in a broad sense, by the top management team and responsible for coordinating various subtasks. Their role is managerial, although their membership may also participate in various project teams.

Project Teams

Project teams (or task forces) are usually temporary groups used for a limited period to either solve specific problems or to develop new products. They may be responsible for both planning and implementation, as in the case of a team that deals with an annual marketing plan. If they are dealing with important problems and issues, they may involve senior personnel and they will report to the highest level possible. Their distinct advantage is often that they enable the organisation to respond to problems and issues with a group approach without creating permanent, and thereby expensive, structures.

George (1977: 72) provides specific examples of the organisational activities in which they might be involved, and these include new product development, manufacturing processes, new marketing programmes, cost reduction ideas, facility planning, and new business ventures. One such example is from a manufacturing organisation that produced parts for shipment abroad. Customer orders would come into Marketing which would pass on the information to Customer Services. This department would coordinate a number of activities, including purchasing, production and inventory control, and planning. There was usually a forty-eight hour delay before a response could be given to the customer, and then the Traffic Department would book the shipping. Apart from the difficulties of coordinating this information, critical decisions had to be taken on which customers to satisfy and which orders had a higher priority. A task force was set up with the specific purpose of finding a way of dealing with enquiries and orders within twenty-four hours. The task force decided the only way to proceed was to bring together the various operations and look for solutions in each department to cut the time taken.

Generally, such teams comprise people with the range of skills necessary for the task and, as we saw in the case above, they may be drawn from different organisational subunits. They may or may not have a designated leader and can enlist the involvement of members of senior management as and when required. One example may be a team established for an engineering project. The task team may comprise a design engineer, a stylist, technicians, draftspeople, quality and manufacturing engineers, a marketing manager, buyers, and a home economist. Other personnel with relevant skills may be added as the project progresses.

Where project- or task-team management is widely used, there is a need for fluidity and flexibility, since tasks must be accomplished rapidly, and members may have to move on quickly to new projects with different teams. Indeed, Peters and Waterman (1982: 127) see the true power of the small group lying in its flexibility, and they give the example of 3M where a culture has been established in which new product teams can be formed without having to fit into set division boundaries. This, however, can be a difficult prescription for many organisations that seek more stability in their operations, but the rewards can be worthwhile. As George (1977: 78) observed in one organisation, sales increased, commercial market share expanded, production increased, profits rose, and there was an increase in the number of employees. Other important benefits related to human resource development and included greater degrees of involvement and commitment, changes for the better in interdepartmental interaction, less interpersonal conflicts, greater integration of functions, and a reduction in turnover.

The issues of involvement and commitment are important ones. As Kezsbom (1990: 50) notes: "One strategy for creating major improvements in project quality and productivity is the involvement of all team members in the up-front development and subsequent maintenance of an integrated project plan; a plan that defines functional interfaces and generates team member commitment."

There are less optimistic views of task-team approaches. Individual accountability may be missing, with most decisions requiring the input of at least several people. Meetings, therefore, are prevalent and can cause severe time pressures. There can also be tensions where individual skills are in great demand across projects, each one trying to assume priority over others. Peters and Waterman (1982: 128) draw attention to certain dysfunctions that have been reported:

> Paper pushing and coordination took the place of task-directed activity. Stodgy, formal, paperbound, rule-driven institutions layered the task force on a maze that lay beneath, rather than using it as a spearable, action-inducing chunk. Task forces became nothing more than coordinating committees – with a different name. Like other management tools adopted in the wrong context, the task force made things worse, not better.

Such drawbacks, though, have to be seen against the distinct advantages of efficiency in terms of staffing, effective decision making, and flexibility in coping with change (George 1977: 80). With a ready acceptance of fluidity, the task force can be a remarkably effective problem-solving tool (Peters and Waterman, 1982: 128). And Kezsbom (1990: 50) describes the 'lean and mean' project team as "the corporate success factor of the 1990's". Speed and efficiency are two criteria that 'horizontal' teams can meet. As Peterson (1991: 84) notes, organisations that direct their energies and resources to horizontal teams can ensure that products are better made, more appealing and more reasonably priced.

Peters and Waterman (1982: 130) also offer some useful advice on the effectiveness criteria of task forces. Their duration is limited (a maximum of six months), they are assembled rapidly with little fuss, action is very swift, and documentation is minimal. Their operation, therefore, is consistent with the environment in which they operate, a complex, multifunctional and dynamic one. Other advice is also given by Peterson (1991: 84): the team should be given authority, members grouped in one location, the team should be customer-driven, and team effort should be spread throughout the organisation.

Referring to the education environment in particular, Holmes (1992: 9) draws attention to the need for task forces to have a cooperative structure and then lists five elements of cooperative groups:

1. Positive interdependence
2. Face-to-face promotive interaction
3. Individual accountability
4. Social skills development
5. Group processing

Teams formed with the purpose of solving problems have become more widespread in recent years. They may discuss issues related to work quality, efficiency, and improving working conditions. Johnson and Johnson (1991: 435) note that: "Problem-solving teams have been found to reduce costs and improve product quality, but to have little effect on how work is organized or how managers behave."

The same authors also mention what they call special purpose teams, formed to improve work processes, introduce new technology, meet with suppliers and customers, and to link different areas of work. Into this category probably fall the types of teams mentioned by Holmes (1992: 8) who refers to the professional context and mentions collegial support groups and *ad hoc* decision-making groups. The former would comprise two to five employees and the goal would be to improve one another's professional growth. The emphasis is on collaboration, cooperation and interdependence. The latter – small decision-making groups – can be formed as part of a larger decision-making body. Giving the ideal size as three, a triad, Holmes suggests such triads are an excellent strategy in collaborative decision making, since they can facilitate discussion and expedite decision making. Where meetings have become unwieldy, triads can form to enable more members to have an input, and the findings of discussions can be fed back into the main forum.

Such teams may deal with both serious and less serious issues. They may also be temporary or permanent. For example, an organisation may have the equivalent of an employees' advisory team, which would comprise a cross-section of the company's employees and would meet with the chief executive on a regular basis to represent the views of the rank and file. This type of team might raise issues such as the provision of a childcare centre, cutbacks in overtime working, smoking policy, working uniform, and using the telephone for emergency personal calls. There may also be teams to deal with employee recreation, canteen food provision, and safety. While some of these areas may seem peripheral in relation to the more critical aspects of organisational life, they may be important to a range of employees and be major causes of satisfaction or disquiet.

Working Groups

Working groups form the basic team unit. Where the team concept is applied, the emphasis is usually on extending the scope for participation amongst work group members, and on using the creative ideas and suggestions that members can offer. Anantaraman (1984b: 220) suggests that the manager's role should become that of team leader, where team work is facilitated rather than directed. Peterson (1991: 37) describes the benefits of using such teams at Ford where regular meetings were held to discuss ways in which improvements might take place in workplace arrangements, production processes, and the lines of communication. He refers to tens of thousands of highly worthwhile ideas being contributed, and maintains that his company's revitalisation would not have been possible without the input of those contributions. The benefits of a creativity enhancement programme in the mid-1980s at Frito-Lay were able to be expressed in hard cash terms: cost reductions of US$100 million over four years, with $50 million of that coming in a single year (*Straits Times*, 7 April 1992). Such claims inevitably generate considerable interest in working groups, which can take several forms.

Quality Circles

A special type of work team, and one that has become popular across a whole range of organisations, is the quality control circle, widely used in Japan and now many other countries. Quality circles generally comprise groups of workers who meet on a regular basis with supervisors to discuss problems and recommend solutions. Such recommendations are often forwarded to higher-level teams for further discussion and resultant actions are implemented with considerable employee involvement (Davidson, 1985: 16). The two major concerns of such teams are productivity and morale. Members look at problems that relate directly to their work and make recommendations for improvements.

There are certain implications for establishing such teams. They must be properly conceived and implemented, and this means getting management guidance and support. It is claimed that they make work more interesting and challenging, and enable individuals to understand their colleagues' work and feelings better. Benefits may not always be expected in terms of financial savings, but in improved morale, confidence, pride and motivation. The major implication is that adequate training is necessary. Team members need to be able to analyse data, brainstorm, and critically evaluate options. These sorts of skills do not emerge overnight.

Two examples of the way that quality control circles might be usefully employed are as follows (*Straits Times*, 6 August 1992):

1. A computer systems manufacturing company was having problems with the wrong orders being shipped out. The job flow was not systematic and complaints started coming in from customers. The quality circle designed a form which would gather all the necessary information and erected three notice boards. One tracked shipments to the various destinations, one monitored the number of days required to complete orders, and another listed the number of deliveries to be made in any one day. As a result of implementing the new system, complaints went down to zero, which was the most important effect. The participants reported other benefits too, like getting to know one another better and learning to understand problems on the production line and in the shipping department.

2. A group of purchasing officers formed a quality circle in an electronics components company. The company had contracts with other companies to provide service maintenance, office equipment and spare parts. Each purchasing officer would deal with his own contracts, but would sometimes forget that a contract had expired. This meant that the company did not have the upper hand in renegotiating these contracts. The circle came up with a scheme which involved one person monitoring all contracts and generating a computer report each month showing the status of the contracts. It was estimated that this simple idea saved the company $100,000 in one year alone.

These are examples of the way in which quality control circles may be used successfully, but it has to be remembered they do not have the power to simply make decisions and implement them. They are advisory in nature and cannot be seen in exactly the same light as those teams that are able to manage their own affairs and assume responsibility for goal achievement. This may be one reason why there appears to be a decline of interest in quality circles in some organisational environments, although derivatives of the original concept continue to operate successfully in many organisations.

Lawler and Mohrman (1987: 42), in an article aptly entitled 'Quality Circles: After the Honeymoon', believe that: "The problems with quality circles typically develop after they become an organization-wide activity and an effort is made to sustain them over a period of years". While acknowledging this and other weaknesses of quality circles they suggest that certain strategies can be employed to strengthen and revive the process. They suggest that organisations can:

1. expand the kind of decisions that are made by participative groups into the areas of strategy, design and operating decisions.
2. move from a model of shared decision making to one in which authority is delegated downward to the groups performing the work, by establishing work teams.
3. treat the quality circle as the basic building block of participation and alter relevant aspects of the organisational context to support successful circle funtioning (p. 49).

Problems associated with quality circles have led to the alteration and refinement of the original concept.

Quality Circle Derivatives

Some organisations have adapted the quality circle concept and used their own names for the teams. One such example is a multinational manufacturing company that uses the acronym STEP which stands for Success Through Employee Participation. The objective, as the name implies, is to improve productivity through involvement. In the course of one year, the company had thirty-two task forces in operation. The system entailed deciding the problems that needed looking at and then planning the task forces for the year. All the problems were work-related and could have an impact on productivity. They included housekeeping, cost reduction, shift work improvement, tracking orders, reducing the cost of scrap or wastage, refining the standard tour of the plant for the company's customers, processing prompt petty cash payments, and preventive maintenance.

Each task force comprised between six and eight members, and meetings were held on average about once or twice each month. While the company accepted there may have been occasions when external consultants could help, there were distinct advantages in using the workforce to solve problems, because they would know the intricacies of the job and they would accept ownership of the problem.

The structure involved a steering committee comprising department managers and facilitators, who were generally section managers and superintendents. The committee would meet every few weeks to give direction, evaluate task-force performance and give feedback, and emphasize and support certain important programmes. Facilitators would attend task-force meetings and help in the solving of some problems. They would also attend steering-committee meetings four times a year to give feedback about progress in the task groups for which they were responsible. Each task force would have a leader who would know the group's schedule, objectives, and details of the problem. The leader would undergo training at a central training agency and group members would receive training from facilitators in process skills, such as data collection and brainstorming.

This scheme is worthy of note because it provides the type of training that is necessary for such a programme to succeed. It also has management support and involvement, and it provides appropriate incentives and displays of appreciation. Despite the undoubted benefits, it does not endow the groups with a large degree of power.

Self-managing Work Teams

An emerging trend in many organisations has been the proliferation of self-managing work teams. These generally have a small number of members and they are responsible for a clearly defined area of work. Jessup (1990: 79) lays out the main characteristics of such teams: "The work of self-managed teams has clearly defined inputs and outputs and clearly defined customers, either internal or external. The teams often use multiple skills for enhanced flexibility. They are accountable for the traditional measures of performance, such as product or service quality, on-time delivery, productivity, and cost control." As these teams mature, they may be afforded extended responsibility for aspects of the job that affect them, while teams that have shown themselves to be highly effective and capable of handling advanced responsibilities may take over some of the more critical duties usually associated with their superiors, such as appraisal and goal setting. Peters and Waterman (1982: 127) refer to findings that teams are more likely to be successful if they set their own goals, comprise volunteers and are of limited duration.

Self-managed teams, or what Barry (1991: 33–6) calls 'Bossless Teams', can also be project teams or task forces. He discusses such teams operating as project teams, problem-solving teams and policy-making teams. Barry claims that existing leadership models are incapable of explaining or assisting self-managed teams to operate or develop and suggests that the leadership roles come from within the team itself and fall into four clusters; envisioning, organising, spanning and social.

Kidder (1981), in his book *The Soul of the Manager* described how he established the equivalent of a self-managed team. He set certain parameters and deadlines, stayed out of inter-team disputes, did his best to provide resources and protected the team from organisational politics. He considered them to be both effective and productive and credited them with building the team by themselves, without any real help from the leader.

Johnson and Johnson (1991: 436) refer to substantial productivity and quality increases where these teams are given the autonomy to take over all aspects of management, including work and holiday scheduling, ordering materials, and hiring new staff for the team. They provide the opportunity for employees to have control over their jobs and they may enhance development by allowing team members to learn all the associated tasks and to move from job to job. As Johnson and Johnson observe, these appear to be the wave of the future.

Such teams are often associated with the word 'empowerment'. In other words, they have the authority and autonomy to get the job done. There are many favourable reports, mainly from major corporations, some claiming "it revitalises jaded employees, boosts morale, increases productivity, improves quality and even reduces turnover" (*Straits Times*, 9 April 1992). Concepts associated with empowerment and with self-managed teams complement and reinforce one another. By empowering people, leaders engender the following ideas (Betof and Harwood, 1992: 32):

- People are part of the management and can help the organisation improve.
- Good ideas they have will be implemented.
- Suggestions they make will be appreciated and rewarded, even if not accepted.
- People can be trusted with responsibility.
- They are respected for their ideas and judgement.

The necessity for fostering such values in the overall organisation can make the job of forming and developing self-managed teams much easier.

Empowerment in terms of teams means that members are seen as being capable of making decisions, of being innovative and able to contribute ideas, because they know the job better than others higher up in the organisation. The difference between this concept and related ideas (like quality circles) is that it gives people real, not imaginary, authority. It is more than just power, however. It involves a major cultural shift for the organisation, necessitating changes in attitudes and behaviours, and in structures, processes and practices. It is essential, therefore, that any move towards this kind of operation stems from the top and is given full support. It cannot be approached half-heartedly. The first step is for the chief executive to devolve real power to the senior management team and this should lead to a condition that can best be described as 'management by consensus'.

Not all reports are so positive. There is resistance from managers, not surprisingly, who may not be prepared to relinquish such an amount of power, and there is also resistance from employees because of the considerable responsibility involved and the decline in promotion opportunities because of a decrease in the numbers of managers. There may also be a cultural barrier, where people have become used to accepting directives, and the new operation may impose conditions of ambiguity that are unfamiliar and threatening. Individuals may be afraid also that others can do their work, and this can threaten their perception of indispensability. Barry (1991: 46) warns that self-managing teams can easily become chaotic and turn into political battlegrounds. Since such teams typically lack a hierarchical leader they must be given time to develop their own system of distributed leadership.

The constraints, however, should not override the immense advantages. Managers and supervisors do not lose their jobs, but they may experience a redefinition of their roles, and the proponents of autonomous work teams suggest that they enjoy considerable benefits in terms of higher-quality work and improved interpersonal relationships. Where self-managing and empowered teams have worked well, and people's energies and abilities have been harnessed, the reports of success are very persuasive.

Summary

As we have seen, there are several different types of teams, but not all fit neatly into categories. For example project teams or quality circles can also be self-managed teams, as can more senior management teams.

Consideration of the type of team that needs to be formed or developed, however, is important. No one particular model is ideal or appropriate in all situations. In his book *Game Plans,* Keidel makes some comparisons between organisational and sports teams. He focuses on baseball, basketball and football teams and then shows their counterparts in business. Although we warned earlier against the overly simplistic comparison of sports and other teams, his observations serve to illustrate the situational differences between teams, and these have implications for development.

1. In a baseball team the players tend to operate independently. The business equivalent may be basic research teams in a telecommunications firm.
2. In football teams the manager tends to make the play decisions. An equivalent may be a McDonald's franchise or a car assembly plant.
3. In basketball the players coordinate themselves as a flexible group. The manager usually acts as a catalyst. Business equivalents may be R&D units in computer firms or other project teams.

Even from these limited examples, it is possible to see how a team may be entirely independent, firmly controlled or self-coordinated with a certain degree of external facilitation. Such differences need to be accounted for in planning appropriate development strategies.

In this chapter we have discussed top and mid-management teams, project teams and various types of working teams. The underlying theme throughout our discussion has been team development and the utility of various types of teams depending on the organisational need and task purpose. In the next chapter we examine what makes teams effective, what their purposes are, and some aspects of the performance and quality of teams.

3

EFFECTIVE TEAMS AND THEIR PERFORMANCE

IN CHAPTER 2 we examined the different types of teams which may typify the organisational environment. During our discussion we referred to why and how different types of teams may be useful. Perhaps one of the most interesting topics to study in relation to any type of team and its development is that of effectiveness. The search for an answer to the question 'What are the characteristics of an effective team?' provides the basis for any development focus. The answers can be quite varied and range from the sublime to the ridiculous. Effectiveness is almost trivialised in some texts.

In this chapter, we concentrate on the characteristics of effective teams, the purposes and benefits which may accrue from using and developing teams, and team performance and quality.

Characteristics of Effective Teams

It is not easy to identify the precise characteristics of an effective team. Even a perfunctory scan of the organisational, political or social environment will show that different types of teams are considered effective, or not effective, depending on the criteria applied. Despite this, there are certain general criteria which emerge continually from discussions on teams.

Anantaraman (1984b: 220) believes that a clear description of what constitutes the ideal team must be available, and with this in mind, he offers a model of effectiveness:

> An effective team would have clear, cooperative goals to which every member is committed; accurate and effective communication of ideas and feelings; distributed participation and leadership; appropriate and effective decision-making procedures; productive controversies; a high level of trust, acceptance and support among members; a high level of cohesion; constructive management of power and conflict; and adequate problem-solving procedures.

Carr (1989: 177) refers to working together as a team and the ability to manage itself, a sentiment that rings true for those involved in teams, but such prescriptions may be of little utility to those charged with the responsibility for improvement. He does go on, however, to explain the importance of common goals and recognising members' special skills. Identifying isolated attributes without adequate justification, however, provides little basis for development.

The literature is rich in its assertions about the features of success. Kazemak (1991: 15), for example, provides a model that is comprehensive and that lists ten effectiveness criteria:

1. Goals and objectives are understood and agreed.
2. Conflict is dealt with constructively.
3. Members share the leadership role.
4. People's abilities are used.
5. Communication is open and participatory, and members know what is going on.
6. Members support the team's controls and procedures.
7. They have well-established problem-solving and decision-making approaches.
8. Experimentation and creativity are encouraged.
9. They evaluate their functions and processes regularly.
10. Members understand their roles, responsibilities and authority limitations.

Hitt (1988: 71–4) presents what he believes to be the distinctive attributes of a productive team:

1. Common agreement on high expectations for the team.
2. A commitment to common goals.

3. Assumed responsibility for work that must be done.
4. Honest and open communication.
5. Common access to information.
6. A climate of trust.
7. A general feeling that one can influence what happens.
8. Support for decisions that are made.
9. A win-win approach to conflict management.
10. A focus on process as well as results.

While these lists were arrived at intuitively on the basis of work with teams, most of the criteria are strongly supported in the literature generally. Some of the items appear in Margerison and McCann's (1985: 63) characteristics of high-performing teams, a list which, it is claimed, was based on research, and which includes high output and high-quality targets, member satisfaction, cooperation, respect for the leader, membership balance, autonomy for the team, the capacity to learn from mistakes, client orientation, problem solving skills and motivation.

Some authors, in contrast, restrict themselves to a more limited range of emphases. Buhler and McCann (1989: 14), for example, draw the sports analogy and emphasize the importance of membership. There is little point, they maintain, in having a limited range of skills because the team would be unable to adapt to the various situational and strategic changes that unfold. Assembling a blend of talent and setting a common goal, therefore, is a prerequisite for success. Koehler (1989: 15) is similarly restrained and dwells on understanding objectives and appreciating the skills and experience of team members. George (1987: 129) emphasizes unity of purpose as the main distinguishing characteristic of successful management teams, and adds several other contributory features, including mutual trust, respect, warmth, common goals and the feeling of group oneness. Members should have a shared reality and a common way of seeing and valuing their work. Petrock (1990: 9) is quite forthright in claiming successful team characteristics are unmistakeable: "Members interact with, rather than react to, the leader; they trust each other and share leadership; they place the group's goals above their own." These may be worthy ideals, but whether they may be found universally amongst effective teams is a matter for conjecture.

One or two other items and emphases are added to the above array of features by other writers. Johnson (1986: 48), for example, includes leaders leading by example, personal freedom for members, self-establishing high standards, and self-discipline as worthy attributes. Robbins (1991: 279) focuses on effectiveness variables in explaining why some group efforts are more successful than others, and brings further considerations into the arena, including group size, and the internal pressures on team members to conform to the group's norms. Drawing on the work of Douglas McGregor, Wynn and Guditus (1984: 209) identify one other effectiveness characteristic not mentioned frequently elsewhere, that of selective use of the team. A team is unlikely to be effective if it is involved in problem-solving and decision-making areas which are not part of its domain.

Woodcock (1989: 12) dwells on the importance of openness and honesty as the key ingredients of effective teamwork, since these two features lead to meetings characterised by high involvement, and confidence and trust in the leader. People are able to express themselves without fear of retribution. He also identifies a number of supporting characteristics, including the following: mistakes are faced openly and learnt from; difficult situations are confronted; competition and conflict are used constructively; there is pride in team achievement; good relationships exist within and outside the team; new ideas abound; leader-member relationships are sound; development is highly rated; there is understanding about objectives and roles; external help is drawn on when it is needed; and there are regular reviews. Again, like many other frameworks, these ideas are based on a combination of experience, personal beliefs and references to the literature. Woodcock calls them 'building blocks' because they can be used in a practical way to build effective teams.

It is interesting to note that where effectiveness characteristics are derived from members' personal experiences and from participants' views on team development programmes, there is usually a heavy emphasis on the role of the leader and the talents of the members. An example of this comes from Zapp (1987: 8) who records the responses from one teambuilding session, where the criteria identified were: "the excellence of the leader, the greatness of the players, the mutual caring and bonding among team members, and the team's pride in their success". Also recording the comments of the session's leader, she identifies three characteristics, in this case called 'themes', that are present in the workings of typical successful teams:

1. Team members have a sense of mission and set themselves high-achievement expectations.

2. They know what they need to do to succeed.
3. Rewards are shared and members feel they are contributing to team success.

To these three themes are added trust, communication, group decision making, and clear procedures – factors already evident in several of the lists above. It is claimed that the themes are based on research findings, but we have already hinted at the methodological problems associated with research into teams and their development, and one must assume, therefore, that characteristics such as these are based more on personal understanding of team success and good common sense than rigorous inquiry.

Huszczo (1990: 38), like Kazemak and Hitt earlier, provides a broad list of characteristics, but reinforces it with detailed explanations in the form of a set of critical questions that can form the basis of a systematic team assessment. He covers the following areas:

1. **Goals:** Direction should be clear and relate to the wider organisation. There should also be commitment from members.
2. **Talent:** The team should have the talent and complementary skills for the task. There should be encouragement for members to develop further.
3. **Roles:** Members should understand their roles and the unique ways in which they contribute to team success. There should be commitment to those roles and clarity about individual contributions.
4. **Procedures:** Effective and efficient operating procedures should be in place. Meetings and planning should be effective, and members should know how to make decisions, solve problems, and share and receive information as a team.
5. **Interpersonal relations:** Team members need to relate well to one another, communicate and resolve conflicts. They must both support and challenge one another. There should be evidence of care and concern, and constructive feedback should be provided so that skill levels are enhanced.
6. **Reinforcement:** Effective reinforcement systems are needed for enhancing teamwork. At a personal level, appreciation might be expressed, and it is important to notice team-oriented behaviours. The organisation is also responsible for reinforcement.

7. **External relations:** Constructive external relationships with the external environment should exist, and there should also be healthy relations with other units within the organisation itself. The team also needs to scan the environment to identify relevant threats and opportunities.

A list with a slightly different focus is provided by Thamhain (1990: 14) who looks at the effectiveness criteria of project teams. He refers to the importance of communicating organisational goals, comprehensive planning, involvement of those at all levels, the involvement of the team in deciding its own staffing, the establishment of an appropriate team structure for the task, building a healthy team image, providing interesting work and a conducive work environment, obtaining senior management support, clear communications, team commitment, management commitment, appointing the right leader, engaging in team development and avoiding potential problems before they become mature and dysfunctional.

One of the important criteria for Johnson and Johnson (1991: 445) is 'positive interdependence'. Team members understand the way their efforts must be linked with those of others in an effective team; they therefore work together, share ideas and resources, support and help one another, and celebrate their collective successes. There is a sense of mutuality. They have mutual goals, are trying to achieve mutual benefits, feel mutually responsible and accept that outcomes are mutually caused. They understand their mutual obligations and they make mutual investments of effort.

Such high levels of interdependence do not simply happen; they have to be structured. Goals have to be set in such a way that they demand interdependent actions; rewards should be based on combined (rather than individual) efforts; responsibilities should be assigned so that everyone is critical to group success; tasks must be given that represent important links in the whole chain; and individuals should be given a necessary chunk of the total resources or information so that their respective contributions are essential.

An effective team, then, can mean different things to different groups, depending on the criteria applied. There are, however, a number of broad conditions which encompass much of the literature and provide an outline, albeit sketchy, of an effective team. Effective teams might aim for the following conditions (Stott and Walker, 1992: 25):

- A common understanding of purpose and direction
- Quality relationships that are both supportive and challenging
- A sense of mutual responsibility and accountability
- Leadership that balances demands within the team

If the question of effectiveness is one of the most interesting issues, an equally important consideration is that of purpose, or the reason for having teams. The key question is: What purposes do teams serve? In the next section we attempt to answer this question. Tied closely to any discussion of the purpose of teams are the benefits their proper utilisation brings to those involved and to the organisation.

Purposes and Benefits of Using Teams

When considering the purpose and benefits of teams, two perspectives become obvious. These are related to the organisation and to the individual. Although we discuss each separately, in reality, both purposes and benefits are inseparable, and they support, enhance and interact with each other.

Purposes

Anantaraman (1984a: 148) mentions three purposes or benefits for the individual: satisfaction, support and information. Satisfaction is derived from the reinforcement gained for one's value system, because there is a sharing of values. The individual can also gain psychological strength through drawing on the strength of others. Membership of the team gives status in the form of membership of an exclusive 'club'. The team provides a forum for sympathetic listening and for self-expression. Teams also meet the needs of those who desire power and the social needs of those who wish simply to feel that they are part of a group. In terms of support, there is protection for the individual through the team, and also the opportunity to protest safely. Finally the team, as a source of information, helps the individual to meet two basic desires – to know and to understand.

Traditional motivation theories tell us that to be valued and recognised are important needs, and it is evident that teams are capable of providing the sort of care and compassion that can lead to individual satisfaction. Emotional support can also be provided at times when it is demanded.

It is easy to see from this that teams can play a considerable part in meeting the personal needs of individual members. From the organisation's point of view, the purposes are more diverse and complex. One obvious purpose is to pool the collective resources to arrive at better decisions, assuming that members' abilities and experience are used profitably. With the relevant information, it seems likely that wiser decisions can be arrived at. The collective strength of the team may also enable decisions to be made that incur an element of risk, but which may not be considered by an individual alone.

A team may also serve the purpose of giving protection against careless actions through the critical scrutiny of ideas and plans. Team effort may have a part to play also in implementation by engendering commitment to goals. Associating commitment with collectivity in this way supports the notion of involvement leading to ownership. As Kizilos and Heinisch (1986: 6) note: "A boss cannot obtain by decree the creativity, initiative, and dedication needed to do a job properly; such allegiance can come freely only from people who have a sense of 'ownership' of the organization's goals."

Teams are able to deal with and coordinate complex information. This is an important purpose because, as we have seen in discussing the work of top-management teams, certain factors may combine to provide information flows to the organisation that are difficult to process. Using the right combination of skills can facilitate this deciphering process.

Teams also have a greater capacity for creating and developing ideas than individuals working alone. Ideas can be expanded and developed, and, equally importantly, they can be subjected to rigorous evaluation. The claim for innovation is supported by Huszczo (1990: 37): "Small groups have been found to be terrific at coming up with innovative ideas and high-quality solutions to problems."

Benefits

Closely linked to the purposes that teams serve are the benefits they might deliver if they fulfil those purposes. Arajs (1991: 76), for example, talks about quality and productivity improvements through drawing on collective energies and wisdom. She suggests that strong teams lead to strong organisations, a persuasive benefit for developing teamwork if it is indeed true.

The claim for increased productivity is supported by several authors. Chance (1989: 18) cites the impressive cases of Keithly Instruments in Ohio (where output increased by 90 percent and absenteeism fell by 75 percent) and Xerox (where a team looking at an uncompetitive work area saved the company US$3.7 million).

In fact there are many claims in the literature for the benefits of team organisation. The same author says teams may "avoid duplication of effort, increase cooperation, spur new ideas, help people solve problems, maintain motivation, improve product quality, and, not incidentally, increase profits". George (1977: 78) too mentions production and profit increases, and several personnel-related benefits, while Timmons (1979: 200) refers to the evidence that teams are the key to building high-growth ventures. Those in the high-technology sector launched by teams were enjoying considerably more success than those having lone founders. As a writer for *The Economist* recently noted, "A successful leadership team will outlive the visionary leader who put it together" (Staff, 1990: 67).

An equally dramatic benefit is identified by Greco (1988: 38) in claiming that teamwork can help a company survive a crisis, because people will put in the extra effort without being asked. This may be because team members' commitment is strengthened through team effort (Kizilos and Heinisch, 1986: 6).

Several of these ideas are taken up by Margerison and McCann (1989: 3) who discuss improvements in productivity, commitment and output, cooperation, communication, creativity, and energy levels. They also draw attention to the added benefits of more time and less stress for managers, two highly persuasive features, while Todryk (1990: 17) focuses on the project management environment, and suggests that an effective teambuilding process will "measurably reduce schedule delays and cost overruns while improving the quality of team morale and increasing productivity".

Other claims may be more difficult to substantiate. Whether the existence of teams has a favourable impact on the organisation's micropolitical activities is a debatable point, but Peterson (1991: 38) maintains: "An environment where people are working together instead of just for themselves also discourages internal rivalries and back-stabbing, by keeping everyone concentrated on his or her own role as part of a team."

While Johnson (1986: 48) focuses on several of the benefits already mentioned, she looks in particular at the benefits that might accrue from developing the work of teams and shows how one thing is linked to another:

> Improve the way team members interact, and you improve their ability to solve problems. Better problem-solving means better efficiency in general. Increased efficiency tends to boost morale and productivity. It also helps to decrease stress, turnover and operating costs. And all of these improvements bolster the organization's public image.

The rationale for some of these linkages is not clear and may be quite dubious, but the point that many factors are interrelated is worth noting.

Bradford (1990: 49) too focuses on the effects of team development and identifies a set of benefits. As a result of the teambuilding process, teams can resolve territorial dilemmas more effectively, managers can solve problems with a sense of common purpose and less emphasis on their own agendas, productivity increases, grievances and absenteeism decrease, service quality improves, and people are more confident about their ability to handle organisational politics and still give high quality service while keeping morale high. This is an impressive list of possible outcomes, but one must be cautious in attributing them all to successful teambuilding interventions. Some of them are supported by other writers. Kirkpatrick and Smith (1991: 8), reporting on a two-year programme of teambuilding, record the comments of a senior executive who observed an astonishing growth of maturity in interdepartmental relationships with contentious issues being frankly discussed, and an emphasis on problem solving rather than fault finding.

Drawing on the work of Douglas McGregor, Wynn and Guditus (1984: 18) identify several advantages of teamwork. If it is effective, it provides the best possible environment for individual development, increasing skill in problem solving and improving social interaction. They also advance the claim that significant objectives and measures of performance can be devised for the group which cannot be applied at the individual level. Also, like Peterson, it is suggested that the effects of adverse political activities can be minimised. The authors also note that systemic coordination of decision making may be increased where there is a consensual approach to team management (p. 141).

Hitt (1988: 81–3), concentrating on the role of the team leader, suggests that teams yield benefits in terms of improved communication, better use of human resources, more creativity, better leadership development and improved job satisfaction. He continues: "Collectively, these five intervening variables can be expected to have a substantial impact on performance" (p. 83).

Benefits, however modest, do not appear with immediacy. It may take some time to feel the positive effects of teamwork. Wynn and Guditus (1984: 214) refer to Likert's observations and suggest that it may take a year before the results of participative approaches become widely felt in the organisation. This is a sobering thought for those who seek instant gains.

In summary, correctly utilised, formed and developed teams may be able to provide both the organisation and the individuals involved with the following benefits:

- Reduced duplication of effort.
- Increased cooperation.
- New, more innovative ideas.
- Better, wiser and more complete decisions.
- Motivated colleagues.
- Improved product and service quality.
- Increased productivity and profits.
- Added flexibility to allow easier adaptation to changing circumstances.
- Increased commitment to implementation.
- Reduced destructive conflict.
- Improved interpersonal and inter-unit relations and communication.
- Higher standards of performance.

The most critical benefits of team operation, then, are concerned with member satisfaction and with performance. Attempting to delineate performance effectiveness carries many pitfalls. We now turn our attention to this complex issue and look briefly at several performance-related considerations, including those of improvement and quality.

Performance

In connection with the research into team development, the word 'performance' is mentioned frequently, since it is the team's performance that is the main determinant of success. One way of conceptualising performance and attempting to reach effective levels of team achievement is by identifying blockages. Many instruments are available. Francis and Young (1979), for example, have a team review questionnaire containing 108 questions, and blockages are identified under 12 categories, namely, inappropriate leadership, unqualified membership, insufficient group commitment, unconstructive climate, low achievement orientation, undeveloped corporate role, ineffective work methods, inadequate team organisation, soft critiquing, stunted individual development, lack of creative capacity, and negative intergroup relations.

Johnson and Johnson (1991: 466) refer to 'obstacles' to performance and identify maturity, history, mixed motives, and obstructive individual behaviours as the significant barriers. Maturity refers to the time required for the team to establish useful patterns of working. History refers to traditional norms that may impede progress. Mixed motives become a barrier when individuals' drives are not entirely cooperative. They may, for example, wish to pursue their own advancement ambitions as well as work towards team goals. The final obstacle, obstructive individual behaviours, refers to all those behaviours that interfere with team effectiveness, such as dominating discussions, being stubborn, and losing track of the task. The literature indeed identifies a whole range of problems (e.g. Petrock, 1990: 9) but these are very much intuitive, and appear to have little empirical foundation.

A diagnostic instrument that may be used in examining the team's condition and in identifying factors that obstruct effective performance is reproduced from Stott and Walker (1992) and is called a Team Condition Assessment (see Figure 3.1).

Hellriegel et al. (1989: 211) identify seven factors that can influence group behaviours and performance. The factors are group size, member composition and roles, group norms, goals, cohesiveness, leadership and the external environment. The authors suggest that each factor does not stand alone but interacts and influences the others. Although the relations between the factors can become quite complex, an example serves to demonstrate the interrelatedness. Cohesiveness is the degree of commitment team members have to the group and have to remain active members of the group: "Cohesiveness is influenced by the degree of compatibility between group goals and individual members' goals"

(p. 218). Team members wanting to remain as a group and willing to accept its goals would be considered highly cohesive; on the other hand, those unwilling would not be. Low cohesiveness as such would retard goal achievement which in turn would influence performance negatively.

Thamhain (1990: 7), looking at new product team performance, identified a number of 'driving factors' (rather than obstacles) which could be associated with effective performance, which was defined in general terms as new product success. These were: clear objectives, stimulating work, professional growth potential, direction and leadership, mutual trust and good interpersonal relations, proper plans, good communication within and outside the team, organisational stability and security, adequate resources, and management involvement. Thamhain's work has utility because the success criteria associated with innovation had been identified. These were: the number of innovative ideas adopted or taken to the market by the organisation; agreed goals met; adaptability to changing requirements and conditions; and commitment (p. 10). His model is a useful one in understanding the linkage between input variables (expressed multidimensionally) and performance. The model is shown in Figure 3.2.

Not all studies have given us the same level of precision, and performance improvement, therefore, may be an elusive concept and may remain largely intuitive unless there is clear information on the level of performance before any developmental intervention. As Huszczo (1990: 39) notes, in the absence of pre-data, it is difficult to ascertain whether a training effect has taken place. The same problem applies to the normal work setting, where performance may never have been considered in terms of effectiveness. Indeed, Maddux (1989: 10) observes that there is a widespread contentment with group performance, because thinking has not progressed beyond present accomplishment to what might be achieved.

Performance does not have to be expressed solely in terms of results criteria, of course. Other dimensions, including processes and relationships, may be part of the performance equation. Weisbord (1985: 29) takes up this point: "Results and good working relationships are linked inextricably in the minds of anyone who has ever had to work with others."

The word that has been associated with performance more than any other in recent years is that of quality.

Figure 3.1 Team Condition Assessment

	Strongly disagree	Disagree	Agree	Strongly agree	SCORE
Tick the appropriate box for each statement. *Do not write anything in the circles yet.*					
1. The team is prepared to air differences of opinion.	☐	☐	☐	☐	◯
2. Meetings are focused and don't waste time.	☐	☐	☐	☐	◯
3. The team leader draws contributions from all members.	☐	☐	☐	☐	◯
4. If an input from outside is needed, someone who can help the team is brought in.	☐	☐	☐	☐	◯
5. Concern is shown for fellow members who are experiencing personal problems.	☐	☐	☐	☐	◯
6. The team likes to dream up new ways of doing things.	☐	☐	☐	☐	◯
7. The leader understands what influences team members.	☐	☐	☐	☐	◯
8. There is confidence that problems and difficulties can be overcome.	☐	☐	☐	☐	◯
9. Members are made to feel equal despite status and experience differences.	☐	☐	☐	☐	◯
10. Problem redefinition and creative solutions are encouraged.	☐	☐	☐	☐	◯
11. The team searches painstakingly for all relevant information.	☐	☐	☐	☐	◯
12. All suggestions are treated seriously, even if later discarded.	☐	☐	☐	☐	◯
13. Each team member is brought into discussions.	☐	☐	☐	☐	◯

	Strongly disagree	Disagree	Agree	Strongly agree	SCORE
14. Accomplishments are constantly measured against goals.	☐	☐	☐	☐	◯
15. Members are encouraged to play 'devil's advocate' so that ideas can be rigorously tested.	☐	☐	☐	☐	◯
16. Conflicts are defused and differences reconciled.	☐	☐	☐	☐	◯
17. High standards are set.	☐	☐	☐	☐	◯
18. Members' respective skills, knowledge and abilities are utilised appropriately and productively.	☐	☐	☐	☐	◯
19. Risks are taken when necessary.	☐	☐	☐	☐	◯
20. Members communicate effectively with one another.	☐	☐	☐	☐	◯
21. Members are open enough to deal with sensitive issues.	☐	☐	☐	☐	◯
22. All necessary talents and abilities are available in the team for effective task completion.	☐	☐	☐	☐	◯
23. Members are open and honest with one another.	☐	☐	☐	☐	◯
24. Members know what they are supposed to be doing.	☐	☐	☐	☐	◯
25. Members understand perfectly what their contributions to the team are.	☐	☐	☐	☐	◯
26. The leader is committed to a participative approach.	☐	☐	☐	☐	◯
27. The team can work well with other teams and share ideas.	☐	☐	☐	☐	◯

	Strongly disagree	Disagree	Agree	Strongly agree	SCORE
28. Team members enjoy being part of the team.	☐	☐	☐	☐	◯
29. Members often ask whether actions and procedures are the best.	☐	☐	☐	☐	◯
30. Members enjoy their successes.	☐	☐	☐	☐	◯
31. There is a good mix of people in terms of personal characteristics.	☐	☐	☐	☐	◯
32. Members help one another when difficulties are experienced.	☐	☐	☐	☐	◯
33. Meetings have clear intentions and productive outcomes.	☐	☐	☐	☐	◯
34. Members can all state the team's prime goal clearly.	☐	☐	☐	☐	◯
35. Members feel they gain personally through being involved in the team.	☐	☐	☐	☐	◯
36. Members don't rest on their laurels, but constantly review the team's operation.	☐	☐	☐	☐	◯
37. Even small successes are celebrated.	☐	☐	☐	☐	◯
38. Members are enthusiastic.	☐	☐	☐	☐	◯
39. Meetings invariably end up with people having to take action.	☐	☐	☐	☐	◯
40. Members work well together.	☐	☐	☐	☐	◯
41. The team leader is supportive.	☐	☐	☐	☐	◯
42. The team evaluates the way it works and rectifies matters.	☐	☐	☐	☐	◯
43. The team produces quality results.	☐	☐	☐	☐	◯

	Strongly disagree	Disagree	Agree	Strongly agree	SCORE
44. Members seem to understand one another's moods and feelings.	☐	☐	☐	☐	◯
45. Individual efforts are well coordinated towards the team effort.	☐	☐	☐	☐	◯
46. Individual differences are recognised and used to effect.	☐	☐	☐	☐	◯
47. Complex information is deciphered by the team and difficulties are unravelled.	☐	☐	☐	☐	◯
48. Individual suggestions are taken and developed towards a solution.	☐	☐	☐	☐	◯
49. Various options are considered in arriving at a team decision.	☐	☐	☐	☐	◯
50. There is trust and confidence in the leader.	☐	☐	☐	☐	◯

INSTRUCTIONS

Now you can write points in the circles. Award points as follows:

Strongly agree	4 points	Disagree	2 points
Agree	3 points	Strongly disagree	1 point

140 – 200　You probably have a management team which is in good shape. Try to identify any obvious weaknesses from the statements.

100 – 140　The team is probably proficient in some areas and not so good in others. Look at the low scoring statements and see if there is a common link. Performance may have to be reviewed in these areas.

Less than 100　The team may not be fulfilling its role in key areas. If the scores are high in some areas but are only ones or twos in others, then examine the latter for linkages. If the team is going to achieve anything, a serious effort will have to be made to assess and improve the way it develops targets, its interpersonal relationships amongst members, the level of cohesion and the way in which the leader reconciles the demands of task, team and individuals.

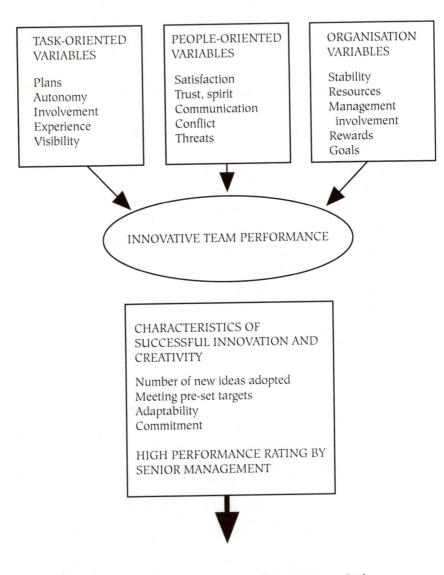

Figure 3.2   Input-Output Model of Innovative Team Performance
(**Source:** Thamhain, 1990: 13)

Quality

Peterson (1991: 142) takes an almost obsessive stance on the quality issue and explains how it is central to any consideration of team performance at Ford, both externally and internally. Performance affects internal customers. Even mundane chores may have an impact on those who receive the work. The impact may also be felt within the team itself, since the interdependencies mean that members rely on colleagues for quality work. Performance, therefore, may have to be considered in terms of the quality of all aspects of the team's work. Indeed, Peterson sees it as the preeminent goal, with improvements in quality performance driving the work of teams forward, and leading to advances in products and services.

The Total Quality Management (TQM) movement has had a definite influence on many organisations (we have already discussed Quality Circles which are one approach to employee involvement in *quality*). Our purpose here is not to examine the TQM movement from its Japanese roots in detail, but, because of the prevalence of the approach and its dedication to teamwork, it is important to highlight a number of aspects which relate to teams.

In essence, TQM is about improving customer service and the quality of services (and goods) and about involving workers in their work. It also demands a scientific approach to data collection and problem analysis. Although many hybrids have developed, a vital aspect of TQM is that everybody in the organisation, regardless of his or her level, should be involved in ensuring and improving quality. At this point, any enthusiasm should be tempered by one piece of research, cited by Tom Peters in *On Achieving Excellence*, which showed that 80 percent of TQM programmes produce little or no benefit (Peters, 1992; cited in Brandt, 1992: 1). Commenting on this, Brandt (1992: 1) says "that disappointing finding suggests that leaders of many organisations never got the message. They weren't prepared to change their basic attitudes; most were probably just looking for innovative management techniques by which to squeeze more productivity out of their workers."

Despite this, there are positive features relevant to our discussion. An integral part of the process is the formation of what Crosby (1986: 106) calls 'Quality Improvement Teams'. Indeed, most basic models of TQM are represented by a triangle with the aim, 'quality', at its apex and 'teamwork' (variously labelled) and 'scientific approach' at the two other points. TQM has at its heart participative teams dedicated to improving quality. In a recent study, Ramsay *et al.* (1991: 94) concluded that "companies with a high level of employee involvement are likely to experience rapid problem solving, fewer defects and a higher level of job interest", and "the team approach to problem solving is considered time saving and economical. It encourages interdependence and facilitates, through improved communication, a greater exchange of ideas and information".

Quality teams, no matter what they are called, are developed within a participative, collaborative culture where all team members are responsible for setting and meeting performance goals. The place of teams is seen as integral in 'quality' organisations. It is considered to be so not only for their ability to produce results but also because of their educative qualities. The TQM movement continues to gain momentum increasingly in public sector organisations, and its reliance on teams supports the importance of team development.

Synergy

Another expression that has been widely associated with performance (and TQM) is that of synergy, a term borrowed from biology and which refers to an effect of an action of two or more substances that is different from the individual summation of those substances (Robbins, 1991: 296). In many cases, the performance of a team is less than the sum of the abilities of the members within it, and this is referred to as 'negative synergy'. This may be due in part to findings that have shown group productivity to rise with increases in size, but individual productivity to fall. The output of the individual team member is not maintained at the same level when it is added to that of others. This is an important concept and obviously has implications for the way in which individual contributions to the team are assessed. Where members combine to produce performance which is in excess of their individual inputs, this produces 'positive synergy'. The search, therefore, must be for performance that is characteristic of this condition. This concept is related to much of the discussion on team roles in Chapter 10.

One troubling aspect when discussing team performance is how and indeed, if, individual performance can be assessed.

Individual Performance

There are various ways of considering individual performance in the team setting. One way, suggested by Lanza (1985: 50), is to conduct an assessment exercise in which each individual's efficiency and effectiveness are evaluated by every team member. A scale is provided and covers the full range of performance from marginal to outstanding. It is really for the team and leader to decide if this is useful, because such a process has to be handled sensitively.

But what if it is apparent that a member is performing poorly? There are several things the leader or members of the team must do. The first is to diagnose the reasons for the inadequate performance. Is it a motivational issue or one caused by an inability to do the job properly? This means identifying the causes rather than the symptoms. For example, if a teacher has an unruly class, the un-controlled bedlam is a symptom, but the problem may be either the teacher's inability to keep control or a lack of concern for doing so. The problem is best identified through discussion with the marginal performer. Possible options for solving the problem can then be explored. It is important to address the issue and to insist that some action be taken – the existing situation cannot be allowed to continue. Where the individual does not understand that his or her performance level is unacceptable, the evidence has to be based on hard facts. The purpose of all this is to reinstate the individual member as a full and active, high-performing member of a high-performing team, and this will necessitate agreed action plans supported by regular reviews of progress. Treated in this way, it can be demonstrated how individual performance is directly linked to team performance.

The issue of individual assessment in a team situation can be problematic, at least if we view teams from an idealised perspective. In such a scenario, a team is a unit that decides how it will approach a task, socialises its own members and is held accountable for its outcomes or performance, as a team. If management starts examining each individual member of the team and assessing performance, the very purpose and structure of the team may be threatened. Members may ask why they are working in a team, which theoretically involves open sharing and risk-taking, if they are to be singled out one at a time for performance appraisal. It may be that strong teams are in the best position to identify and deal with individual weaknesses themselves, without 'outside' interference. Teams which have trouble with some members to the extent that performance and relationships suffer, and they are unable to deal effectively with the trouble, may need to undergo comprehensive development activities or, in other cases, be re-formed.

Summary

In this chapter, we have concentrated on discussing characteristics which typify effective teams. We have also attempted to describe the purposes of teams and the benefits which may accrue to individuals and organisations. The last section of the chapter tackled the difficult issue of team performance and what it may involve. In Chapter 4 we look in depth at several issues related to team development.

4

TEAM DEVELOPMENT

SENGE (1990) believes that the organisations with the best chance of survival and growth are what he calls 'learning organisations'. These are organisations where people, processes and systems are dedicated or subject to ongoing learning or improvement. This thought is a useful prelude to our discussion of the central theme of this book, the growth and development of organisational teams.

In this chapter, we shall be looking at several issues relating to development. We present a model that provides the conceptual foundation for the book and that emphasizes the multidimensionality and the relatedness amongst dimensions of team development. Since the model is concerned with team problem solving, that is, discovering the areas of operation which interfere most with effective performance, we shall also look at the issue of problem diagnosis and identification. Another section examines research into teambuilding and discovers that, on the whole, the current state of research is largely inconclusive. We then examine some of the problems associated with development both within the team and amongst teams, and look briefly at 'outdoor management development', a technique of training that has enjoyed a remarkable surge in popularity in recent years. 'Teambuilding' is referred to frequently in this section, and we therefore attempt to explain its meaning and relevance for modern organisations, and the way it might be broken down into models that reflect particular emphases.

First, however, an understanding of the teambuilding intervention should start with a look at the wider concept of Organisation Development, generally known as OD, since teambuilding is a much used OD strategy.

Organisation Development

The process of OD is largely concerned with finding better ways to get work done by drawing on the skills and abilities of an organisation's human resources. Although OD practice is aimed at improving performance, its main focus is development; the fulfilment and well-being of people in the organisation. It "uses knowledge and techniques from the behavioural sciences to improve performance through trust, open confrontation of problems, employee empowerment and participation, the design of meaningful work, cooperation between groups, and the full use of human potential" (Daft, 1992: 268). OD is basically an approach to bring about change in an organisation; often an attempt to build a desirable organisational culture. We discuss culture in more detail in Chapter 18.

Ends and Page (1977: 188) identify four key features of OD:

1. **Planned change intervention.** It is usually applied when there are problems. Such problems are seen as the result of organisational ineffectiveness, and are, therefore, symptoms. Systematic diagnosis of the organisation takes place and improvement plans are made.

2. **Effectiveness.** OD aims to help the organisation adapt to and cope with environmental changes. It does this by considering appropriate modifications in structure, systems and processes, and in attitudes and personal relationships amongst organisational members.

3. **Planned interventions in processes and tasks.** Interventions are made in those aspects of operation that were earlier diagnosed as ineffective. The organisation is seen as a total system and any aspect of it may be the target of a planned intervention.

4. **Importance of teams.** One of the major assumptions of OD is that teams are the basic building blocks of organisations. It is the team that is changed in the OD concept.

As can be seen from the above points, OD is not a single technique but a collection of techniques designed to improve both organisational effectiveness and job satisfaction. Hellriegel *et al.* (1989: 555) list the basic tenets of OD which differentiate it from other organisational change strategies:

- OD tries to create self-directed change to which employees are committed. Workers themselves identify the issues and problems which need attention.
- OD is an organisation-wide change effort. It recognises that it is impossible to change one part of the organisation without changing the whole. It acknowledges that to make the organisation more effective for the long term, system-wide issues must be clearly understood.
- OD attempts to solve both short- and long-term problems. It recognises that for change to be effective in the long term, employees must be equipped to solve future problems.
- OD emphasises a collaborative approach to data collection, diagnosis and action.
- OD can lead to organisational restructuring and changes in relationship patterns that deviate from more traditional bureaucratic models.

There are a number of techniques or interventions that typify the OD approach to produce organisational change. These include: survey feedback, team building, quality circles, job enrichment, inter-group activities, managing cultures, quality of work life, transactional analysis, sensitivity training and process consultation (Daft, 1992: 269; Hellriegel *et al.*, 1989: 560; Mondy and Noe, 1990: 324; Mukhi *et al.*, 1988: 408; Roberts and Hunt, 1991: 566–8).

People, therefore, are the focus of OD, and the team is a large part of this. In the same way that OD takes a system-wide view of the organisation, an equally wide view might be taken of the team and its operation. Development at team level has to account for the factors that together contribute to performance. This issue will be taken up in detail later in this chapter.

Now we turn our attention specifically to teambuilding, the dominant intervention in a large number of OD programmes, and one which is aimed at heightening performance by improving the coordination of effort amongst members.

Teambuilding

Several benefits have been noted with regard to teambuilding. Todryk (1990: 21), for example, referring to project team development, identifies the following gains:

- Increased ability to respond to project needs.
- Rapid and accurate responses.
- Highly motivated teams.
- Increased work and decision quality.
- Increased collective team strength, leading to projects being completed on time.
- Increased commitment to personal effectiveness on the part of team members.

Linked to these benefits, Anderson (1984: 580) describes the areas in which teambuilding is used to improve team functioning:

1. Identifying goals the team should be pursuing and its performance to date in reaching its goals.
2. Identifying the strengths and weaknesses of team performance, ways in which weaknesses can be eliminated, and ways in which strengths can be maximized.
3. Actually making the improvement in the group by focusing on its process, decision-making styles, and communication. The role of each person and his or her responsibilities are clarified during this step. The impact each person has on others is also explored.
4. Resolving conflicts in the group. Conflicts may be between group members or between leaders and members. Team building tries to build skills into the group so that conflicts can be resolved within the group itself, without the help of outsiders.

Anantaraman (1984b: 217) condenses the above into a definition that describes teambuilding as "a method under which groups experientially learn to increase their skills for effective team work by examining their structures, purposes, setting, procedures and interpersonal dynamics". Johnson and Johnson's (1991: 435) definition is equally comprehensive: "Team building emphasizes the analysis of work procedures and activities to improve productivity, relationships among members, the social competence of members, and the ability of the team to adapt to changing conditions and demands."

Although, by most standards, reasonably clear definitions, they still lack the operational clarity to test the intervention, and this is indeed a difficulty with most definitions of teambuilding. De Meuse and Liebowitz (1981: 358) provide some examples that highlight the vagueness and lack of precision widely evident:

> Team building is the process of helping a work group become more effective in accomplishing its tasks and in satisfying the needs of group members (Huse, 1980, p. 511).

> Team building is an intervention conducted in a work unit as an action to deal with a condition (or conditions) seen as needing improvement (Dyer, 1977, p. 4).

> Group development is a process by which members of a group diagnose how they work together and plan changes that will improve their effectiveness (Beer, 1980, p. 140).

This lack of clarity of definition is exacerbated by the fact that there are generally acknowledged to be several foci or models of teambuilding, amongst them: the role model, the goal-setting model, and the interpersonal model. In some texts, these models are explained as variables. Johnson (1986: 48), for example, refers to goals, roles, procedures (e.g. making decisions), and relationships. Efforts to improve the work of organisational teams have tended to focus on one of these emphases. Beer's (1976) conceptual scheme, which incorporates the three models mentioned above, helps to explain these different emphases.

Goal-setting Model

The first, often called the goal-setting model, attempts to improve performance by forming goals and then devising action plans for attaining them. It may involve participation in goal setting and incorporate principles of such techniques as Management By Objectives. An approach based on the tenets of this model is described by Davidson (1985: 16). It focuses on actual organisational tasks and starts off by attempting to gain consensus on team problems in order to develop a mission statement. It then goes on to consider how the mission might be achieved and how obstacles can be overcome. Ideas are generated and action plans devised, followed by bargaining and conflict resolution sessions. Eventually, realistic, quantifiable individual performance goals are defined which lead to team goals.

Davidson suggests that by encouraging members to divert all their energies into team goal accomplishment, harmony and cooperation are generated as *effects* of the approach. This, of course, represents a highly optimistic view of the model, and one that assumes that members will give their undivided attention and support to team mission attainment. Whether that is realistic or not is a matter for debate. We look at goal setting in more detail in Chapter 7.

Interpersonal Model

The interpersonal model, as the name suggests, emphasizes the improvement of interpersonal relations in the team and thus the climate of the group. Activities might include conflict resolution and problem solving with the aim of elevating the levels of trust and openness amongst group members. As Tolle (1988: 278) observes:

> The systematic 'building plan' of the interpersonal relations model of Team Building assumes that most organization problems arise from personality differences, a lack of openness and candor, team members holding one another in low regard, the withholding of feelings or emotional data from one another, or varying degrees of all the above.

Various strategies might be used to deal with such difficulties. Horak *et al.* (1991: 70), for instance, highlight the activity of confrontation, where deep-seated issues can be brought to the surface through a process of perception exchange. This is just one of a number of powerful techniques that can be applied in the model.

The model evolved from techniques such as 'sensitivity training' and 'T-groups'. One of the problems with T-group training was the transfer dilemma, in other words, transposing the behavioural changes that take place during the training episode to the job. In team-building, this may be less of a problem, since the development of interpersonal skills can take place while participants are engaged in solving workgroup or organisational problems. As Huszczo (1990: 40) notes, however, the transferability to the 'real' situation *must* be present.

In the interpersonal model of teambuilding, there are often considered to be four foci:

- Interpersonal skill improvement
- Giving and receiving feedback
- Heightening self-awareness and learning to express feelings
- Encouraging individuals to open up about their team interactions

It is important to note that the values of openness and trust in interpersonal relations are central to teambuilding efforts, and the aim of the interpersonal model is to promote growth in such a way that these values feature prominently.

The model often demands the use of trained facilitators to assist in some of the techniques and to act as impartial conflict mediators. They are frequently used to ensure that the key issues are confronted and they are also required to act impartially.

Other Models

Given the number of consultants around who are involved in teambuilding, it is not surprising that a large number of models are available. Whereas it is not our aim to describe them here, two other models are worth mentioning. The role model uses meetings and emphasizes the clarification and development of team members' roles. A variety of issues may be explored, including leadership, power, and relationships between teams. Chapter 10 is devoted to exploring team roles. Lastly, and closely related to the role model, the Managerial Grid model is part of a wider scheme of whole organisation development, and emphasizes an examination of both task and interpersonal issues in work teams.

As our model will show, it is possible to effect integration amongst these different approaches. Weisbord (1985: 27) goes along these lines in suggesting the need for a dual focus – on the task and on the processes by which it is achieved. Referring specifically to teambuilding meetings, he indicates that there must be an aim for outcomes at both levels: means and ends. The notion of, and need for, integration will be developed later but first, it is important that we acknowledge some of the problems associated with teambuilding. Perhaps the most appropriate point to begin this is by discussing some of the research that has been conducted into team development.

Research into Team Development

In keeping with the widespread support for teams in organisations in times of change, team development has also received much attention. Situations have been defined in which it might be appropriate to employ intervention approaches. It should be noted that the reasons given often relate to the results of organisational responses to environmental conditions. Bradford (1990: 38), for example, suggests a number of factors that might determine the appropriateness of teambuilding:

- After size reduction when new management teams must be formed.
- At the beginning of productivity drives.
- As part of a quality enhancement programme.
- To introduce technological change.
- As part of a major policy and programme shift.

These are reasonable suggestions, but there are no guarantees that development efforts will be successful, even at significant times such as these in the organisation's operation. Research has little to say on the issue, and is largely inconclusive. We move on now to look at what evidence there might be to support claims for the effectiveness of development interventions.

It is difficult to make assertions about the link between development activities and performance for two key reasons. First, as discussed earlier in this chapter, there is no universally accepted definition of teams, much less teambuilding or team development. We shall see later how development might be seen as a multidimensional construct and how different practitioners may have different emphases in terms of development foci. It is not possible at present levels of understanding, therefore, to refer to teambuilding as if it were a standardised activity. Second, what research has been conducted is methodologically weak, and indeed the reason for this may be partly attributed to the absence of a satisfactory definition.

One of the few exceptions to this criticism may be Eden's (1985: 94) field experiment, in which experimental and control groups were used to test a team development intervention. The design permitted three different tests of a hypothesis to be conducted, described in order of ascending rigour. Eden admitted, however, the more rigorous criterion of objective performance data was not employed.

Other researchers have made efforts to elevate the rigour of their studies. Margerison *et al.* (1988: 53), for example, in a major project which examined the effects of a development intervention for teams of airline pilots, indicated the intention in a follow-up study to conduct blind trials, so that observers would not know whether their subjects had been part of a team development intervention.

Apart from these occasional attempts at rigorous inquiry, the predominant way of documenting interventions has been in the form of anecdotal evidence and simple reaction measures. For example, the success of team development episodes has been, and still is to a large degree, judged on the basis of participants' remarks following the intervention. For various reasons, there have been increasing calls for more rigorous evaluation.

This raises another issue. Much of the research into teams and participative decision making has been experimental and conducted with heterogeneous groups working under laboratory conditions (Wynn and Guditus, 1984: 112). This may be far removed from the real context. For example, we may wish to understand the relationship between cooperation in teams and performance amongst permanent groups of professional managers who are dealing with complex managerial problems. Under these conditions, it may be difficult to transpose the findings of empirical research to the actual context.

Another problem evident from the research is the prevalence of vague reporting (De Meuse and Liebowitz, 1981: 359). Details about the precise activities implemented are not given, and often other important items of information such as sample sizes, personnel involved, and the time frame of the research are not recorded.

Horak *et al.* (1991: 70) also highlight several weaknesses, including lack of experimental controls, failing to check the reliability and validity of instrumentation, and lack of definitions of the variables used. They also mention the possibility of bias in the responses, and we shall see below how bias may be built into the evaluation design.

De Meuse and Liebowitz (1981: 364) analysed a number of studies and provided some useful information about the dependent variables used to assess the impact of the interventions. The variables identified were as follows:

1. **Initial reactions:** These are remarks made soon after the event and relate to the perceived usefulness of the team development

effort. As a dependent variable, it may be useful in deciding whether to continue the effort.

2. **Attitudinal and perceptual changes**: The variable is concerned with subjective assessments of changes in the group's condition, and may include such factors as climate, openness, trust, and relations between members. Many of the studies that the authors examined measured this variable, but there was a vast range of concepts covered (p. 365).

3. **Behavioural changes**: These are concerned with the behaviours of team members that might have been changed through the team development event. Such behaviours included work group performance, turnover, and critical incidents.

4. **Organisational changes**: Unlike the first three, which are all concerned with intra-group responses, these relate to the wider organisation. It is proposed that changes in a team will have an effect in the wider organisation of which the team is a part. Measures used included productivity, turnover and conflict.

The findings from the above studies are interesting. More studies found positive behavioural and organisational changes than attitudinal changes. "Thus, these results *suggest* that team development is consistently effective for enhancing individual attitudes and perceptions and improving individual and organizational performance, with a greater emphasis on the latter" (De Meuse and Liebowitz, 1981: 369).

While the findings may be of interest, caution must be exercised in drawing firm conclusions, since the evaluations were far from rigorous, and this is a fact that has indeed characterised most of the research. One of the most notable weaknesses is the common practice of the programme leader also being the evaluator. Since most interventions using outside consultants represent a source of livelihood to the practitioners, it is unlikely that they will promote evaluations that may turn out to be unfavourable. It is in their interests to elicit measures that offer support for the intervention.

Large sums of money have been spent by organisations on teambuilding activities, but as Margerison *et al.* (1988: 54) so aptly sum up their major research project into air-crew team management development: "It remains to be seen whether all of this converts into more effective performance." It seems strange that even in times of resource scarcity, organisations are prepared to invest substantial amounts in training that only 'may' have the desired effect. Research can have a major part to play in arriving at more solid conclusions. However, it is clear from the preceding discussion that if research into team development is to be of more utility, there have to be substantial methodological improvements. Horak *et al.* (1991: 70) suggest evaluations of long-term effectiveness may need to take place, rather than the short-term measures currently made. As Wolff (1988: 6) observes in discussing interpersonal teambuilding, there is no data to support the belief that lasting benefits are produced, and it is this long-term perspective that is vital in considering development. Horak *et al.* also suggest comparative studies involving different approaches, and conducting studies using different mixes of participants. Perhaps this relates to the fact that most teams studied have comprised production workers rather than professional managers. This may be a severe limitation if one is expecting to transpose the findings of a particular study to a different setting.

Probably the critical factor in improving the state of research into team development is arriving at an agreed definition of the intervention with standardised activities. This, however, is unlikely to happen and it may be inadvisable anyway, since the diversity of approach is both its strength and its attraction to those who demand its benefits. We now look more closely at problems with team development.

Problems with Team Development

There are several problems that have emerged from the practice of planned team development. The first concerns the 'events' that take place. In some ways, the word 'intervention' when applied to teambuilding can imply a misleading note of finality. If it is to be effective, it is better seen as a process rather than an isolated activity. It is worth emphasizing that development takes place across time and team development must, therefore, be seen as an ongoing strategy (Huszczo, 1990: 41).

A second problem is the nature of the event. Games and exercises feature prominently in teambuilding training programmes, and people often remember these vividly. One of the strengths of 'outdoor management development', as a case in point, is the quality of exercise format: participants come away with memorable experiences of the exercises themselves, which, in many cases, do help to highlight important points about interpersonal relationships, systematic planning, and a host of other team-related issues. Teire (1982: 204) indeed sees advantages in moving away from the organisational problem context, because members often 'can't see the wood for the trees'. It may be argued, however, that such exercises should supplement, rather than replace, realistic development activities:

> Team members need to spend time during their developmental activities actually negotiating with each other, discussing issues, identifying together the goals of the team and the commitment level of team members to those goals, identifying the roles each member should play to accomplish goals, and reviewing and establishing procedures that the team will use to become more effective (Huszczo, 1990: 41).

All that seems to be more relevant when applied in the workplace.

On this point, Kezsbom (1990: 51) observes that teams may have little time to engage in separate teambuilding events, and the development, therefore, needs to be integrated into the real team processes. Such processes include planning sessions, review meetings, and informal updates about the status of projects. She provides some practical advice in the form of steps that can be followed while these 'normal' team activities are taking place. They include creating a positive climate, establishing a common vision, determining responsibilities, understanding interdependencies and identifying tradeoffs and risks.

A further problem relates to the consultants and facilitators who generally lead training events. Adair (1986: 139) observes, somewhat alarmingly, that teambuilding may have more to do with their needs and values rather than an analysis of what the team really needs. In pursuing this line of inquiry, he lists some of the reasons that consultants might give for running team development sessions. They include: enjoyment, being good at it, being flattered by being invited to do the job, receiving good feedback, professional kudos, financial reward and power gains through operating in familiar territory. Many of these reasons are concerned with the needs and skills of the facilitator rather than the client team. From this, it is obvious that a rigorous assessment is needed of whether team development is necessary and, if so, in what areas it is needed.

Intra- and Inter-team Development

The emphasis in models of teambuilding is on the improvement of work *within* the team. On this note, Barner (1989: 47) appropriately distinguishes between 'intra-team building' and 'inter-team building'.

It is obviously important to determine where the focus of the team-building effort should lie. In the former, some of the key issues that development interventions might address are decision making, role clarity, and communication between team members, all important features of one or other of the above models. Inter-team building efforts, in contrast, concentrate on the interface issues between teams, the problems that they might face in relations because of interdependent functions and responsibilities. Such issues might include the need to increase the understanding amongst teams of their respective missions, priorities and roles; of the ways in which they might service and support one another; of their inter-actions in working with external customers and suppliers; and of the application of common work procedures across interdependent functions.

We mentioned earlier 'outdoor management development'. This is a technique that is used widely in teambuilding and, in view of the rapid expansion of this type of intervention in recent years, it is worth taking a brief look at some of the features of this process.

Outdoor Management Development

It is claimed that Outdoor Management Development provides a powerful and stimulating tool for learning, where the effects of decisions are felt with immediacy. It uses outdoor exercises to help participants, amongst other objectives, develop teamwork skills. "Classroom teaching we can neatly allocate (relegate) to an appropriate memory file...physical and real experience is more likely to perturb" (Mossman, 1982). By putting people in problem situations, which are very real in themselves (as opposed to paper exercises in the classroom), the effects of decisions are felt in a real way. For example, a group of senior managers was given the task of navigating some un-familiar terrain. Some critical decisions had to be taken about directions and time. Had the decisions been inappropriately conceived, they could easily have been lost for several hours. The consequences would have been at least uncomfortable. Under these circumstances, learning is intensified and it is argued by leading exponents of the system that learning is a speedier process than by any other method of training.

Where the focus is specifically on 'management develop-ment' the training is concerned with collective performance. It is argued that an understanding of colleagues' behaviour in high-pressure situations will help managers understand one another better at work when difficult tasks emerge.

One problem with such programmes is that there may be a greater emphasis on the physical activities themselves than the learning which should take place in relation to team development. Using a suitable framework for planning, action and reflection may go some way to diverting attention away from the physical activity (used simply as a vehicle for learning) and more firmly towards the transposition of learning to the practice of teamwork.

There are considerable resource demands in terms of personnel, facilities, equipment and time. The right people have to be involved in the design and delivery of the programme. The key designers must have expertise in outdoor exercise design and in development. The consequences of inappropriate exercises (from either a safety or learning experience viewpoint) are too serious to be taken lightly. Group facilitators (those who work with small groups of participants, observing them and guiding their evaluation discussions) must have a thorough understanding of the processes involved and the way in which learning is heightened before, during and after the experience. Their part in reviewing exercises is of the utmost importance and Mossman (1982) claims that the quality of review hinges on the skill and sensitivity of supervising staff.

It is claimed that the key to the success of Outdoor Management Development lies in its effectiveness in fulfilling chosen objectives in terms of improved performance in the workplace, although it has to be said that this transaction is difficult to substantiate. Nevertheless, those providers and clients who have had an extended association with the method claim intuitively that it works and that it has a considerable effect on performance.

A Multidimensional Model

Major Propositions

The basis of the multidimensional model outlined in this section emerges from a distillation of the available literature on team development in organisations, with an attempt to integrate various propositions in the theory; from several episodes of small-scale research in the field; and from intuition and experience of both individual and team development.

The model has five major propositions:

1. Team development is best seen as a multidimensional construct, where the conditions in one dimension critically affect the conditions in other dimensions.
2. For effective team development to take place, attempts must be made to consciously optimise the conditions in each dimension.
3. Teams need to identify those dimensions that are in need of attention and to employ appropriate development strategies. Performance will depend on accurate diagnosis.
4. Relative emphases in dimensional development will be determined in part by the development level of the team.
5. Responsibility for team development should lie largely with the team itself.

It will be noted from the above propositions that we use the word 'dimension' frequently, and this word is synonymous with what might be termed 'models' of team development, described earlier in the chapter.

These models, in our scheme, form the basis for our understanding of dimensions. They show that different foci may exist in looking at team development. We have chosen to call these dimensions: 'individual', 'task', 'team' and 'organisation'. These will be explained in detail in the next section.

The first proposition suggests that these dimensions are inextricably linked and that it is unrealistic, therefore, to see them as discrete teambuilding foci. They each have a significant impact on the other. If, for example, interpersonal relations are unsatisfactory, it is argued that this might have an important effect on *task* performance and accomplishment. Conversely, if the team is unsystematic in its efforts to process tasks and thereby experiences little success, *team* morale and relationships amongst members may suffer.

The second proposition states that teams need to have satisfactory conditions in each of the above dimensions. This is supported by Buller (1986: 156): "Teams that address multiple forces (that is, task, interpersonal, organizational, and so on) may outperform teams that address only one set of forces such as task or interpersonal."

The third proposition, which is closely linked to the previous one, implies that teams must give attention to dimensions 'selectively'.

In other words, it is inadvisable to employ development strategies across the board. Some dimensions will need more attention than others. The team's success, therefore, may hinge in part on identifying needs accurately and applying development efforts to the right dimensions. This, again, is confirmed by Buller (1986: 156): "The model predicts that, to the extent the team can recognize and solve those problems interfering *most* with task performance, its performance will be improved."

The fourth proposition is that the variations in dimensional development needs may be attributed partly to the level of development (or maturity) of the team. Team membership composition obviously has an impact on team development needs, but the degree of maturity of the team as a group is a factor that is often overlooked. Huszczo (1990: 40) too notes: "Even teams that are playing the same 'sport' should not necessarily be coached and developed in the same manner. If a team has more new members than long-term veterans, training may have to focus on the skills needed to improve quality rather than efficiency."

The final proposition assumes that the team itself is often in the best position to identify and decide upon its own developmental focus, especially in regard to the task and organisational dimensions. Although this does not exclude outside assistance, advice or analysis, we hold that if teams are to develop on a continuous basis and are to be responsive to an unpredictable environment, they should be encouraged to take charge of their own development.

We now return to the concept of dimensions.

The Four Dimensions

Using four areas of consideration is only a convenient way of directing our thoughts. The dimensions are not mutually exclusive and, indeed, we have found no framework of team development in the literature that satisfactorily separates models. This is because the activities that contribute to a particular aspect of development within any given model are often related to improvements in other dimensions. For example, if attempts are made to elevate the motivation levels of individuals (we have included that activity in the 'individual' dimension), the effects may be felt in the team (the 'team' dimension) and there can be a considerable impact on the quality of task accomplishment (the 'task' dimension). It is necessary, therefore, to accept large areas of overlap amongst the dimensions. This reinforces the view that the model of team development presented is a holistic, integrated one.

Despite the inter-relatedness, the activities within dimensions are more likely to have a major impact on their own dimensions. For example, by concentrating on development in a number of task dimension activities, the greatest effect will be on improvements in the way the task is carried out – the 'task' dimension. We would suggest this is more likely to be so when several or more activities within a dimension are being developed.

We have used the word 'activities' so far to indicate the items within dimensions. That label is inappropriate to apply across the board. Some items are 'processes'; others are 'factors'. For example, clarity and ambiguity are 'factors' in the task dimension, but influencing and coordinating are 'processes' in the team dimension.

The model draws on some of the literature relating to participative decision making and small group theory, thus accounting for such factors as team characteristics, member skills and contributions, team processes, and the environment in which the group operates.

Using force field analysis as the basic framework, Buller (1986: 157) produced a model that described the relation of team building to task performance. Our model accepts the force field conceptualisation, that by recognising and dealing with those forces that interfere most with performance, the team may have the most significant impact on performance improvement. We also accept Buller's four factor framework. We have extended the model, however, to incorporate more items within each factor area. Some of these items may be critical to success. There is another significant difference. We have added a temporal or maturity dimension. Teams may be thought to progress through a series of stages of development. They start off as relatively incohesive and immature (in team terms). Some teams, however, progress to the point of being outstanding in their work. The matter of 'phases of development' is discussed fully in Chapter 19. At this stage, it is important to recognise that the needs for development may vary according to the development level of the team. A team that is mature and effective will require different development emphases to one that is newly formed. The model accounts for these differences and suggests those areas that might need more attention at any given stage. The list of dimensions and items is shown in Figure 4.1 and the model is shown in Figure 4.2.

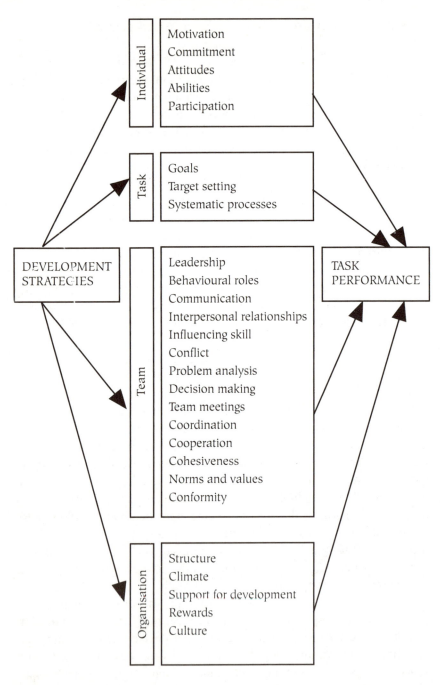

Figure 4.1   An Extended Model of Team Development
(**Source:** Adapted from Buller, 1986)

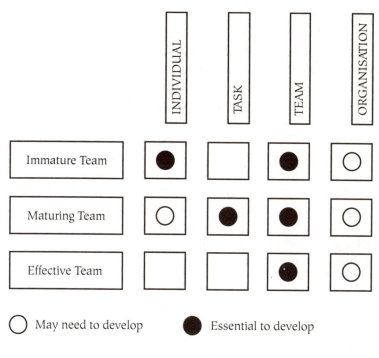

Figure 4.2   Model of Team Development Emphases
According to Team Maturity Levels

Force Field Analysis

Lewin's (1951) well-known concept of force field analysis, a diagnostic technique useful in decoding confusing and complex situations, is a helpful way of conceptualising the process of team development. Lewin proposed that successful organisational change should follow three phases. The first involved 'unfreezing' the *status quo* and moving to a new state, and then 'refreezing' the change to make it lasting. Lewin did not see change as an event but rather as a balance of forces working in opposite directions. He claimed that the *status quo* was in fact a state of equilibrium resulting from a combination or balance of forces pushing against one another. Certain forces, which he labelled 'restraining forces' retard movement from equilibrium, while at the same time 'driving forces' direct behaviour away from equilibrium; the result – equilibrium. If change is to come the agent must manipulate the current equilibrium of forces. This can be done by increasing the driving forces, decreasing the resisting forces or by combining the two approaches.

Lewin's work has had a profound effect on organisational change strategies but, like many models, it was developed in a time when change may have been more predictable than it is today. His framework assumes a planned, problem-oriented, systematic, and system-wide approach to managing change.

Buller (1986: 151) used Lewin's work to explain the dynamics of his problem-solving model, and the similarities with Lewin's work are obvious. According to the concept, the team can be thought of as being in a state of balance, which is a result of driving forces pushing for change in one direction, and restraining forces that push in the opposite direction. The analysis of these forces, to determine whether they help or obstruct progress, breaks down perceptual barriers and provides a clearer view of where the deficiencies are and of how to reach predetermined goals. Strategies can be employed to modify the forces either side of the balance line. This is shown in Figure 4.3.

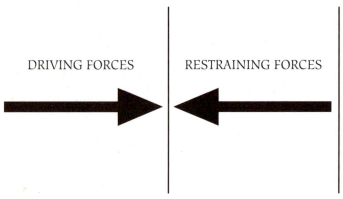

DRIVING FORCES   RESTRAINING FORCES

Present performance level   Desired performance level

Figure 4.3   Force Field and Performance
(**Source:** Adapted from Buller, 1986)

From this perspective, by trying to reduce the restraining forces, advances can be made towards the desired level of performance, and this may explain how teambuilding strategies elevate performance effectiveness. This is explained by Anantaraman (1984b: 220) in describing teambuilding as "the deliberate working through of all blockages to progress until a working group becomes an effective team. These blockages may exist in the domain of leadership, goal-setting, role clarification, interpersonal relations or intergroup relations."

Zenger and Miller (1974: cited in Buller, 1986: 151) explain three groups of forces that might support improved performance levels:

- Personal motivations: Within each individual is a force leading to higher achievement, growth, and personal fulfilment. While this force varies in strength, there does seem to be a drive in most individuals to work and be productive.
- Interpersonal effects: In any organization there is some degree of cooperation on the part of supervisors, colleagues, and subordinates that reinforces positive personal motivation.
- Organization pressures: The power of the organization to give or withhold compensation, status, and responsibility is another performance elevating force.

The same authors then identify the following counterforces:

- Personal: While there are strong forces upward, individuals some-times underestimate their own capabilities, or they may not clearly see how what they do (or fail to do) affects the organization or team performance.
- Interpersonal: As people work together, minor misunderstandings arise and in time build up to hostility unless they are periodically cleared away. Those whose job it is to motivate others sometimes try to do so in a way that actually offends or demotivates.
- Organizational: At times the carrot-and-stick power of organizations is misused or its intended effects are misunderstood. Resentment, bitterness, or apathy ensue, and performance drops.

Buller, in his model, adds forces relating to the task, and identifies the following sub-forces: clarity of expectations and goals, and job requirements; knowledge, ability and skills available; and the nature of the tools available. The countervailing sub-forces are: the complexity, difficulty, ambiguity, and degree of structure of the task; the need for interdependencies; and outdated tools and technology. Some of these may truly be forces against effective task completion, but some are questionable. For example, ambiguity may be both a curse and a blessing, depending on the nature and preferences of the members.

By decreasing the restraining forces, the team can go nearer the desired performance mark. Therefore, if individuals learn to under-stand their own capabilities, if task goals are specified clearly, and if up-to-date tools are provided, it follows that performance will be lifted in these areas. The same applies equally to the other sub-forces, processes and factors. Other frameworks offer varied perspectives to change and development.

Other Frameworks

Several frameworks adopt a broader perspective from which to approach team success. A comprehensive model of factors affecting group performance is advanced by Jewell and Reitz (1981). They list a range of factors associated with performance. Team member characteristics (skills, abilities, knowledge), team characteristics (size, cohesiveness, behaviour norms, maturity level, membership mix), team processes (decision making, coordinating, communicating), team environment (nature of the task, goals and targets, rewards), and organisational structure and policy, all combine to affect team performance.

Another framework worth noting is advanced by Thamhain (1990: 11) who looks at the characteristics of an innovative work environment. He identifies three primary issues: task definition, people management, and organisational support. These correspond closely with other models, but the people-related factors might be divided into individual and group considerations. The interesting point to note from Thamhain's work is that the task-related factors are most likely to have the greatest effect on innovative performance. Such factors include clear goals, technical direction and leadership, autonomy and professionally challenging work, experienced and qualified team members, and team involvement and project visibility. Although concerned with the special case of innovative product teams, the work throws useful light on the development focus and performance linkage.

The multidimensional model we present, by taking a holistic view of team development, follows the approach adopted by Buller (1986: 156) and "enhances the likelihood that the team will identify and solve critical debilitating problems, and thereby function more effectively. Moreover, by developing a general problem solving capacity within the team, the problem solving approach may foster continued performance effectiveness after the formal team building intervention is concluded."

We must now turn our attention to the problem-solving process just mentioned. Whilst one approach to solving the problems of teams depends on a third party consultant carrying out a planned intervention, in this book we are looking at a broader approach in which teams diagnose their own needs and then plan strategies to improve performance.

Although teams may choose to use consultants, we suggest that the most worthwhile development comes from the team itself and not from outside. We believe teams should aim for internal and external relationships which encourage constant learning and development within the team and that, as far as possible, this should be self-guided. Development should become a part of the team's 'way of doing things' and not involve action only when problems arise. Our model attempts to account for this. We also propose that many of the strategies may be useful to teams that are not intact or permanent, and, in that respect, our approach differs from others.

If teams are to take more control of their own development, being able to recognise and diagnose problems is paramount to their success.

Diagnosis

In this scheme, the team identifies problem areas, gathers data to aid the diagnostic process, then devises strategies to reduce or remove the deficiencies. By attacking the major problems, the process is economical. In other words, it does not expend effort on those dimensions that provide little or no hindrance to effective performance. As Barner (1989: 46) notes: "A team-building effort should address only those performance issues that directly affect the entire team and issues that lie within the control and direction of the team."

This last point deserves further elaboration. Many team development episodes are led by expert consultants who have preferences in terms of a teambuilding model. There is little diagnosis. Consequently, problems may be tackled that do not really exist. For example, those with a preference for interpersonal models will tend to work on interpersonal issues, whether or not they realistically demand attention. Those who prefer systematic goal models will work regardless at improving goal setting and action planning. These are the only problems they see. Teams then end up with a narrow range of skills.

On this note of inadequate diagnosis, Tolle (1988: 279) questions whether the improvement of interpersonal competencies amongst management teams will really impact on the operational performance of the organisation. He goes on to note that:

> anything further than this is pure happenstance unless diagnosis of the organization's ills has determined the cause to be the underdevelopment or use of interpersonal skills among the team members. Otherwise, the organization with operational problems before team building will likely

have many of the same problems after team building except that the team members will behave in a more friendly and cooperative way.

Huszczo (1990: 39) observes that much team training is conducted without any preliminary diagnosis at all. The likelihood of success, he notes, is low. Development needs to be tailor-made. One reason for avoiding diagnosis may be the fear of stirring up conflict when the more searching diagnostic questions are asked. Another reason may be the inability of people involved in teambuilding to deploy data gathering and analysis skills.

Ends and Page (1977: 172) advocate a preliminary diagnosis by the leader which can then be presented to the team as a starting point for discussion, leading to a more accurate diagnosis by the team as a whole. Such a process attempts to answer the question, collectively: What is standing in the way of more effective performance?

The use of an instrument as a starting point for discussion is useful, since it may give some indication of where development efforts should be directed. The questionnaire in Figure 4.4 presents some statements that can be assessed by participants, on an individual basis, on the bipolar scale.

In line with our belief that development should largely be team driven, diagnosis cannot be seen as a one-off process. Within the team, especially if it is fairly permanent, there should exist a 'challenge' mentality. Members should be scanning continually both the internal and external environment in an effort to predict and identify problems or challenges. In terms of development, diagnosis can be seen as crossing and including task, individual, group and organisational dimensions depending on the needs of the team. As expressed earlier, events in one dimension will almost inevitably affect other dimensions. Constant scanning and diagnosis allows problems to be identified in one or more domains, thereby allowing the required development to be planned for. There are a number of methods available for diagnosing team development needs.

Computer Software

A recent advance in team diagnosis is reported by Meyer (1991: 40). He describes the use of a software program to analyse a group's composition and dynamics, and suggests it may be particularly useful for application before a team actually forms. It is claimed the software can report information on interpersonal factors causing stress, dissatisfaction and

Do individuals work interdependently or independently? Do they understand the need for mutual support?

1	2	3	4	5	6
Serious weakness				Major strength	

Is time wasted struggling over issues of territorial rights, or are members concerned more about personal gain than team accomplishments?

1	2	3	4	5	6
Serious weakness				Major strength	

Do team members feel a sense of ownership of team goals? Are they involved in setting them and is there real commitment?

1	2	3	4	5	6
Serious weakness				Major strength	

Do team members wait to be told what to do or do they willingly make suggestions and genuinely contribute their talents and abilities to the team?

1	2	3	4	5	6
Serious weakness				Major strength	

Do team members work in a climate of trust where they feel able to openly express their ideas, opinions, feelings and dissent, or are they afraid to disagree for fear of recrimination?

1	2	3	4	5	6
Serious weakness				Major strength	

Do team members exercise great caution in what they say or are they honest and open? Do they try to understand one another and accept that there are inevitably many different views?

1	2	3	4	5	6
Serious weakness				Major strength	

Are team members encouraged to develop their skills for the good of the team?

1	2	3	4	5	6
Serious weakness				Major strength	

Is conflict viewed positively, as an opportunity to develop new ideas and creative approaches to problems? Is it dealt with constructively?

1	2	3	4	5	6
Serious weakness				Major strength	

Is decision making of a high quality with all members participating, or is conformity more important?

1	2	3	4	5	6
Serious weakness				Major strength	

Figure 4.4　　　Diagnosing Team Strengths and Weaknesses

poor morale; the behavioural role preferences of team members; team values; informal communication networks; individual personal and professional characteristics; team member perceptions; and work-flow patterns and mismatched responsibilities and authority.

Perhaps computer software's most productive use may be as an aid to the selection process. It does not cover all possible dimensions of team activity, but it does seem to have utility: "The program can make team managing a more objective, scientific process, eliminating much of the guesswork, time, and amateur psychoanalysis used by managers trying to understand a team's dynamics. Team members are themselves the source of feedback, and the computer performs the tedious analytical work" (Meyer, 1991: 43). Used as a comple-ment to other diagnostic measures, this approach may provide a useful tool.

Simulation

Another useful implement for diagnostic purposes is the realistic organisational simulation (Kaplan *et al.*, 1985: 242). The advantage of simulation is that the observation can be controlled and limited to a specific time and place. The characteristic of the technique is that it is realistic, unlike some of the 'simulations' commonly used with manage-ment teams. "It reproduces the pace, pressure, and fragmentation of managerial work. It is freely interacting, allowing participants to take their roles and relate to one another entirely as they please." The simulation produces behavioural data, but more important is the system set up to collect, assemble and interpret data.

The benefits of one realistic simulation episode are recorded by the same authors (p. 249):

> Herein lies the unique contribution of the simulation: It uncovered the configuration of actual behavior that impaired the team's effectiveness. The simulation enabled the managers to go beyond recognizing that they disposed of problems poorly, for it also showed them how it hurt their performance as a team. Thus, the simulation helped clarify the team's understanding of itself.

The participants expressed improvements in lateral communication and cooperation, more direct contact with one another, better results and quicker response and a higher degree of morale.

It should be made clear, however, that these findings were based essentially on reaction measures, and like most interventions, there is no guarantee of real performance improvement over time. There are, nevertheless, distinct advantages of this approach over some others. Despite the compelling benefits of realistic simulation, it requires a sizeable investment of time and energy, and it may be best used only for special circumstances.

Interpersonal Teambuilding Efforts

The focus in most teambuilding efforts has tended to be on interpersonal issues, often dealing with conflict among group members. These are undoubtedly important, because personality differences and uncontrolled episodes of conflict can have an adverse effect on performance. As Tolle (1988: 279) notes, it is easier to observe who is in conflict with whom rather than the underlying issues that led to the problem episode, and it is no surprise, therefore, that managers rely on the interpersonal emphasis to see them out of difficulties.

In some cases, however, there may have been an over-emphasis on simply improving the way people 'get along'. As a result, team-building is seen as 'soft' and not directly related to real improvements in organisational performance. This 'softness' may be an image generated by observation of some activities that some practitioners use:

> And some of them are perhaps a little silly. At one team-building session, for example, the consultant had team members toss a whiffle ball back and forth to break the ice. Then team members wrapped string around a finger while telling the rest of the group something about themselves. (Wrapping string was supposed to make you less self-conscious about talking about yourself.) No doubt there are team-building programs in which people are led blindfolded or fall backward into the arms of their fellow team members, as in the encounter groups of decades past and the Outward Bound groups that continue to be popular. But the touchy-feely approach does not seem to be the rule in team-building sessions (Chance, 1989: 25).

The problem of softness is also identified by Huszczo (1990: 42) in looking at responses of people who have gone through team-building programmes: "'We got to know each other better,' 'We learned that we need to communicate more with each other,' and 'We learned that no one is perfect and we just have to accept each other more.' Such 'safe' (socially desirable), broad statements are difficult to follow up on." Such statements are probably familiar to many of us. To exacerbate the problem, a great deal of training is not even documented. Teambuilding in the outdoor management development field is a case in point (Laabs, 1991: 63). Subjective evaluation, through observation (some of it informed) and reaction questionnaires, seems to predominate.

Huszczo (1990: 42) suggests that the appropriate counter-action is to demand 'harder' statements: "We need to dedicate time to helping teams draw up concrete statements of expectation before leaving training sessions. We need to help teams identify who will do what, with or to whom, and by when." This is consistent with a target or goal-setting approach which is discussed in Chapter 7.

Whilst there are many claims (mostly anecdotal) for the successes of interpersonal development approaches, Wolff (1988: 6) notes there is "no data supporting the belief that interpersonal team building produces lasting benefits for the organization. It can even mask more fundamental weaknesses in your management system." Drawing on Tolle's experiences at IBM, Wolff observes that the focus should be diverted from interpersonal issues to task-related considerations. He concludes that:

> interpersonal team building can change people's attitudes and behaviors enough to make a friendlier, more cooperative, more cohesive group. But this doesn't necessarily mean it will be a more effective group insofar as the larger organization is concerned. "The more critical factors of team effort revolve around all members understanding and agreeing on the *mission* or purpose of the team effort, commonly held *goals* and *objectives* and each member's possession of sufficient knowledge and skills to perform their individual *responsibilities*. Feelings of competency, camaraderie, and interpersonal intimacy are more likely to be effects of successful team efforts than the causes of success."

These sentiments are supported also by Chance (1989: 25) who suggests the focus should be on teaching people how to work with one another; and by Crouch and Yetton (1987: 126), who state when discussing team development: "Within the conventional team development approaches management training in behavioural skills is (also) divorced from training in task skills".

There may, of course, be organisational reasons for improving interpersonal relationships. Managers may want people to comply with plans and actions already decided, and getting employees to have good personal relationships may strengthen the capacity to achieve compliance.

This is a widely practised, but highly dubious, strategy. As Huszczo (1990: 37) observes:

> Most of us have worked on or with teams in which members have gotten along well with each other, but weren't all that effective. They weren't able to accomplish the required tasks, to use team members' talents to the best advantage, or to interact effectively with other elements of the organization.

There are indeed many cases of teams, after a teambuilding intervention, coming away able to confront interpersonal conflict and other related issues, but being helpless in dealing with individual issues (such as motivation), with task design, and with the degree of organisational support. Hence, when the balance of problems changes for the team, it is unable to cope with the new difficulties. Our approach, in contrast, looks at a whole range of issues associated with performance and encourages general problem-solving skills in the team which, it is reasonably claimed, may lead to long-term effectiveness.

Summary

This chapter has focused on development and the various emphases that might be applied. In looking at the available research, we highlighted the problems of drawing conclusions from less than rigorous investigations. The picture need not be an entirely pessimistic one. There is much to support the effectiveness of teams. Kanter (1983), for example, points to decades of socio-psychological research and corporate experience in suggesting that participative teams are the most appropriate structure for keeping ahead of change. We accept that unreservedly. Our question is more concerned with the relationship between development efforts and performance.

We have also attempted to demonstrate that it may be inappropriate to think of team development in terms of a single dimension. Nevertheless, it is easy to see from the lists in Figure 4.1 that there may be an enormous amount to cover even within one dimension, and that dimension alone can take up all the time allocated to a teambuilding effort.

It is worth reiterating two points, however. First, a team would not usually need to give equal attention to each item in a dimension. The problem-solving procedure, therefore, is selective. Only those items that are impeding effective performance should be the focus of development efforts. Second, team development is concerned, amongst other things, with having the right individuals with appropriate skills, with systematic approaches to task accomplishment, with effective interpersonal and communication processes and with a high degree of support from the organisation. In other words, it has to be seen from a multidimensional perspective. As Buller (1986: 166) observes, "team building is a complex, multifaceted intervention that may affect performance in a variety of ways".

The following sections of the book now examine each dimension and its component items in detail. We explain the nature and relevance of these topics to the team and identify the implications for managers in terms of improvement. By drawing on the literature, we show the strategies that can be employed to effect improvements in each aspect of team operation.

Section 2

The Individual Team Member

5

MOTIVATION

MOTIVATION basically involves looking at why people do the things they do, or why they behave the way they do. It is about people's drives, wants and needs. "Motivation refers to the idea of directing people's behaviour towards a given goal, or set of goals, and in encouraging them to invest more of themselves into that goal directed behaviour" (Dingley, 1986: 21). If teams are to work together effectively toward goal accomplishment they must want to do it and feel the outcome will be worthwhile.

We are not proposing that there is any such thing as team motivation. Rather, there is an amalgam of individual attitudes and motivations that integrate to provide a spirit or drive in a team. Motivation necessarily focuses on individuals and how their contribution can be made more meaningful. In the final analysis, motivation applies to the distinctiveness of each individual. Individuals must then be combined into a team. "The manager's job becomes one of identifying the right chords to play to influence each group member to achieve the group's goals ... to mold a team spirit, a common identity, that creates not only shared goals but also shared motivations for achieving them" (Roberts and Hunt, 1991: 435).

To understand and improve motivation we need to gather a basic understanding of its central tenets. Then we must look at the role of the team leader (and members) in providing a climate that is conducive to motivation. Next, we have to learn how to identify the ways in which individual members in teams are motivated. Finally, we shall explore some of the ways in which motivational levels might be increased.

The Concept of Motivation

An individual's performance is essentially determined by three factors: ability, work environment, and motivation. This is commonly expressed by the following equation.

Performance $= f$ (Ability x Motivation x Environment)

For a person to perform effectively he must know how to do the job, must want to do the job and must have a conducive, well-supported environment. If any one of these three factors is absent it is unlikely that employees will be truly effective (Griffin, 1984). While we look at each of these areas separately, it should be realised that team and organisation structure and leader behaviour have a substantial impact on what Margerison (1973: 59) calls 'motivational balance'. In this section, we concentrate on the second of the three factors, and one of the key issues relating to both individuals in teams, that of motivation. We look at the question of individual abilities and experience a little later, and the issue of organisational support in providing a satisfactory environment (that is, the social and physical milieu in which the employee works) is covered in Chapter 17.

In a thoughtfully constructed team setting, it is likely that the combination of members will have the abilities to perform a task. Whether they are motivated or not is a different matter. Managers are responsible for providing a conducive physical environment but, in many ways, this depends on the team itself and the culture of the organisation. Both of these are inexorably linked to motivation. There are a number of ways of looking at motivation but most promote similar ideas.

People can be motivated by three generic types of needs or forces (some writers call them *drives*):

- Personal forces
- Push forces
- Pull forces

Personal forces come from within people themselves. For example, if we hold strong religious or political views, these can have a considerable influence on our behaviour. If something is a matter of personal importance, therefore, it becomes a motivational force.

Push forces come from other people such as family, colleagues, superiors or subordinates. If any of these groups put the individual under pressure to follow a course of action, it becomes a push force. In a work team situation, this sort of force is likely to originate from superiors, fellow workers or clients.

Pull forces come from external factors, those which exist outside the individual and which form an attraction. Items such as a car, a house or a holiday usually impel people to earn or save money. Such forces may act by 'pulling' the individual to seek, for example, a promotion in order to meet an external want or demand. The concept of 'push' and 'pull' forces may seem somewhat paradoxical in the light of our claim that motivation is an internal condition. There is a subtle difference, however. Such forces may have an effect on the individual's thinking, but the willingness to respond comes from within, and it is only by activating this response process that action takes place. This view reinforces the notion that we have to look at motivation essentially from the perspective of the individual and how he or she 'becomes' motivated.

The relevance of forces from the team's point of view is that help may have to be given to the individual in satisfying his forces in such a way that they tie in with organisational or team goals. Such a situation, where team and individual goals are optimised, might best be described as 'integrated'. This is more likely to lead to a high level of cohesion in carrying out team tasks.

Motivation might best be thought of as a cyclical process which starts and finishes with individual needs. Each individual has certain *needs*. For example, a team member may need to be recognised by the team leader for his accomplishments. These needs create certain *wants*. Wants then trigger *actions* or behaviours in order to achieve certain *goals*. The achievement of these goals results in *accomplishments*. The accomplishments ensure that the original needs are satisfied. Teams may fit the same cycle, but as a group of connected individuals. Such a process is shown in Figure 5.1.

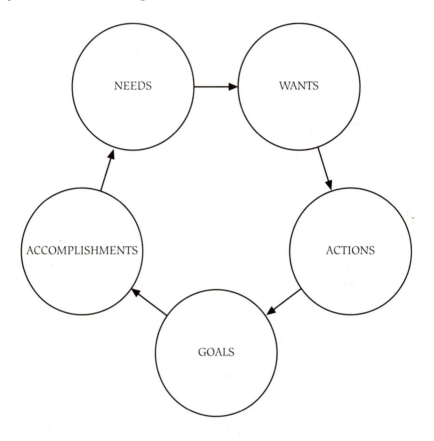

Figure 5.1   The Motivation Cycle

Motivation and Teams

What is it about motivation that is so important, specifically in a team environment? The 'good things' that Wynn and Guditus (1984: 161) refer to when motivation levels are elevated are persuasive benefits for any team. Referring to the motivated individual, they observe: "Generally, he works harder than he used to, thus usually improving his job performance; his readiness to learn skills needed for increased work effectiveness grows; and he tends to find work more satisfying." Indeed, performance, effectiveness and satisfaction are words that will enter the discussion frequently.

Whilst it is tempting to focus on the team leader as a motivator (a highly popular concept in many spheres of team operation), the emphasis may be misplaced. True, the leader has an important part to play, but it seems unlikely that motivation is externally imposed. It is not something that can be administered like medication. As Wynn and Guditus (1984: 161) note: "It is, of course, unlikely that anyone can directly motivate another person", and "Motivation comes from within the individual. If an individual changes her behavior, it is probably not because someone else has motivated her but because, with or without outside influence, her perception of the situation has changed."

Roberts and Hunt (1991: 435) eloquently support this point:

> Even if influenced as by a kick in the butt, motivation is essentially voluntary rather than coerced. The prisoner who follows the prison routine is not motivated but obedient. The employee who studies on her own to learn advanced features of a new computer program is motivated to increase her skills, perhaps because of a desire for promotion.

This is an interesting perspective on motivation, because it helps us to see lack of motivation in a different light. Wynn and Guditus (1984) propose that what we often interpret as an absence of motivation is not that exactly, but motivation in a different direction. All behaviour is motivated. It is incumbent on teams, therefore, to discover what motivates people and, if necessary, to redirect their motivations.

It is reasonable to assume, then, that individuals are self-motivated and do things for their own reasons, not those of the team leader or the organisation. Thus, motivation may have to be viewed from the personal benefits angle: that a response is made when gain is perceived. Ends and Page (1977: 75) reinforce this point: "It takes a fairly powerful stimulus to motivate an individual to overcome inertia. Clearly, unless one believes there is really some personal gain in it, one will not exert the effort."

This is not to say the leader is helpless, but it has to be recognised that the will to work and succeed comes from within. Rewards and incentives may be offered which are considered motivators, but unless they are viewed as desirable by the team member they will have little effect. Whether such benefits are desired by the employee depends on the needs, values and priorities he, as an individual, brings with him to the team (O'Mahoney, 1984).

This, of course, does not mean that the team leader cannot work towards motivating the members. In fact, we would suggest that he has an important role in setting up the conditions in which motivation can thrive. Individual motivation is strongly influenced by leadership style, so it is vital for the leader to establish an environment that supports motivational behaviour. Perhaps even more importantly, it means that the leader must attempt to identify the members' needs, values and priorities, and work towards helping them attain them. The condition we are seeking from this point of view is one where individuals are intrinsically motivated (which represents a more lasting perspective of motivation) and the leader's role is that of structuring situations so that people can motivate themselves.

Team leaders, some would argue, can also work towards motivating team members, often through the power of charisma or personality. In fact, motivation and inspiration are sometimes used synonymously (Kotter, 1990: 61-73). Lee Iacocca (1984: 9), when discussing his managerial beliefs noted:

> I've always felt that a manager has achieved a great deal when he's able to motivate one other person. When it comes to making the place run, motivation is everything. You might be able to do the work of two people, but you can't *be* two people. Instead, you have to inspire the next guy down the line and get him to inspire *his* people.

One could, however, question the lasting effect of inspirationally induced motivation. What happens if the leader moves on? Can people be continually 'inspired'? Whereas inspiration may have a place in motivating a team, we would question its long-term effectiveness.

A more interesting perspective, although presented somewhat simplistically, is Hitt's (1988: 149) equation of motivation and empowerment. The concept is appealing, especially with regard to teams. His basic premise is similar to that discussed in earlier chapters – giving people the responsibility and 'power' to accomplish something may be one of the most powerful motivational strategies managers have at their disposal. We will examine this point later in the chapter.

It is useful for teams to understand motivation so that strategies might be developed for increasing motivational levels. On a practical level, we now look at a motivation framework that can be applied in the team setting. The framework comprises four stages and is shown in Figure 5.2.

The stages are:

- understanding some of the basic concepts of motivation;
- accepting that the leader (and each team member in some cases) plays a vital role in increasing team motivation;
- identifying the needs of individuals in the team, or finding out how they are motivated;
- acting to consciously improve the motivational levels.

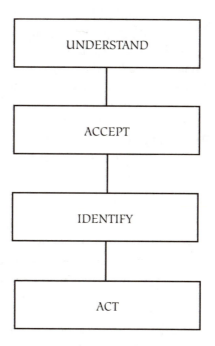

Figure 5.2   A Framework for Motivation

Understand

If motivation is one of the vital ingredients of successful teamwork, it seems necessary to understand some of the different approaches to motivation, and this necessitates a look at some of the major theories. Some of these theories are quite similar, while others adopt substantially different emphases. If team leaders and members are to have an impact on motivational levels, they need to understand the approach or emphasis they are adopting.

We present below a brief summary of some of the major motivational theories that are relevant to teams and which have influenced management thinking. We have avoided going into excessive detail, but chosen instead to draw out those parts which have relevance to the work of organisational teams. We divide the theories into Content Theories and Process Theories.

Content Theories

Maslow: Needs hierarchy

Maslow's theory is one of the most well known and asserts that human beings have certain needs and that these needs are arranged in a hierarchy of importance. This is shown in Figure 5.3.

He suggested that our needs can be viewed as being in five categories and that they all have the potential to act as motivators. Firstly, our most basic needs, such as those for food, water, sex and air, were labelled *physiological needs* – in short, basic survival needs. His second category, which he called *safety needs*, includes needs such as a secure emotional and physical environment. *Belongingness needs*, related to social processes such as love, affection and acceptance, comprise the third category. The fourth category he labelled *self-esteem needs*, referring to our need for self-respect and recognition from others. Maslow's final category, *self-actualisation needs*, refers to needs for reaching our full potential and continued growth. These needs focus on individual development.

Maslow arranged these needs in the form of a hierarchy. His theory stated that once lower order needs, such as food and security, were satisfied, other higher level needs, such as that for self-esteem, become dominant motivators. Once lower order needs have been satisfied, they no longer act as motivators. If lower order needs are not satisfied, it is unlikely that higher order needs such as self-actualisation will dominate. A simple example: If someone lives in abject poverty and expends all his energy acquiring food and shelter, he is unlikely to be too concerned about whether or not he is being challenged in his job.

In the team setting in modern organisations, the higher order needs obviously assume the most importance, but these are often neglected. As Ends and Page (1977: 137) observe, "the need for esteem is seldom met to the individual's satisfaction. If someone clearly sees an opportunity to help satisfy that need by participating in team activity, he or she will generally jump at the chance." Weisbord (1985: 28) takes a similar line, but the emphasis is more on the social belongingness needs: "Most of

SELF-ACTUALISATION

Maximise skills and abilities   Risk taking

                                             Autonomy

ESTEEM

Self-esteem   Social

Esteem from others   Professional

                                             Rewards

BELONGINGNESS

Acceptance   Family

Appreciation   Friends

                                             Social groups

SAFETY

Security   Salary

Order and rules   Insurance

BASIC

Food and clothes   Given for most

Shelter

Figure 5.3   Maslow's Needs Hierarchy

us want to belong, to be valued, to have tasks that matter and to be recognized as insiders by others. The more 'in' we feel, the better we cooperate."

In terms of higher order needs, one thing that teams can do for their members is to provide adequate challenges and opportunities for them to develop their abilities and skills. Another is to provide the reinforcement that people need, and which can come from team members with similar goals, interests and concerns (Peterson, 1991: 38). This emphasis seems to be more essential then focusing on lower level needs.

Robbins (1991: 275) takes up this issue and identifies six needs which must be met by the team: security, status, self-esteem, affiliation, power, and goal achievement. He looks at the importance of gaining reassurance from interaction with other members; of inclusion in a team seen as important by others; of providing recognition and status; of being accepted by a highly-valued group; of meeting the need for friendship and social relations; of being associated with power through the strength of the team; and of being able to pool talents and knowledge to get a task completed well.

Herzberg: Two-factor theory

Herzberg discovered that there were certain factors associated with job satisfaction (motivation factors) and a completely different set of factors associated with dissatisfaction (maintenance or hygiene factors). For example, he discovered that an inadequate salary could cause dissatisfaction at work but that a high salary would not necessarily cause job satisfaction.

Herzberg's work challenged the assumption that job satisfaction was uni-dimensional, ranging along a continuum from satisfaction to the opposite end, dissatisfaction. Instead, he found motivation to be two-dimensional. His theory, which has been labelled the 'two-factor theory' is summarised in Figure 5.4.

MAINTENANCE FACTORS	MOTIVATION FACTORS
• Supervisory methods • Salary • Relationships with colleagues • Working conditions • Company policy, administration • Personal life • Status • Interpersonal relations	• Challenge of work • Promotional opportunities • Sense of achievement • Recognition of job done • Sense of responsibility

Figure 5.4   Herzberg's Two-factor Theory

Herzberg claimed that maintenance factors, if correct, do not cause dissatisfaction, but neither do they motivate workers. However, when they are not right, they lead to dissatisfaction and exert negative impact.

The implication for teams is that when true motivating factors, such as recognition, acceptance and responsibility are present, team members are likely to be highly motivated. If these factors are ignored, motivation is likely to be low, even though the 'maintenance' factors may be adequate.

The theory also implies that motivation is not increased by simply removing the causes of dissatisfaction. The basic ideas proposed by Herzberg are presented in Figure 5.5.

MAINTENANCE FACTORS		MOTIVATION FACTORS	
EFFECTS OF FACTORS			
WHEN RIGHT	WHEN WRONG	WHEN RIGHT	WHEN WRONG
No dissatisfaction	Dissatisfaction	Job satisfaction	No job satisfaction
Do not motivate	Negative impact	Increased motivation	No dissatisfaction

Figure 5.5   Maintenance and Motivation Factors

Achievement motivation theory

McClelland too was concerned with the issue of needs and isolated three basic ones, *achievement*, *affiliation* and *power* as the most significant motivation-influencing needs.

The best known is perhaps the need for achievement. Put simply, workers are motivated to do well in their job by a need to achieve. McClelland found that workers with high achievement needs had:

- a desire to assume personal responsibility;
- a tendency to set difficult targets for themselves;
- a need for specific and immediate feedback;
- a preoccupation with the task (Griffin, 1984).

The need for affiliation is about acceptance and companionship. Members in which such needs are dominant work best in teams that provide social interaction and friendship.

The third need involves a demand for power: a need to control and influence one's environment. People who have a strong need for power and achievement tend to become the leaders and superior performers.

A questionnaire and accompanying scoring chart designed to diagnose the dominant needs pattern for any individual can be found in Stott and Walker (1992: 66). It may seem from the above descriptions that people with high achievement needs may be the most difficult to integrate in the team environment. This is partly true, but it also means that teams may have to recognise this type of need and provide the scope in operation for such people to derive satisfaction from their team membership. They are high performers and, nurtured in the right team conditions, can transpose their performance attributes to the team setting effectively. As Margerison (1973: 59) notes, it is an organisational (and team) responsibility to allow scope to progress for those people who are motivated to achieve high goals and effective performance.

McGregor: Theory X and Theory Y

Although McGregor's well-known theory was not developed as a theory of motivation, it has particular relevance to team leaders and, in some cases, team members. The theory draws attention to our assumptions and how these can provide a strong basis for our actions. The basic tenets are shown in Figure 5.6. Theory X represents a rather pessimistic view of people, one which suggests colleagues will take advantage unless they are watched closely and tightly controlled. Even team members may be somewhat loathe to entrust their colleagues with important task components if they operate from Theory X assumptions.

There is a strong case for examining our assumptions and questioning their validity. They can lead to teams arriving at the wrong conclusions about what motivates their members, with a resultant lowering of motivational levels.

If team leaders operate on the basis that members must be coerced, controlled, directed and threatened to put in effort, leaders' behaviour will probably revolve around bullying, instructing and bribing employees. It seems unlikely that teams can be very pro-ductive in this sort of environment. An appropriate way of dealing with the problematic issue of assumptions may be, in the first instance,

THEORY X LEADERS ASSUME:	THEORY Y LEADERS ASSUME:
• Team members are fundamentally lazy.	• Team members enjoy work and achievement.
• They are interested only in their own benefits.	• They like to help others.
• Punishment gets results.	• Punishment is counterproductive.
• Members have no real interest in their work.	• Most members are basically interested in their work.
• They are basically dishonest.	• They are basically honest.
• They are cunning and sly.	• They are open with others.
• They need discipline and control.	• They work well when they have freedom of action.
• They are not interested in team goals.	• They are interested in team goals.
• Members will avoid responsibility	• They enjoy responsibility.

Figure 5.6   McGregor's Theory X and Theory Y

to examine and question beliefs, and then to employ strategies that enable a new set of positive assumptions to be supported. Such assumptions may be built on the premise that team members can exercise self-direction and control in the pursuit of team objectives.

Although needs theories have been very influential, they have been criticised because they fail to look at the process of motivation. Four well-known theories that try to address this 'process' perspective are 'expectancy', 'equity', 'reinforcement' and 'goal-setting' theories.

Process Theories

Expectancy theory

Expectancy theory proposes that motivation is a function of an individual's expectations. It suggests that an individual's motivation depends on two things: how much he actually wants to do something and how likely he thinks it is that he will be able to do it. In considering the relevance of such a theory, there are several factors that have to be taken into account:

1. the situation;
2. the rewards;
3. the likelihood of being able to perform in ways that will secure rewards;
4. the likelihood of actually being 'paid' – even if satisfactory performance is achieved (O'Mahoney, 1984).

Expectancy theory expands needs theories by going beyond, or expanding, their content perspective. It acknowledges that different people have different needs and will try to satisfy these needs in various ways.

Porter and Lawler (1968) extended expectancy theory by including an intrinsic addition. They stated that values or outcomes could be intrinsic (accomplishment, recognition, self-concept), as well as extrinsic (promotion, pay rises).

What relevance has this theory to the work of teams? Nadler and Lawler (1983) looked at the theory from an organisational viewpoint and made a number of recommendations for managers. These can be easily transposed to the team setting:

1. Work out the outcomes each employee may want.
2. Decide on the performance necessary to meet organisational goals.
3. Ensure desired performance levels are attainable.
4. Tie desired outcomes and desired performance.
5. Examine the situation for varying expectations.
6. Ensure rewards are tempting enough.
7. Make sure the system is fair to all employees.

The last item on this list draws attention to the issue of equity and appropriately takes us into another set of theories which approach motivation from the fairness angle.

Equity theory

A consideration for team membership is whether the reward system is seen to be fair. Equity theory assumes that people want to be treated fairly and that each individual tends to compare his contributions and rewards to those received by others. The basic theory can be shown in the following equation:

$$\frac{\text{Outcomes by a person}}{\text{Inputs by a person}} = \frac{\text{Outcomes by another person}}{\text{Inputs by another person}}$$

Equity theory, as its name implies, is based on the following principles, which we have adapted from the organisational context to that of the workteam:

1. If members perceive that they are not properly rewarded by the team, they will be dissatisfied and not work to their full ability. They may even try to leave the team.
2. If members believe they are adequately rewarded for what they do, they will maintain the same level of output.
3. If members perceive the rewards as more than they consider fair, they will probably work harder. However, they may also discount the reward (Koontz and Weihrich, 1988).

These, of course, are based very much on perceptions. The individual, therefore, may overestimate his own contribution or he may assess the rewards others receive inaccurately. Whether this theory is accepted or not, it seems necessary for team leaders to be aware of perceptions of inequity, since they have the potential to give rise to quite dysfunctional behaviours.

Reinforcement theory

Reinforcement theory proposes that reinforcement conditions behaviour and sees behaviour as being environmentally caused. The theory discounts the intrinsic needs and what initiates behaviour, and concentrates on what happens to a person when he takes some action. Leavitt and Bahrami (1988: 11) observe that its emphasis is on how people *learn* from their experiences. An example serves to clarify the basics of the theory:

Two workers with identical motives go to work in similar companies in similar positions. They turn into different workers depending on the successful or unsuccessful events they experience. The first worker gets acknowledged, or reinforced every time he develops an innovative approach. The second worker gets no acknowledgement when he innovates, but frequent reinforcement when he adheres exactly to company rules. The first worker becomes more innovative and open to risk taking, while the second becomes more of a stickler for the rules. The example would be equally meaningful if we included instances of negative reinforcement.

Classical reinforcement theory then focuses on outside influences, and in this context, how the leader does or does not reinforce particular behaviours. As Robbins (1991) states, most scholars would disagree that reinforcement is the only influence. The theory, if applied wholly and manipulatively, is contrary to recent moves towards collaboration and self-development. Team leaders adhering to classical reinforcement theory may find they do not lead very happy, productive teams.

Goal-setting theory

We provide a very brief explanation of goal-setting here as it is covered in greater detail in Chapter 7. Goal-setting theory is a rational approach to motivation and is related to expectancy theory. It proposes that behaviour can be understood in terms of setting goals focusing on three issues: goal specificity, goal difficulty and goal acceptance. It states that three factors influence performance: competition, participation and feedback. In simple terms, the theory argues that workers will improve their performance if they have specific goals, rather than spurious objectives, to aim for. Robbins (1991: 210) comments that, whereas setting specific goals does lead to higher performance, there is no evidence that this is associated with increased job satisfaction.

In this section we have dealt with only a number of the major motivation theories. There are certainly other movements influencing thinking about motivation. Some of these, such as Attribution theories, Self-Concept theories and Self Efficacy theories, are commanding increasing attention. Other movements relate to Social Action or Information Processing perspectives. As Dingley (1986: 21) writes, "The theory argues that the understanding of behaviour needs to be expanded beyond an understanding of inner psychological needs to an understanding of the wider social setting in which behaviour takes place". As with equity theories, social information processing theories recognise the possibility that people's perceptions of other organisational actors help determine behaviour.

It can be seen from the above how an understanding of motivation can help determine the emphases we might wish to adopt in improving the level of motivation in the team setting. Following an understanding, there needs to be an acceptance by team members of their responsibility for motivation.

Accept

The advantages of having highly motivated team members are obvious. People work harder and enjoy their involvement more. The team becomes more productive. The commitment and desire to work often leads to considerable effort on the part of members. Kotter (1990: 73) describes motivated or inspired employees as "a group of people who exhibit a level of energy, intensity and determination far above what is considered normal". He also expounds their possible impact as being "able to overcome major economic, bureaucratic and political obstacles that stand in its (their) way".

The leader obviously has a significant part to play in improving team motivation and he must accept that role unreservedly. But the role can be shared in part by all team members, and if they can accept their involvement in promoting a strong motivational climate, the potential for success seems even greater.

Identify

Having developed some understanding of motivation and accepted the responsibility for doing something about it, the next step is to identify the needs of team members. This is part of the process of people getting to know one another better. If team members can develop an awareness of the strongest motivational factors for their colleagues, their behaviours might be more appropriately directed.

Identifying why people work is not easy, mainly because different team members have different needs. "People work for a variety of reasons. What is important to one person may have little significance to another. Motivation is personal and supervisors must get to know individual employees in order to learn what motivates them" (Maddux, 1988: 28).

On this point, Ends and Page (1977: 135) raise several questions that draw attention to the various reasons that people might have for team membership: What do they expect to derive from their membership? What is important to them? Are they seeking companionship? Do they expect recognition? Are they hoping to gain skills? Are they looking for friendship and acceptance? Are they trying to prove something? Are they there simply because they have to be?

Team leaders often jump to conclusions about what is important to their members and, as a result, may find that their strategies are not very effective. There are diagnostic instruments that can be used to address the issue of motivation factors, but a useful starting point is to discuss as a team the individual motivational preferences of members. It is helpful to have a checklist, and we have provided some ideas in Figure 5.7 that team members can prioritise and then discuss.

Team members should also learn to be observant, to notice what appears to contribute to individuals' motivation. Which processes bring out the best in them? Do they have a need to be involved extensively in decision making, for example? Do they like very specific targets or do they thrive in conditions of ambiguity? Answers to these questions will contribute to an understanding of how individuals in the team might be more effectively motivated.

Preferences in terms of tasks may also need to be identified. Margerison and McCann (1989: 28) found high levels of demotivation where there was a serious mismatch between work preferences and assigned tasks. Achieving a degree of congruence, therefore, may be essential to keep individuals satisfied, and this congruence can be achieved only by discussing personal preferences and expectations.

Act

Kotter (1990: 72) provides advice on what motivation involves at the organisational level:

1. Communicate visions and strategies on a regular basis.
2. Communicate beyond simply informing; it should excite employees by connecting to their values.
3. Involve employees in deciding how to implement the vision – make the involvement real, not manipulative.
4. Provide support so employees can succeed in making progress towards the vision.
5. Ensure rewards and recognition are sincere.

Team members should consider carefully the points below and identify the *six* factors that are the most important in influencing their motivation. They should then rank those factors 1 to 6, 1 being the most influential factor, and 6 being the least important of the six.

1.   Pay scale   ☐

2.   Promotion prospects   ☐

3.   Participation in decision making   ☐

4.   Supportive leader   ☐

5.   Clear team direction   ☐

6.   Comfortable working conditions   ☐

7.   Support from managers   ☐

8.   Fringe benefits   ☐

9.   Recognition of achievements   ☐

10. Task challenge   ☐

11. Job security   ☐

12. Respect of other team members   ☐

13. Flexibility of rules   ☐

14. Position in the team or organisation   ☐

15. Love of the job   ☐

16. Support from colleagues and team members   ☐

17. Freedom of action   ☐

18. Involvement in setting goals and targets   ☐

19. Opportunities to develop skills and abilities   ☐

20. Trust in the leader   ☐

Figure 5.7   Individual Motivation Factors

Looking at team goals and strategies, giving real involvement to team members, helping and supporting them, and recognising achievement are indeed as important to the team's operation as to the organisation as a whole. Combining this broad advice with efforts to understand members as individuals may help to ensure that motivational strategies are well-directed.

We now turn our attention to several strategies drawn from various theories that can have an impact on the level of motivation of individuals in the team. Some of these may not be possible, perhaps because of the lifespan of the team, but others may be useful in meeting the needs of particular individual members. It is advisable to relate these strategies, therefore, to information about individual team members' motivation factors.

Motivation Strategies

Task Enrichment

Providing challenging and meaningful work is a powerful motivational strategy. Bradford (1990: 39) appropriately claims "that people want to see their jobs as personally meaningful, and as something they can share in with other members of the team". Task enrichment, therefore, means increasing the capacity for challenge and achievement. Depending on the nature of the team, this can be done in several ways:

1. By providing discretion in task areas which lend themselves to some flexibility of operation.
2. By actively involving members in decisions.
3. By providing personal responsibility for tasks.
4. By showing team members that their roles are valuable.
5. By demonstrating to team members how their respective contributions fit into the overall team effort.
6. By providing prompt feedback on performance.

The need to provide meaningful work may be even greater if team members are well-educated or have high expectations. If the purpose is not made clear and understood, there is likely to be disaffection and demotivation (Margerison and McCann, 1989: 27).

Involvement

The literature is very persuasive about the benefits of involvement in organisational life, and it seems even more necessary in the team setting, since teams are formed essentially to benefit from the involvement of members. Anantaraman (1984a: 156) relates involvement and participation to the meeting of higher order needs. "It immediately satisfies the individual's need to belong since he is now an integral part of the team. His esteem needs are also satisfied because the fact that his ideas are sought after, accepted and implemented, means high ego involvement."

Involvement can be encouraged in a number of ways. Seeking opinions and ideas, and consulting members about important matters, can have positive effects. An important point to note here is that involvement must be real and not a sham, otherwise it may be difficult to secure cooperation in the future.

Achievement

We all know the feeling that comes from having achieved something of value and this can be a powerful source of motivation. Unfortunately, this sense of accomplishment does not last very long. Opportunities need to be provided, therefore, for team members to experience achievement regularly.

The occasional large dose of achievement is desirable, such as that experienced after successfully completing a major task. At the same time, relatively minor incidences of achievement help to promote motivation on a regular basis and to keep people going.

The satisfaction gained from achieving something is related to the challenge of the task. Challenges should neither be set so high that they are unattainable nor so low that they can be achieved without real effort. Tasks which do not challenge workers can breed lethargy, and those set too high can cause frustration and 'giving-up'. Part of the purpose of teams (e.g. quality teams) is to help prevent challenges from becoming useless by encouraging a constant search for improvement through collaboration (Newsom, 1990: 52).

Recognition

Recognition is a strong need in most people. Recognition can be simply acknowledgement and appreciation of a person's contribution to the team. The occasional supportive comment or pat on the back may not seem very much, but it can have a powerful motivational effect. Strangely, team leaders and members are often slow to acknowledge achievement, and this can be demotivating. This type of situation is a breeding ground for unhappiness and discontent.

Closely related to recognition is consistency. An important point about recognition is that it should be given only when it is deserved. Maintaining consistency can have implications for the motivational level of team members. If the team has a designated leader, he must take care to ensure that all members perceive they are treated equitably and fairly. If inappropriate or sloppy work is recognised, the wrong message will be sent. The ideal situation in a team is where each member is making contributions that are worthy of acknowledgement and team members are showing the recognition to one another.

Responsibility

The leader may have responsibility for the work of the team, but individuals too have responsibilities for task completion, and indeed many thrive on such responsibility. The keys to developing responsibility are risk-taking and trust.

However, it is not always too difficult or dangerous to give responsibility. It is often a matter of perception. What may seem like a major responsibility to one person may be relatively insignificant to another. One of the key properties of responsibility is that it is both a powerful and ongoing motivator. It is also a way of showing recognition of a team member's ability and competence.

Support

Motivation may hinge to some extent on the degree of support the individual is given. Support may involve the provision of resources such as materials, finance or time. It may also be reflected in help with carrying out certain tasks and the degree of interest shown by team colleagues. It is doubtful whether adequate resource support in itself can be a great source of motivation, but where it is absent, it can be demotivating.

The issue of support also raises the question of the team's environment and whether the physical conditions are satisfactory. Again, this is not an important motivational factor, but may need attention since it can easily form a source of distraction. As Margerison and

McCann (1989: 27) point out, if people are working in an environment that is dirty or uncomfortable, the team may become demotivated.

It is interesting to note that teams often complain about the physical work environment, but this can be symptomatic of other problems. Team members who are highly motivated and committed to their roles seldom complain about working conditions.

Other Motivation Factors

Finally, it is worth providing more detail on a number of important points about motivation in teams. Effective teams achieve a high level of integration between team goals and individual goals. This notion of goal congruence is an important one. As Barrett (1970: 98) reports:

> Individuals who rank high in the extent to which they see their personal goals as being integrated with the organization's objectives also tend to rank high in their motivation to come to work and to work hard, in their satisfaction with the organization and their job in it, and their feelings of loyalty to the organization and commitment to its success.

Integration is unlikely to happen by chance, however. There has to be a conscious matching of team intentions with individual needs fulfilment, and this is where the leader's skill in effecting integration is paramount. The leader can help individuals to see that by "willingly striving to attain organization objectives they will also satisfy some of their personal needs, such as self-esteem, esteem from others, a sense of competence, a feeling of belonging, a feeling of personal significance, and a feeling of growth" (Ends and Page, 1977: 47). Integration may also mean achieving a high degree of congruence between the individual's abilities, ideas and needs, and the team's task requirements. As Margerison (1973: 58) notes: "Where ... there is little overlap between the abilities of the person and his job, it is not surprising if motivation is low".

Robbin's (1991: 303) emphasis in terms of the individual's satisfaction is very much on the task. Team members, he predicts, are likely to be satisfied and motivated to work hard when relatively high-level skills are needed; the work is meaningful with a visible outcome; the outcomes have significant consequences for other people; there is substantial autonomy for deciding how to go about the work; and there is regular and trustworthy feedback on performance.

Effective teams, it may be argued, have leaders who themselves are motivated, who are sufficiently interested in, and aware of, the factors which determine the motivation of their team members, who believe they can help their colleagues develop, who role-model their beliefs, and who support and trust their staff. "They must help their people accomplish something and make everyone on the team feel as though the work of each individual is important" (Tarkenton, 1986: 31). Margerison (1973: 59) takes up some of these points in signifying the importance of leaders' roles: "to recognise the efforts of their subordinates, to provide challenging work, to give increased responsibility and facilitate an individual's growth and development."

Adair (1988: 140) reinforces these views and provides a useful summary of how employees should feel if motivation and job satisfaction are to be good rather than merely adequate. Each individual must:

1. feel a sense of personal achievement in the job he is doing, and that the contributions he makes to team or organisational attainment are considered worthwhile;
2. feel that his job is challenging and demands his best effort. He must feel that the job provides him with the responsibility to match his capabilities;
3. receive adequate reward and recognition for his achievements;
4. have considerable control over aspects of the job which have been delegated to him;
5. feel that he is developing as a person and that he is advancing his ability and experience.

Much of what Adair advocates draws together some of the essential points from the major motivation theories. He talks about achievement, contributing in a genuinely worthwhile way, doing challenging work, taking on responsibility, enjoying appropriate recognition and reward, and feeling the benefits of moving forward in terms of development. Common sense dictates that these are worthy ideals, based on a highly positive view of individuals in the team, and capable of contributing in no small way to a stimulating motivational climate for team endeavour. They inevitably lead to commitment on the part of individuals, and that is a highly sought after condition, one which we shall now consider briefly alongside the closely related issue of morale.

Commitment

"Commitment to a goal means that an individual finds a specific goal desirable enough so that he or she is willing to invest some time, energy, and abilities to help achieve it" (Ends and Page, 1977: 48). We have used the word commitment frequently in this text, and it is a serious consideration in team performance. The same authors go so far as to describe it as the first concern when trying to achieve team goals (p. 174). Individual members must be committed to goals. They should see the goals as desirable and be prepared to work to achieve them.

The literature generally supports the notion that commitment is more likely to occur if team members have some part to play in the goal formulation process. Leavitt and Bahrami (1988: 173) call this the 'I-love-my-own-baby' proposition and suggest that it holds true in a wide range of situations. Commitment leads to a feeling of ownership, a view supported by Maddux (1988: 40) who sees commitment as self-generating, a state that cannot be forced and a condition most likely to be developed through a feeling of involvement. Ownership comes about through involvement in problem solving and goal setting, and through responsibility for outcomes.

It is clear from the above that commitment is concerned with individuals choosing consciously to identify with the group and group goals. From this perspective, Wynn and Guditus (1984: 114) take us a step further and suggest several factors that might strengthen this bonding. Apart from the factor of goal sharing, they also identify the following: perceived high prestige of the team; high frequency of interaction; high number of individual needs satisfied; and low competition amongst members. Commitment and its relation to team decision making is discussed in Chapter 14.

Individual Goals

We saw when we looked at motivation how it is felt generally that the chances of commitment are heightened if, rather than thinking in terms of team goals *or* individual goals, there can be a congruence or integration of goals. George (1977: 79) suggests such an integration is possible, since they are similar anyway: "Growth, profitability, market leadership, being the innovator, and producing a high-quality product ... these are company goals which come close to matching goals of most individuals in the company ... personal growth, performance rewards, high personal standards of excellence, a job with a winner, and opportunities for larger responsibilities."

This view may be somewhat optimistic in the light of Wynn and Guditus' (1984: 129) observation that a gap of varying degrees may exist between organisation and individual goals. They also note that each set of goals may have different motivational strengths. It may also be unrealistic to ascribe the same motivations to most individuals. Individual goals may be substantially different and this can easily lead to conflict situations.

Nevertheless, the leader may have a responsibility to try to effect such an integration. Referring to the work of new product teams, Thamhain (1990: 16) claims that ways should be found to "satisfy part of the team member's interests by bringing personal and organizational goals into focus and perspective". This is an effort worth making if Wynn and Guditus' (1984: 129) assertion about the value of goal congruence is true: "When individual and organizational goals are perfectly integrated, there is an idyllic state of affairs. One can satisfy one's own needs and the organization's expectations with the same behavior. This results in high morale and high job performance."

The same authors, however, go on to explain the conventional wisdom that goal integration is unlikely to be a complete process. It is more likely to be a question of degree.

Morale

Closely related to the issue of commitment is morale. It refers to the confidence a team has in its capacity to reach difficult goals. Confidence comes from not only having the essential skills in the team but also the commitment to work together in order to achieve. In a high-morale environment, each team member can depend on all the others to work to capacity in order to ensure team success. Team leaders should be concerned about morale, because a feeling of confidence and commitment can be a self-fulfilling prophecy. There are a number of indicators related to team morale. Probably the best one is enthusiasm, since it is reasonable to assume that a team with highly enthusiastic members is a high-morale unit. The quality of communication is another useful indicator. If team members are open, friendly, positive and show integrity, there is likely to be high morale.

Much of this, of course, suggests that people's attitudes have to be right. Members have to display the right attitudes to the task and supportive attitudes to their fellow team members. Attitudes, therefore, are important, and we now discuss individual attitudes and two closely related considerations, those of expectations and attitudes to change.

Attitudes

The attitudes of people in the team are an important component of the individual dimension. This may determine their readiness to take responsibility for effective performance. If they have immature attitudes, several things may happen. Teamwork may be used to pursue goals and targets which are not relevant to the team. Members may set different work limits and priorities, and follow their own agendas. If they have been set up to manage their own work, they may even resent what they consider abdication of responsibility and force the manager to manage (Carr, 1989: 181).

Research has generally distinguished between three types of attitudes: cognitive, affective and behavioural.

> The cognitive aspects of attitudes are the properties attributed to the object; a job could be viewed as challenging or boring, full of pressure or worry free. Affect, the most widely studied component of attitudes, is how much an individual likes the object – how does the employee feel about his job. The behavioural component, the person's behaviour toward the object, is usually measured by what a person says she intends to do (Roberts and Hunt, 1991: 506).

Since attitudes are closely related to feelings of job satisfaction, it is important for team leaders, and members, to be aware of how they influence motivation.

This raises the issue of motives in determining attitudes. Some may have personal motives which take precedence over those of the team. Peterson (1991: 101) notes in his matter-of-fact way that not everyone will have supportive attitudes to team effort. "A lot of people pay lip service to it, but they're really only interested in themselves. This is most evident when times get tough. Whatever notions of teamwork were around go right out the window, and everybody starts heading off in his or her own direction."

Ends and Page (1977: 96) neatly separate attitudes into two types: those concerned with how members feel about their ability to achieve targets; and those concerned with members' feelings about one another. Attitudes to completing difficult and challenging assignments, and to winning in competitive situations are important. With appropriate attitudes, team members may feel they are part of a winning team and this in turn leads to what is generally called high morale. Such attitudes are related to expectations and, as such, can have a dramatic impact on success. The authors suggest that leaders need to keep a watchful eye on the attitudes of individual team members, since, if low morale becomes evident, failure can easily accrue. Team members' attitudes to one another are equally important. If they enjoy one another's company, there is more likely to be cohesion and this can (though it is not inevitable) lead to high performance.

In terms of team development, it seems more important that team members can extend their understanding of their own attitudes than to merely rely on leaders and managers to identify low morale. Self-examination of attitudes can lead to successful changes in behaviour. As Johnson and Johnson (1991: 448) suggest, people need to develop an awareness of their own experiences in order to appreciate their role in determining success.

The relationship between inappropriate attitudes and dysfunctional behaviour is well illustrated by Kazemak and Albert (1988: 108):

> Sometimes we belong to groups that violate our expectations for efficiency and assault our standards for quality. Our patience with interdependence wears thin, and our fantasy of rugged individualism emerges to haunt us. Most of us choose one of two tactics in managing this interpersonal mess: we mentally withdraw from the group, distancing ourselves from responsibilities; or we wage war on other individual group members, attacking them openly or behind the scenes.

This serves to alert us to the danger of ignoring attitudes.

Ends and Page (1977: 184) too provide a list of behaviours that are detrimental to the team. They label them: attacking, blocking, competing, pleading, clowning, handclasping, striving, isolating, and honeymooning. The activities associated with these behaviours include blaming others, arguing too much about isolated points, trying to talk the most, supporting their own pet concerns, disrupting the work of the team, holding private dialogues, trying to call attention to themselves, being excessively formal, and pretending there is perfect harmony when there is really disagreement. Other attitudes and behaviours that may be described as typical are identified by Miller and Phillips (1986: 55): pointing the finger, embarrassing people, not listening, nit-picking and continually harping back to old mistakes.

It is evident from these lists that many behaviours may be symptomatic of the team's inadequacies to satisfy members' personal needs. For example, where there is extreme rigidity, people may hold tight to their positions (Schutz, 1989: 8). Such rigidities are often based on "personal fears, often unconscious, of such possibilities as being ignored, humiliated, or rejected; or of feeling insignificant, incompetent, or unlikable". Schutz maintains that flexibility is a function of a strong self-concept.

It may be mistaken, therefore, to assume that behaviours are necessarily the causes of team dysfunctions. As Tolle (1988: 285) notes: "The manifestations of these disruptive behaviours are more likely to be the effects of the organization's management system than causes of organizational dysfunction."

Johnson and Johnson (1991: 468) separate behaviour problems into four categories:

- Passive uninvolvement
- Active uninvolvement
- Independence
- Taking charge

Passive uninvolvement is when members are simply not involved and show no interest in the team's activities. Strategies to counter this problem include: ensuring that each member has information the others need; giving passive members a vital role; and distributing rewards based on the team's performance rather than the performance of individuals in it.

Active uninvolvement is where team members talk about things other than the task at hand or refuse to play their full part. Remedial strategies that might be used include: finding rewards that such individuals find attractive; structuring tasks in such a way that all members must play their part for the team to achieve success; and giving members specific roles.

Independence occurs where members work alone and fail to take part in team discussions. The leader can restrict the supply of resources so that it is difficult for members to work in isolation; arrange materials and information in such a way that interaction is necessary.

Taking charge, as the expression implies, is when one person does most of the work, issues orders and makes decisions without checking for agreement. Strategies available include: arranging resources so that participation has to be wide and members' views have to be listened to; assigning roles so that other team members have more powerful positions; and rewarding the team based on its lowest level of performance. This encourages the team to support all its members. In a team development exercise we designed, the team had to navigate a course and find certain markers using directions on a map. The team's time was based on the last person to arrive. This ensured that full support was given to those members who needed it most.

Other dysfunctional behaviours may emerge through bad attitudes, such as fault finding, pulling rank, dominating and striving for power (Petrock, 1990: 9). The way forward may be for the right attitudes to be supported and for individuals to be convinced that it is in their best interests to adopt attitudes that enhance the pursuit of goals and the interpersonal processes in the team. It is probably the leader's responsibility to convince team members that they will achieve more for themselves and their areas of concern by displaying collaborative attitudes (Watts, 1988: 103). Another way of helping to avoid more serious dysfunctional behaviours may be to keep a watchful eye between team meetings for signs of ill-feeling, frustration and low spirits.

Not all behaviours can be viewed as either supportive or dysfunctional. Some are part of the psychological make-up and need to be understood. In terms of team members' responses to the leader, two behaviours may be worthy of note, those of dependency and counterdependency (Adair, 1986: 69). Dependency is where people look to others to tell them what to do. This can be frustrating for the leader who expects members to use their ingenuity and to readily accept responsibility. Such individuals may need to be encouraged and coached to take a more independent stance. Counterdependency represents a resistance to authority and attempts to restrict their freedom. The wrong response from the leader is to use the muscle of authority, for that can be an alienating strategy. The informal sources of power seem to have more potential for dealing with these people, and we shall be examining this issue in detail in Chapter 12.

Expectations

Expectations are a complex form of attitudes. The expectations team members have about their own behaviour and performance, and the expectations that others have of them combine to produce a powerful influence on behaviour. Ends and Page (1977: 79) note that members' responses to the expectations of others are complex, since they reflect a measure of esteem and regard for them as individuals. As a result, they have a profound effect on behaviour.

The issue of expectations should not be taken lightly. Such is the effect that people are often able to achieve seemingly unattainable outcomes. The expectations of the leader will usually be supported by team members and it is important, therefore, for leaders to consider seriously their beliefs about performance. Expectations may take many forms, sometimes subtle, and their communication can lead to a high-performance climate. The converse is also true, that where expectations are low, there is likely to be poor performance and minimal effort.

Probably the best way of dealing with the expectations issue is to bring them into the open and allow the team to discuss what every individual expects. This then provides an opportunity to help individuals revise expectations in accordance with desired performance and individual gains. On this point, it seems reasonable that expectations should be neither too modest nor too ambitious. The former may lead to little progress or gains in performance, while the latter will probably lead to failure. Expectations may best be set at a level so that meeting them necessitates some stretching of effort.

In this context, we have looked at expectations in relation to individual behaviour and performance, but they can also relate to values and beliefs, attitudes and feelings. These, again, can have a considerable impact on how the team functions.

Change

Still related to the question of individual attitudes is the issue of change and individual team members' responses to situations that involve changes. From what has been said about teams so far and the contextual factors that make teamwork necessary, it is apparent that individuals are needed who are prepared to respond positively to many aspects of team change. Where there is excessive resistance, it can be highly dysfunctional.

Ends and Page (1977: 75) cite five reasons for resistance to change: inertia, past experiences, self-concept, risk of failure and the perception of psychological disadvantage.

Inertia can be a serious problem, because it is built up through habit, and habits are difficult to break. Only by seeing obvious personal gain can the effects of inertia be overcome.

Past experiences may also provide solid defences. Such experiences may have been successful and support beliefs that things are being done well. Under these circumstances, it becomes difficult to convince people that change is genuinely needed and to secure commitment to it. A fundamental change in attitudes may be necessary to develop open and receptive minds.

Also, people may be unwilling to operate in ways that are inconsistent with their preferred patterns of working. For example, some members may have a great attention to detail, and to insist on quick work that is less than perfect may interfere with their self-concept. This would suggest that tasks given to team members should be compatible, as far as possible, with such self-concepts.

The fear of failure can be very real for some people and a source of great distress, especially if it could incur a loss of self-esteem. Nevertheless, conservative approaches are not always appropriate and an element of risk-taking may be necessary for successful team development. Ends and Page suggest the problem can be minimised by making the changes incrementally, in small steps, so that the risks are small. The process may also be aided by giving adequate help and support.

The final factor concerns the perceived advantages of a course of action to the individual. Team members have perceptions about the personal gains for them. What the individual believes is a gain may depend on how the situation is perceived in terms of rewards and punishments, and how much the outcome can be influenced by personal effort (p. 78).

How can resistance to change be overcome in the team situation? Several strategies have already been hinted at above. Tasks may be given that are consistent with the self-concept. Risks can be kept at acceptable levels to the individual. Personal gains can be identified and emphasized. On this point, Ends and Page (1977: 78) note:

> This source of resistance can often be avoided if the manager will only take the time to discuss suggested changes thoroughly with subordinates.

The most critical objective of the discussion is to make sure that all subordinates clearly see that it is in their own best interests, and that of the organization, that it is to their psychological advantage, to make the suggested changes in behavior.

This may come about by enabling team members to perceive the gains as greater than the risks, and the rewards proportional to the effort required (p. 79). This calls for leadership skill in understanding people in the team and the way they interpret a given situation. In short, it demands considerable 'empathy'.

Despite the problems outlined, there is evidence to suggest that change may be facilitated through team approaches and that it becomes longer lasting (Wynn and Guditus, 1984: 151). Participative approaches may also reduce resistance.

Todryk (1990: 21) draws on work by Leon Martel in identifying elements that might be integrated into a strategy for mastering change. The elements are:

- recognise that change is occurring, even in times when things appear to be in a state of equilibrium;
- identify those changes that will affect the team's work, and the individual's professional and private life;
- decide on the type and pattern of each change;
- rank changes according to their potential levels of impact and the likelihood that they will occur;
- make use of the changes in implementing strategies for successful work assignments.

Summary

We have limited our discussion of this important field of motivation to its relevance to teams. Further discussion in other chapters about collaboration, empowerment, collegiality and participation are all pertinent to the topic. The fact that people are brought together in team settings, as we have seen, is motivational within itself. Having a real say in decisions and having one's point of view valued by colleagues and the organisation may be claimed to be one of the most powerful motivators of all. In this chapter, we have attempted to provide an introduction to some influential motivation theories, a brief description of motivational strategies and some further discussion on other important motivational factors.

In the following chapter, we develop the theme of the individual team member by discussing the effective utilisation of individual resources.

Summary of the Implications for Managers

- It may be argued that unless personal gain is perceived by the individual, effort will not be forthcoming. Leaders should therefore ensure that team members can understand how they, as individuals, might stand to gain from their contributions.

- The leader indeed has a major part to play in elevating the level of team motivation. With personal gains in mind, he can identify needs, values and priorities of people and help them to achieve them. He can also set up the conditions in which motivation might thrive and where people can be self-motivated. If the leader can help individuals satisfy their own motivational forces and at the same time tie these in with team goals, we can say that effort is integrated and more likely to result in success.

- Managers can provide challenges and opportunities for members to develop their abilities and skills, and they can also give reinforcement and reassurance. Furthermore, managers may be in a position to raise the status of the team, and this can be an important motivational consideration, since being part of a team which is seen widely as important may act as a strong stimulus. While setting up conditions for friendships and good social relations are important, the leader's willingness to show recognition and acceptance, and to give responsibility, is more likely to lead to high motivation.

- Members' needs may be different, and scope may need to be provided for people to satisfy their needs for achievement, affiliation or power. Achievement-oriented members, in particular, are often motivated towards high goals and achievement, and need the stimulus of challenging assignments and responsibility. This may necessitate a belief in people and what they can do: they are often capable of exercising self-control and direction in working towards team goals. Indeed, it is probably wise to involve members widely, and to encourage them to accept that they too have a vital part to play in the team's motivation.

- One of the important motivational strategies is task enrichment, and this means increasing the capacity for challenge and achievement. Some of the actions that can be taken include: giving discretion in some task areas; involving members in decisions; giving individuals responsibility; demonstrating to members that their roles are valuable and how their contributions fit into the team plan; and giving regular, helpful and supportive feedback.

- Several of these points are worth explaining. Involvement means seeking opinions and ideas, and consulting people regularly. Achievement should be experienced often, even if it is in small doses. Recognition is best given when deserved and it should also be shown by members to one another. Giving responsibility means risk-taking and trust, and many managers are unwilling to go this far. It should be noted, however, that responsibility is a powerful and ongoing motivator, since it demonstrates a recognition of ability and competence. Providing support may involve the manager in finding adequate resources in terms of materials, finance, time, and a pleasant working environment to enable the job to be done well.

- Some general points that are common to a number of motivational theories should be noted. People's skills should be needed and the team's outcomes should be perceived as significant. The work should be meaningful, and individuals should be given autonomy in how to do the work. They should receive helpful feedback and they should feel that they are developing in ability and experience as part of their team membership.

- Ownership is a word that is often associated with commitment. It is likely to come about through involvement in the goal formulation process, involvement in problem solving, and through responsibility for the team's outcomes. Commitment needs situations in which there is frequent interaction, in which individual needs are satisfied, and in which there is low competition amongst members.

- Managers and team leaders have to watch out carefully for symptoms of low morale, and this may become evident through signs of ill-feeling, frustration or just low spirits. It seems more likely to occur where people's involvement is either unnecessary or marginal. Because of this, it is best to ensure that people have information others need and arrange tasks so that involvement by all is necessary. This may necessitate distributing resources accordingly. Rewards should be distributed to the team and not to individuals; this means they will be based on the lowest performance level. Where individuals appear to be over-dependent, they might be encouraged to take responsibility.

- Leaders should consider their beliefs about performance. A high performance climate might be established by setting high expectations, but they should not be so high as to be unrealistic. Individuals should also be allowed to express expectations in the team forum and then to revise them in accordance with the team's desired performance and the individual gains that are sought.

- Some team members may be afraid of change because of the possibility of failure. Leaders can help by minimising the risks through incremental changes, and by giving plenty of help and support. Tasks might be allocated that are consistent with the self-concept, and risks can be kept at acceptable levels. Personal gains should be perceived as greater than the risks involved. As we mentioned earlier, the skilful leader is able to integrate organisational and personal interests, but it is profitable to emphasize the latter to team members. Any form of change needs discussing amongst the team membership and this is likely to lead to a healthier attitude to the whole process of change.

6

USING INDIVIDUAL RESOURCES

It is obvious by now that a team, however it is viewed, is a collection of individuals. Each team member brings certain strengths, weaknesses, skills and abilities into the team setting. The team or (if there is one) team leader's responsibility is to identify, encourage and develop individual skills and abilities, build on strengths and reduce weaknesses. Effective use of individual resources towards team attainment is vital. In this chapter, therefore, we discuss individual team members in terms of their abilities and skills, look briefly at some adult learning principles, and discuss further the importance of participation.

Abilities and Skills

It is important to recognise that people's abilities and skills must be used if their efforts are to influence team outcomes. As Greenberg and Greenberg (1988: 58) state: "The most effective teams recognize each individual's particular talents ... and create environments which enable those talents to unfold." It makes sense that certain skills and abilities need to be present according to the nature of the team's work. The importance is aptly summarised by Robbins (1991: 282):

> Evidence indicates that individuals who hold crucial abilities for attaining the group's task tend to be more involved in group activity, generally contribute more, are more likely to emerge as the group leaders, and are more satisfied if their talents are effectively utilized by the group. Second, intellectual ability and task-relevant ability have both been found to be related to overall group performance.

Robbins goes on to mention the relationship is not a strong one, however, and that other factors also influence performance.

In order to make use of existing skills and abilities, a matching process may have to take place between individual preferences and task demands. As Margerison and McCann (1985: 5) note, this may be critical to both individual and team effectiveness. The matching can take place both ways. Sometimes the task can be adapted to fit individual abilities, while on other occasions, the individual may need to receive training and guidance so that he can meet the demands of the task. On the point of adapting the task, Weisbord (1985: 28) observes that there is wide potential in most teams, but jobs are often defined so narrowly that people can use neither their intellect nor their skills. Tasks, therefore, may have to be defined more flexibly to accommodate the abilities present.

Another consideration in relation to individual abilities is that of complementarity. There needs to be the right mix of skills. As Robbins (1991: 294) notes: "Most group activities require a variety of skills and knowledge. Given this requirement, it would be reasonable to conclude that heterogeneous groups – those composed of dissimilar individuals – would be more likely to have diverse abilities and information and should be more effective". This point also relates to the behavioural role preferences of team members and is taken up in detail in Chapter 10.

The abilities we refer to above are mostly concerned with task-related skills. But there are other process skills that relate to the effective functioning of the team. There may, of course, be some overlap between the two. Bradford (1990: 47) provides a 'repertoire' of such skills and abilities:

- Relating to one another
- Problem solving

- Acting independently
- Listening and giving feedback
- Networking
- Focusing on interests rather than positions
- Generating multiple options
- Scanning the environment appropriately
- Promoting results-oriented communication
- Defining and using independent standards
- Using empathy
- Separating people from the problem

Teire (1982: 201) too talks about basic skill requirements and includes such abilities as listening, being aware of others' needs, recognising and resolving conflicts, setting priorities, promoting trust and honesty, and taking responsibility and initiative. We discuss a number of these skills in this book, but note that it may be more appropriate to talk about 'desirable' skills rather than 'necessary' ones. It is unrealistic to expect each member to have or to develop a level of expertise in all the above.

We have already mentioned the word 'experience' in connection with the team's resources. The question needs to be asked: What experiences have team members had that are relevant to the team's task? This suggests that team leaders need to become aware of a great deal of information about their members in terms of experience, skill and ability.

One more issue needs addressing in looking at the resources individuals bring to the team, and that is 'personality'. When we discuss leadership in Chapter 9, we outline the drawbacks of approaches that dwell on personality traits, but it would be wrong to imply that personality characteristics have no part to play in team effectiveness. As Robbins (1991: 282) indicates, group productivity, morale and cohesiveness may all be related to the more positive personality attributes. Thus, such characteristics as perseverance, sociability and self-reliance may have an important effect. Conversely, less desirable attributes such as dominance, impatience and authoritarianism may have negative effects. Such traits influence interactions amongst team members. It is important to note, however, that personality characteristics play an important part in determining team behaviour only when they are taken together, and not in isolation.

In team development efforts, therefore, individual skills and abilities need to receive adequate attention. If individuals are to develop the behavioural patterns of high achievers, support may be needed in examining their individual development needs. A set of questions may be asked in the form of a checklist, and these include the following:

1. Is there a belief on the part of the team member that knowledge, skill or ability is needed?
2. Does the team member desire to acquire the skill?
3. Will the team member have responsibility for the outcome?
4. Are individual goals realistic but challenging, and do they account for his ability, experience and confidence? (Ends and Page, 1977: 91.)

Developing an individual's abilities and skills is paramount to overall team development, and ties in very closely with the notion of 'the learning organisation' (Senge, 1990). Individuals need to extend their abilities and learn new skills in order to expand the team's resources. From this perspective, individual development is an integral part of team growth. "If a team is to be effective it needs to be continually developing itself and this in part means constantly facilitating individual as well as team development" (Woodcock, 1979: 6). Members need to develop a range of skills and abilities to contribute more effectively to the work of the team. Similarly, the enhancement of team performance usually leads to gains in individual growth.

Ends and Page (1977: 85) suggest there may be two important conditions when considering adult learning. One is that learning goals must not be threatening. The risk of failure must be low. This is best achieved by allowing learning to take place in safe easy steps. The other condition is that learning goals must be congruent with the team member's self-image. Johnson and Johnson (1991: 435) refer to individual development and claim that individuals must learn how to coordinate actions, identify problems in working together, and improve the integration of their efforts. All this, of course, refers to collective effort, with individuals being true participants in the team. When discussing individual development within a team setting, it is necessary to be familiar with some of the central tenets of adult learning which might relate to team development efforts.

Adult Learning

To understand fully and attempt to meet the development needs of team members, it is necessary to have some understanding of how adults learn, grow and develop. Although it appears obvious, the first step in building a collaborative team culture is to consciously recognise that team members are adults and not children. Brookfield (1986), one of the 'gurus' of adult learning, identifies six general observations concerning the nature of learning (p. 30):

1. Learning is a life long process.
2. Learning is personal.
3. Learning involves change.
4. Learning is partially a function of human development.
5. Learning pertains to experience.
6. Learning is partially intuitive.

In addition to these general tenets, adults also exhibit four essential characteristics which they bring with them to the learning environment. Such characteristics provide important considerations in structuring team development.

1. Adults have multiple roles and responsibilities (e.g. work role, home role, spouse role, service role, etc.) which result in a different orientation to learning from that of children.
2. Adults, throughout their lifetime, have accumulated many and diverse life experiences. These result in distinct preferences for ways or methods of learning and learning environments.
3. Adults pass through a number of developmental phases (physical, psychological and social) and transition from one stage to another provides for the reinterpretation of past experience.
4. Adults experience anxiety and ambivalence in their orientation to learning.

Boud (1987) discusses adult learning and the role of the facilitator. In a team setting, the facilitator may be the leader or another member. He believes that the role of the facilitator (in this context, the team leader) is to encourage and guide development of individual skills and ability rather than imposing rigid ideas. Boud also discusses the role and intricacies of the facilitator in adult learning settings and suggests he or she may have to adopt different roles depending on the learner and the situation (p. 235):

- Presenter of expertise
- Democrat and worker-centred guide
- Provider of access to personal and material resources
- Supporter and encourager
- Critical friend and stimulator of critical reflection
- Challenger of taken-for-granted assumptions

Moore (1988: 3–4) provides a number of suggestions extracted from her work into adult learning that may guide the direction of development efforts for expanding individual skills and abilities of team members. The same guides may also be useful when thinking about any development strategies for the team as a whole:

1. Have a climate of success.
2. Have a collaborative mode.
3. Help team members achieve self-direction and empowerment.
4. Capitalise on members' experience.
5. Foster participation.
6. Foster critical, reflective thinking.
7. Foster learning for action.
8. Foster problem posing and problem solving.

In summary, adult learners may be very different from child learners. Current trends in adult education emphasize, among other things, experiential approaches, action learning, critical thinking, and collegial and cooperative processes.

Many of the ideas discussed about adult learning, and related to the consideration, utilisation and development of individual resources, promote the concept of participation. For members to feel comfortable and productive in their team, they must feel that their skills, abilities, ideas and experience are worthwhile and valued. Perhaps the best way to foster this is to develop a culture of participation within the team. We now examine briefly a rationale for participation and involvement, and mention some of the ideas that might be used to encourage and support true participation amongst members.

Participation

> An individual likes to be master of his own house. If this is denied,
> if the landlord exercises his legal right to paint the wall some obnoxious
> colour, the tenant may be forced to accept the situation, but he will
> be less likely to protect those walls, to guard them from damage (Handy,
> 1976: 312).

Participation is about commitment, and is certainly not a new concept. It grew from the human relations movement in the 1920s and
1930s after the Hawthorn Experiments indicated that 'human' factors
such as involvement rather than manipulation of the physical environment led to increases in productivity. The search for methods of
creating involvement caused serious consideration of how people liked
to work and worked best. It is interesting to note that the concepts of
participation and the formation of teams in work settings evolved in
tandem. Leavitt and Bahrami (1988: 263) describe the search for
techniques for creating involvement:

> Two key developments emerged. The first key was the idea of *participa-
> tion;* essentially, 'people support what they help to create.' In other
> words, people love their own babies more than other people's. The second
> was a technique – the *small group*, the team, as a mechanism for
> generating involvement. The group could serve almost as a substitute for
> authority. By participating in groups, people would develop loyalty to
> one another; they would develop commitment to their groups and the
> group's tasks.

Participation may be conceptualised in two dimensions: the extent
of participation and the scope of it (Anantaraman, 1984a: 154).
Addressing these two issues inevitably raises the question of
whether participation is real or simply token. In terms of its extent,
if true participation is to be practised, members need to be involved
in both decision making and problem definition. As Handy (1976: 125)
tells us: "Participation increases commitment (only) if the individual
considers participation worthwhile and legitimate". Participation must
cover areas that are significant and of importance. Indeed, "it should
be extended to vital production areas such as change in technology
and timing of its introduction, production planning scheduling, and
even performance appraisal".

Gibson and Hodgetts (1986: 78) suggest that the four major benefits
of collaboration or participation are greater knowledge and/or infor-

mation, increased number of approaches to problem solving, increased commitment to implementation and more comprehensive analysis of problems. Anantaraman (1984a: 154) states that participation leads to better decisions (through pooling talents and resources), individual ownership of the decision increases, commitment and involvement to implementation is elevated and follow-up activity is more meaningful. These views are also supported by Margerison (1973: 30) who proposes that participation in goal setting leads to concern for implementation. Also, Arajs (1991: 76) identifies improvements in quality and productivity arising from effective participatory approaches, a view supported strongly by Kezsbom (1990: 50).

Thamhain (1990: 15) looks at the issue of participation in relation to innovative team efforts and emphasizes the involvement of members even during the problem definition stage. The benefits from this extent of participation are better understanding of task requirements, stimulation of interest, team unity improvements and commitment to the project plan.

There may also be more far-reaching benefits. Earlier, for example, we looked at the ideal of goal integration and attempts to reconcile team goals and individual goals. If people are allowed to participate in team management, it might be argued that greater integration between individual aspirations and team goals is achieved. An orientation towards participation may also be reflected in a series of attitudes or actions by those in positions of power. There may be concern for personal needs, general supervision, training for advancement, support, recognition and a willingness to keep people informed. From this point of view, participation is an integral part of the team rationale.

There are also considerable benefits to individual team members. Wynn and Guditus (1984: 114) draw extensively on the research to outline some of the desirable effects that participative decision making might have on members. These include increased productivity, reduced resistance to change, higher levels of motivation and satisfaction, increased sense of mutual interdependence, stronger commitment to decisions and the setting of higher performance goals for individuals and their teams.

Apart from considering extent and scope, and emphasizing the managerial will needed to establish a climate of participation, in what other ways might participation be supported? At a practical level, we suggest in other parts of this book that all contributions to the team should be considered seriously, this being particularly relevant to those situations requiring creativity, but it is also important in encouraging participation. As Graham (1991: 52) advises:

> However outlandish a person's views may be, they will contain grains of truth embedded in his logic and prejudices. It is much more fruitful, much more productive to bring the differences into the open, to extract these grains of truth and use them. It is in this way that managers will build their team into the group that grows and develops, making each one a participant in the action.

The leader's role in promoting participation is of paramount importance, and Anderson (1984: 157) draws on some research into the characteristics of participative leaders. Such leaders:

- are easily approachable;
- are concerned about morale improvements;
- keep members informed;
- encourage sharing in decision making;
- train and develop members;
- communicate effectively;
- are considerate;
- are willing to make changes;
- support people when they make mistakes;
- show their appreciation for good performance.

Although the above discussion paints participation in glowing colours, the case must not be overstated. Indeed, as participative structures came more and more into vogue, many companies attempted to institute participative mechanisms everywhere, regardless of their utility. Many of these organisations found out to their cost that participation was not always necessary or productive. Roberts and Hurst (1991: 334–5) report literature which questions the value, in terms of productivity, of participation. Many of the cautions appear realistic but perhaps relate more to the unthinking and inappropriate use of participation by organisations. We would certainly agree that forced or contrived participation cannot only be useless but also destructive. We discuss this issue further in Chapter 14, but it is worth noting Handy's (1976: 312) general criteria for using participative methods as we remind ourselves that participation is not necessarily always 'good':

1. The invitation to participate must be genuine. If team members feel a decision has already been made or their input will be ignored they may 'turn-off' and simply comply with the leader.
2. The problem must be worth the time and effort in the eyes of all concerned. Obviously, participation uses a lot of time. If the issue is perceived as trivial, foreclosed, does not concern the individual or is beyond his control, participation will probably be meaningless.
3. The 'contract' must be clear. If the team is asked to make the decision in participative fashion, this is what must happen. If it is asked to merely provide advice, this should be stated at the outset.
4. The individuals concerned should have the necessary skills and information so they can participate effectively.
5. The organisational culture must communicate participation and, if it is to be meaningful, the team leader must believe in it.

Summary

Participation then is seen as a desirable technique, not only for arriving at better decisions and fostering greater commitment, but also as a powerful way for allowing individuals to use and develop their own skills, abilities and experience for their own and the team's benefit. Issues related to this, such as target setting and communication, are covered in later chapters.

In this chapter we have emphasized the importance of team members having the opportunity to use their individual skills, abilities and experience, and that these should be continually developed. We discussed briefly some principles of adult learning and how these must be recognised in any developmental considerations. Finally, we examined the issue of participation, emphasizing that any participation must be, and be perceived to be, real and meaningful. We complete this chapter with a summary of the possible implications for managers when using and developing individual resources, and then we move on to several chapters which discuss issues connected with team tasks.

Summary of the Implications for Managers

- The literature is generally clear that abilities must be recognised and used, and work environments should be created that allow talents to benefit the team. Leaders need to become aware, therefore, of people's experience, skills and abilities. With this knowledge, sometimes it may be appropriate to match the task to individual abilities, and this involves flexible definitions of the task. Other circumstances may dictate that the task cannot be adapted, and individuals, therefore, may need training and guidance so that their skills might become consistent with task demands.

- With training and development, the learning goals in an adult environment must not be threatening, and the risk of failure must be kept low. This means that learning should take place in short easy steps and account for other principles of adult learning.

- If participation is to be meaningful, there should be involvement in problem definition and decision making, and generally in matters of significance. All contributions to the team effort should be treated seriously and recognised. Leaders need to keep members informed, to show consideration, to support their members when they make mistakes, and to show appreciation when work has been done well.

Section 3

The Task

7

GOALS AND TARGETS

"Cheshire Puss, would you like to tell me which way I ought to walk from here?"

"That depends on where you want to get to," said the cat.

"I don't care where," said Alice.

"Then it doesn't matter which way you walk," said the cat.

"So long as I get somewhere," said Alice as an explanation.

"Oh you're bound to do that," said the cat, "if only you walk long enough."

From *Alice in Wonderland*

TEAMS eventually get somewhere, but it may be a long way from the intended destination. One of the key issues in looking at team tasks, therefore, is that of goals or targets. Like Alice, a team may be operating without any clear intention and purpose, and is unlikely to be effective in achieving the task. This would suggest goals and targets are essential, must be clearly defined and play an important role in the 'complete' team picture.

This chapter begins the section on the 'task' by discussing the setting of team targets or goals. Noone (1984: 76) stresses the importance of task emphasis in teambuilding and development. He questions the apparent disproportionate emphasis on the interpersonal side of team functioning:

> When we do consider the team as an entity we often concentrate on interpersonal relationships rather than task and goal. We make much of topics such as 'conflict resolution' and 'human relations'. Could it be that interpersonal conflict is a symptom of lack of role clarity? ... Are we diverting attention from successful accomplishment of team goals and the task interdependence of team members, by concentrating on the individual and interpersonal domain?

Jessup (1992: 65) makes a similar observation, but broadens the issues by tying teamwork to organisational goals: "Much team building focuses only on internal processes; it fails to energize the team by focusing on the organisation's mission and how team members can contribute to it." Whereas we would not entirely agree with Noone and Jessup, we strongly support their conjecture that team development needs to balance the human and task domains.

Team Goals

Goal or target setting is a process designed to specify desired outcomes towards which teams should work. Goals need to be clearly defined, a view reinforced by Shonk and Shonk (1988: 76) who, in drawing a parallel between work teams and athletic teams, advance some keys to success:

- Making goals a living document that constantly guides individual and team effort and is frequently updated to remain relevant.
- Clarifying goals for both the team and the individual players.
- Ensuring ownership of individual and team goals by all team members.

A number of questions might be raised in relation to team goals. For example: Who should determine the goals? What is the most effective process? What should the relationship be between individual and team goals? What should be the relationship between team goals and those of the overall organisation?

The last two questions in particular are interesting and raise the issue of integration. The literature generally advocates the need to ensure effective integration between the goals of the team and those of the organisation (Anantaraman, 1984a: 152) and between those of individual members and the team (Noone, 1984: 75).

Margerison and McCann (1989: 6) in referring to organisational mission statements confirm the need for integration by emphasizing it is important "at the team level that members know not only the overall mission but the way in which it specifically applies to their team". Johnson and Johnson (1991: 445) discuss this theme of integration in terms of 'mutuality': team members should have mutual goals and be mutually responsible for one another. This sort of internal goal integration is linked to the degree of cohesiveness in the team, and referred to as 'positive goal interdependence', where "members perceive that they have a mutual set of goals that all are striving to accomplish and that success depends on all members reaching the goal". Jessup (1992: 66) supports this notion stating: "The basic objectives of any team are defined by the expectations of a large group of stakeholders."

The same author, while accentuating the importance of overall organisational awareness believes that newly formed teams often focus on internal or 'housekeeping' matters for which they are often rewarded with success. However, their real worth is measured by their contribution to organisational goals which are often neglected.

For teams to be successful, as we have stated earlier, members must have common goals. Of course, members will also have individual goals, but these are usually tied to the team goals within which they work. In a team situation, success is gauged on the outcomes produced by the team rather than the individual – if the team succeeds, the individual succeeds. Individual (work-related) goals are formed by the team member both to satisfy himself and the team, causing the goals to interact and overlap. As Noone (1984: 75) states: "The team members are task interdependent ... the team can be truly successful only if all members agree on what the team exists to achieve and are prepared to place their individual work roles within that context".

The need for goals and targets, general, specific or otherwise, in all spheres of life is widely accepted. In terms of teams, without them, efforts may lack direction and focus. Too many teams in organisations, it may be argued, tend to follow the design of Christopher Columbus:

> When he set out, he did not know where he was going;
> when he arrived, he did not know where he was;
> when he got back, he did not know where he had been;
> and all this done on public money.

From Brunt (1987: 217)

It may not be public money necessarily that is being wasted, but undoubtedly valuable resources are often used inefficiently and unproductively in teams, in large part due to lack of goal clarity. This very problem is aptly highlighted by Wynn and Guditus (1984: 130) in drawing attention to the extreme difficulties caused by goal ambiguity in the education sector. They discuss the surge in interest in pursuing the goal of returning to 'basics'. They rightly point out that there is little agreement about what the 'basics' are and that this has led in some cases to the proliferation of even more ambiguous goals and possibly wasted effort.

We have already indicated some of the problems that people working in teams face in relation to the task. These tend to revolve around lack of clarity, being unaware of team purpose, and lack of involvement. Such problems for team members might include:

1. being unclear about what is expected;
2. being unsure what they are accountable for;
3. being unable to focus on the job;
4. being unaware of the team's central purpose;
5. being unable to contribute effectively to the team's decision making.

It may be reasonable to assume that some of these can be overcome through appropriate involvement in decisions about how tasks are undertaken and by giving responsibility for achieving targets to individual team members. This sharing of power is an important feature of teams for some writers. Kizilos and Heinisch (1986: 12), for example, relate it to getting the best out of people. "When 'work' is not an assignment handed down by the boss but the application of everyone's efforts to the task at hand, people are more likely to care about the outcome and to view the organization's goals as their own."

It is difficult to generalise about the extent of goal or target specificity. Much will depend on the type of team and the purpose for which it was formed. For example, a team which has the brief of distributing an extra thousand cars to government departments over the next twelve months can plan and set targets relatively easily. On the other hand, an experimental product team asked to invent new products for the computer market cannot be as specific. Despite this, all teams need some form of target to guide their progress.

Target Management (Stott and Walker, 1992) takes up these issues of involvement and accountability, and attempts to promote participation in goal setting processes and to locate responsibility in the most appropriate quarters.

Texts generally use expressions like 'goals', 'objectives' and 'targets' interchangeably, although some have attempted to effect some discrimination between the terms. One is no better than another, but the word 'target' seems to conjure up a powerful and precise image. It conveys the notion of specificity and this is important when we look at the way in which tasks and subtasks are managed.

Target Management

Target Management is derived from a traditional Management By Objectives (MBO) approach, first named by Peter Drucker in 1954, but it differs in several ways. MBO fell into disfavour in some spheres in the 1980s, partly due to the fact that it had become overcomplicated and that organisations tended to rely too heavily on the process. Target Management has attempted to condense and generally simplify the process, and is arguably more practical. The number of steps have been reduced in order to facilitate understanding and implementation. It lends itself quite readily to the work of teams.

An explanation of how Target Management is used in the superior-subordinate relationship in the whole organisation context is given in Stott and Walker (1992). The approach is slightly different when used in teams. The concern is more firmly located with task issues rather than personal development, although admittedly the latter cannot be seen in isolation from the former. The focus, however, is on completing task and subtask assignments. The second significant difference is that the target setting process can be carried out between team leader and individual member, or between team members themselves. In the context of this volume, we see the process as a team one. Buller and Bell (1986: 307) see the team-focused model of MBO as overcoming two of the major deficiencies in the individually focused model: "First, the team model explicitly recognizes the interdependencies between jobs. Second it encourages integration of goals among individuals who must work together rather than placing the entire responsibility for coordination on a common superior."

Despite these differences of focus and operation, the essence is still the same. The process clarifies what is expected of people, in this case, as either individuals or members of a team, and holds them accountable for the outcomes.

The emphasis is on results rather than specific activities or processes. In other words, the intended outcome is defined before the means of attaining it. This is consistent with similar approaches. Margerison and McCann (1989: 36), for instance, explain the necessity to know what the outputs are. These should indicate:

> what has to be achieved, by when, by whom, and within what specific parameters. Once we know that then the focus can be on the inputs to achieve these outputs. The resources required can be identified – the people, the money, the equipment – so that the outputs can be achieved in the most efficient and effective way.

Target Management, when applied to teams, starts off with the team's overall purpose or mission. As Todryk (1990: 18) notes, a strong mission statement calls team members into action and creates a good framework within which to establish goals and schedules. There are many examples of failures in the business world where goals and values are not articulated clearly enough (Timmons, 1979: 202). In the same way that the author advocates prospective partners in business ventures working on a business plan to identify conflicting goals and values, teams too may need to look at their 'partnerships' from the same perspective. Goal setting is indeed extremely dependent on individual values, and these values are difficult to change. Achieving clarity from the start, therefore, is important.

How is this clarity achieved? Wolff (1988: 6) provides useful advice in preparing a team's mission statement or its declaration of purpose. It should:

- be succinct;
- be clear in language;
- explain what the group does and why it exists;
- identify what is unique about the team;
- support the overall organisational mission;
- leave issues of quantity, quality, cost and time for the more specific goal or target statements.

This advice gives some indication of the difference between team purpose and targets. The former is more general and will probably endure for some time, whereas targets are highly specific and may have to change frequently. Tolle (1988: 282) explains the nature of team mission (described as 'goals') in terms of characteristics. Some of these are listed below:

- They are ideal states to be achieved at some unidentified future time.
- They relate directly to the organisational unit's mission.
- They are concise.
- They are neither time-bound nor do they necessarily deal with measurable results.

Obviously there will be substantial differences between the purposes of permanent senior management teams, for example, and temporary task forces set up for a single task. In the case of a top management team, the mission may be, say, to become the market leader in a particular product line. A temporary workteam, in contrast, may have as its purpose to improve the way customers are dealt with in the reception area. Despite the differences in scope of these aims, they nevertheless form the starting points for setting highly defined targets.

Such targets are aptly characterised by Wolff (1988: 7). They should be:

- realistic, possible to achieve;
- specific and unambiguous;

- bound by time so that you know when to expect results;
- specified in terms of quantity, quality and cost;
- directly related to your mission and goal statements.

The target setting process follows four basic steps. It is presented in Figure 7.1.

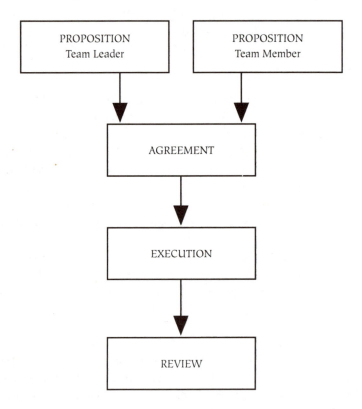

Figure 7.1   The Steps in Target Management

Proposition

At this stage, the intention is to arrive at some realistic targets. These are guided by the team's overall purpose and the specific contribution that the individual can make. They may also be affected by the degree of specificity of the team's brief. For example, if the team is 'to reduce by 20 percent the spending on stationery requisition items by the end of the next quarter' there may be less scope for target setting than if the brief were 'to seek improvements in the efficiency of office procedures'. The scope is, therefore, controlled to some extent by the level of clarity or ambiguity of the overall purpose statement.

Assuming that the task needs to be broken down into components, it is best if the individual (or small group of team members) suggests target statements and these can then be modified by the team as a whole, relevant members, or by the leader. Using one of the examples above, the process may unfold something like this:

- Team goal: To make improvements in the way in which customers are treated at reception.
- Framework: At the last team meeting, it was decided that one way to tackle the problem would be to provide training for reception staff.
- Team member responsible: An external consultant will be sought by the end of the month and three half-day sessions of training will be arranged within two months. I shall meet with all reception staff for one hour each week during this period to discuss problems and concerns and to reinforce some of the main training points.

It can be seen how the proposed target statement is consistent with the overall team goal to improve the quality of customer service in the reception area. The next step is for the leader or team members to become involved in refining the statement.

Agreement

The input from other team members may be invaluable at this stage. On the other hand, it may not be necessary to change the proposed statement very much, if at all. The important thing is that a statement emerges that covers a *key result area*. The other important criteria are that targets must be realistic, tied to team goals, and be within the boundaries of member and resource capabilities. They must also be attainable. It makes sense that the team member responsible should have the final say, since he has the commitment and responsibility. At the same time, the team must exert some influence in ensuring that targets are appropriately located within team goals.

We said earlier that the focus in team target setting is on the task. This is true, but the development of team members cannot be overlooked. Target setting, approached skilfully, can be a powerful force for individual development. Indeed, it is designed in such a way as to support the integration of personal needs in terms of development and team or organisational goals, a substantially more productive approach than focusing exclusively on team goal achievement (Wynn and Guditus, 1984: 129). Responsibility in itself, achieved through the target setting mechanism, is an excellent vehicle for development, but the targets, and the level of challenge they offer, also provide the opportunity for development.

Once the individual and team members have agreed on a target, the individual (or, in some cases, a small group of individuals) should be allowed to decide *how* to do the task. With the responsibility for successful subtask completion comes the responsibility for determining the means that will be used. This may necessitate support from the team, team leader and maybe the organisation in providing the necessary resources and authority.

The end of this stage should result in clarity about the steps to be taken. Using Ends and Page's (1977: 56) criteria, the targets should be clearly defined, perfectly understood and accepted by all those involved.

Execution

The next stage of the process involves the team member in working to achieve the target. The team leader should not become involved in excessive monitoring, but should operate in a supportive capacity, offering help and advice when it is needed. Some monitoring, of course, is required and checkpoints will have been agreed on. The leader and other members may also be available for consultation.

Review

When the task has been completed (or when it was supposed to be finished) is the time for review. If things have not gone according to plan, it may be necessary to 'dissect' the process and learn from the experience. If on the other hand the task was successful, the review session provides an occasion to acknowledge the effort and consider appropriate rewards.

This may also be a time to set new targets and to iron out difficulties. For the system to work, however, skill must be acquired by all team members and there needs to be a high degree of commitment to seeing it through. In Figure 7.2 we review the process of target setting and identify the key practical points.

IN A GOOD TARGET MANAGEMENT PROGRAMME:

- Team members must have clear task descriptions.
- Individual performance must be tied to team goals.
- The leader must provide sufficient resources for targets to be attained.
- Target setting is best used as a developmental process as well as a system for achieving team goals.
- The system should contain both rewards and sanctions for achievement or non-achievement of targets.
- Sufficient time must be provided.
- Once targets have been set the team member should be responsible for the 'how'.
- The system should be flexible and allow for crisis situations.
- Progress towards target attainment should be reviewed at agreed points and the leader should be available for consultation.
- Team members should be held accountable for target attainment.

Figure 7.2   Target Setting: The Key Practical Points

Hellriegel *et al.* (1991: 415) suggest that team-focused target setting will be truly successful only if three conditions are present:

- A real need for integration among individuals must exist.
- Top management must cooperate and offer mutual assistance instead of engaging in political power struggles.
- Participants must have some degree of skill in group processes and interpersonal relations.

The final point reinforces the main thrust of this volume: Team development must be considered in a number of interrelated areas – individual, task, team and organisation – if teams are to realise their full potential.

Benefits and Drawbacks

There appear to be some distinct advantages to adopting such a participative approach to the target setting process:

1. Those involved are required have to consider results and relate these to team purposes. The outcomes, therefore, are important. As Bechtel (1980) observes, a key weakness in some target statements is the emphasis on the 'how' rather than the 'what'.
2. Teams are more likely to see themselves with clearly defined roles and as having an important part to play in decisions. This may promote a greater sense of commitment.
3. There may be an improved understanding of what is required and expected.
4. The process separates the important from the routine, thus directing effort into key result areas. The less significant parts of the task are relegated in importance.
5. Ownership of the process may also contribute to motivation levels, and setting realistic targets means success is usually attainable, which is a powerful motivating factor in itself. Additionally, the involvement may increase satisfaction in the job and contribute to improved morale.

Such systematic processes are not without their problems, and some of these are highlighted below:

1. Target Management can be time consuming, especially in the initial stages when a team is learning how to set appropriate targets and consider the related issues.
2. It can also lead to the generation of mountains of paperwork and this may need to be kept in check.
3. The setting of measurable and attainable targets can also be problematic. As Bechtel (1980) indicates, if people overestimate their own capabilities and set unworkable or unrealistically

high targets, the process may collapse. If, on the other hand, they are too low, satisfaction may be limited and capabilities remain unchallenged. The high achiever, suggest Ends and Page (1977: 88), manages to fall neatly between the two extremes. He selects goals with a moderate degree of risk but which are nonetheless realistic. They represent a challenge sufficient to draw on the individual's best efforts. He is neither a speculative gambler nor a rigid conservative. "While the goals set may appear to be quite risky to an onlooker, the achievement-oriented person sets goals very carefully with respect to his or her self-confidence in the ability to achieve them by exerting a reasonable amount of effort and skill. The goals therefore represent a level of performance for which the high achiever is willing to hold himself or herself accountable." This type of goal or target setting behaviour may be an adequate model to follow.

4. Yet another difficulty is inflexibility and the inability to respond to operational crises. At the same time, such events may divert attention away from target achievement inappropriately.

5. Failing to review progress periodically can lead to targets drifting and becoming increasingly diffuse.

6. A major difficulty (and this applies to any rational goal-oriented approach) is the tendency to focus on those results that are easily measurable. These may divert attention away from more important result areas which are less easy to define.

Other problems identified by Bechtel (1980) are lack of clarity about who is ultimately responsible for the outcome, setting targets that are more in keeping with leader preferences rather than team purpose, failing to abandon or modify unworkable or irrelevant targets, setting over-optimistic time schedules and being unable to justify a target adequately. Hellriegel *et al.* (1991: 414) cite a number of criticisms, interestingly, of individually focused MBO. Those which do not duplicate items noted previously include a warning that the process turns into a win-lose situation between superior and subordinate. The process tends to be controlled from the top, allowing minimal opportunity for worker involvement, and that too much emphasis is placed on a reward-punishment psychology. They also mention that the emphasis on individual performance and targets works against the need for collaborative group goals, pushing individuals to concentrate on individual goals at the expense of team or organisational goals. Noone (1984: 74) would disagree with this, believing that individual and team goals are necessarily interdependent.

With these problems in mind, we now address a practical issue which often gives rise to concern: the writing of realistic, verifiable targets.

Writing Target Statements

A cursory glance at some of the documents from organisational teams' planning meetings will generally confirm there is a great diversity in the quality of goal or target statements. The following two examples, both taken from the record of actual meetings, illustrate the point:

1. The coordinators' sub-committee will improve the orientation process.

2. The course team will plan a one-day orientation unit, and this must be done within the cost limits of previous events. The plan must be submitted by the course team leader at our next meeting on 11 May.

The first statement, of course, is very imprecise. Although it does give some indication of where responsibility lies, it does not define improvement, nor does it specify what must be done. The second statement, in contrast, shows that planning must be done, what the resource constraints are and when everything is to be completed. It may not be perfect, but it provides most of the essential outline details. The problem with the first statement is that it lends itself to multiple interpretations, and the outcomes, therefore, may be at variance with what was originally intended.

Figure 7.3 summarises the important criteria of a clear statement.

It can be seen that a good target states the *what, when, who* and *maximum cost*. However, it avoids feasibility and the *how*. The operational or action plan developed for the target will deal with the how and test the feasibility. Simpson (no date: 9) recommends that

---

- It has an action word.
- It states the team member responsible.
- It outlines the cost in terms of time and money.
- It sets a completion date.
- It specifies a measurable end result.

Figure 7.3   Characteristics of a Target Statement

the following questions be considered (by the team) when targets have been set.

1. How significant is the target in terms of the known objectives of the organisation?
2. How urgent is the target?
3. To what extent is the target measurable? (Consider the yardsticks you have developed.)
4. How clearly is the target described? Does it precisely describe the end results expected?
5. To what extent is the target attainable?
6. To what extent does this target statement describe an *activity* leading to a target as opposed to a real end *result*?
7. What should the target completion date be?
8. To what extent is this target challenging as opposed to being routine? To what extent does this target stretch you?

The requirements for a good target statement can, of course, be even more detailed and specific. The more precision there is, the less likelihood there will be of misunderstanding, confusion or avoidance of responsibility. At this point it may be worth noting Simpson's warning that trying to achieve any more than six targets in any given period is unwise and can lead to failure in some or all. He reminds us that "targets are priorities, special tasks to be achieved over and above the routine work" (p. 8).

For target statements to be measurable they must be stated in concrete and explicit terms. It is preferable if the target outcomes can be quantified. This is not always possible, however, and qualitative outcomes may be necessary. Target statements can be tested against the checklist shown in Figure 7.4 to ascertain whether they include the essential elements.

Does it state what has to be done?	☐
Does it state what the target is meant to achieve?	☐
Does it state who has the responsibility for doing it?	☐
Does it state a completion date?	☐
Does it give details of the resources needed?	☐
Does it contain a brief statement explaining the approach?	☐
Does it state who will coordinate different parts?	☐
Does it include a justification for the target?	☐

Figure 7.4   A Target Statement Checklist

Summary

In summary, Target Management is a useful participative process that can involve all team members in focusing their respective efforts. Like many of the strategies in this book, it is based on a very positive philosophy about people and their willingness to contribute to the team effort. It assumes that team members want to be involved in making decisions and in how to achieve their targets. It is firmly based on the premise that real involvement leads to commitment, a feature of all shared goal-setting approaches. Target Management, therefore, aims to take advantage of people's natural willingness to learn, achieve and work, and to aid the integration process between specific team targets and overall team purpose. In the following chapter we describe a scheme for planning team tasks systematically.

Summary of the Implications for Managers

- One way for teams to approach the target-setting process is for individuals to suggest target statements and for these to be then modified by the team. Such statements should cover the key result areas. They should be realistic and attainable, tied to team goals, and be within team member and resource capabilities.

- Target statements should be clearly defined, perfectly understood, and accepted by all those team members. In terms of content, they should deal with the what, when, who and maximum cost. They should be as measurable as possible.

- Despite the high level of definition recommended for setting targets, individuals should still be able to decide how to do the task. The leader's role is best seen as a supportive one, helping and advising, and avoiding the pitfall of excessive monitoring.

8

TACKLING
TEAM TASKS
SYSTEMATICALLY

THE OUTPUT of a team is undoubtedly the most significant indicator of success, and most of the other considerations in relation to team development are concerned with supporting performance. Some teams are primarily concerned with longer term and ongoing issues, while others are formed to complete specific assignments. These sorts of teams in particular are often under time constraints and other limitations, and it is crucial, therefore, that the approach adopted is systematic and economical. All teams, however, can benefit from adopting an approach which is consistent and which covers the steps towards task completion in a systematic way. In this chapter we describe a scheme which teams might employ to guide their planning.

A Scheme

The scheme suggested in this chapter encourages teams to address assignments coherently and it will be seen that a large part of the scheme is concerned with planning. Team performance indeed has to be a planned event. As Ends and Page (1977: 150) advocate, five major aspects have to be positively planned; these are:

1. establishing team performance goals,
2. planning the work,
3. negotiating roles,
4. establishing performance criteria, and
5. planning performance feedback.

These are very similar to the four fundamental components of team planning advanced by Margerison and McCann (1985: 65), namely, agreeing mission, setting objectives, analysing performance, and allocating work. These aspects are all accommodated in our scheme.

The components above apply equally to the work of permanent teams and, indeed, Margerison and McCann (1985: 70) suggest team planning must be done on a regular basis: some dimensions of planning may be done on an annual basis, such as the team's mission, whilst others may have to be tackled on a daily basis, such as task allocation and operations review. Planning, at whatever level, is seen as vital to effectiveness.

It is worth noting at this stage the importance of planning in teams and how much it is an avoided activity. Most operations seem to be reactive rather than proactive: the evidence is plentiful: running out of stock; machinery breaking down; failing to consider contingencies. Numerous Mintzberg-type (1973) studies (Kotter, 1982) have shown that, despite the folklore that managers spend their time carefully planning, staffing and organising, reality is different. Managers' work is actually characterised by pace, brevity and variety of activities, and fragmentation. In the real world of management, managers are reactive and spend little time planning. And teams are often little different, being less than systematic when confronted with new tasks.

Even where planning takes place, it is often less than successful or is even discarded. Some of the reasons might include the following (Kezsbom, 1990: 50):

- Overall organisational mission and goals are not fully understood by team members.
- People with important information are missing from the planning process.

- Planning stops at the general level and fails to address specifics.
- Plans are made using insufficient data.
- Work activities and tasks have not been defined.
- Progress checkpoints have not been set.
- Intended outcomes are not defined.
- Insufficient time is given to planning.

The scheme, called the '7D Scheme for Team Action', concentrates very much on adequate planning activity and attempts to overcome many of the problems identified above. Essentially there are several phases of short-term planning activity followed by the phases of implementation and review. We mention several topics such as creativity and generating options, but cover them only briefly, since we go into considerably more detail about such issues later in the book and particularly in Chapter 14. At this stage, our concern is to present a usable, sequential framework for project-type tasks.

The scheme has been developed with three basic ideas in mind. For a team to complete a task successfully, the members must:

1. carefully plan what they are going to do and how they will do it;
2. ensure that the plan is implemented as far as possible in accordance with its original design;
3. evaluate the plan and the process itself to see how it can be improved, either while it is in action or after the task is completed.

In reality, the seven steps which comprise the scheme should not be viewed as discrete steps, since there is considerable overlap depending on the nature of the assignment. It may be necessary on occasions to modify the sequence. By sticking loosely to the order of steps, however, the chances of successful task completion will increase. There are many other similar 'staged' schemes which might best be described as team problem-solving approaches. For example, Margerison and McCann (1989: 26) have a system which they call SADIE. The stages are: sharing information on problems and opportunities; analysing information; developing options and making a selection; implementing the decision; and evaluating the results. Hunt (1979: 148) suggests planning involves establishing objectives, collecting data related to these objectives, examining alternatives or courses of action and selecting the most desirable course of action. Such schemes cover the essential elements, but the 7D scheme gives more detailed attention to several stages and breaks them down into separate components.

The 7D scheme (displayed in Figure 8.1) is concerned essentially with tactical or short-term plans rather than longer term strategic plans. It is essential to differentiate between these two general types of planning. Strategic or long-term planning is vital for continued organisational success. Seiler and Said (1983: 16) describe strategic planning as the process of positioning the organisation so that future prospects are maximised and future risks minimised. They define it as "the identification of choices concerning possible future positions in which the organization may find itself, and their evaluation such that one possible position is selected over others". Strategic planning then is concerned with the way in which the organisation sets and progresses towards long-term goals. It involves a series of steps which lead to formulation of appropriate strategies. If, however, strategic plans are not operationalised through shorter term processes, long-term goals may remain unattainable.

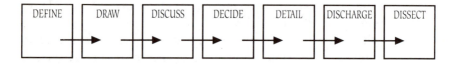

Figure 8.1   The 7D Scheme

The fact is, especially in times of rapid change, many teams are more likely to be concerned with shorter term planning on a more frequent basis. Short-term or operational plans are highly specific and relate to the intended outcomes for the team. They tend to cover eventualities (as far as is realistically possible), are quantifiable in terms of performance and timescale, and have checkpoints so that performance can be evaluated along the way. The seven phases of the scheme are explained below, followed by a summary of the key action points after each phase. These can be used as a form of checklist when undertaking team tasks.

1. Define

In this phase the task is defined precisely and clearly delineated. The team members should know what it is and what it is not. This first stage sets the scene for the success of the team's subsequent action. It is also important to explain *why* the task needs to be done. Commitment is unlikely to be forthcoming unless members understand the value and relevance of the task. This point is reinforced by Graham (1991: 50):

> It is not only the 'how' but also the 'why' of the task that must be shared with all those involved in it. Full commitment cannot be had, unless everyone in the group knows the whys and has taken a part, however small, in the decision-making process that went to make up the objective.

Dwelling on the theme of commitment, she goes on: "People simply cannot commit themselves wholeheartedly to aims they do not share and have not taken a part in developing."

It is also at this stage that the issue of problem definition may need addressing if the team is involved primarily in problem solving. This, for many teams, presents considerable difficulties. As Drucker warned as long ago as 1954: "The most common source of mistakes in management decisions is the emphasis on finding the right answer rather than the right question ... The first job in decision making is to find the real problem and define it" (Drucker, 1954; cited in Wynn and Guditus, 1984: 105). If the problem is identified correctly, arriving at a relevant solution is a more straightforward process.

Included in this phase is an explanation of the time available for the task's completion and also for the specific phases of planning. The team also needs to be made aware of the other possible constraints. These may include political obstacles, such as an important person's opposition to particular courses of action or the lack of cooperation the team might face from individuals or other groups.

This phase of the scheme requires exact communication and at the end of it all team members should be clear about the task and intended outcomes. Specificity, therefore, is important. There should be a statement of what constitutes success. The phase also represents an opportunity to unravel the difficulties by encouraging questions and discussion so that a high level of clarity might be achieved. The defining stage then 'gets the ball rolling' for the team by defining its direction and purpose.

DEFINE

- Explain the task.
- Explain why the task needs doing.
- Gain commitment to the task.
- Unravel the difficulties.
- Specify the time available.
- Spell out the known constraints.

---

2. Draw

The second phase involves the drawing in of information and all the available data necessary to make informed choices. Poor planning often results from failing to acquire all the relevant knowledge that is available. It may not be possible or realistic to gather together all the information, but if it is readily available it should be acquired. Obviously, the nature of the data is dependent on the type of task, but information can be collected about such things as competitors' products and prices, technical specifications, market data, the likelihood of opposition to certain ideas, and political information that could affect what is and what is not possible.

Other types of information may include details of resources available to the team. For example, it is important to know in detail what is available in terms of people, equipment and facilities, materials, services and energy, money and information. It may also be considered how additional resources can be acquired if they would improve the effectiveness of the team's operation.

The question of human resources is an important one. It may be possible, for example, to draw on expertise from outside the team. If specialisms are needed that do not exist in the team, this can be valuable information. Equally valuable is the capacity to seek specialist advice.

In this information-gathering phase, it is also an opportunity to conduct an 'internal audit' by assessing the skills and experience amongst team members that might contribute towards successful task completion. While recruiting expertise from outside may be desirable in some circumstances, some team members may benefit from the provision of development opportunities, and it is possible at this stage to audit preferences in terms of task contributions.

DRAW

- Seek relevant information.
- Check the resources available.
- Consider whether additional resources can be acquired.
- Assess members' task-related skills and expertise.
- Seek knowledge and expert advice.

---

3. Discuss

The discussion phase is inevitably (and appropriately) the longest stage in the scheme. Ideas, methods and possible solutions can be aired, and opportunities given for all members of the team to contribute. Apart from the specialist functional skills that members may bring to the team, their contributions, as will be seen in the next section of the book, will hinge very much on the roles they prefer to play. Some may come forward with creative ideas, others will look at suggestions critically, and yet others will be able to coordinate separate inputs and put them together into some semblance of order.

The discussion phase is an ideal time to foster creative inputs, and the strength of the team's performance may depend to a large extent on its capacity to foster these. If creativity is to be supported, it is probably advisable to avoid constraining assumptions at this stage of the discussion. Suggestions, however impractical, may need to be treated seriously, and there are many techniques for trying to think beyond the bounds of normal thought patterns. One of these is the well-known process of brainstorming, and we have looked at this separately as part of the decision-making process. Another strategy which can be used is what we call the 'Clean Sheet' method. Team members are given a clean sheet of paper and informed that, if there were no constraints at all, an ideal solution would be possible. They can be asked to identify and write down such ideal solutions.

Then, they are asked to consider how constraints might be broken down or accommodated.

Creativity might best be fostered in an environment where questioning is encouraged, where individuals can challenge ideas, assumptions and processes without fear. Peterson (1991: 86) talks about freeing minds and dreaming up new ways of doing things: "Tell them to question the things about your business that have always seemed unquestionable. If employee involvement and participative management have truly permeated your company, people will already be in a frame of mind to do some real breakthrough thinking."

Liberating the team environment for a free flow of ideas probably means that dissent might surface, and it is probably advisable to encourage rather than suppress it. The quality of ideas and their use may hinge on the intensity of debate. As Alfred P. Sloan, then President of General Motors, is reported to have said at a meeting of one of his top committees:

> "Gentlemen, I take it we are all in agreement on the decision here." Everyone around the table nodded assent. "Then," continued Sloan, "I propose we postpone further discussion of this matter until our next meeting to give ourselves time to develop disagreement and perhaps gain some understanding of what the decision is all about." (quoted in Adair, 1988: 88)

During the discussion phase, options or alternative solutions are generated. This is an 'open' process where plenty of ideas might be encouraged. The evaluation of options, in contrast, must be systematic and based on sound critical judgement. It is a useful technique to record against each option the resources needed, the resources available, the possible outcomes and the estimated chances of success. This may not be easy to gauge, but a helpful procedure is for the team (or individual members) to make an assessment out of ten. This represents the perceived possibility of success. In this way, participants have to state preferences quantitatively and explain the reasons for their judgements. A form similar to that shown in Figure 8.2 can be used for this purpose.

When the various options are being evaluated, the consequences of different courses of action can be thought out. This scrutiny should lead to a shortlist of viable options which can then be tested for applicability. This systematic approach should enhance the chances of consensus when a final conclusion has to be reached.

OPTION:		
Resources available	Resources needed	Predicted outcomes
Chance of success	Why?	

Figure 8.2   A Form for Evaluating Options

This phase of the scheme demands considerable leadership skill. An effective leader probably has to be adept at promoting open discussion whilst keeping it on line, and encouraging members to challenge ideas. Apart from technical and interpersonal skills, the leader may need to be proficient in synthesising and summarising. Synthesising skills "allow you to take things that appear separate and see a unifying pattern to them ... You have to take the separate individuals and skills (and ideas) in your workgroup and pull them together" (Carr, 1989: 208). Regular summaries clarify progress and indicate the direction in which the discussion should go.

Two further related issues need to be covered during this phase. First, potential pitfalls can be identified. This represents an assessment of what could possibly go wrong and helps to prepare for the eventuality. Second, contingency plans need to be considered in an attempt to make the plan as foolproof as is realistically possible. A discussion of these issues leads naturally into the decision phase.

DISCUSS
- Set the priorities.
- Encourage ideas: Brainstorm alternative solutions.
- Generate options.
- Explore different viewpoints.
- Challenge ideas.
- Summarise contributions.
- Synthesise: Build on suggestions; coordinate contributions.
- Consider consequences of different courses of action.

---

4. Decide

Depending on the team's brief, it is likely that a decision must be arrived at. If the preceding phases have been conducted effectively, the decision should be soundly based. A problem that teams often face after going through these processes is the unwillingness to actually make the decision. There is often a tendency to revisit the ground covered in the previous phase. Margerison (1973: 44) highlights this same problem:

> We have all attended long meetings where an idea has been discussed fully, but no decision taken. This is a major facet of avoidance behaviour, where people postpone a decision that they regard as risky or painful. One of the classic organizational devices for dealing with such problems is to refer them to sub-committees.

Such delaying tactics can go on indefinitely, but once the previous three phases have been completed, there is a need to make an incisive decision. The leader's role at this point is to move the team firmly towards an outcome. If a consensus is sought, it may not be possible to take short cuts such as vote-taking, and the leader's skill is again of great importance in completing the process efficiently.

Consensus is often talked about lightly but it can be difficult to achieve. As Ackoff (1986: 160) rightly notes: "It is frequently easier to get managers to agree that consensus is desirable than it is to obtain it. The additional time and effort more than compensate for the reduction in time and effort required to implement the decision it produces and the increase in the effectiveness of that implementation." We shall discuss the process of consensus in detail in Section 4.

Even after consensus has been achieved and a firm decision made, there may still be an inclination to return to the discussion which preceded the decision. Discipline needs to be exercised, however, in accepting that the decision is final and there is little point in wasting time and effort in covering old ground. At this point, the effort has to be directed into constructing a simple and workable plan that can be understood by all team members.

It is unrealistic to set plans in concrete. They may need to be adapted as situations change. This is not an excuse for imprecise plans; they should be carefully thought out in all the relevant detail. At the same time, contingencies need to be considered should any problems eventuate. An element of flexibility, therefore, is probably advisable.

Having reached a decision, considered some of the things that could go wrong, and drafted a plan of action, the team is now ready to look at the finer detail of the plan and move towards implementation.

DECIDE

- Try for consensus.
- Prod members to an incisive decision.
- Make a simple and workable plan.
- Make a contingency plan.

---

5. Detail

Ends and Page (1977: 151) refer to this phase as 'planning the work', and consider the issues of subtask identification and member participation. We too would reinforce the need for active participation but have used the word 'detail' because it involves other essential elements such as breaking down the task and looking at some of its specifics and components. The three key aspects of the phase then are:

- dividing the task up and delineating individual responsibilities;
- briefing the team;
- defining the ways in which performance is to be measured.

Some tasks are sufficiently large and complex to lend themselves to be broken up into subtasks for the attention of individuals or team subunits. Such subtasks might include collecting information, seeking people's opinions, or drafting advertisements. Other types of task may require the whole team's attention throughout, and the task may be broken down, therefore, into manageable and logically sequential parts.

Having made decisions about such detail, the assignment of sub-tasks should be systematic, and on this note, Carr (1989: 44) provides some sound advice. Write down every task that has to be done. Besides each task, write the name of the person who will do it. If more than one person, identify the person with overall responsibility. Then brief the team.

A similar process, which also deals with the issue of individual accountability, is called 'responsibility charting' and is explained in Wolff (1988: 7). The first step involves listing the essential processes; the examples given by Wolff are as follows:

- **Responsibility:** This one person is responsible for starting things off and seeing that every action is carried out properly.
- **Approval:** This person can approve or veto.
- **Support:** This person provides supporting resources.
- **Inform:** This person must be informed but cannot interfere.

The second step is to list the subtasks or actions. For each subtask, a decision is made as to who has responsibility. The advice is given that it should be someone as far down in the ranks as is possible. The final step is to decide which people should be the approvers, the supporters and those who must be informed. The chart is best displayed in the form of a grid as shown in Figure 8.3.

The briefing process is an important component of this phase. Members need to understand their roles in task implementation, and the briefing, therefore, needs to be clearly communicated. Full explanations are essential to all involved, as is the opportunity for clarifying questions in preparation for implementation.

A vital part of the briefing process involves determining how performance will be measured. A team needs feedback about the level of its performance and 'markers', therefore, are essential. These need to be specified in such a way that the team knows whether it is on course, below expectations, or exceeding the planned levels.

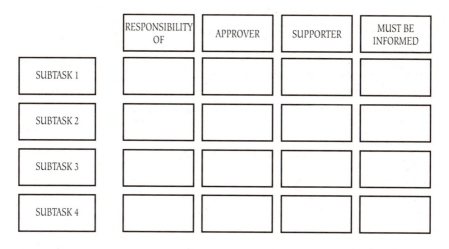

RESPONSIBILITY OF   This refers to the person who has overall responsibility for the subtask.

APPROVER   This person has the power to override actions or decisions of the above individual, and his or her approval must be sought.

SUPPORTER   This person has the resources that support the subtask.

MUST BE INFORMED   This person may not be capable of influencing the subtask, but must be informed.

Figure 8.3   Subtask Responsibility Grid

It is equally important to define requirements for individuals or subunits, and to set 'progress checkpoints'. Progress towards defined targets may need to be evaluated alongside predetermined standards of performance. These may take the form of minimum performance standards that can be tolerated without affecting the team's goals (Ends and Page, 1977: 152).

One way of dealing with action plans, incorporating much of the information outlined above, is shown in Figure 8.4. Such a summary plan shows the team's goal, how it relates to the organisational mission, the specific tasks or subtasks, the resources needed, the personnel responsible and the completion date. The plan, based on an action plan in Snyder (1988: 203), also specifies the monitoring and review mechanisms.

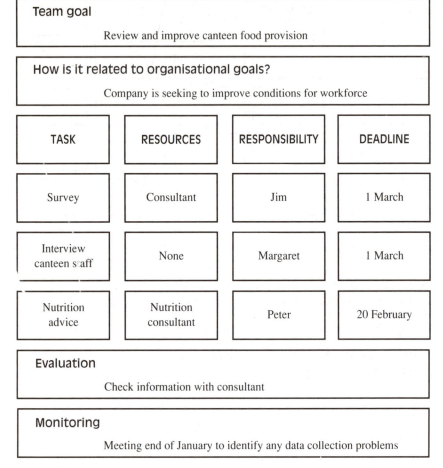

Figure 8.4   A Sample Action Plan

The skills involved in this phase as the process moves towards implementation are essentially those of clarifying, establishing, and communicating. Clarity refers to team members being aware of the steps involved in implementation and the actions that have to be taken. Establishing clear targets and timeframes is also necessary and individuals must know and understand their contributory roles. The success of these processes largely hinges on effective communication amongst team members to ensure that roles and outcomes are fully understood.

With individual or subunit responsibilities delineated, the team briefed, and control mechanisms in place for ensuring that the plan progresses as closely as possible to original intentions, the team is ready to 'discharge' or implement the plan.

DETAIL

- Assign responsibilities and ensure individual work is challenging.
- Brief thoroughly: give careful explanation to the group.
- Allocate specific tasks.
- Check members understand their individual contributions.
- Distribute resources.
- Explain contingencies.
- Set 'progress checkpoints'.
- Specify 'performance markers'.
- Specify individual targets.

---

6. Discharge

If the previous phases have been dealt with effectively, discharging the task should be a smooth process leading to successful task completion. It is not always so. Sometimes, decisions are taken but subsequent action is less than effective. As Margerison (1973: 44) says: "It is essential, not just to take decisions but to ensure that people feel involved and committed to making the decision effective by acting upon it". Converting plans to action is of crucial importance.

The activities, of course, should be those that have been planned, and the control mechanisms should ensure this occurs to a greater extent. At the same time, it must be remembered that an action plan is simply a best guess (albeit an informed one) of what will work, and it may need some modification along the way. In this light, the intermediate measures of performance and progress should be responded to appropriately. Progress can be checked at the predetermined intervals, using standard control mechanisms such as meetings, output checks, production records, and reports. A useful tool to aid this process is the 'progress report', and a suitable format is suggested in Figure 8.5 which again shows the subtasks, asks for the current position and then suggests new plans in response to events so far.

The leader's role in this phase is to observe progress and to keep the 'big picture' in focus, but occasional involvement in items of detail may be necessary.

The monitoring process involves checking the 'actual' against the 'intended'. If a discrepancy between the two is discovered, it needs to be decided if any action should be taken. The deviation may not be very significant and it may be decided to tolerate it. On the other hand, it may be crucial to organisation performance, in which case something needs to be done about even the smallest deviation. Such deviations, it should be noted, are not always on the negative side. Sometimes, performance

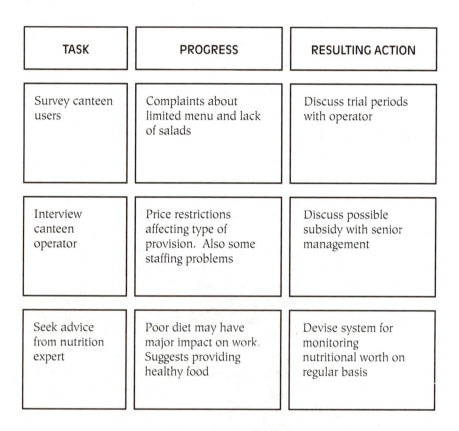

TASK	PROGRESS	RESULTING ACTION
Survey canteen users	Complaints about limited menu and lack of salads	Discuss trial periods with operator
Interview canteen operator	Price restrictions affecting type of provision. Also some staffing problems	Discuss possible subsidy with senior management
Seek advice from nutrition expert	Poor diet may have major impact on work. Suggests providing healthy food	Devise system for monitoring nutritional worth on regular basis

Figure 8.5　　Sample Progress Report

may exceed expectations, and the decision then is whether to revise targets in the light of new information. This sort of change should be handled with care, however, since individuals may modify their standards of performance to account for new measures, and may compromise quality for the sake of quantity.

Sometimes, it is a positive decision to do nothing, especially if the discrepancy is minimal. If it costs more to solve a problem, either in human or resource terms, than the benefits it would reap, it may be expedient to take no action. Another option, albeit a radical one, is to abort the plan, and this may be appropriate in extreme cases. If events are leading to a final outcome that is completely short of the standards planned, it may be wise to cut losses and go back to the drawing board. Abandoning a plan can be difficult, especially if considerable energy has been committed to the process, but team members must ask whether it would be advisable professionally, financially or personally to take such a course. There are some situations, however, where decisions to implement are irreversible and that means proceeding despite the obstacles and setbacks.

Monitoring, from the leader's point of view, is best seen as a facilitative rather than an inspectoral role. Apart from the formal procedures, informal review is important. It involves casual conversations and polite enquiries about progress. Control that is too tight can be construed as unreasonable interference and lead to unpleasantness, whereas too little attention may give rise to quality and performance problems. If intervention is needed, it should be made with immediacy. Of course, it is not necessarily a leader's job to carry out control procedures. Team members themselves may take this on effectively. Whether leader or team takes responsibility for monitoring, however, there is a danger that control mechanisms can become more important than the task itself, and this is a malady that needs to be avoided.

There are several other aspects to this phase. Team members need to be kept informed of progress and this might best be done on a whole team basis so that the overall task is kept in view. It is also important for team members to receive encouragement and reassurance, probably even more important when things are not going quite so well as expected. Good examples of teamwork, small successes and the meeting of dead-lines need to be acknowledged, and this again can be done by the leader or the team generally. Occasionally, the phase also necessitates some disciplining of members if they are not fulfilling their obligations and commitments satisfactorily, and this might involve reminding them of agreed targets, appealing to their team spirit, or even reassigning them elsewhere.

The discharge phase, then, covers the implementation of the plan and its progress in line with agreed targets. If all goes well, a successful outcome should result. That is not the end. There is still one more step.

DISCHARGE

- Check actions are related to targets.
- Look for discrepancies between actual and planned.
- Intervene and help where necessary.
- Guide and train where necessary.
- Check standards of performance.
- Monitor progress towards targets.
- Keep members informed of progress.
- Give reassurance and encouragement.

---

7. Dissect

Unless reflection takes place, there is unlikely to be much learning. Experience cannot be built on unless people consider carefully the actions they have taken and the events that have happened. Johnson and Johnson (1991: 448) draw attention to the importance of review in making the team more productive. A team should set aside time to discuss progress in relation to goal achievement and working relationships between team members.

Dissecting, according to the *Longman Dictionary of Contemporary English*, means to cut up and study the shape and relationship of the parts. It also means to study very carefully in order to find the faults. And this is what this final phase entails. It is not really a separate stage in the scheme. The review process should take place during several other phases as well as at the end of the task. Plans, for example, need to be 'studied carefully and faults found' during formulation. Objectives need to be checked and the feasibility of preferred options must be reviewed. In the 'defining' phase, for example, it can be asked whether the definition of the task is appropriate. In the 'draw' phase, the sufficiency and relevance of information acquired can be reviewed.

It is also necessary to 'cut up' performance at the end in order to answer questions about outcome success, team interaction and cohesion, individual performance and behaviour, and a number of related issues. This, of course, is intended to lead to learning, so that future performance is improved. Improvement is the focus of Peterson (1991: 85), former president of Ford, who sees serious review as a vital factor in ensuring progress:

> The emphasis in all these efforts was (and still is) on examining all of the many processes used in manufacturing cars and trucks and challenging every one of them. Is a given process even needed? Can it be simplified? Are better processes available that we can adopt? Are we taking steps in the right sequence? This is difficult, conceptual thinking, and it takes the best minds you have, but unless you make the effort to improve your processes, your well is going to run dry.

Such a positive 'dissecting' process can lead to a team experiencing real learning. This can occur only if the process is well managed. On this score Johnson and Johnson (1991: 448) provide some useful guidelines:

1. Allow sufficient time for review to take place.
2. Make it specific rather than general.
3. Keep members involved in review and working collaboratively.
4. Communicate clear expectations for review.

The first point deserves some elaboration. Reviews are normally held during team meetings, but time pressures invariably prevent adequate discussion taking place. Yet it is important for the team to evaluate its progress on a regular basis. With this in mind, Margerison and McCann (1989: 25) suggest arranging separate review meetings which should last at least half a day, and which should have only one item on the agenda, namely, the question 'How well are we doing in relation to our task?' This then gives time for adequate analysis to take place and discussion of what needs to be done to stay on track.

The same authors (p. 29) also point out the dangers of focusing only on 'what' has been done, rather than 'how' it has been done. They suggest discussion should also include the factors that lie behind the team outcomes, and this may lead to a consideration of vital behavioural factors.

The sorts of activities that might characterise the review process include regular summaries, asking for close scrutiny of plans and testing possible consequences. They also include assessing the value of individual contributions and giving appropriate feedback.

Feedback is an important part of the review process. Individuals can report progress to the leader or team colleagues and assistance can be provided if required. This is one type of feedback. Another is where the leader provides feedback to individuals and to the team as a whole (Ends and Page, 1977: 152). At an individual level, it may involve assessing performance and the value of individual contributions. It may also include praising and rewarding productive, worthwhile contributions and discussing how inadequate effects or results can be improved next time. It is preferable if these points can be identified through monitoring and corrected in the earlier phases of the scheme. Informing a team member that his performance was substandard after task completion is much less powerful than trying to correct it during the process itself.

The issue of individual feedback is important, and one which Johnson and Johnson (1991: 447) associate with accountability. They claim that accountability exists when individual contributions are assessed and given back to both the individual and the team. In part, they see it as a strategy against inertia or 'getting a free ride'. With effective feedback mechanisms, people are more likely to do their fair share of the work. They advocate assessing how much effort each individual is contributing to the group's effort, providing feedback to individuals and the team, ensuring everyone is accountable for the final outcome, and highlighting and clarifying the responsibilities of each team member.

This final phase gives an ideal opportunity to identify successes as a team and to learn from failure. Successes may need to be rewarded for motivational purposes, but a great deal of good can also emerge from incidences of failure. Failure is best looked at positively, heeding the words of Henry Ford: "Failure is the opportunity to begin again more intelligently."

From the point of view of team development, it is vital for the team to stand back and consider its effectiveness. It needs to look at whether members are on top of the job and it needs to diagnose malfunctions and barriers to successful task completion. The process element is critical. As Weisbord (1985: 27) notes: "Members step back from the task long enough to observe the team's strengths and weaknesses, how satisfied they are with their work, and steps they might take to improve it."

Review and reflection may also go a stage further in exploring the important fundamental values and views that people hold about their work. On this score, it is appropriate to note the words of Adair (1986: 136) on the issue of the leader's role with regard to informal listening sessions:

> Reflections on issues and careful exploration of individual views implies a philosophy of teamwork which is far removed from the various 'instant teamwork' recipes offered on one day courses to managers. In many organisations people are encouraged to have as few meetings as possible and to get on with the 'real work'. But work which ignores individual values and perspectives can lead to superficial activity. In such low-performance teams, members are not committed to the activity, and the quality of the team's life is not enriched by the range of experience available within it.

A challenging thought indeed to those who choose to ignore the importance of reflection and of making the team a 'learning team'.

DISSECT
- Summarise progress.
- Replan where necessary.
- Ask for feedback on the process and outcome.
- Give feedback to the team and individuals.
- Assess the value of individual contributions.
- Identify successes.
- Learn from failure.

Using the Scheme

The scheme is simply an attempt to present a systematic approach to dealing with a problem or issue that needs a decision and eventual implementation of that decision. It may not be necessary to use the scheme in its entirety nor each part of every phase, but it provides a useful checklist to ensure that no important steps or processes are omitted. At the end of a team task, if performance does not match up to expectations, it can be useful to look back at the scheme and

assess whether any one of the phases was omitted or underempha-
sized.

A planning team in an organisation used this scheme to cope
with a real task. The team was formed for the sole purpose of organising the company's annual dinner, and, in the words of the
managing director, it had to be a successful event that year:

> The leader explained to the team of volunteers, which comprised one
> supervisor, a clerical officer and three production operatives, that
> they had been given three months, and one meeting a month using
> an hour of company time to plan the annual dinner. It had to be
> better than the previous year's highly disappointing event. A
> budget of $50 per employee was available. Any form of entertain-
> ment would have to be acceptable to a wide taste and not be
> offensive in any way.
>
> The leader then asked what experience team members could
> offer. The clerical officer said she had bought prizes in previous
> years and could organise the prize giving ceremony. The supervisor
> said he would like to take charge of reception, as that was an
> opportunity for him to meet people from other departments. One
> of the operatives felt he could offer some skill in providing security
> support by organising a group of colleagues to staff the reception
> area and prevent gatecrashers from entering. These were useful
> offers, but the leader was more interested in getting the important
> items of information at this stage. It was agreed that he would
> telephone a number of hotels to check on availability on the date
> that had been set for the dinner. He would also ask the human
> resources manager whether he could contact friends in other
> companies to get details of good agencies and acts that had
> been enjoyed. This information would be brought back to the next
> meeting. Team members also agreed to speak to their colleagues,
> obtain ideas, and find out whether they were willing to help with
> the event in any way.
>
> At that next meeting, the leader asked for ideas. A number
> emerged and these were discussed seriously. The list was even-
> tually narrowed down to two widely attractive ideas: a spit roast
> followed by entertainment, or a conventional sit-down meal with
> a theme evening on which the entertainment would be based.
> Through discussion, the theme evening generated much support
> and members built on the idea by suggesting a few themes.

The leader had arranged during this meeting for an entertainment agency to make a brief presentation and answer questions from the team. When they were invited in, they showed photographs of some of the theme evenings they had organised in the past. As a result of this, several theme options emerged, and after discussing the advantages and disadvantages of each, the team agreed that it should be a 'Back to School' evening, with school uniform being the official dress. It was also decided that no pressure would be put on those who did not want to dress up, but the big prizes would be connected with dress.

Specific tasks were then allocated. Those who had offered to organise reception, prizes and security were detailed, and they agreed to have certain things done in time for the next meeting one month later. Other members were to look into other important parts of the project, such as seating arrangements for the dinner and contingency plans in case anything should go wrong.

Not every item in the scheme was covered, but the team followed a systematic process generally. They defined what the task was, considered how much time they had and what constraints were imposed. They then obtained relevant information about hotels, entertainment and the views of other employees. They listened to ideas, built on suggestions and generated several options. They set priorities for action and reached consensus on a decision. They then assigned responsibilities and set targets in preparation for the final planning meeting.

Evidence, as we have seen at the beginning of this book, suggests that teams are proliferating in organisations and that the tasks they are asked to manage are becoming increasingly complex. It must be emphasized that complexity needs even more coherence in planning, not less, and a scheme such as the one outlined above contributes to this coherence by enabling a set of simple, but essential, steps to be approached in a systematic way. It is argued that adopting a systematic approach will help team members plan more effectively and ensure that their efforts and skills are appropriately harnessed for successful task completion.

Summary

The scheme described here is intended to guide action towards improved team performance. We have recognised the fact that plans rarely, if ever, proceed exactly as intended. Teams need to remain flexible and be prepared to adjust their actions throughout the scheme. We maintain, however, that unless initial planning is carefully and sequentially constructed, effective task completion may be jeopardized. As such, even teams that are highly cohesive and relate well on a personal level may not be effective unless they have consciously developed their planning skills. The next chapter begins the section devoted to issues concerning the team.

Summary of the Implications for Managers

- Team leaders need to approach tasks systematically. In general terms, this involves defining and clarifying the task; obtaining relevant information; encouraging the formation of ideas, generating options and reaching agreement; developing a plan of action; assigning responsibilities and setting progress markers; implementing the plan and monitoring it; and reviewing performance.

- Sufficient time needs to be allowed for reviews to take place, and team members need to be actively encouraged to reflect on their performance and that of the team, and to discuss it openly. By considering 'how' the task was handled and discussing barriers to effective performance, malfunctions may be avoided in the future. It is also of lasting benefit to explore members' fundamental values, since these may have a considerable impact on ways of working and what is possible.

Section 4

The Team

can get others to commit themselves; and the provision of clear objectives with adequate resources.

Other complications arise from the ingrained tradition of leadership being vested in an hierarchical position. In decades past there has been little recognition that all members of a group could take a leadership role, depending on the situation. Current moves promote concepts such as *shared leadership* and *empowerment*. The ideals behind shared leadership appear to fit neatly within a team situation. We have mentioned earlier in the book that leadership may shift, depending on the issue at hand and that it need not necessarily reside in any one person in a static hierarchical position. Harris (1986: 28) suggests that leadership should be shared, but does so in the context of developing a concern amongst all team members for task accomplishment and team maintenance factors. Peterson (1991: 101) takes a similar line and suggests leadership is not just the responsibility of one or several people, but has to permeate the team and the organisation. It seems a worthy ideal to have individuals who can adopt such leadership behaviours. We examine briefly some of the newer approaches to leadership later in the chapter.

First, after discussing briefly some traditional theories of leadership, we describe one productive way of approaching the team leadership problem. Our main aim, however, is to present some ideas which may assist team members in developing a range of skills in several key areas in order to meet the requirements of effective team leadership.

Theories of Leadership

Trait Theory

Probably the earliest of the traditional approaches is that of 'trait theory', an approach that still enjoys a degree of support. Trait theory is essentially about personal qualities and proposes that there are certain qualities which make a good leader. Its basis is that leaders are born and not made and that there are certain qualities, therefore, that good leaders must possess. From this perspective, an effective leader can be assessed on the basis of the presence of predetermined qualities. Such qualities are far-ranging. Stogdill (1948), for example, listed: *intelligence, scholarship, dependability, responsibility, social participation* and *socio-economic status* as characteristics of leaders, while other researchers listed *intelligence, supervisory ability, initiative, self-assurance*, and so on.

A major problem of trait theory was that there was little agreement about which qualities were relevant. Stogdill reviewed a large number of trait studies and came to the conclusion that the approach had produced inconclusive and confusing findings. Research found that many traits tentatively identified as critical in one study were not important in others. In some organisations, effective leaders were quiet and restrained, whereas in others they were reflective, assertive, aggressive or decisive. In short, there has been little agreement on which qualities were relevant and that an almost unlimited number of leadership traits could be identified.

Another failing was that the notion favoured *selection* rather than *development*. Yet there is good evidence to show that leaders can be developed. The approach also failed to account for the different contexts in which leadership (and, indeed, team leadership) is practised. Situations can be vastly different. Owens (1987: 126) makes this very point:

> The characteristics of the group being led (for example, maturity level, level of trust, cohesiveness), the nature of the group's tasks or mission (for example, clarity of goals, complexity of tasks), and the psychological environment in which leadership is attempted (for example, levels of ambiguity, uncertainty, threat, and conflict), are illustrative of variables that differ from situation to situation and that have an impact on the ability of individuals to lead effectively.

This draws attention to the need to consider leadership from a more contextual perspective, and we shall look later in this chapter at an approach which expressed leadership as being 'contingent' on the situation in which it was applied. We return briefly, however, to the traits or personal characteristics approach.

Despite the reservations, the qualities approach can be quite compelling, and it is tempting to add many other desirable attributes to the list. For example, intelligence, at first glance, seems essential in view of the leader's role. This, however, may be misinterpreted as a call for educational qualifications. While there is little to suggest that effective leadership is directly connected to scholastic achievement, it does seem necessary that a team leader should have the ability to conceptualise the sorts of problems with which the team deals.

Trait studies continue (Yukl, 1981: 69). The emphasis now is not on distinguishing between leaders and non-leaders (thereby attempting to predict who will become leaders), but on the relationship between traits and leader effectiveness. The divide between largely spurious qualities and real actions appears to have narrowed, and successful 'characteristics' – for example, drive for responsibility and task completion, ability to influence others, willingness to accept consequences of decisions – have a distinctly practical flavour. We now move on from the traits approach to another popular concept of leadership, Behavioural Leadership theories.

Behavioural Approaches

One of the most famous episodes of leadership research was undertaken at Ohio State University where leadership was defined in terms, not of characteristics, but of performance. Hoy and Forsyth (1986: 122) summarise the essence of the behavioural approach:

> Here the emphasis is not on traits but rather on performance. Behaviour is described directly through observation. Once the descriptions of leader behaviour are established, then comparisons of the behaviours of effective and ineffective leaders using a variety of criteria can be made. Hence, the critical elements of leadership can be identified and their relations to important organisational outcomes can be explored.

The approach defined two basic functions (many names were given to these functions by various researchers): 'consideration' or 'human relations', which relates to the extent of care and concern for the staff, and 'initiating structure', which is associated with the task. The latter relates to defined relationships, roles and patterns of working.

From this perspective, failing to emphasize the initiation of structure may inhibit team effectiveness; neglecting consideration may seriously inhibit the satisfaction of team members. Being able to maximise both orientations would suggest an effective approach, although there may be situations where one might be emphasized to a greater extent than the other. As Hoy and Miskel (1991: 268) note: "The matching of leadership style with the appropriate situation in order to maximize effectiveness is a knotty problem."

These two categories – interpersonal relations and task achievement – have indeed dominated much of the literature, despite its immense diversity. As indicated above, the general basis of the work was that effective leaders were those who gave evidence of behaviour high in both dimensions, and this has been widely accepted as common wisdom. There are, however, a number of inherent weaknesses.

Firstly, it may be a somewhat optimistic expectation for all leaders to develop such attributes, and it may be argued that some are able to compensate for their weaknesses by demonstrating considerable strengths in one of the categories. The suggestion, though, that leaders weak in both dimensions are likely to be ineffective is a reasonable one.

Blake and Mouton (1964), famous for *The Managerial Grid*, advanced the notion that effective leaders are those who can develop good relations with their staff and initiate new ways to solve problems. Advocates of the approach may describe effective leaders as 'high on task, and high on people'. It simply means that they get things done well and at the same time care for the needs of people. The grid has been a highly popular tool for analysis and for identifying the alternative emphases available to the leader.

While it may make sense to expect the team leader to care about the quality of the task execution and at the same time care for the needs of team members by keeping them satisfied with their endeavours, the approach can be problematic. These two dimensions (task and people) may not be mutually compatible. For instance, a tension may exist between task accomplishment and looking after the welfare of staff. There may even be different expectations. Senior colleagues may view only the outcomes as important, and little else. Team members, in contrast, may expect an overriding concern for their well-being and their working conditions, and expect the leader to be preoccupied with their protection. Middle managers in particular suffer from this tension created by conflicting demands.

It may be unrealistic in some situations to expect a single individual to reconcile these two tensions. A solution that seems to have worked well in a number of settings is to have two people fulfilling the leadership role, although one is the officially appointed leader. For example, the leader may be one who is very much task-centred and who focuses on achieving organisational goals, while a colleague may concentrate more on the social and emotional needs of the subordinates.

The problem of leader 'imbalance' is a prevalent one in teams, and this may point to a need for a greater awareness of how roles should be deployed. Adair (1986: 120) aptly provides a warning that "it is fatal to select people to work with you who are clones of yourself. You should deliberately choose individuals who have strengths, knowledge and experience which you do not possess in considerable measure." We shall be addressing the topic of such roles in the following chapter.

While success in achieving results is important, how it is done is equally important. There are undoubtedly many team leaders who use their power of position to force decisions, to supervise closely and to interfere in every activity. Effective leaders, in contrast, are more likely to show a concern for their team members' needs and to lead by consent. This point is aptly taken up by Weisbord (1985: 28) in noting the problems of task-centredness. Leaders often assume that doing things harder and faster produces better results. They may pressure people to work overtime, chide members for not cooperating, and reiterate goals for rapid implementation. The missing link in this sort of thinking, however, is that the people dimension is ignored, and instead only outcomes are considered. Leaders may feel they are managing a system technology or a product; in essence, however, they are managing a team of people. As obvious as it seems, this point is often missed.

Despite the persuasive attractions of such behavioural theories, there is no consistency of relationship between the leader's effectiveness and the two measures of 'consideration' and 'initiating structure'. They also lacked strong theoretical foundations, and that partly explains why alternative models with greater descriptive powers were developed.

It is generally accepted that leadership has passed through three key stages. The first of these, the 'trait' stage, was highly influential and lasted until about the middle of the century, although, as we have indicated above, it may still be exerting an influence even now in some quarters. The second stage is usually referred to as 'behavioural' and is largely concerned with leadership style in an attempt to draw conclusions about which style is most effective across the board. The third stage, known as the 'contingency' or 'situational' phase, looks at the interrelationship of three factors: the leader, the subordinates (or followers) and the situation. Whereas 'behavioural' theories tend to emphasize the effectiveness of leader behaviours, characterised by high concerns for task and for relationships, or 'one best way', 'contingency' views propose that there is no best style which works in all situations and that leadership effectiveness is evaluated in the unit's success in achieving its objectives.

Contingency Approaches

Contingency theories of leadership maintain there is no one best style: it largely depends on the fit between leader variables (personality and behaviour) and situational variables (nature of task, available skills, attitudes, etc.). Such approaches attempt to predict the type of leadership that might be effective in a given situation.

House's Path-Goal theory (Hoy and Miskel, 1991: 252) shows how leaders influence paths to goal attainment: they are effective when they can improve acceptance, satisfaction and motivation amongst team members. Four basic types of leader behaviour are delineated: directive, achievement-oriented, supportive, and participative. The first two relate to initiating structure, while the last two are concerned with consideration. An important feature of the model is that leaders can change their behaviour to fit the situation.

Situational variables in this theory are considered in terms of team member characteristics and environmental pressures and demands. Effectiveness is not defined in terms of task accomplishment, but the satisfaction and motivation of team members.

Fiedler was one of the earlier proponents of 'contingency' leadership, considering critical contextual factors for the practice of leadership (Hoy and Miskel, 1991: 274). He classified situations in terms of their 'favourableness' (later expressed as 'situational control' by Fiedler) to the leader, and identified three key factors which would determine this:

1. The quality of the relationship between the leader and the team members
2. The extent to which the task has clarity
3. The powers that the leader possesses

The most important factor in determining the leader's influence over the team is the quality of relations. Two factors are evident: the quality of interpersonal relations, and the level of informal authority. The leader's personality and behaviour are the key determinants of relations between leader and team. In contrast to House's theory, Fiedler's criterion of effectiveness is simply the extent to which the team accomplishes the task. Other aspects are contributory elements, but they are not in themselves performance criteria.

Fiedler developed three major propositions from his contingency theory:

1. In those situations where there is high control, task-oriented leaders are the more effective.
2. In moderate control situations, a relationship orientation is more effective.
3. In low control situations, a task orientation is more effective.

The model described above, while intuitively appealing, fails to explain what actually produces effective performance. Fiedler and Garcia (1987) noted this deficiency in their later work and developed 'cognitive resource theory'. In an ideal situation, the leader's cognitive resources (intellectual abilities) are the major source of decisions guiding the team's actions (Hoy and Miskel, 1991: 283). Intelligence and competence, therefore, according to Fiedler, are essential attributes of leadership, and there is an assumption that leaders with intellect determine more effective plans, decisions and strategies. Communication is in the form of directive behaviour.

'Situational leadership theory' (Hersey and Blanchard, 1977), which might be appropriately described as an offshoot or extension of the contingency approach, is not really a guide to research, but more a basis for leadership training. It extends the 'Managerial Grid' and draws heavily on Reddin's (1967) '3-D Management Style Theory'.

Hersey and Blanchard's work had two categories of behaviour: the first, 'task behaviour', was closely related to 'initiating structure'; the second, 'relationship behaviour', corresponded largely with 'consideration'. Task behaviour was concerned with the leader's arrangement and definition of team members' roles. It was characterised by delineating the what, when, where, how and with whom of each task. Details are clearly laid out, including whose permission should be sought before an action can be taken, and there is generally little ambiguity. Relationship behaviour on the other hand is concerned with the extent to which personal relationships between leader and members are maintained. There is scope for contribution through open communication, and the provision of emotional support is seen as important.

Hersey and Blanchard's theory is useful to the understanding of leadership by dwelling on the importance of team member characteristics in determining the appropriateness of leadership style. The significant characteristic is that of maturity (of the team or the individuals in it) and this is considered one task at a time. In terms of the members' capacity to set challenging goals, the willingness to accept responsibility, and their education or experience, they may be considered very mature on one task, but comparatively immature on another. Maturity in this model has two components: job maturity, which is concerned with the skills and knowledge to do the job; and psychological maturity, which is related to self-confidence and self-respect.

The way that Hersey and Blanchard's model addresses the problem of effectiveness is by prescribing appropriate leadership behaviour for the situation. As team members' level of maturity increases (up to a moderate level) the leader should use more relationship and less task behaviour.

As maturity continues to increase, there should be less relationship (and still less task) behaviour. Leadership might even take place in the group. A description of the basic tenets of the prescription is given in Yukl (1989: 107–8).

The same author also highlights the inadequacies of the model, pointing to the weak conceptual basis and the lack of a coherent rationale for the assumed relationships. Situational variables which may be relevant to leader behaviour are also ignored, and maturity is defined too broadly. But on a positive note, the work has made an important contribution to the field. People have to be treated differently and in different situations. Leaders can also actively change the situation by building the maturity of subordinates. This is an important role. The aim is to encourage the team to develop skills, knowledge and confidence to be able to complete tasks without strong leadership interventions. Thus, the leader's influence might diminish over time. Finally, the prescription for effective leadership behaviour in a given situation may be advanced, but the leader still has to have the skill in employing that behaviour (Yukl, 1989: 108).

And this is one of the major problems of the theory. Understanding the theory and actually applying it are two different things. Some leaders find it immensely difficult to modify their styles even when they know what the situation demands. For example, there are many who find it problematic to reduce their task-centredness, even when a stronger relationship style is called for. Similarly, even when the team may be extremely mature (individually and as a unit), some find it impossible to fade into the background and allow team members to share in some of the leadership activities. It is easy to see, therefore, that the model demands considerable flexibility, and much practice may be needed in changing style comfortably.

Other important questions arise. A team may be mature on one task but immature on others. Also, the leader may have to consider not only the maturity of individuals in the team, but also the maturity of the team as a whole. This can be important in those situations where the two are distinctly different.

Owens (1987: 152) too draws attention to some possible problems. Some leaders for instance may actually force immaturity on team members by being inappropriately directive and failing to provide the opportunities and conditions in which growth and development can take place. And again, some leaders may give responsibilities to members who are not ready, and who have neither the job maturity nor the psychological maturity. Despite the drawbacks, the theory demonstrates a useful incremental approach for taking the team through a series of steps to a high level of maturity.

We have already mentioned briefly the issue of effectiveness in relation to the theory. It needs to be reiterated that it is a complex concept that incorporates performance and conditions. It includes the extent to which the task is achieved (in terms of both short-term and longer term objectives) and the psychological state of team members.

Caution must be exercised in accepting without question the tenets of such theories. Despite the obvious attractions, there is a lack of rigorous evidence and it is wise, therefore, to avoid definitive claims about relationships between effectiveness and contributory variables.

Whilst there may be differences between various theories and their conceptual derivations about which situational factors are the most influential, there has been increasing agreement that leader behaviour is difficult to separate from contextual considerations. Despite the absence of a firm and proven prescription for leadership in any given situation, as Yukl (1989) indicated, there are skills which must be acquired before any choices about behaviour can be made. This may be the way forward and, on this basis, several key actions of leadership can be identified, and then skill attained in employing those actions. This forms the basis of a comprehensive approach to the practice of team leadership.

Although understanding of leadership was enhanced by approaches such as those discussed above, many of which continue to be popular and improved upon, they have been widely criticised and their utility for modern times questioned. Watkins (1989: 9–11) lists a number of concerns:

- Traditional approaches to leadership assume a static one-directional view of leadership in which the 'boss' leads an unquestioning group of subordinates. It ignores the reality that others in the organisation may be leaders in their own right.
- Through its concentration on management, traditional research implies that managers are more variable than workers and thereby more worthy of study.
- Most research conducted serves management and administrative power thereby reproducing the *status quo*.

- Traditional leadership research assumes rationality to systems but not to people.

Working in teams necessitates shared leadership in various forms at differing levels. The approach presented below involves actions. We see the approach as operating within a collaborative atmosphere where all team members are valued for themselves, their abilities and skills. We see the team, especially if it is a long-term unit, as a group continuously learning and improving performance. The approach suggested sees the leader depending on 'real' collaborative mechanisms rather than depending on hierarchically based authority, if this exists.

A Comprehensive Approach

In this approach, the theme of needs is taken up, and the needs are addressed in three key areas. The approach also lays the emphasis not on what leadership is, but what the leader does. It takes into account not only the leader, but the demands of the team's task, the team as a unit, and the individuals who form that team. Underlying the approach is an acceptance that leadership may 'shift' and can be shared by team members. However, it also admits that in most situations, at least one member of the team will be in a hierarchically superior position to the other members.

A Framework for Leadership Action

John Adair's (1986) work on teambuilding and leadership is well known in management circles and, intuitively, seems to make sense. The 'action centred leadership' approach has been successfully adopted by many major companies who have put their managers through programmes based on the model.

The essence of action centred leadership is the move away from what leaders *are* and more towards what they *do*. It will be recalled that the quotation from the book *In Search of Excellence* at the beginning of this section identified things the leader does rather than what he is. By focusing on the actions that leaders take, Adair is clearly implying that leaders can develop. The emphasis in this approach, therefore, is on identifying key actions in three interrelated areas, which will ensure that leadership is effective. These areas are shown in Figure 9.1.

First, there is a demand to achieve the task, the purpose for which the team exists. Second, there is a need to attain team cohesion. Third,

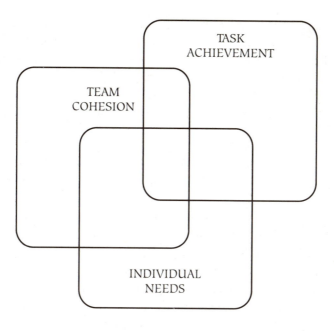

Figure 9.1   Three Interrelated Demands

there are needs and demands which individuals bring with them into the team and which, if met, provide them with job satisfaction.

These are important considerations. Highlighting the importance of the team and the individuals in it, Hemphill (1949) tied in leadership with the degree of cohesion felt amongst team members and their satisfaction as individuals derived from their membership. Being together and taking pride and pleasure in membership is therefore associated with the team's leadership. As Adair (1986: 59) notes:

> Achieving a balance between the interests and self-expression of each individual on the one hand and of the group on the other, is one of the most challenging tasks of leaders. It is best done by reference to the third dimension – the common task. For it is the value of that task which draws us together and underpins our unity.

Task Needs

Achievement of the task is crucial to the team's success. The leader in many team situations is held accountable for the team's performance and thereby the quality of the outcomes, although in other situations the team itself is the unit of accountability. Wherever the onus lies, teams must be clear of their purpose: "Highly developed teams without an aim will quickly degenerate into groups of people without a task and will never be able to practice true teamwork" (Woodcock, 1989: 29). One of the key activities in this area must be that of achieving goal clarity, so that team members know precisely what it is they are trying to accomplish.

A set of questions needs to be asked in relation to the task. Adair (1986: 196) provides a useful checklist for addressing the relevant issues, and the questions include the following:

- What is the purpose of the task?
- Have the objectives been agreed with superiors?
- Are the working conditions right?
- Are resources adequate?
- Are there clearly defined targets for team members?
- Is accountability delineated?
- Are there any important skill deficiencies?
- Is time planning clear?
- Is there a monitoring and evaluation schedule?

Although the task represents the key need, it cannot be seen in isolation, and team leaders must recognise the presence of other needs that demand their attention.

Team Needs

If the team is to achieve the quality outcomes for which it is held accountable, it must be held together as a unit. This can be a difficult challenge for the leader. If members choose to ignore any need for interdependency or coordinated effort, the sum of the disparate contributions is unlikely to lead to the desired outcomes. Obviously the contributions may need to be different, but they have to be seen as complementary, and it could be interpreted as part of the leader's remit, therefore, to bring these inputs together and to achieve a high level of cohesion. The need for interdependence should be reinforced regularly, and this might be done by either simply identifying the importance of individuals' performance or by rotating assignments.

Part of the process of facilitating cohesion is learning to understand the team as a unit and being able to assess what it is capable of. This requires a different type of thinking to that required for simple addition sums. There is little to be gained from simply totalling up the respective contributions of team members. From this integrated perspective, the leader may need to understand how the strengths and weaknesses of individuals interact to produce a coordinated group effort.

Again, Adair (p. 197) provides some helpful questions in relation to team maintenance. These include:

- Does the team understand and accept the goals?
- Are members clear about standards of performance?
- Is the team size about right for the task concerned?
- Is there a need to break into subgroups?
- What opportunities are there for developing team spirit?
- Is there fairness in imparting rules?
- Are disruptive issues dealt with promptly?
- Are ideas and suggestions welcomed?
- Is briefing about plans and progress adequate?
- Are the team's feelings represented outside?
- Is there good enough support when the team is apart?

Individual Needs

The needs that individuals bring to the group are very complex. Motivation theories, which were discussed earlier, draw attention to such needs. Herzberg *et al.* (1959), for example, linked satisfaction with the needs for achievement, recognition, responsibility and job interest, while Maslow (1954) identified such higher order needs as group acceptance (social), status (self-esteem) and the opportunity to use one's ability (self-actualisation).

Individual needs for growth and development may be met partly through coaching and supervision. In order to ensure individual performance is at an appropriate level, the leader may need to help members gain in competence by providing the necessary coaching support. The leader must also encourage members to pursue development opportunities they believe are personally beneficial and lead to increased job satisfaction. Encouragement and support is founded on a strong concern on the part of the leader for the self-image of team members, and a desire to help individuals achieve and perform to higher levels than they could on their own.

The leader who sees the importance of meeting individual needs is more likely to lead the team through collaboration and by consent. In this climate, the leader can effect the integrative process by helping them understand "that by willingly striving to attain organization objectives they will also satisfy some of their personal needs, such as self-esteem, esteem from others, a sense of competence, a feeling of belonging, a feeling of personal significance, and a feeling of growth" (Ends and Page, 1977: 47).

All this would suggest that the leader must have an intimate knowledge of individuals in the team. In working towards group goals, members are trying to satisfy their personal goals, and the leader who can understand those and integrate them with team goals is likely to enjoy success. There is also a need to understand value systems, motivational patterns, prior experiences (and their impact), and perceptions. In short, the effective leader must get to know what affects individual behaviour. Adair (1986: 123) points out that there must be understanding about what members share in common and what differentiates them. He observes that leaders do not have a 'right' to know everyone, but they have a duty to try to do so. In practical terms, it means investing time in getting about, meeting and talking to people, and, most important, listening to them.

This need for understanding is reinforced by Greenberg and Greenberg (1988: 59) who suggest that the best leaders "are those who thoroughly understand their own motivations, as well as the motivations, strengths and limitations of those individuals who report to them". It is also confirmed by Maddux (1988: 27): "Establishing yourself as a strong leader requires an understanding of people and what motivates them. Those who understand can create a working climate in which team members can meet individual needs while achieving team goals." Such a working climate is set by leaders who recognise the efforts of their team members, provide challenging work, give increased responsibility, and make it possible for members to grow and develop (Margerison, 1973: 59).

The questions Adair (p. 198) raises in relation to the individual in the team include:

- Have targets been agreed and quantified?

- Is there understanding about how individual work relates to the team effort?
- Is there clarity about responsibilities?
- Has sufficient authority been given?
- What needs are there for training?
- Are successes emphasized?
- Are development and career opportunities understood?
- Is performance reviewed regularly?
- Are rewards appropriate?
- Is the right person in the right job?
- What are the individual's distinctive differences?
- Is time spent listening, developing and counselling?
- Does the individual have the necessary resources?

Integrating Needs

If the team's task purpose is fulfilled, this model of leadership suggests the effect will be the creation of a sense of unity in the team and the satisfaction of individuals. Similarly, if individuals are fully involved and motivated, they will contribute much more to the team and the team is much more likely to achieve the task.

By contrast, if there is failure in any one of the need areas, it is likely to impact on the other two. For example, lack of team cohesion affects the achievement of the task and the needs fulfilment of individuals. From this, it can be seen how the three sets of needs are closely interwoven. But it would be mistaken to believe that each need should receive equal attention. At certain points in time, one need may have to be emphasized over others.

Similar models have been implied elsewhere, but without the depth of detail and explanation of interrelatedness. Zapp (1987: 7) refers to a workshop source and claims that, in order to be an effective leader, it is necessary to work at three levels: individual, team, and organisational. With these three levels aligned, there is greater chance of a high-performing team. The notion of integration is also confirmed by Ends and Page (1977: 176) who discuss the related processes of group interaction and individual growth, and suggest that performance growth leads to personal growth.

The model, therefore, proposes that the leader has to be conscious of task, team and individual needs and has to engage positive actions to assist members in satisfying those needs.

Before leaving this section it is important to point out that the approach discussed cannot stand alone. This is mainly because it concentrates on the internal dynamics of the team and ignores, except perhaps for an implicit suggestion in the task section, the external environment. At the beginning of this book, we mentioned that one of the driving forces for the growing popularity of teams is that they are necessary in a turbulent environment. To be effective, the leader also needs to ensure that the team is acutely aware of what is happening in relevant parts of the external environment. In terms of teams, this may include both the organisation within which the team operates and the wider market environment. If you substitute 'team' for 'organisation', the following statement by Dunphy and Stace (1990: 148) provides a worthwhile guide in this area for team leaders:

> As the organisational environment becomes more turbulent, managers must increasingly look outward from their organisations and spend more time monitoring the organisational environment and seeking to maintain their organisations' strategic fit. At the executive level in particular, environmental scanning has necessarily become a central preoccupation, demanding a consequent radical delegation of operational duties.

Team Leader Roles

With the above in mind, we now turn our attention to the specific role of team leader. Maddux (1988: 43) sees it as being a challenger, prober, coach and enabler. It is almost certainly facilitative rather than directive, with the "overall aim of chanelling the more creative energy towards benefiting the organization rather than blocking its progress" (Anantaraman, 1984b: 220). This facilitator of creativity role is confirmed also by George (1977: 75) who adds that the leader in a project team setting must be able to integrate functional expertise and to manage time, budgets and people in a disciplined manner.

Such a view of the leader's role implies strong capabilities in team members. Peterson (1991: 108) maintains that the leader, in a team meeting, often knows the least. There is more knowledge in the combined membership of the team than in the leader alone. On this basis, it is important to openly reveal lack of knowledge so that individuals can feel free to contribute.

Facilitating creativity is even more crucial in those teams whose existence depend on innovation. Thamhain (1990: 13) identifies the key roles for team leadership in these conditions: understanding the factors relevant to success; being action oriented; providing necessary resources; planning and directing implementation; and helping in identification and resolution of problems. The effective leader of innovative workteams

> is usually a social architect who understands the interaction of organizational and behavioural variables and can foster a climate of active participation and minimal dysfunctional conflict. This requires carefully developed skills in leadership, administration and organizational and technical expertise. It further requires that the project team leader is able to work effectively with upper management to assure organizational visibility, resource availability, focus and overall support for the innovation-oriented activities and programs throughout their life cycles.

The leader's role is indeed far-ranging and demanding.

Perhaps the key role is managing the decision-making process, and this is substantially different from making decisions. The decision-making process is discussed separately and in detail. It is worth noting here, however, that such a role implies a heavy emphasis on participative processes and collaboration rather than on position, power and domination.

Avoiding domination and becoming part of the team may require the learning of a new and unfamiliar role. For example, it may involve a willingness to withhold opinions, lest they are accepted too readily and without criticism. The leader's contributions to the group need to be evaluated on merit, like everyone else's, if the quality of decision making is to be upheld.

The role also involves affecting the team climate (how the team members feel about and react to one another). Ends and Page (1977: 52) suggest this can be done through personal example and by addressing problems associated with attitudes, feelings, and behaviour on the part of individual team members. This might lead to a climate in which "team members' energies can be devoted to constructive effort rather than wasted on defensiveness or destructive attacks on others in the group" (p. 178). This aspect of the role suggests a need to manage situations characterised by conflict. Yukl (1989: 134) draws on diverse literatures as evidence to conclude that conflict management behaviours are highly relevant to effectiveness.

Leading by example is an important consideration in climate setting. Evidence suggests the leader's behaviour norms have a considerable impact on team norms. From this perspective, if the leader expects members to share views openly and honestly, he too must do the same. In short, the desired behaviours and attitudes must be modelled by the leader, and he must be very much a part of the team (Woodcock, 1979: 5).

Another major element in the establishment of team climate is how power and authority are used by the leader. Authority is the right to issue orders and directions, and we shall see how this might be used or abused when we look at leadership styles. Power is more concerned with the ability to influence team members' behaviours, and this is the subject of a separate discussion in Chapter 12. The methods used to exert influence have a considerable impact on the team climate, and it is a subject, therefore, that should receive serious attention. Wynn and Guditus (1984: 167) claim that power should really lie with the team, and the leader's role is to mobilise this power collectively in order to achieve team goals. To do this requires a view of the leader's role that extends beyond just leading and towards providing the scope for members to grow and to contribute to team achievement.

There are many leaders who, sadly, are unwilling to give up part of their power. They perceive that, by doing so, they will have less or themselves. That is a myth. Indeed, the same authors suggest it can be *expanded* by sharing it with others, and that there are vast reserves of latent power that can be energised. This is a notion that receives wide support from the proponents of participative styles of team leadership.

Yet another dimension to team climate is the demand for loyalty and supportive relations. Loyalty, of course, might be promoted through the leader's actions in mobilising power, as described above, and through showing concern for personal needs and opinions. This ties in closely with the integrated model we described earlier in this chapter. To consolidate these sorts of relations may also require other strategies, and these might include spending periods of social time together, a strategy commonly employed by Japanese management and coaches in sports operations.

Sharing power and granting involvement may be closely linked with securing commitment, and this can be described as a major leadership role. It involves integrating individual members' preferred contributions with team goals. If an individual is satisfied with the role assigned, there is more likely to be commitment. This obviously relates to the notion of individual gain, and the leader's task is to provide situations in which individual benefit may be gained in the pursuit of team goals.

In terms of such goals, much of the literature is clear that leader expectations are critically important. Ends and Page (1977: 151), for example, state that: "In high performing groups the leader always expects more from the group than they initially believe they can deliver;" and "Leaders of high-performing, high-morale groups typically have higher performance standards for the team than do the individual members" (p. 50). In setting high, but not unrealistic, expectations, the leader is issuing a challenge and an opportunity to both individuals and the team as a whole. But the story does not end with expectations. Similarly high standards of performance must be sustained when tasks get under way.

Team Leader Skills

The word 'skill' has been mentioned on several occasions. What are the skills that might support the leader's concern for the three inter-related areas identified in the above framework? Ends and Page (1977: 129) suggest the following six skill areas in which strength should be developed:

- **Communication**: The ability to communicate with team members on both a one-to-one and a group basis needs to be developed.
- **Planning**: The leader must be clear about goals and the means of achieving them. He must be able to plan strategies and actions, and the sequence in which they should occur.
- **Organising**: This involves matching individual preferences and abilities to the various tasks; checking for understanding about task definition, timescale and methods; and coordinating the contributions across the team.
- **Coaching**: This may involve demonstration, helping individuals in target setting and the measurement of progress, helping diagnose performance problems and taking remedial action, and providing feedback.
- **Persuading**: This skill may include the sub-skills of selling, convincing, inspiring and encouraging. The ability to use empathy is an important component of the skill.

- **Negotiating:** The leader typically negotiates with individuals in the team about such matters as tasks and roles, and with agencies outside the team but with a bearing on the team's work.

It is not clear how the authors arrive at this list of skills, but it provides a useful framework from which to commence a programme of skill development. Within each skill area could be included many sub-skills, some of which are quite important. For example, communicating covers a whole field of relate skills, including listening, paraphrasing and presenting. Also, some of the above skill areas are interrelated. Negotiating, for instance, could be considered a specialist component of communicating skills.

It is probably appropriate that communication appears at the top of the list, since this represents one of the more significant skill areas for the team leader. It is concerned with interactions and relationships with team members. Questions that might be usefully addressed in assessing leader skills in the area relate to the nature of such interactions, whether the leader is an initiator of involvement, whether there is always an insistence on taking the leading role, and whether there is genuine warmth and friendliness towards team members.

Another dimension of communication is the skill of understanding and acting on feedback. The leader can acquire much information from interactions with members and this can lead to improved leadership behaviour. Much of the skill that might be developed in terms of influence depends on the accuracy with which feedback is read.

Skill must also be applied in giving feedback. At the individual level, it might be given in order to intercept difficulties and thus prevent further wasted effort. It can be used also as a means of confirmation that effort is appropriately directed. By giving feedback to the team as a whole, there may be an increase in enthusiasm and morale.

Part of the feedback process is giving praise. Maddux (1988: 66) suggests the successful leader helps members feel good about themselves by giving periodic praise when job requirements have been met, and by giving it in a sincere way that members can understand. He also suggests praise might be given to both individuals and the team as a whole. Praise can be a strong contributor to motivation.

We have already signified the importance of motivation, and a vital skill is understanding the behavioural patterns of team members. This can be developed by observing the situations in which they become enthusiastic or uninvolved, how they respond to ideas and suggestions, and the factors that control their interest. Such observation can help determine the types of needs individuals are trying to satisfy, and the leader can then respond appropriately. For example, an individual who is driven by the need for achievement may respond positively to criticism.

Observation is a critical skill for the new leader of a team. The initial phase is one of uncertainty with much essential information missing. Looram (1985: 29) identifies some of these details: strengths and weaknesses of members; temperament; operating problems; and perceptions of the new team leader's style and beliefs. This phase can be unproductive as the leader gets the feel of the operation.

A particularly useful device for smoothing the passage during this stage is what Looram calls the 'transition meeting', in which the team considers both its internal processes and also its concerns about the new leader. By going through this or a similar process the leader can gain a clear picture of the major issues and personalities. He can also correct perceptions where they are inaccurate. With a firm exchange of information such as this provides, it is easier to move on to realistic goal setting and other work-related issues.

The basis of Looram's argument is that the introduction of a new leader represents a special phase in the life of a team, and one that needs handling differently from other phases.

> The name of the game has literally been changed. A tremendous amount of renegotiation must take place between each team member and the new boss and among the team members themselves. The negotiations will deal with the roles each person will play, the tasks that will be taken on, the amount of influence each will now have, the amount of information each will have access to, and so on. In short, the team will have to be rebuilt, and this approach offers one of the most cost-effective, low-risk methods for doing so (Looram, 1985: 36).

Whether rebuilding is necessary is debatable, but the message is clear, that the presence of a new leader can be dysfunctional unless the situation is well handled. The leader must have the skill and willingness to confront the major issues and to set the sort of climate in which open discussion can take place.

Team Leader Styles

In our brief review of some of the major theories underlying the development of leadership understanding, we mentioned the subject of 'style' in connection with several approaches. One of the key considerations in team leadership relates to the degree of involvement that the team leader affords to members. The issues of participation and involvement are discussed separately and also receive attention in Chapter 14: Team Problems and Decisions. It is worth noting here, however, that a common theme in any discussion about participation is that of the context for the decision. This draws on the contingency perspective. A style appropriate in one set of conditions will not necessarily be appropriate in another, and very different, situation.

Before we describe the different styles it is necessary to note that we have not disregarded the criticisms of contingency type approaches discussed earlier. We are not suggesting that a team leader can automatically alter his behaviours to suit any situation. Although we obviously promote the 'Sharing' style of leadership we do not

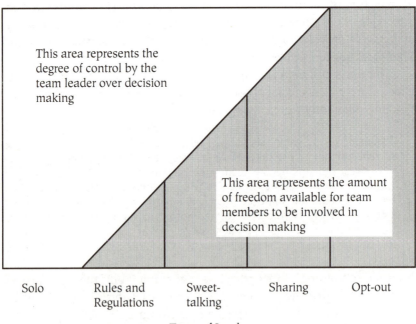

This area represents the degree of control by the team leader over decision making

This area represents the amount of freedom available for team members to be involved in decision making

| Solo | Rules and Regulations | Sweet-talking | Sharing | Opt-out |

Types of Leader

Figure 9.2   Team Member Involvement in Decision Making

claim it is the 'one best way' but suggest that it is an ideal for which teams might aim. The other styles may have their place, but should be regarded only as guides for some contexts.

For ease of understanding, we have tried to simplify the conceptual material about style and have provided five 'discrete' categories. They are not really discrete, of course, but more appropriately seen on a continuum. They do help, however, to illuminate preferred approaches and thereby to heighten understanding of how leaders might typically choose to behave. Figure 9.2 shows some of the options.

The options shown are generally referred to as *styles*. It is probably true that many team leaders operate predominantly in a given style. Below is an explanation of the terms used in Figure 9.2.

Solo

> You cannot expect a soldier to be a proud soldier if you humiliate him. You cannot expect him to be brave if you abuse and cower him. You cannot expect him to be strong if you break him ... I enjoin you to be ever alert to the pitfalls of too much authority (from a speech by Lieutenant General Melvin Zais, USA, now retired; cited in Peterson, 1991: 171).

The *solo* leader, in the extreme form, is an autocrat, one who simply gives directions, operates almost entirely alone, and prefers to stay detached from team members. In team meetings, this type of leader dominates the discussion and is insistent that his views are accepted. He may have the expectation that members will be aware of his views and that they will not suggest any contrasting or dissenting opinions. His influence is pervasive and members may be reticent about contributing to discussions. In such situations, members may form a cohesive group that excludes the leader, and this may lead to mistrust and ineffectiveness. Even worse, as Peterson (1991: 69) claims, things may fall apart:

> An autocratic manager, a schemer, or someone driven only by selfish instincts can do a pretty good job catering to people above him, toeing the company line, taking instructions from a boss, and so on. He might even get away with being a bastard to his subordinates. But a manager who doesn't deal openly with his peers and who isn't trusted is in trouble. His peers won't share information, and they won't want to work with him. Actually, they'll avoid him if possible.

The type of approach characteristic of the solo leader may be useful in those situations where time is not available for drawn out discussion, but there may be team members who are intolerant of such an approach and, as a result, may fail to perform optimally. Indeed, Robbins (1991: 283) notes that there are some situations where a group, guided by a directive, autocratic leader, will outperform groups run along participative lines. Performance is obviously a key variable. At the same time, short-term effectiveness in performance needs to be considered against longer term gains, and it may be too simplistic, therefore, to specify that one style is preferable to another based on limited outcome criteria.

Rules and Regulations

The *rules and regulations* leader may also be fairly directive, but instructions are based on rules and laid-down guidelines. Consequently, there is little room for initiative. The leader can enjoy reduced accountability, because the system can be blamed in part for imperfections in performance.

Under such leadership, there is likely to be fairness and impartiality, and team members can usually expect a fair degree of clarity about their roles. The style may be appropriate, therefore, for those with a low tolerance for ambiguity. It can also be intensely frustrating when quick, responsive action is needed or when a solution necessitates actions that are not consistent with the rules and procedures.

Sweet-talking

The *sweet-talking* leader has a persuasive disposition and is ever the diplomat. Plans and actions that are in the team's interests may also be made to sound in the individual's interests. The authority weapon is seldom used so as not to compromise popularity. Personality and political skills are used to achieve the desired ends. Sometimes described as 'charismatic', this type of leader is adept at drawing on personal attributes and skills to support a strategy designed to get things done with little personal damage.

Sharing

The *sharing* leader is generally broad in outlook and socially inclined. Sharing in problem solving and decision making is encouraged, and individual team members are given considerable freedom of action. Individual interests are looked after, and efforts are directed at establishing and maintaining a congenial team atmosphere.

It has to be recognised, however, that sharing takes time. Time is not always in ample supply. With this in mind, skill has to be applied in deciding what should be shared and what should be retained within the leader's decision-making domain.

Opt-out

The *opt-out* leader is very active at first in setting guidelines and deadlines, but then withdraws from the scene. There is little monitoring or evaluation. Team members, therefore, enjoy a considerable degree of freedom, and the leader may save himself the attendant worry and stress. There are likely to be difficulties with this style when things go wrong. As Blanchard (1988: 6) notes, the team may, at least, lose direction, and, at worst, drift into anarchy. Having chosen to abdicate responsibility, there are few, if any, checks on progress in order to spot such potentially damaging dysfunctions before they magnify.

In some team situations, members may thrive on having almost complete freedom to tackle assignments without any sort of interference. Blanchard observes that if the leader does not remove himself from the authority role soon enough, the team may become frustrated and make hasty decisions. Such teams may comprise, for instance, highly skilled and experienced individuals (probably professional workers), who have the political know-how to understand when matters should be referred upwards. Nevertheless, it may be argued that at least a modicum of interest from the team leader is essential.

Directive Versus Sharing

As mentioned, the styles cannot be seen as discrete, and indeed, there are many frameworks, some of which span the gaps between the above styles. Margerison's (1973: 21) summary reflects situations in which managers might command, negotiate or bargain, consult, represent, or solve problems jointly. This framework, in particular, draws attention to bargaining and voting activities.

Some styles have won widespread support, while several receive criticism. In episodes of organisational revitalisation, for example,

Peterson (1991: 106) sees the autocratic style as being potentially destructive, and claims that real team leaders are required, those who can enthuse and involve colleagues in the challenges they face. Ends and Page (1977: 65) also implicitly condemn the 'solo' approach in the team setting by defining leadership skill as "the ability to influence the thinking, the attitudes, and the behaviour of subordinates without use of coercion." It is indeed difficult to see any substantial role for strongly directive team leadership in the context of modern teams, and much of our discussion points to the overriding need for more democratic types of operation.

Despite the obvious advantages of the sharing approach, however, there are also benefits to be derived from other styles in certain situations. It is not possible, therefore, to propose an approach which is accepted as universally the best. As Reddin (1967) posited, the effectiveness of any style is dependent on the context, and that pressures from five potential sources will determine the context in which leadership style has to be employed. It is important, therefore, for team leaders to understand their contexts: the ways in which organisational superiors, team members, colleagues leading other teams, the nature of the team's work, and the culture of both the team and the organisation all affect the situation.

Some of these sources of demand were accounted for at an earlier date by Tannenbaum and Schmidt (1958) who identified three sets of characteristics: those of the manager (team leader), the subordinates (team members) and the situation. Amongst the leader's characteristics are personal values, confidence in team members, style preferences and the ability to cope with the uncertainty that arises when decisions are shared. The team members' characteristics include the level of their independence, their tolerance for ambiguity, their knowledge and experience, and their expectations about participation. Amongst the situation characteristics are the culture of the team and the larger organisation (in other words, how things are customarily done), the nature of the problem (whether it is relatively simple or complex), and the amount of time available. These correspond approximately to Reddin's sources, since the demands from superiors and colleagues, and the nature of the work, may be incorporated in the situational characteristics.

Since it is evident that team situations change, it may be argued that leaders need to account for these influencing factors by developing skill in more than one style and by applying approaches that are relevant to the contextual variables. For example, a sharing approach with experienced and knowledgeable employees may be effective, whereas a directive style may be counterproductive. Similarly, an approach that gives team members a great degree of latitude may be inappropriate if they have a low tolerance for ambiguity. The need for flexibility is indeed confirmed by Tannenbaum and Schmidt (1958) in stating that strong leadership is called for in some situations and a more permissive style in others.

Apart from adaptive capabilities, there is also a need for leaders to develop an awareness about their own behaviour and their impact on individuals. This provides the basis for development. It can only happen when leaders consciously acquire information from their colleagues and ask the relevant questions. Such questions might be about: the degree of fear of the leadership position; the amount of respect members have; expectations of the role; whether the leader is perceived as autocratic or democratic; the degree of fairness shown; whether there is too little or too much criticism; the extent of perceived competence; the political dynamics within the organisation and the group and whether the leader is seen as friendly or antagonistic. Many other issues could be addressed, but it seems essential to gather at least a basic understanding of team member perceptions.

Leadership today, as always, is an elusive subject and the search for increased understanding continues unabated. Although our purpose here is not to cover comprehensively recent developments in leadership thought, it is important to have some understanding of its direction, as such developments will undoubtedly continue to influence issues related to team leadership. In a number of ways, current thoughts on leadership mirror team workings much more closely than the more dated approaches.

Developments in Understanding Leadership

Leadership is a topic of continual and universal interest. Even comparatively recent developments are being superseded by new conceptualisations of leadership, some of which may have a profound impact on furthering our understanding of team leadership effectiveness. Schriesheim and Neider (1989: 19), for example, draw attention to the fact that behavioural and situational theories have not really accounted for the broad managerial roles that are generally carried out and that style has been treated in a simplified way. They indicate that current research is more managerial in its emphasis, with leadership as a part of the job. The authors also identify influence processes and the conceptualisations of style as topics for investigation. In terms of the broader managerial role, delegation is an issue central to leadership, and they indicate (p. 21) that preliminary data is pointing to the effectiveness of middle ground delegational strategies. This means that the leader neither retires completely from the scene having delegated a task, nor indulges in excessive interference by checking up and having team members request permission for every move. The data is pointing to member job satisfaction and organisational commitment if this approach is practised.

In relation to the second focus, influence processes, Schriesheim and Neider (1989: 21) advocate the integration of such processes (with special attention being given to 'rational' strategies) into leadership development, and suggest "investigating other influence styles to determine more effectively which styles are most appropriate under varying situational and subordinate characteristics. Ultimately, such research should lead to a set of prescriptions for new managers concerning how best to achieve organizational goals". We examine the issue of influence strategies and their relevance to the team context separately.

In addition to the two strands just outlined, leadership is being looked at as a 'multidimensional, dynamic interpersonal process.' Fiedler, previously associated with pioneering work in contingency approaches, has more recently been developing the process by which leaders achieve effective group performance (Fiedler and Garcia, 1987). "To achieve high performance, these authors now contend that organizations must enhance group support for managers, select experienced managers for high stress positions and train intelligent leaders to be more directive in their interactions with subordinates" (Schriesheim and Neider, 1989: 22).

It is worth mentioning a few other developments that have been gathering momentum. Accompanying discussion of the need to differentiate between management and leadership have been similar differentiations between 'transactional' and 'transformational' leadership. Transactional leadership is viewed as the technical or routine side of leadership. It is about routine managerial tasks. "Transactional practices [are] central in maintaining the organisation – getting the day-to-day routines carried out" (Leithwood, 1992: 9). Although

Leithwood continues to state that "such practices do not stimulate improvement", he and most other writers admit that they are necessary for continuation and stability.

Transactional leadership in times of rapid change, however, is not enough. Leadership must also be transformative. Transformational leadership provides the incentive for people to attempt improvements. Avolio and Bass (1988) and Sergiovanni (1990) refer to transformational leadership as 'value-added'.

Tichy and Devanna (1986) suggest that transformational leaders take their organisation through three phases on an ongoing basis:

1. They recognise the need for revitalisation and the need for change in order to keep pace with the uncertain environment and to remain competitive.
2. They visualise changes that need to be made and then motivate people towards making them a reality.
3. They guide people towards the vision until the change becomes institutionalised.

Lussier (1990: 153) neatly summarises the characteristics of transformational leaders: "They see themselves as change agents; they are courageous individuals who take risks; they believe in people and motivate them; they are value driven; they are life-long learners; they have the ability to deal with complexity, ambiguity, and uncertainty; they are visionaries." Viewed in this light, the transformational approach is highly relevant to the team situation.

There have been many derivatives of the transformational leadership approach and there has also been a growing recognition of the place of ethics in leadership. Much recent leadership inquiry has focused on the influence the leader might have over subordinates. There is also increasing interest in the effect culture and language have on our understanding of leadership. It is argued that culture is important, because it helps the leader read the team and understand its workings. It also helps the leader understand how change might be introduced and accomplished. Certain leader strategies, for example, might be incongruent with prevailing culture and make change difficult or impossible.

In conclusion, despite the crucial part the leader has to play in team effectiveness, it would be wrong to imply that the leadership skills of one person guarantee success. As Wynn and Guditus

(1984: 208) appropriately note: "The determining variables of group effectiveness lie with the group itself and in the milieu in which it works. The leader may influence those variables but never control them absolutely."

Team leadership is full of complexities. We have tried to demonstrate by reference to the theory that the multiplicity of variables, each with a potentially substantial impact on the situation in which team leadership is practised, makes the role a particularly difficult one. Team leaders, therefore, may need to become reflective, knowledgeable and adaptable. They may need to consider, first, their typical behaviours and preferences, their values, and the nature of the team setting; second, the approaches they might adopt in pursuit of team goals; and third, how they might adapt their behaviour and actions to achieve congruence with the changing situations teams might face. Change and development are constant features in the lives of modern teams, and in such conditions, there appears to be a great need for team leaders who are willing to develop the requisite skills.

It must be said, however, that leadership may be, in part, enigmatic. It may go beyond the actions, behaviours and characteristics that have formed much of the discussion hitherto. Hoy and Miskel (1991: 299) make this very point in relation to institutional leadership, but their observation may be equally related to the leadership of teams:

> Leadership is cultural and symbolic as well as instrumental and behavioural. Successful leaders infuse value into organizations, thereby creating institutional meaning and purpose that go beyond the technical requirements of the job. The institutional leader is responsible for articulating the mission of the organization, shaping its culture, and protecting and maintaining its integrity.

Summary

In this chapter we have attempted to provide a brief overview of the history of leadership thought and suggested a model that may act as a useful guide to the sorts of actions a team leader can take. We also discussed a number of areas related to the leader's role, skills and team leadership styles. We concluded the chapter by mentioning briefly some of the more recent developments in leadership thought. Throughout the chapter we have mentioned a preference for shared leadership. In line with this the next chapter examines the various roles present and necessary in a team. The discussion will reinforce the point that a team cannot operate with one person leading and telling others what to do. For a team to be effective, it needs a mixture of skills, abilities, behaviours and personalities.

Summary of the Implications for Managers

- In terms of the task, the leader needs to consider its purpose, the resources needed and the essential skills. Individual targets need to be defined and accountability clearly delineated. Monitoring and evaluation procedures have to be established.

- The leader also has to focus on team needs. The need for interdependence has to be constantly reinforced, and this may be achieved by emphasizing the importance of individual contributions and by such practical strategies as rotating assignments. The leader must ensure goals are understood and accepted, and that standards of performance are clarified. The team size may have to be reconsidered for some tasks alongside the possibility of subdividing the task. Disruptive issues need to be dealt with quickly, and ideas and suggestions need to be welcomed. The leader is responsible for briefing the team regularly on plans and progress, and for representing the team in the larger organisation.

- At an individual level, the leader provides coaching support and helps team personnel experience achievement and perform at high levels. He needs to know individuals, their needs and motivations, their value systems, prior experiences, and perceptions. This inevitably means talking to people, getting around, meeting them and listening to them. Efforts should be recognised and challenging work provided. The leader, above all, should give responsibility and provide opportunity for growth and development. He understands how individual work relates to the team effort and is able to identify appropriate training and development needs. Authority is given to do the job properly, successes are emphasized, and rewards are given where appropriate. The leader constantly asks whether individuals have the right resources and whether they are doing the right tasks to ensure overall team effectiveness. Probably the greatest skill lies in being able to integrate individual benefits with the pursuit of team goals.

- The leader needs to develop skill in communicating with in-dividuals and the team, and such skills include planning, matching people's abilities to tasks, coordinating, coaching, persuading and being empathetic, and negotiating. Helpful feedback should be given to both individuals and the team as a unit, and everyone might benefit from praise when it is fairly given. The leader also needs to be the skilful observer, noting when individuals become en-thusiastic or uninvolved, how they respond to ideas and suggestions, and what interests them.

- Self-awareness is a great asset in the leader, and he may need to consider the impact of his behaviour on others. Knowing how others perceive the leader's style, the degree of fairness displayed, competence level, and whether he is friendly or antagonistic can help to improve performance.

- Much of what has been said above may be summarised in three attributes: the skilled leader is reflective, knowledgeable and adaptable. Flexibility is of utmost importance. The team leader should consider a range of factors that impact on the situation, and these include his own preferred behaviours, values and the team setting. His approach may have to be modified to achieve certain goals, and he may have to display considerable flexibility in adapting behaviour and actions to changing situations.

10

TEAM ROLES

We have indicated throughout previous chapters that team members have an important contribution to make in terms of their expertise and knowledge to the team. For example, they may be experts in marketing, information systems or any other aspect which is related to the task in hand. The contribution which they are expected to make is relatively straightforward and has been labelled their functional role in the team.

Members also have another part to play in the team and that is related to their behaviour. How they behave has a considerable impact on the effectiveness of the team's operation. Robbins (1991: 282) points out that, while any one personality characteristic is not a predictor of group behaviour, when taken together, personality factors do have a significant impact. Peterson (1991: 60) takes a similar line and, in discussing personality differences, points to the problems of people being different, thinking in different ways, and arriving at decisions differently. Much of what is attributed to poor communication stems from these differences.

Behaviour can influence not only performance but also the degree of satisfaction which they themselves and other members derive from the team. The two, performance and satisfaction, are linked. This point is emphasized by Anantaraman (1984a: 145) in discussing intellectual and emotional roles. Facilitating the task is intellectual, while maintaining group harmony is emotional. The roles are seldom present in one person, and this points to the need for them to be covered by different members.

If members do not feel happy about the team and its work, they become ineffective in carrying out their assignments, and this leads to further dysfunctional behaviours (Dyer, 1980). The team's success, therefore, might be thought of as the product of a combination of the functional skills and the behaviours which members typically employ in the team setting. We call these behaviours *roles* and we argue that they are critical to team effectiveness.

A role is "a set of expected behavior patterns attributed to someone occupying a given position in a social unit" (Robbins, 1991: 283). The key word in that definition is 'behaviour'. The presence of behavioural roles is referred to by several writers in emphasizing the contributions which members bring to the team. For example, Hastings *et al.* (1986) state: "They contribute a much wider range of acquired know-how and inbuilt qualities many of them paradoxically opposites which they balance and apply with fluid ease." Margerison and McCann (1989: 18) refer to them as 'work preferences', described as the different ways that individuals approach tasks.

In this section, we shall explain the significance of individual roles to team performance, demonstrate how preferred roles might be identified and then developed, and finally show how roles might be used in combination to build an effective team.

Roles in Teams

A number of role frameworks have been postulated. Buhler and McCann (1989: 15), for example, refer to a need for the roles of innovator, organiser, troubleshooter, communicator and strategist in management teams. Ends and Page (1977: 178) describe roles as services or contributions. The task-oriented services are energising, searching, polling, evaluating, and summarising; the group process services are encouraging, including, standardising, and ventilating; and the combined group task and group process services are evaluating, diagnosing, testing, mediating and conciliating.

Margerison and McCann's (1985: 17) framework is divided into behaviours and roles. The two aspects to behaviour are 'exploring': searching, creativity, contacting, etc. – what they call 'diverging' activities; and 'controlling': concern for detail, precision, standards, rules, planning – these are all 'converging' activities. The roles are first, 'advisory': provision of support and information, planning, research, training, and other areas needed to get the task done; and second, 'organisational': setting up systems and procedures, putting pressure on people for output and delivering the product or service. Behaviours and roles are arranged on two dimensions and it is suggested that individuals have behavioural and role preferences that must be balanced for the benefit of the team. Added to the above four activities is a fifth, 'linking', which involves bringing together members in an integrated and coordinated way, and these form five fundamental activities that make up their Team Management Wheel. The model is used in considering team composition and performance. It will be seen later how many of the above items correspond with the model of team roles presented in this section.

The work of Meredith Belbin is arguably the most significant piece of research into team effectiveness undertaken to date. Since his highly influential book *Management Teams: Why They Succeed or Fail* came out in 1981, Belbin has been continually refining the Team Roles. Before the work of researchers such as Belbin, common wisdom dictated that if the best people are put together, a high-performance team would inevitably result. Traditionally, the most skilled people, therefore, would be selected for the team. This approach is still prevalent in most organisations and there are many examples: a committee which comprises distribution experts; an urban redevelopment task force which comprises the best architects in the field. Even cheque book-waving football managers tend to believe that top performance comes from acquiring the best individual players available. It has been found, however, that such an approach does not guarantee success. Belbin indeed discovered that factors other than technical ability were more important in determining the success of a team.

It was originally thought that there may be a personal characteristics mix which produced the right formula. This was a reasonable assumption; some people like one another and enjoy working together, and there seems to be a sort of 'chemistry'. It is this chemistry which Belbin tried to investigate by conducting a series of psychometric tests on people working in teams. He found that some combinations of personality mix could be put together and the team would be successful most of the time. Other combinations were less successful and, in some cases, disastrous.

It is true that some teams, through sheer expertise alone, should succeed, but the results are often disappointing. This may be explained by the similarity of approach to problems. For example, a group of intelligent professionals may fail due to the members' high critical analysis capacities. Everard and Morris (1985) indeed draw attention to this phenomenon in groups of secondary school heads and teams of higher education academics in the UK. Whilst it may be necessary that a team should comprise people who have relevant knowledge in the task area, there are other factors that may determine the extent of the team's success.

In considering team membership, we call for the need for hetero-geneity, for skills and abilities to be complementary rather than duplicated, and this may be a key factor in team success. Selection, therefore, becomes a crucial component in the equation. Selecting team members against inappropriate criteria may do little to enhance team performance. For example, the selection of 'capable' colleagues or those of sufficient seniority is widely practised, while in many cases, people assume team membership as of right by virtue of position. As the following discussion will show, this may be less than ideal in pro-ducing high-performance teams. It is a situation, however, that is unlikely to be changed in many organisations, and more complex strategies may be required to weld a diverse group of people into a cohesive unit.

In order to gain an initial assessment of preferred behavioural roles, the form shown in Figure 10.1 can be completed by team members. The scores will be interpreted later in this chapter. First we look at some general tenets of team roles theory, followed by a description of each of nine team roles.

The Basic Premise of Team Roles

The dominant premise on which team roles theory is built is that individuals tend to have distinctive preferences in terms of behaviours, and these are essentially a function of their personality make-up. Hurst *et al.* (1989: 93) note: "Although individuals may be able to exhibit a variety of behaviors it is unlikely they will be equally able at each set of behaviors, or indifferent amongst them. They will have a preference." Thus, individuals have much more to contribute than their professional skills or expertise. It is important, therefore, to identify these preferences and develop them into strengths that can be used in the team. In order to do this, roles (both functional and behavioural) need to be clear, since power struggles and rivalries may occur where there is ambiguity (Belzer, 1989: 12).

Figure 10.1   Self-description Statements

Award marks to these statements according to their applicability to you. You have 25 points to use which may be distributed amongst a maximum of *three* boxes. You may want to give all the 25 points to one statement or you may wish to spread your points out over two or three boxes.

Award
points

1. You like to lead the team. You want to involve others and you are democratic, but you know when you have to take control. You keep an eye on your team's targets and that you stay on course. You know what the priorities are and you ensure your team members know their roles. You are very practical and you cope well with pressure. You like to do things properly.

2. You like to lead from the front. You like quick results and members who will follow your orders. You make incisive, no-nonsense decisions and push your own ideas. You can put up with not being popular because you get results. You tell people when they are not doing things right. You are impatient, but people respect your drive and enthusiasm.

3. You are an ideas person. You make creative suggestions. You are self-confident but not too diplomatic at times. You are not too pleased if someone criticises your innovative suggestions. Sometimes, you feel it is better to opt out of the team rather than stay there and antagonise other people.

4. You have an analytical mind. You like to examine ideas and suggestions critically and see whether they fit in with the team's goals. You are serious and shrewd. You find the flaws that others overlook, but sometimes you are accused of being negative. At least, you stop the team from doing things that won't work. You have the brains to interpret very complex information and to make the best decision.

5. You are a practical person who gets on with the job. You look for clear goals, practical work routines and tangible results. You are not too concerned with exciting ideas. You work with care and determination. You are more concerned with thoroughness than speed. You wish that people would stop changing things occasionally and let you get on with a good, solid job.

6. Your first concern is for people and their feelings. You can spot their strengths and weaknesses. You hate friction and you try to console those who are upset. You don't see why people should compete with one another. You like to develop people's talents and you are able to draw reticent colleagues into discussions. Ideally, you like the team to be a nice, happy family.

7. You have an enquiring mind. You explore ideas outside the team and like to find out what others are doing. You develop many contacts. You use your colleagues' talents well. You need plenty of variety or you become bored. At times you are a bit impulsive. You are really good at exploring new possibilities and you have the ability to persuade and motivate team members.

8. You are an anxious sort of person and you have plenty of nervous energy. You like to see jobs finished and finished well. You like things to be done on time. You nag your team mates and don't allow them to become complacent. You keep people on their toes. You spot mistakes and have an attention to detail. At times, you tend to irritate others, but you stop them becoming careless, over-confident or lazy.

9. You are an expert with highly developed technical or professional expertise. You have the ability to describe complex concepts in simple, easy to understand terms, and you encourage others to think objectively. At times, you may lose your patience with those who don't under-stand. You tend to be sensitive to criticism. You are self-directed and dedicated and, at times, stubborn.

The underlying premises of team roles theory are as follows:

1. People working in teams tend to adopt particular roles.
2. They tend to prefer these roles and stick with them.
3. Certain combinations lead to more effective teams.

In order to develop effective teams, therefore, it is necessary for individuals to be given opportunities to:

1. become aware of their role preferences;
2. understand how they can use these role preferences for the good of the team;
3. develop their role preferences so they are more effective.

We now move on to describe in some detail the various roles.

Team Roles: Descriptions

The following descriptions are our interpretation of the roles originally delineated by Dr Meredith Belbin (1981) in his well-known research at Henley and subsequently built on by him. This interpretation has also taken into account the work of Belbin's co-researchers, and the authors' experience of working on development programmes with teams of managers. It should be noted that the descriptions are presented in their 'pure' forms, representing the extreme form of each role. In reality, such forms are unlikely to occur to that extent, but showing them in this way helps in understanding the central behavioural features characteristic of each role.

It should be noted that each ideal role includes a number of weaknesses associated with the role. Belbin calls these 'allowable weaknesses' and notes that these are acceptable in a team setting. They can be described as the payments which are made for the strengths inherent in the particluar role. It may be counter-productive to work on these weaknesses as, in many cases, they are closely intertwined with strengths. It is better to deal with weaknesses by delegating certain responsibilities or roles to others or, in some cases, recruiting a new team member to fill the void. Often this can be done by encouraging a team member to strengthen a secondary role. This point will become clearer as you read through the role descriptions. Below each description, we have included a summary of the key behavioural points of the particular role.

The Coordinator

This role is one of the two team leadership roles. It is substantially different from that of the more directive leader, called the 'Shaper', and described below. The Coordinator likes to identify people's skills and abilities, and use them. He will involve colleagues in decision making and will genuinely share whenever possible. But he does not lose control and things do get done, because he retains a focus on the task. He politely brings discussions back on line and ensures that contributions are relevant to the matter at hand. In a management meeting, for example, a manager who enacts the Coordinator role will give colleagues the feeling that their contributions are important and that their skills are there to be recognised and utilised. The Coordinator will seldom simply announce decisions, but seek an input from interested parties.

He is usually quite intelligent, but this can be problematic if his intellect far exceeds that of other team members. He is emotionally stable, not showing much concern for the problem of others taking on leading roles, because he is basically secure. He can be assertive and is quite pragmatic. The Coordinator has faith in his colleagues to do a good job.

The Shaper

The Shaper is in direct contrast to the Coordinator. He is brash and has a sharp, sometimes uncontrolled, tongue. He makes rapid, incisive decisions and gives direct orders, which he would probably argue are more productive and less time consuming than participative episodes. Essentially, he is an action man and wants to see quick results. He likes 'yes people' and has no time for those who question his decisions. He is extremely task-centred and people's personal needs tend to take a poor second place. He is not very popular with colleagues, but he at least makes sure that things get done promptly.

His no-nonsense approach gives rise to impatience, intolerance and competitiveness. He may be emotionally insecure and seems to have boundless energy. He is often critical of others but is incapable of accepting criticism himself.

Some people can accept this, but some team members may have their own ways of reacting to what may be seen as a bullying style. It is unlikely that the Shaper heading a professional organisation or unit will get lasting commitment and cooperation from colleagues, unless another colleague adopts a more conciliatory role. There are situations, however, where the Shaper role may be necessary to shake things up and make rapid changes.

The Plant

The Plant is the ideas person and can take a team out of a condition of dull mediocrity into new realms of performance, but only if other team members are prepared to listen and respond to him. The main activity for the Plant is what Ends and Page (1977: 179) call 'energising': suggesting new ideas, proposing solutions to problems, advancing new approaches and formulating new ways of organising data. Lau (1988: 14) suggests purposely selecting one such creative personality for the team who is known for not sticking to the norm: "That person usually will serve as the springboard toward innovative thinking and fresh solutions."

The Plant, as the above clearly indicates, has a highly creative mind and likes to search for new ways of doing things. But this does not always go down too well with some of the other roles, namely, the Shaper, the Monitor-Evaluator and the Implementer. As a result, the Plant is quite likely to disappear into the background unless there is a skilful team leader who can draw on his creativity and at the same time direct it into activity which is in line with the task objectives. Rejecting the Plant is injurious to the team, since the unit will almost certainly lack that vital spark which is the hallmark of high performance. Jacobs and Everett (1988: 13), though, suggest that rejection is all too prevalent:

> Most executives who dissent from the established team ideology or view of the world are likely to be sanctioned for their lack of loyalty or commitment to that view ... They will be held in lower esteem by the team, and in more extreme cases may be shut out of many of the team's activities.

The Plant is a loner who may not like to be bound by such group norms nor restricted by petty rules and procedures. In systems that are largely bureaucratic, it seems difficult to provide the conditions in which Plants can be nurtured. In these circumstances, Plants may be few and far between. It is also interesting to note that Plants may be in short supply in cultures that promote a narrow focus in their educational systems and provide little support for activities that might be described as 'creative'.

The Plant can be problematic to the rest of the team, is often undiplomatic, and his radical ideas seem to be divorced from reality. He is also intensely sensitive to criticism, which suggests that the team may have to pay a high price in terms of tolerance if it is to enjoy the benefits which the Plant inevitably brings.

As many teams seem to operate at the level of mediocrity, the role of the Plant may be of crucial importance in feeding new ideas to both senior management and other organisational teams. As Buhler and McCann (1989: 15) note:

> This person will stimulate and challenge others in your organization to elicit the great concepts. This is the individual who develops the ideas or concepts and keeps your products, services and organization competitive. This individual is usually a risk taker, willing to accept occasional setbacks in order to keep pushing your organizational 'frontier' forward.

The importance of innovatory activity to the organisation is also highlighted by Jacobs and Everett (1988: 13): "As the high-tech marketplace becomes more competitive, and budgets and staff resources become tighter, organisations need Innovators and innovative strategies more than ever, as they continue attempting to adapt to their turbulent environments." The same authors go on to suggest serious problems for teams and organisations that cannot accommodate the unique contributions which such individuals bring to the team setting: "Innovators and innovation must be inhibited by this apparent inability of teams in general to encourage, accept and manage effectively a certain amount of 'healthy' dissent and division. The failure to share fully the differences in perception must certainly reduce their capacity to cope with, and successfully adapt to, change."

Managers at all levels, therefore, may be well advised to seek out those colleagues who provide this role preference and make full use of their special skills. These special skills are highlighted by Watts (1988):

> If you have a Plant on your team you have probably already experienced both the benefits and disadvantages they can offer. A strong innovative disposition and an effective thinking ability of a high order are considerable assets to any management team but they must be managed with great skill if negative side-effects are to be avoided. There may, for example, be long periods of non- or low contribution. The Plant is a talented midfield player who is always one step ahead of the others. Once your team learns to match the Plant's attributes with its collective efforts and stops demanding a continuous work rate, you are on your way to success.

In promoting the cause of the creative talent, we are not condoning excessive individualism, because team membership demands that the team's interests be put first, even if only for a short while. Nevertheless, it has to be accepted that such talents are likely to be associated with individualists, in the sense that they pursue independent courses in thought and action. They still need to be accommodated in the team (Adair, 1986: 54).

Finally, it is worth noting some findings from a study by Berelson and Steiner (1964, cited in Anderson, 1984: 135) which give some insights into the nature of the creative person:

- Creativity may appear in spurts.
- Intelligence, in itself, is not enough for creative ideas.
- Highly creative people like complexity and novelty.
- They are less conforming and need to take risks.
- They produce their best work early in their careers.
- Most creative work in any one field is done by relatively few people.

The Monitor Evaluator

If the Plant is the one who creates the ideas, the Monitor Evaluator is the one who breaks them down and often discards them. He provides a quality control mechanism, meticulously finding the faults in proposals and suggestions, and rejecting any idea which has not accommodated the necessary constraints and limitations. As a result, he can easily incur the wrath of the Plant and can indeed antagonise the rest of the team by an over-critical and negative attitude. This is not always the case, of course, but the role does demand providing a sort of filtering mechanism, so that only those ideas which meet rigorous criteria are allowed to pass through.

The Monitor Evaluator has a great capacity for interpreting complex data and, more often than not, is able to choose the best decision from a range of alternatives. He deals with confusing information in the same way children tackle game puzzles: it is a stimulating challenge. He is an excellent planner and he invariably keeps team goals in mind. He is not a risk-taker, but errs on the cautious side, which can be frustrating for the Plant. His role becomes dysfunctional when he starts to take pleasure in antagonising 'ideas people', and this type of behaviour can indeed become destructive to the team. This may be especially true where assumptions are made about barriers, whether or not they really exist, and in some cases, assumptions may become reality. This is a problem that is not confined to the domain of the Monitor Evaluator.

There are many Monitor Evaluators to be found amongst teams of professionals, which is not surprising in view of the fact that the role demands intellect and analytical capacities. Whilst a negative picture has been painted of the role in its more destructive form, the Monitor Evaluator is of great value to teams in all spheres, but particularly to those teams in organisations that face considerable complexity and uncertainty, since he will probably prevent colleagues from taking on projects that are inadvisable and that are not aligned to company mission. At operational, rather than strategic, levels, he will certainly have a clear idea of what will work and what will not.

The Implementer

This role is reflected in Johnson and Johnson's (1991: 437) team worker, one who is involved and committed, who tries to upgrade knowledge and skills, and to ensure high quality work and products. The Implementer is a solid, reliable individual who thrives in a stable, little-changing environment, so he may not be particularly well disposed towards the Plant. He is down-to-earth, conscientious and disciplined, and as such, can easily accept rules and procedures, seeing them as necessary constraints. Totally unlike the Plant who can thrive on ambiguity, the Implementer likes to be told what to do. In return, he will get on with the job and work carefully for good results. He is also meticulous about quality and quite determined, which means that he does not like to be coerced into doing a quick job, and this may bring him into conflict with the Shaper who may not share the same concern for quality.

The Implementer is considered essential to the effective functioning of the team, but despite his admirable qualities, his limitations can be frustrating. He lacks vision and reacts badly to situations that may involve ambiguous information and change. He may also react against new ideas, which can make the atmosphere uncomfortable if several team members are pressing for change.

Like the Monitor Evaluator, there are many Implementers to be found in management teams. They are seen as good, reliable people who will get jobs done. They are highly thought of in organisational cultures that emphasize conformity and the application of tried and tested solutions to problems. But the team must be careful unless it settles for simply maintaining the *status quo*, which may be totally inappropriate for the team's context and the organisational conditions.

Development can take place only if the Implementer is shielded from the ambiguity and given specific meaningful tasks to carry out. The most difficult situation occurs when this person becomes the team leader, because leadership, by its very nature, demands vision and the capacity to look beyond the immediate. The Implementer, in contrast to this requirement, may be comparatively myopic. There are many organisations that put Implementers in charge, because it is part of their culture to reward experience and a declared willingness to toe the company line. This is almost certainly detrimental to team effectiveness. At the top of the organisation, in particular, it can be disastrous if an Implementer takes a strong hold, and, for this reason, it is critical that senior management team members recognise the relevance of roles to their work so that they can modify their behaviours if the situation dictates.

The Team Worker

The Team Worker is everyone's friend, but may be less concerned about getting the task completed than other, more task-oriented colleagues. He has effective interpersonal skills and is adept at developing team cohesion. He is good at 'reading' people, being able to understand their moods and feelings. He works quietly to achieve harmony and will address discord if it threatens to surface.

He is emotionally stable and without a strong competitive streak. He is sometimes seen as being too soft, which may be true in some situations where a much harder line and some discomfort would be more appropriate. For example, a departmental team may be under-performing and may need shaking out of its complacency, but the Team Worker is not the person to do this, preferring instead to emphasize harmony.

His complementary role has to be used well, so that he can help build team spirit and heal the wounds caused by interpersonal differences.

It is good to have a Team Worker in management teams, especially where they (the teams) are predominantly task-centred. Apart from such individuals' ability to build and maintain relationships between people, they are good at promoting development and, when in senior positions, they are usually effective delegators, providing the sorts of opportunities for colleagues to gain development experiences valuable to their careers. They are not over concerned about others being able to do their jobs.

The Resource Investigator

This role provides the link with the outside world, since the Resource Investigator is the one most likely to seek ideas and develop contacts with other units and organisations. The purpose of these activities is to ensure that the team acquires the best ideas and that it does not suffer the effects of insularity.

The Resource Investigator, like the Coordinator, likes to develop people's talents, but is not quite so stable as the latter. He is impulsive and can lose interest quickly. He needs lots of variety in his work, challenge and constant stimulation. He also needs people around to maintain his interest, because he is certainly not one to become involved in long tedious paperwork tasks which demand perseverance and attention to detail.

It is this tendency to become bored quickly that can be problematic, alongside a failure to stay closely focused on the relevant issues. Despite this, the team may benefit considerably from his outward looking orientation and the capacity to keep in touch with life outside the team.

In a competitive environment, the person who adopts this role may look for examples of good practice in other organisations, either by visiting and observing them or by being constantly in social contact with colleagues outside. He may hold membership of professional associations and is usually enthusiastic about introducing ideas acquired from conferences and training or development sessions outside the place of work. He is also the person who may devise innovative ways of linking up with the outside world for the benefit of the team and the organisation by, for example, inviting customers to make an input into new product development or by getting recipients of goods or services to meet with the team to offer advice.

The Completer

The Completer is one of life's 'naggers'. He can be infuriating to team colleagues, often turning up at the wrong time and pestering for work to be completed. In fact, his boundless nervous energy is primarily used to this end. He invariably meets deadlines and makes sure that others do so. He communicates urgency and many colleagues learn to dread his frequent appearances as time deadlines approach. He can easily upset people with his persistence, but he certainly prevents complacency and poor work.

Some aspects of organisational life can be highly complex and there may be many initiatives that teams at all levels have to deal with. Whilst intentions are good, it is understandable that some things either fall behind schedule or fade completely into the background. Where the Completer has a part in a project, however, this is unlikely to happen, since he will ensure colleagues are constantly reminded of the task's status and what they must do to reach a satisfactory conclusion.

His influence extends beyond time deadlines, however. He has great attention to detail and will often take on the task of checking everything himself so that mistakes do not pass through unnoticed. With a Completer in the team, it is more than likely that the output will be accurate and on schedule, and that nothing important will be omitted. It does not mean that the work is necessarily creative or that it incorporates particularly stunning ideas: that is not part of his role.

Apart from his nagging, which can easily lower morale amongst team members, he is likely to be at loggerheads with those who are casual, clumsy or fail to meet his expectations of urgency and meticulous accuracy.

The Specialist

The Specialist, as the name implies, is the team member who provides the expertise and knowledge which is so often vital for effectively completing tasks. The specialist plays a somewhat different role from other members, in that his personal attributes do not affect his inclusion or exclusion. In this way, the specialist may be seen as playing a more functional role, with his behavioural role being secondary in a team sense. Because of his expertise, the Specialist's inclusion is a must and other members must learn to live with him. The Specialist's task is to provide professional or technical information which the team needs for specific projects and does not otherwise possess. Due to the nature of the role, the Specialist may not be a member of fairly permanent or long-term teams, but may join temporarily as the occasion arises. He is more likely to be a permanent member only in shorter term or project teams.

The Specialist is self-motivated, somewhat opinionated, and dedicated (even dogmatic) to his own particular area of expertise. He can usually provide a great deal of specialised knowledge which the team would otherwise not have or even consider. Specialists can only contribute in a focused area and tend to concentrate on sometimes trying technicalities. This role is essential when specialised and technical decisions need to be made and is useful for providing technical information to the team and helping the team remain objective. The Specialist should be adept at translating complex information into 'lay' terms and assisting other team members in understanding technical problems. He can also supply a professional perspective to problem solving and other discussions.

Assessing Role Preferences

The form shown in Figure 10.2 allows an analysis to be made of the scores given earlier for the role 'descriptions'. This is only a preliminary analysis and it is better to have team members discuss role perceptions with one another. It is possible to assess the role preferences for each member of the team and this is usefully done on a team basis, with each member having some input into each of the other team members'

The three scores given in the Self-description Statements form should be entered in the boxes below. The numbers refer to the statements. The initials refer to the roles.

1. CO	☐	5. IM	☐
2. SH	☐	6. TW	☐
3. PL	☐	7. RI	☐
4. ME	☐	8. CF	☐
		9. SP	☐

Figure 10.2　Team Behaviour Roles Preliminary Analysis Form

assessments. It may release new insights into the relationship between team performance and behaviour, and thus enable some constructive adjustments to be made at a later stage to either team membership or role preferences. It is then possible to total the scores given for each role, divide them by the number of people in the team, and then arrive at an average score for each role. This can be done using the form in Figure 10.3. For the interested reader, it is worth noting that more in-depth analyses can take place, and this service is offered by registered Belbin Consultants using state-of-the-art computer software.

Each team member can complete one of these forms. Scores from other team members are entered into the small boxes. They are then totalled and divided by the number of people in the team to yield an average score.

Roles	Scores	Total	Average
COORDINATOR	☐ ☐ ☐ ☐ ☐ ☐	☐	☐
SHAPER	☐ ☐ ☐ ☐ ☐ ☐	☐	☐
PLANT	☐ ☐ ☐ ☐ ☐ ☐	☐	☐
MONITOR EVALUATOR	☐ ☐ ☐ ☐ ☐ ☐	☐	☐
IMPLEMENTER	☐ ☐ ☐ ☐ ☐ ☐	☐	☐
TEAM WORKER	☐ ☐ ☐ ☐ ☐ ☐	☐	☐
RESOURCE INVESTIGATOR	☐ ☐ ☐ ☐ ☐ ☐	☐	☐
COMPLETER	☐ ☐ ☐ ☐ ☐ ☐	☐	☐
SPECIALIST	☐ ☐ ☐ ☐ ☐ ☐	☐	☐

Figure 10.3   Team Roles: Perceptions of Other Team Members

The Ideal Team

First of all, the question needs to be asked: Is there such a thing as an 'ideal' team? There probably is, but it may only be ideal for a particular situation. For example, where a team is operating in an uncertain environment, facing competition and having to move quickly, an active Resource Investigator may be essential if the team is to be 'ideal'. In other circumstances, the presence of that role may not be quite so important and he may even be a liability if he becomes bored with the lack of action.

Most of us, of course, are unlikely to encounter a team which is perfect in every respect. We know a great deal about the technical skills which our teams require, and the team roles research presented here is sufficiently persuasive to lead us to believe we could construct the ideal team, but reality tends to be different. If we had a clean slate and were to apply some of the principles of team composition outlined in this chapter, we could possibly form teams which approach the ideal. Obviously, it is not possible to dispense with everyone who does not fit into prescribed team roles, however, so teams have to make the best out of their available resources. Despite this, there are situations where it may be wise to move one or two people in or out of teams, because their presence (or absence) may be critical to organisational or subunit success.

What can be done about the team that is already formed and operating, and which could not be dismantled in any way? The first task is to analyse the individual team members' preferred roles. This is the starting point. The next step is to assess the balance of the team and see whether it contains the required roles. Balance is important. With a too high level of homogeneity, performance is likely to suffer. Such teams may manage in the short term, but over a longer period, they need to establish role balance to succeed. Margerison and McCann (1985: 59) provide a typical example of imbalance, where the team comprises what they call 'controllers', (similar to some of the elements of the Implementer and Completer roles). In such a case, other essential roles may be neglected and lead to failure. The symptoms of failure are that relevant information is not acquired, new ideas are not aired, there is no exploration activity for opportunities or resources, and there is little development.

The theme of balance is expanded by Watts (1988: 117) who identifies several essential team characteristics, most of which relate directly to adequate role provision. These characteristics are: balance, leadership, task and target orientation, creative problem-solving ability and positive synergy. Acknowledging the near impossibility of finding the 'perfect' team, it is suggested that role development can be undertaken on an evolutionary basis, by developing people in the job.

Assessing the team's role balance can be done by using an analysis form such as that shown in Figure 10.4. By calculating the index, it gives an approximate indication of how balanced the team is. It must be emphasized that it is only a guide and should not be used for any purpose other than gaining an initial impression of how appropriate the membership is.

The notion of balance would suggest that the presence of all nine roles would make the perfect team. Belbin's experiments supported the view that it is desirable to have most of the roles represented. The exception to this relates to the leadership of the team. The presence of both Coordinator *and* Shaper is not advisable, since it may create unproductive tension in the team's leadership. Whilst the ideal may point to everyone having different roles, role duplication may be acceptable in some circumstances, although care must be taken that confusion and competition do not occur. It largely depends on which role it is. There are some team members (Coordinators are probably good examples) who can use their role characteristics to good effect in other parts of the team, but there are some roles that seem very limited in the extent to which they can be compromised for the sake of team balance.

On the analysis form, there may be two or more members occupying the same role slot, with some blank boxes alongside several of the other roles. This creates role 'gaps' or deficiencies. Whilst this is not ideal, it is still possible to overcome the difficulties by assigning people to secondary (or even tertiary) roles. Hurst *et al.* (1989: 95) reinforce this possibility: "If, however, there exists within the group an awareness of the need for different types of cognition and behavior, as well as some capacity to perform the role, then it is possible that one or more members of the team may spontaneously assume the 'vacant' role." It need not be spontaneous, however. An individual who is already duplicating another role, for example, can be asked to adopt a secondary role more prominently in order to fill the void. Some can do this.

Coordinators, as we have mentioned, are very adaptable and can often fill in the missing spaces. Team Workers too have adaptive capabilities and, being friendly by nature and good at interaction, can often take on the task of discovering what is going on in the outside world (Resource Investigator). A Specialist is a very necessary part of the team if the task or tasks necessitate complex technical or professional input.

In the table below, enter the names of your team members alongside their preferred roles. Their highest scoring one will go under primary role, the second highest under secondary role, and so on. You can have more than one name in any box.

TEAM ROLE	PRIMARY	SECONDARY	TERTIARY
COORDINATOR			
SHAPER			
PLANT			
MONITOR EVALUATOR			
IMPLEMENTER			
TEAM WORKER			
RESOURCE INVESTIGATOR			
COMPLETER			
SPECIALIST			

Add up the number of completed boxes in the Primary column [ ] X 2 = [ ]

Add up the number of completed boxes in the Secondary column which were not already filled in the Primary column [ ]

Add a bonus point each if you have Innovator or Monitor Evaluator in the Primary column [ ]

TOTAL [ ]

If your score is greater than 10, you may have a reasonably balanced team, although a score approaching 15 indicates a more extensive range of roles.

Figure 10.4   Team Balance

With increasing specialisation in many industries and organisations today the role of the Specialist may well become more vital. Depending on the specialisation required, it is unlikely that another team member could easily adjust his role to become a specialist. On this front, it is interesting to note that Belbin's original team roles did not include the specialist. It may well be that its addition reflects recognition of the growing complexity of the market-place.

Robbins (1991: 282) in fact draws on the notion of 'role identity' (attitudes and actual behaviours consistent with a role) to propose that "people have the ability to shift roles rapidly when they recognize that the situation and its demands clearly require major changes". This may be true and it is not inconsistent with the concept of role 'preferences'. It simply means that individuals may be able to adapt to a new role demand. This is reinforced by 'role perception', a view of how a person is supposed to act in a given situation. It is based on the individual's interpretation of expectations. In this sense, 'role expectations' can be very powerful determinants of actual behaviour.

A note of caution should be entered, however, about trying to transfer some role preferences. Shapers are unlikely to have the capacity to become Team Workers, and such attempted manoeuvres are generally unrealistic. Some roles require the sort of ability which is not easily acquired. Plants are naturally very creative individuals and others cannot be expected to assume this responsibility if they have neither the creative inclination nor expertise. Similarly, the Monitor Evaluator has a clever mind and can make sense of complicated information without too much difficulty, a capacity which is not acquired very easily. Team members with these skills, in particular, need to remain in their primary roles.

What can be done in the situation where individuals are not available to fill the roles of Plant and Monitor Evaluator either through a primary role or a developed secondary role? Watts (1988: 121) points out that it may be possible to use a consultant in an innovatory capacity. Such a move is expensive, but it can be highly successful. It has the advantage that the consultant's services can be dispensed with once the need for innovatory thinking is over. Where the role of Monitor Evaluator is not present, it may be incumbent on the leader to encourage others to play 'devil's advocate'. This can be done on a rotating basis. Members are encouraged to present contrary opinions, to argue them out from the opponents' points of view, and to identify the possible unplanned results of decisions and actions. This is necessary to protect the team from actions that have not been well thought through.

Obviously, it makes sense to utilise individuals' primary roles, which are the result of particular abilities and behavioural preferences. This is where the main contribution to the team's effectiveness comes from. Learning a secondary role can be a difficult and time consuming business, but one that may be necessary in some circumstances.

Constructing the Team

Hurst *et al.* (1989: 95) note that an 'ideal' team needs different types of individuals in order to fill the important roles that are required. They also observe that preferences are stable and hence the need for primary roles in an ideal team configuration. It is highly unlikely that a team of workable size will have all the roles represented as primary preferences, but it may be desirable to have most roles present, even if they appear as secondary and tertiary roles. There are some roles that are probably essential and these are shown in the outline ideal composition in Figure 10.5.

Figure 10.5   Ideal Team Composition

Those in the smaller box are almost certainly vital to real effectiveness. The role of Coordinator is preferred to Shaper although, in some circumstances, the directive approach of the Shaper may be useful. In most cases, however, the Coordinator type is more satisfactory and supportive to the effective functioning of the team. Problems have been experienced in a number of contexts with the leader who expects submissive behaviour:

> Some leaders like people to be dependent and encourage this; some leaders are so task oriented they do not see the counterreactions to them that drain off the energies and creativity and emotional well-being of the members. Hopefully we in leadership positions center our focus on the people and their needs and try to create conditions which allow us to work *with* them rather than over them (Dyer, 1980: 184).

There are other related problems with Shaper-type leadership and these generally relate to team climate. It is best expressed in Dyer's discourse on group behaviour: "In a defensive climate people usually spend their time trying to defend themselves against the authority persons. They do not have time or emotional energy to be creative – to grow and mature – for their energies are dissipated in trying to protect themselves from the punishment, censoring, telling, controlling efforts of others" (Dyer, 1980: 185). This group reaction is often expressed in statements such as: 'If a leader does not lead, he is not doing his job.' But this may hide poor attitudes towards a highly directive leader. Because of the relationship that exists between leader and 'followers', the latter may push all responsibility onto the leader, and this may give rise to a relationship which is wary and antagonistic (Hastings *et al.*, 1986).

Nevertheless, it is possible, and in some cases desirable, to have a Shaper. If there are two in the team, however, there can be severe difficulties. "Even as few as two Shapers in a team can be disruptive and they can spend all their energy cancelling each other out. Male-female Shaper situations are particularly problematical" (Watts, 1988: 118).

The new role of the Specialist tends to be incompatible with Shapers, Plants and Resource Investigators. They also often have trouble dealing with other specialists. Despite this, and because of the Specialist's unique knowledge and expertise, other members must learn to work with him. This can often be difficult and may not be a natural relationship, as the Specialist is usually very single-minded and dogmatic, and sure of his ability in the specialised area. Uninformed team members often see the Specialist's involvement as overly concentrating on minor and insignificant technicalities when they just want to get on with the job.

The creative person may be critical to success. Belbin found that, when 'planted' in an ordinary team (hence the name 'Plant'), he could transform the team from a state of mediocrity to one of high achievement.

This could only occur, of course, when the team was willing to listen to his ideas and use his creative talents. There is a widespread conviction in the management literature that most teams have a need for the Plant. They are, however, in short supply and that may partly explain why many organisational teams are no more than average performers. Not surprisingly, their perceptions of performance may be unrealistically high, but that may be explained by virtue of the fact they may compare themselves with equally mediocre teams.

We have already outlined the key contribution that the Monitor Evaluator makes. The presence of the role is probably as essential as that of the Plant. The role is central to some of the key purposes of teams: processing complex information, sifting ideas for flaws and relevance to the key purpose, and selecting the optimum solution. The presence of someone with the necessary critical analysis capabilities should ensure that high-quality decisions emerge.

The other roles may be described as important contributory elements to effective teams, but not critical. It is more than useful to have the other roles represented once. For example, teams need a disciplined approach to task performance and meeting targets. The Completer and the Implementer are the key exponents of these roles. Similarly, the chances of a congenial working environment and relatively harmonious relationships are higher in the presence of a Team Worker. Without these roles, the onus may fall on others to engage in compensatory activity.

Belbin has recently extended his notion of the ideal team to account for different stages in team activities. In other words, certain roles are more vital at certain stages than others. For example, when a team is going through the process of setting project direction or establishing needs, a Coordinator or Shaper is essential. When they reach the stage of actual planning, however, a Monitor Evaluator is invaluable. Below is a list of particular roles which may be essential at different stages of the task.

Direction and needs: Coordinator, Shaper
Ideas: Plant, Resource Investigator
Plans: Coordinator, Monitor Evaluator
Contracts: Resource Investigator, Team Worker
Organisation: Implementer, Coordinator
Follow through: Completer, Implementer

Regardless of their roles, all team members need to develop. We now examine how team members might improve their roles to enhance overall team effectiveness.

Developing Team Members' Roles

Developing the work of the team through individuals' roles involves, first, an understanding of what the roles involve, and, second, planned strategies to help individuals either to improve their prime preferred roles or to learn roles that are comparatively new to them.

The notes below are designed as an aid to understanding the key elements of the roles, and they suggest how those individuals adopting them might improve their performance and thereby their contribution to the team. While reading the descriptions, it should be remembered that it is not the aim to eliminate role weaknesses, as these, in many cases, may actually be strengths.

Coordinator

As Wynn and Guditus (1984: 101) note in referring to managers in participative systems, the leader's role is one of designing, monitoring and regulating the decision-making structure, rather than making terminal decisions. From this point of view, it is clear that the Co-ordinator has a responsibility to be well organised and to coordinate the contributions of others. Indeed, the coordinating role demands that interventions are best limited to paraphrasing, summaries and the occasional personal contribution, which should be skilfully timed. Providing summaries is a particularly useful contribution to the team, because it helps to tie together all the important points in an easy-to-understand package.

Long periods of time should be spent listening, followed by summaries of the discussion. Even though the Coordinator may have strong personal opinions, an open mind is desirable and it should be accepted that some people may have unusual, even eccentric, ideas. One of the key duties is to ensure that each individual's capabilities are discovered and used.

With this in mind, delegation is an important part of the role. It should be noted, however, that only real responsibilities should be delegated, those that offer a challenge to the individuals concerned. It is not part of the Coordinator's remit to merely dish out work as a way of offloading tedious chores.

Common activities of effective team leaders are those of 'searching' and 'polling' (Ends and Page, 1977: 179). In the former, clarification of suggestions is sought and additional information requested. The purpose of that activity is to secure a better understanding of the issues involved for all team members. 'Polling' involves seeking expressions of feeling about issues in order to decide if there is enough support to continue discussion.

The Coordinator needs to learn incisiveness. When the discussion has gone on for long enough, and all relevant issues have been covered, there should be purposeful movement towards a decision. The role also demands an ability to search for consensus where the situation demands it, rather than to rely on simple vote-taking.

Two of the key features of the role are integrating and coordinating. These are referred to as part of 'linking' by Margerison and McCann (1989: 34), and imply an awareness about team activities, but the Coordinator should not become over-involved. Linking involves knowing when to intervene, how to obtain feedback, how to handle the political elements, and how to establish high levels of collaboration. The same authors identify a list of 'linking' skills, and these are probably highly relevant to the Coordinator's role:

- Listening before reaching decisions.
- Keeping team members informed.
- Being responsive to individuals' problems.
- Helping develop role balance in the team.
- Discovering capabilities and allocating work accordingly.
- Encouraging respect, understanding and trust.
- Delegating appropriately.
- Agreeing high-quality standards.
- Setting achievable targets.
- Coordinating and representing team members.
- Involving members in key issue problem solving.

Margerison and McCann (1985: 52) also list another key skill, that of keeping track of the discussion's time dimension. For example, some team members may have their point of reference in the past, while others are talking about the future. Focusing on how problems have arisen is clearly in the past time dimension, and if others are dwelling on potential solutions, their reference is to the future. The Coordinator, therefore, may need to ensure that the conversation focuses on the appropriate time dimension, and this is what the authors describe as a conversational linking skill.

If the Coordinator is also leader of the team (this is by no means always the case), there may be a tendency to dominate discussions. The problem can be made worse if he is also the 'ideas' person. Meetings can become solo performances and this will do little to support the effectiveness of the team. Sometimes, there may be a need for the Coordinator to bite his tongue and to make a conscious effort to listen, letting others do most of the talking, and drawing quiet members into the discussion.

The Coordinator should learn to:

- organise well;
- listen and summarise;
- discover others' abilities and use them;
- move others to making decisions;
- gain consensus;
- coordinate resources;
- consult and delegate responsibilities;
- exercise personal self-discipline;
- encourage others.

Shaper

As a directive type of leader, the Shaper is responsible for giving drive, enthusiasm and clear direction to the team. Like the Coordinator, though, a coordination role is essential, and the Shaper may have to work at developing the associated skills. He should recognise how each individual can contribute to team success and avoid at all costs ignoring and treating individuals insensitively in his enthusiasm to complete the task.

Being quite objective, the Shaper can stop people getting carried away with their ideas, especially those ideas that are detached from the real purpose. Target setting techniques can be used to ensure that tasks stay on line. It may be difficult for the Shaper to listen and to recognise the contributions of others, but a conscious effort must be made to afford realistic involvement to team members and to make them feel an important part of the team's success.

The Shaper should learn to:

- give clear direction to the team;
- coordinate members' contributions;
- set up appropriate control mechanisms;
- use members' abilities;
- keep discussions on line;
- employ target setting;
- listen to others and support them;
- keep team goals in sight;
- establish priorities.

Plant

The Plant is the 'ideas person', and it needs to be recognised that this person's creativity is a key ingredient in the team's success. Improvement might be made, however, by making ideas more focused. Such focus may point to the need for effort to be directed at the problems which the team is having real difficulties in solving, rather than the peripheral or personally preferred issues. The Plant may also need to develop a thick skin, since some teams may be extremely critical about new ideas, and can easily discourage creative suggestions.

If the Plant also leads the group, conscious effort may have to be made to listen to others. In many ways, it is preferable for the leader to be someone other than the occupant of the Plant role, since it is easy for the organisational and team responsibilities to form a source of distraction; the key contribution is idea generation and that should take prime place.

The Plant should learn to:

- focus ideas on relevant issues;
- concentrate on problems that are hard to solve;
- listen to other views;
- time contributions carefully.

Monitor Evaluator

As the 'brains' of the team, it is the Monitor Evaluator's role to simplify complex issues for team colleagues and to analyse ideas in order to ensure they are related to the team's primary task and that they are workable. The role also involves evaluating potential solutions to problems and ensuring that the best option is selected. There is a danger of becoming too critical, however, and some colleagues may become inhibited, while others may try to compete. The Monitor Evaluator should be encouraged, therefore, to listen to members' suggestions and then build on them rather than knock them down as a first response. In this respect, learning to keep an open mind and considering each contribution on its merits are vital attributes.

It is useful if the Monitor Evaluator can develop a friendship with the creative team member, if there is one. The two working collaboratively can be a powerful force for team success.

As a team leader, the role demands some patience and the effort to avoid being over-critical. Nevertheless, it is part of the role to spot weak ideas and to avoid letting them slip through the net, and this can be done effectively by encouraging critical analysis from others and letting them identify the flaws first.

The Monitor Evaluator should learn to:

- make sense of complicated issues;
- put ideas in simple language to aid understanding;
- look for weaknesses in ideas and assess practicability;
- put problem solutions in rank order;
- listen to colleagues and make constructive remarks;
- work with the 'ideas person';
- help others identify weaknesses.

Implementer

This is the hardworking, reliable colleague, very down-to-earth and practical. Although he likes things neatly laid out and with clear targets, it is best not to criticise those with less tidy minds, and especially those who feed in the creative, if unrealistic, suggestions. In this respect, the Implementer may need to develop flexibility and an acceptance that there may be better ways of doing things.

The most significant contribution that can be made is helping colleagues with the practicalities and keeping a watchful eye on quality and targets. It is also necessary to be pragmatic and advise colleagues about what is realistically possible in terms of planned goals and targets. This can be effected by ensuring targets are clearly defined and that individuals are aware of their responsibilities.

The Implementer should learn to:

- be flexible and accept different ways of working;
- listen to new ideas;
- help colleagues with practicalities;
- define targets and responsibilities.

Team Worker

As we saw earlier, the Team Worker is the harmoniser and relationship healer. It may involve mediating-type activity, such as reconciling differences in points of view and arriving at compromise solutions that are acceptable to disputing parties. The role may also involve conciliatory-type activity, by defusing potentially damaging conflict episodes, and this may be done with the use of humour.

The role demands impartiality, especially when personal disputes surface, and the ability to divert personal criticisms amongst members into task related conflict. It also demands a friendly and supportive attitude, and the willingness to listen and compliment people on their suggestions.

It is as the maintainer of harmony that the Team Worker makes the greatest contribution. The role necessitates the confrontation of conflict, even in those difficult situations when people have cut off communication with one another. In such circumstances, effective counselling skills may be invaluable.

Support can also be given to the team by taking an interest in individuals, something which is seldom done very well. The Team Worker can find out about people's interests and abilities, and can promote these in the team setting. He can help individuals in various ways, by making contacts for them (not the exclusive domain of the Resource Investigator) and by seeking resources. These 'encouraging' activities are described as a 'group process service' by Ends and Page (1977: 180).

The Team Worker is usually seen as low profile and doing a very effective job behind the scenes, but as leader, he has to learn to play on people's strengths and to help them develop as individuals. This may be achieved through skilful delegation.

Petrock (1990: 9), interestingly, implies that the role might be enacted by more than a minority. Indeed, it may be possible for most team members to learn how to support the ideas of others, how to acknowledge contributions, how to relieve interpersonal tension, and sometimes how to energise the group. There is, no doubt, a strong case for trying to improve the interpersonal skills of all team members.

The Team Worker should learn to:

- be friendly and supportive to individuals;
- nip destructive comments in the bud;
- heal relationship breakdowns;
- discover members' interests and abilities;
- consider individual development needs.

Resource Investigator

This role is the link with the world outside the team. A good network of contacts may need to be built up and there should also be efforts to discover how other teams doing similar work operate. Examples of good practice can be observed, for instance. Appropriate materials should be read and he should keep up to date in the field of expertise. Information acquired needs to be disseminated to the team.

Contributions should be clearly related to the team's purpose and care should be taken that the Resource Investigator does not get locked into the social world, which can be a source of distraction. At the same time, the role demands a talent for establishing friendship and productive contacts, and this can easily be wasted through over-regulated time constraints. Being good in developing personal relationships means the Resource Investigator can be used also to help maintain harmony in the team, and this can be done by showing support and encouragement.

Hastings *et al.* (1986: 98), in referring to the role which technical specialists might play, seem to identify such members with the typical Resource Investigator activities. The following description is also apt advice for those who have this role responsibility or preference:

> The members who are technical specialists value their contacts with other specialists and those who use their services. Not only that, they go out and talk to people. They have the skills to develop relationships and build mutual respect and confidence by translating and explaining their specialism to others. They are also eager to find out in broad terms the expertise that other specialists have to offer. They see all the other specialists in their team not as boffins or blockages, but as resources that may help them or the team do the job better. These members' attitude is to 'find out – not keep out'.

Team leaders may often be Resource Investigators and the items of advice above apply to both leaders and team members who possess this external orientation.

The Resource Investigator should learn to:
- build up friendships and contacts;
- find out what other teams are doing;
- discover good practice and investigate it;
- keep up to date in the team's area of concern;
- keep the team informed;
- focus on the team's purpose;
- be supportive and encouraging to team colleagues.

Completer

The Completer is the perfectionist, but so is the Implementer to a certain extent. The essential difference is that the former makes sure that everything is finished on time. He can act as the team's major control mechanism by keeping an eye on progress and standards of performance. Shoddy work should not be accepted, and although there may be pressure to meet deadlines, optimum quality should be sought. Encouragement can be given to team members to keep up with schedules and targets, but they should not be 'nagged' to the point of annoyance. The role involves watching out for mistakes, and although there is a concern about quality and deadlines, it is imperative to avoid letting the finer points of detail become more important than the overall task.

As a leader, the Completer can keep the team well focused on the task and he should be purposeful in seeing things through to completion. There is a temptation to check everything personally and to become involved in error correction, but it is better to apply good delegation principles and trust others to do the work, otherwise damage to team morale may occur.

The Completer should learn to:

- keep an eye on progress and standards;
- communicate expectations about quality work;
- spot mistakes;
- give encouragement to colleagues;
- avoid being submerged in trivial details;
- delegate well.

Specialist

As the expert in technical or professional areas, the Specialist is the one who provides advice and information in very focused areas. He needs to be careful that he does not become impatient if other team members fail to grasp technical intricacies or misunderstand complex explanations. It is because Specialists have such highly developed expertise that they risk explaining concepts too quickly or using too much technical jargon, which confuses other team members.

Due to the technical nature and sometimes intermittent membership in the team, Specialists can become anxious to get their views across and unwittingly communicate this anxiety to the rest of the team. Additionally, because of their specialised role and the fact that they may not be a permanent part of the team, they may misinterpret other members' reactions or feel they are being ignored and be tempted to 'switch off'.

The Specialist should learn to:

- simplify complex concepts;
- communicate effectively;
- be patient with other members.

Related Issues

Those in a position to select the members of teams might well note that "their ability to contribute to the workings of the team needs to be considered just as much as their specialist technical skills" (Hastings et al., 1986: 99).

In our book *Making Management Work* we recorded a case which illustrated the danger of believing that the best 'experts' automatically lead to successful outcomes. It is worth repeating briefly here. A government department decided some radical changes were needed in the higher education provision. A team was set up to re-structure the service. It comprised some of the leading 'brains' in the land with no one holding less than professorial status. They were all very clever, but no one was particularly creative. The outcome was disappointing and in no way radical. It involved calling one institution a different name and moving a few departments round, but the proposed solution failed to deal with the fundamental personnel shortage and the inbuilt access problems to the higher education service.

To relate this to our previous discussion on role preferences, the team may have comprised primarily Monitor Evaluators, Implementers or Specialists. There seemed to be insufficient balance to produce anything like a worthwhile outcome. Had there been a Plant in the team, the result of their work may have been somewhat different, but that assumes that the other members would accept his contribution. Buhler and McCann (1989: 26) support the view that lack of innovatory talent may explain such inadequate performance:

> It is in the more established corporations and government bureaucracies that this member of the management team is often missing. Many of the managers in these situations often feel that their size and mass alone will be sufficient to maintain leadership. But the lessons learned by megapowers proves otherwise.

Putting together people who are all of one type, whether in terms of technical skills or role denomination, can be problematic. The need for balance comes up frequently in the teams literature. For instance, Chance (1989: 22) talks about differences in personality balancing other team members' weaknesses. He refers to 'thinking' types being able to analyse and organise information, and also being able to spot the flaws in arguments and acting accordingly. But they have the weakness of not being able to enthuse others, and they also fail to identify when a product will appeal to customers and to know how to market it. 'Feeling' types, in contrast, have these skills. Hurst *et al.* (1989: 92) also take up the issue of balance in relation to top management teams and the handling of the creative process. Referring to 'cognitive preferences', they imply the need for the presence of intuition (possibilities and patterns, ideas), feeling (people and values), thinking (cause and effect things), and sensation (activities, events) in the team, and these are provided by different individuals.

We have mentioned the need for functional specialisms in the team. The specialist problem raises particular concerns, however, about protective behaviours: "Those very specialisms provide problems for teams because the members' attitudes to their own and other specialisms often prevent the team from performing to its full potential" (Hastings *et al.*, 1986: 98). Despite these problems, it is often necessary for a team to have a Specialist to assist with technical problems. However, they tend to work better with some roles than others. For example, a Specialist works well with an Implementer, Coordinator or Team Worker in charge and with Implementers or Team Workers as colleagues or subordinates. Conversely, they are generally unhappy having a Shaper or Resource Investigator as a 'boss' or a Plant as a colleague or a subordinate. Often, because of their respective disciplines' technical training, they have difficulty in dealing with the creative and, at times, 'off-beam' Plant.

Whilst there may often be a real need for creativity in the team, it seems that there can also be too much of it. An earlier example about a team of architects illustrated this point. It can happen in such fields of employment as research and development units and design offices. In such cases, groups of often highly creative people have to learn to work together and to develop supportive behaviours towards their colleagues. Some, of course, have learned these behaviours and delight in having other creative people around (like a group of ensemble musicians), whilst others see themselves in competition and engage in seemingly irrational behaviours. There are also situations where creative people are actually formed into teams and the results are less than satisfactory. There may be much confusion as they each struggle to find their niche. A useful strategy in these situations may be to give each person clearly defined areas of responsibility.

Teams are generally formed based on specialist knowledge, experience or status. They have credibility. Few dispute their membership or right to operate. Their achievements are usually within the bounds of acceptability. On the whole, it may be difficult to dismantle them. Even when one person leaves, he is replaced by someone who meets similar membership criteria. They seldom achieve anything exceptional, and that may be because they have neither a Plant nor a Monitor Evaluator. They seldom have winning ideas and the ones they do think of are not put to the test of critical scrutiny. They are neither creative nor clever but are possibly seen as 'good people' who have worked their way through the system, always avoiding controversy or causing upset, and generally being good and loyal organisational servants. Essentially, they are conformists. The problem of conformity, though, is identified by Dyer (1980: 181): "We find that if a person is to get along best in these situations he remains submissive, obedient and conforming, dependent, and is encouraged to use only a few of his skills." The problems associated with conformity are addressed in Chapter 16.

Our observations lead us to believe there may be many management teams in organisations comprising almost solely Implementers. It is hardly surprising that the output is mediocre. Individuals are caught in the involvement-submission trap. On the one hand, they may want to be involved in planning their actions, but if they do, conflicts may arise about goals, targets and procedures. They then resort to looking for instructions and directives so that they can put the onus of responsibility on others. Such conformity hardly supports elevated team performance and is more likely to lead to passivity.

A balanced team is likely to be successful because it has the presence of key roles. Intuitively, it seems that a good Coordinator who is skilled in most aspects of the Coordinator's role, a Plant and a Monitor Evaluator can provide the nucleus of a high-performing team. These roles, therefore, are central. Very often, if a few influential team members provide these roles, the team may be successful despite the role gaps and inadequacies amongst the other team members.

A small number of teams are enigmatic. The analysis of roles may suggest that creativity is not present and that there is little balance. Yet they may perform in an outstanding way. The reasons are difficult to explain, but participants often ascribe their success to their capacity to get on well with one another and to gain 'excitement' from being part of a team. There are considerably many more teams with similar membership to those above, but which perform disastrously, so success in this case may have to be a phenomenon which remains unexplained.

Harris (1986: 29) perhaps has part of the answer. Acknowledging the need to achieve complementarity of roles to enjoy success, he adds: "To raise team performance beyond the sum of individual member efforts, a team culture must also be created – one that promotes team spirit, energizes people, promotes cooperation among members and with other organizational teams."

Shifting Importance

Referring to renewal in management teams, Hurst *et al.* (1989: 95) raise the interesting issue of shifting role importance. They suggest there are stages of operation where different roles should assume the dominant influence. This makes sense in other team contexts. Different phases may demand different 'cognitive' inputs, and the needs of the situation should determine the type of influence on the other team. There are times when creativity is needed, especially in the early stage of a problem-solving episode; at other times, the need is for critical analysis, and here, a different role might predominate. "Like strands in a tapestry, now in the front, now in the back, individuals on the team together weave a cognitive fabric, the pattern of which will express their version of a renewed organizational reality."

Role Suppression

The same authors also introduce the notion of role suppression. Through analysis, it may be found that the required preferred roles exist among members, but they are not enacted for one of several possible reasons. Such reasons may include cultural norms (either in the team or the organisation as a whole), power relationships and the reward system. There was a not unusual case, for example, of an individual who, in department meetings, carried out a worthwhile role of questioning policies and identifying the flaws in current practices (Monitor Evaluator). This behaviour was largely condemned by a rigid and traditional leadership, and the individual concerned failed to obtain a much deserved promotion. This led to avoidance behaviour by keeping quiet in meetings – role suppression.

This is unlikely to be helpful to either the organisation or the team. The authors suggest a change of context may help to legitimise suppressed behaviours, if that is the intention. Using such tools as Outdoor Management Development may provide a dramatically different context, which may present an opportunity for preferences, previously suppressed in the work team context, to surface.

Maturity

In Chapter 19, we shall look at the notion of developmental stages, where teams move from a raw state to one of maturity and high performance. It is worth noting that it is likely to be in the later stages, what we have called 'achieving', and what in a different framework is called 'norming' (Petrock, 1990: 9), that members are able to settle in productive roles for the team and to learn to develop them. This assumes, of course, that the team, or its leader, does not set norms that suppress and inhibit role performance.

The subject of team roles is one to be taken seriously. Hurst *et al.* (1989: 103), for example, assert that role (or cognitive) preferences are sufficiently powerful to determine top management team strategy: as these preferences vary, so too does the strategy. Belbin's research has also suggested that team composition has a considerable impact on performance, and the more critical the team is to organisational success, the more economic sense it makes to do something about getting the role balance right.

First, team leaders and members can analyse their preferred roles and learn how to improve their behavioural contributions to the team. Second, some role redistribution can take place where necessary, and if the membership is likely to change in the near future, considerations other than technical expertise can be accounted for in selection. As Hurst *et al.* (1989: 103) confirm, role preferences could be used as a partial basis for team selection and development, and this is reinforced by Watts (1988: 102) who similarly advocates the recruitment of those whose preferred roles might complement and enhance the team. Third, teams can be assessed against those described in the above discussion. For example, some important questions may need to be asked. Is membership simply based on status and experience? Does the team comprise solely people with analytical minds or who are high on creativity? Is the team reasonably successful but still missing that 'spark' characteristic of great teams? Answers to these questions may help in building up teams that are high-achieving and successful in meeting the needs of the organisation and the satisfaction of their members.

The need, as we have seen, is to have diversity and difference in the team. It is more than that, however. As Hurst *et al.* (1989: 103) note: "Difference without synthesis is anarchy. The organization and its members must also have the ability to achieve unity from diversity, the ability to transcend."

Summary

In this chapter, we have explained the significance of individual roles on team performance and demonstrated how preferred roles might be identified and developed. After detailing the nine roles developed by Belbin, we attempted to show how these roles might be used in combination to build an effective team.

Summary of the Implications for Managers

- People with innovatory talents need to be sought out and their special skills need to be supported and used. They can contribute enormously to team success.

- A balanced team is more likely to be effective than one that is homogeneous in terms of individual roles. It may be necessary, in order to achieve balance, to ask some members to adopt secondary roles, and the appropriate behaviours can be learnt and developed. If there is no one in the team who naturally evaluates ideas critically, it is important to encourage someone to play 'devil's advocate' and this can be done on a rotating basis. The member concerned presents contrary opinions, argues things out from the opponent's viewpoint, and identifies unplanned results of decisions and actions. In some circumstances, it may be necessary to 'buy in' certain skills, and this is particularly so where there is an absence of creativity and where innovation is crucial to team success.

- Still on the theme of balance, the three key roles are Coordinator, Plant and Monitor Evaluator. A highly successful team can be built around these, and other team members can adopt supporting roles. Individuals should be encouraged to develop the key features of their preferred roles in support of the team, but it may also be wise in some situations to take the roles issue into account when selecting team members.

11

COMMUNICATION AND RELATIONSHIPS

MOST TEAMS spend the vast majority of their time engaged directly in some form of communication. There can be little credence given to any team effort if communication is neglected or if positive relationships among members are absent. The issue of communication is a very broad area, but here, we focus on the relevance of effective communication to successful team operation. We are largely concerned with verbal and aural communication between team members, although reading and writing skills are important at certain times. In this chapter, we discuss communication in tandem with relationships, because we believe open, honest and productive relationships are dependent on effective communication.

Communication

The ability of a group to accomplish its purpose depends largely on the capability of its members to communicate with each other effectively. Interpersonal communications are the cornerstone for effective team planning, problem solving, action, reflection, and evaluation (Snyder, 1988: 209).

Thamhain (1990: 16) notes that poor communication is a major barrier to effective team operation and innovative performance, and that the free flow of communication in all directions and throughout the team is of vital importance.

According to Wynn and Guditus (1984: 74) communication is "the process of exchanging information, beliefs and feelings among people; it may be oral, written, or nonverbal. Information may travel up, down or horizontally. It permeates every aspect of management and organizational life. The more complex an organization, the more critical communication becomes." Rees (1988: 126) reinforces the importance of communication:

> Even when they (managers) are working alone – for example, studying or preparing reports – they are relying on other people's attempts to communicate with them or they are preparing to communicate with others. Accuracy in decision making depends, in particular, on effective communication. If the communication process is faulty then everything else can be affected.

As a starting point, it is useful to evaluate the quality of communication in the team, asking such questions as:

- How easy is it to get information from other members?
- Do team members consider one another's viewpoints ?
- Do they give information willingly?
- Do team members know what their colleagues think about their contribution?
- Do team members consider one another's feelings?
- Are they guarded and keep their conversations restricted to the job?

These, and other questions, may help to reveal strengths and inadequacies in the team's communication, which may have an impact on cohesiveness and morale. They obviously raise questions about communication patterns: Is there one-way traffic? Are conversations two-way between, say, leader and members? Or is the communication pattern multidirectional, with every member able to interact with all other members?

Ends and Page (1977: 153) provide a list of five characteristics the leader can display that might have a positive effect on the quality of team communication. They are honesty, openness, constructiveness, adultness, and respect. We have discussed some of these characteristics in looking at the leader's role in the team.

Snyder (1988: 209) suggests that most people have received little or no training in communication. Some are from fields where role isolation precludes frequent interaction. She advises, therefore, that conscious attention should be given to the learning of essential skills for cooperative production. What are these skills? Adair (1986: 18) gives a hint of some of the important features in describing the corner-stones of effective speaking as clarity, simplicity, vividness, prepared-ness, naturalness and conciseness, and he describes the good listener as one who looks on listening as a positive, searching, active and cooperative activity. With these points in mind, we would suggest the following items of advice provide a basis on which skilful communication can be built:

- Encode messages in terms that are easily understood by the receiver.
- Use specific examples rather than vague generalities.
- Use simple, clear language.
- Think about and construct the message before sending it.
- Check understanding with the receiver.
- When listening, concentrate and make mental summaries.
- Avoid evaluating the message until it has been completed.
- In the team setting, occasionally summarise what is being said to check for accuracy (paraphrase).
- Ask clarifying questions to check understanding.

Margerison and McCann (1985: 49) discuss some of these points and give advice on enhancing communication. They refer to 'conversational control' – "the ability to identify what others have said and to make an appropriate response in terms of resolving the problems and helping to get the work done". They deal with a number of related skills, like focusing on specifics and discussing problems before solutions. They also look at the important component skill of summarising messages succinctly. What summaries do "is to let the other person know that you recognise, understand and appreciate what they say and do. Most people are usually more willing to help if they feel you understand, appreciate and recognise their position and views" (p. 53).

Snyder (1988: 209) refers to 'in-and-out listening', a technique of listening attentively to others in the team, but at the same time recording one's own thoughts. Since the thought processes are con-siderably faster than speech, there is time to work out personal ideas and listen at the same time. She also outlines the need to para-phrase regularly, since "group participation is nurtured as members build, add on, or refine someone's contribution". Like Margerison and McCann, she identifies distinct benefits in providing these types of summaries, as they communicate to the other person that their contributions are valued, and this leads to motivation and continued involvement in the dialogue. Wynn and Guditus (1984: 82) too advocate probing and paraphrasing, and, drawing on the work of an eminent psychologist, state that such behaviour "will reduce the insincerities, exaggeration, lies, and false fronts that characterise almost every failure in communication. Probing for deeper meaning can be con-tagious: as one person drops defensiveness, others tend to reciprocate and probe for deeper meaning also".

We mentioned in the list of skills the need to delay before evalua-ting. Yet there is a common tendency to ascribe values to what is communicated before it is completely understood. This causes accurate communication to break down. The advice in the literature is to listen, restate the ideas and feelings of the other person, obtain feed-back on the accuracy of those interpretations, and then evaluate.

Much of what is said above clearly indicates that successful communication has to be a reciprocal, two-way process. It is one thing to make a message clear, another to ensure the understanding and acceptance of the receiver. Several of the skills outlined help to check on these elements and enable follow-up action.

Skills can be developed in communication, but some team-building strategies take communication development a stage further and emphasize other ingredients of effective interaction. The interpersonal model of teambuilding we referred to earlier, for example, aims to establish an effective communication system within the team, and this is done by team members following a set of rules of interaction (Anantaraman, 1984b: 225). It is useful to look briefly at these rules, since they provide a basis for the development of highly productive communication. They include:

1. frank expressions of feelings;
2. restating ideas and feelings when emotions are running high. This involves summarising, perception checking and negotiating for meaning;
3. self-disclosing relevant past experiences;
4. giving reciprocal support;

5. listening with empathy and not evaluating;
6. confronting responsibly;
7. inviting individuals to self-examine behaviour;
8. making the past relevant to the present;
9. illustrating points with examples.

An explanation of these rules is given by Anantaraman (p. 225). Although they refer to a special process of relationship development, they give some indication of how communication might be heightened, opening up channels for interaction. This takes us back to the issue of openness, and it may be argued there needs to be openness in communication if the team is to operate satisfactorily. In terms of communication, openness is concerned with the free expression of opinions, ideas and feelings about tasks and processes. Openness in communication is vital in allowing the team to use the knowledge, skills and abilities present in the team.

The openness of communication is closely linked to other elements. For example, if communication is poor and guarded, there will be little cohesiveness. This may result in low morale which inevitably has an effect on performance.

Probably the best pattern of communication to aim for is that shown in Figure 11.1, which clearly shows an open flow of interaction. Each member communicates freely with others and there are no missing links. If one or more lines are missing, communication is incomplete and this may lead to dysfunctions. The pattern is particularly effective when tasks

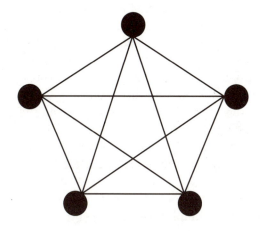

Figure 11.1   The Ideal Communication Pattern

are complex and require specialist and diverse inputs. It has a capacity for verifying and interpreting information. The star pattern also gives rise arguably to increased member satisfaction and higher levels of team morale.

Listening

As simple as it sounds, listening is perhaps the most important communication skill of all. If team members do not listen to one another, it is unlikely they will develop and maintain good relationships or solve problems creatively. The first step when 'learning to listen' is to make a conscious decision to take note of what other members are saying, fighting the temptation to drift off into private thoughts. This is called becoming an 'active listener'. The listener needs to ask questions to clarify understanding, use body language which communicates attention, and paraphrase key points made by the speaker. This not only makes for better understanding, but also shows the other person he is being given undivided attention.

Guidelines for increasing listening skills are interrelated, but require considerable effort on the part of the listener. Widely recognised guidelines include the following:

- There must be a purpose for listening. Ineffective listeners tend to make quick decisions about what is being said and 'switch off' fairly quickly if it does not fit in with their interests. Good listeners, on the other hand, look for meaning and value in what is being said, even if it is of no obvious interest to them.
- Rushed judgements about the message should not be made. Good listeners try to concentrate on the entire message rather than make judgements on scattered pieces of information.
- There should be a focus on the person who is talking and an attempt to block out any distractions.
- The message should be rephrased to ensure understanding.
- The speaker's feelings should be accepted.
- It is advisable to pause before offering a response.
- The whole message should be listened to. It may include content and feeling.
- Positive interest should be shown in what the speaker is saying.
(Brownwell, 1986; Dunphy, 1989: 118, Hitt, 1988: 133; Rees, 1988: 138)

Much of what we have read shows that communication must be active in both directions. This thought leads us into a brief discussion of one aspect of such a reciprocal process, that of feedback.

Feedback

One of the important concepts in relation to communication is that of feedback. Todryk (1990: 19) observes that when a team is not performing very well, feedback is critical. If members have learned how to give and receive feedback, relationships will not be harmed and the team can improve its performance through a process of self-criticism. If the process is handled well, there is encouragement to change. If it is done badly, it can result in a retreat to behaviours that maintain a feeling of security.

It is worth looking at feedback, since it may be used in both the team's normal operations and also in team development activities. Anantaraman (1984b: 226) presents an explanation of three conditions for effective feedback:

1. Understanding
2. Acceptance
3. Ability to act

To enable the receiver to understand, feedback should be specific, it should describe the person's behaviour, and it should be given immediately. The sooner the results of a performance or behaviour are known, the faster the individual can learn.

To gain acceptance for the content of the feedback, it should be responsible, indicating care and concern; descriptive, rather than evaluative; appropriately timed when the receiver is psychologically ready; and it should be valid. This last point is especially relevant when the feedback is negative.

Feedback, of course, is of value only if action can follow. It makes sense, therefore, that it focuses on behaviours that can be modified, and is restricted to several important areas. Karp (1987) reinforces some of these points and provides some basic principles for effective feedback.

- Feedback should be clear and specific, rather than general.
- Feedback must be based on trust and openness.
- Feedback should be discussed with the person receiving it to ensure it is on track and useful.

- Feedback should not include more than the receiver can handle at any particular time.
- Feedback should be timed for when the person is ready to receive it.
- Feedback should include mainly items which the person can do something about.

The mark of high achievers in the team context is that they know how to learn from feedback. They want to know what they are doing well or badly, they want it expressed in precise (often quantifiable) terms, and they want to know immediately. They have learned how to use their experience to improve their performance. Put another way, they have discovered basically how to coach themselves.

Coaching

We now turn our attention briefly to a performance issue closely related to communication, that of coaching. The essence of coaching is based on two central principles. One, the individual must actually want to improve performance. Like the athlete who seeks out a coach who will help him to improve his time or distance, the individual team member must want the coach to help him improve the quality of his contribution to the team effort. This first principle is based on the assumption that the member is capable of higher performance. It also assumes that he simply does not know how to improve. The second principle is fairly self-evident: it is that both the coach and the member must be convinced that the coach can help to improve the other person's performance .

The coach (who may or may not be the leader) may have some idea of the desired level of performance and is aiming to lessen the discrepancy between the desired and the actual levels. It is important, therefore, to be clear about the desired level and be able to define it. Obviously, the performance must be directly related to the team's task and must be realistically attainable. Goals must be set, and they must be defined, understood and accepted by both parties.

Ends and Page (1977: 91) provide a useful coaching checklist which raises some of the important coaching-related issues:

1. Do team members believe they need the knowledge or skill to be developed?
2. Do they understand precisely what is needed?

3. Do they want to acquire the skill?
4. Will they be able to hold personal responsibility for the outcome?
5. Are the goals realistic but challenging?
6. Will the coaching situation provide immediate and objective feedback as a guide to performance?

What are the skills involved in coaching? First, it is useful sometimes, although not essential, if the task can be demonstrated. There is a mistaken belief that the coach has to do this himself. This is not necessary, and it may even be undesirable if the coach is not able to demonstrate exemplary performance. Others can be used for demonstration purposes. Second, the coach must understand how to set performance goals and how to measure progress towards them. Third, like the sports coach, he must be able to detect errors in performance and explain how to correct them. But skill in this aspect means more than simply identifying defects: it involves distinguishing between what is important and what is not, and then prioritising the deficiencies for remedial action. Finally, the coach must have skill in providing accurate and supportive feedback, and this necessitates at least a rudimentary understanding of the central tenets of motivation.

For coaching to be effective, it makes sense that people need to be able to relate to one another well and to communicate accurately and sensitively. This demands a degree of interpersonal competence, and we now turn our attention briefly to the much talked about issue of relationships.

Interpersonal Relationships

The relationships between members of the team is a subject that receives much attention in the teambuilding literature, and it is true to say that the ability of people to relate well to one another has a considerable impact on team processes and the capacity of the team to work productively. Relationships, it might be argued, should be perceived to be supportive by all team members.

Establishing these sorts of relationships demands the development of skills. There are many who are not used to working in a team environment and have not acquired the communicative and co-operative skills needed. Task-related skills may be present, but a good team is also interpersonally competent and promotes the acquisition and use of interpersonal and small group skills.

The skills required in establishing a healthy relationship climate are quite diverse, and so are the typical actions. They may include being flexible when there are domestic difficulties, putting in extra time to help a team colleague finish some work, making appreciative gestures when work has been done well and listening patiently. There are many more behaviours and actions that could be added to this list. The important thing to note, however, is that setting the climate is important. Good relationships are more likely to be the effects of a successful team climate and not a sole cause.

One way of helping to promote relationships through the team climate is with the use of humour, a much neglected topic in the team communication literature, but one that we believe is very important. Westcott (1988: 139) states that "humor has been described as a 'social lubricant' and plays a vital role in the support of group harmony and the communication of information". It is a relatively safe way of raising difficult problems or risky issues.

She describes (p. 141) how humour can assist group dynamics, enhance creative problem solving and relieve tension in conflict situations. She also provides a number of guidelines that may be useful for teams using humour to enhance communication and intragroup relations:

1. See the humour in the things you do yourself.
2. Take your work seriously but yourself a little more lightly.
3. Notice humour and respond to it.
4. Think of humour as having a private and public side. Public humour is shared with others when it occurs. Private humour is experienced when something happens but it is inappropriate to laugh.
5. Use humour to support competence rather than to hide a lack of it.
6. Use humour sensitively so it is likely to be appreciated.

Although seemingly peripheral, these are more than useful items of advice.

In the light of this discussion, the interpersonal climate is a vital concern. Where the climate is unhealthy, developing and maintaining good relationships may be more problematic. For example: "Where people cannot confide in or trust their manager, where they are fearful of him or where their conversations are on a superficial or trivial level, of him or where their conversations are on a superficial or trivial level, then real teamwork is unlikely to exist" (Woodcock, 1979: 5). This leads us to consider two key factors in establishing a strong, supportive team environment: trust and openness.

Trust and Openness

It is important to emphasize that trust and openness are two key ingredients, or what Anantaraman (1984b: 224) calls 'value orientations', in team operation and development. Where there are low levels of trust in a team, dysfunctional behaviours will be evident, including dishonesty, evasiveness and intolerance. Johnson and Johnson (1991: 465) note that the more team members are able to trust one another, the more effectively they will be able to cooperate as a unit:

> Team effectiveness rests on every member's sharing resources, giving and receiving help, dividing the work, and contributing to the accomplishment of mutual goals. Such behaviours will occur when there is trust that everyone is contributing to the group's progress and not using members' openness and sharing of resources for personal rather than group gain. Team members will more openly express their thoughts, feelings, reactions, opinions, information, and ideas when the trust level is high.

Apart from the team level, trust is also the essence of good relationships on a one-to-one basis. "It is a relationship in which neither party feels a need to keep defenses up. It is a relationship in which both parties are open, honest, and respectful. This creates a feeling of rapport which establishes communication and keeps the channel open for constructive influence" (Ends and Page, 1977: 54). At a practical level, this leads to supportive behaviours rather than dysfunctional ones. The latter include those described by Peterson (1991: 107), like criticising people for making simple mistakes, criticising members in public, and criticising them behind their backs. These are more associated with the absence of mutual trust.

It is evident from this that trust is essential. So is openness, which might be a sharing of information, ideas, thoughts, and even feelings. But openness can also be seen on a broader basis, incorporating the openness of the team as a unit and openness on the part of individuals in it. George (1977: 78) explains how the condition might make itself apparent: "This openness is demonstrated in a variety of ways: (a) a receptiveness to new ideas and newcomers, (b) an open sharing of information ... (c) a willingness of individuals to share their professional problems, challenges, and frustrations with others." Woodcock (1989: 86–8), on a slightly different tack, ties openness in a team setting to confrontation. He proposes that developing a climate where members are free to speak their mind leads to positive confrontation and hence higher creativity. He claims that openness and confrontation improve as certain conditions become ingrained in teams. The conditions listed below exemplify the interrelatedness of communication and relationship-building skills. In essence, openness and confrontation improve when:

- communication and feedback improve;
- individuals learn more about themselves and their colleagues;
- conflict is used constructively;
- there is an increase in active listening in the team.

It is worth asking why openness is not evident in many teams. It may be due partly to relationships still being at a superficial level, but it is also apparently missing in many teams where members know one another fairly well and have worked together for long periods of time. In such cases, it may be due to the fear of being open, the consequences of voicing opinions, of making feelings known, or of infringing someone's territorial rights. People may fear the repercussions of disagreeing with the leader and may compromise their personal interests in terms of advancement and esteem. As Schutz (1989: 8) notes, however, this is the height of organisational inefficiency because the more open the team members, the more effective is the work of the team.

Communicating in an open environment is far easier than in one where feelings and views are concealed. But communication is not always practised under ideal conditions. This suggests that communication and interpersonal skills have to be applied flexibly. This is especially true in the special case of communicating with people in order to determine their behaviour, otherwise known as 'influencing'. The next chapter shows how skills have to be applied thoughtfully and flexibly in order to achieve intended outcomes.

Before we leave communication and relationships, it is important to note that both may be further complicated if teams comprise members from diverse cultural backgrounds, something that is occurring more and more frequently. Rees (1988: 140–1) provides a good example of how varying cultural understandings and norms can be mis-interpreted. He tells of Asian males working in a factory in London:

> There was a certain amount of friction when food was being served, part of which was said by the canteen workers to be because of the surly response by the Asians when they received their food. In particular it was commented that the Asians never smiled. Their response to this was initially one of bewilderment as, in their culture, it was seen as being altogether too familiar for a man to smile at a woman he didn't know. Far from trying to create offence they had been trying to avoid it by their impassive expression.

The implications for multinational or cultural teams are fairly obvious. Members not only need to improve communication but also to attempt to understand cultural influences on various values and processes. This important issue is taken up in more detail in Chapter 18.

We have attempted to cover only a small number of narrow areas related to communication and relationships in teams. These, however, are vital to building open, trusting units. Other information about relationship building and communication can be found throughout other chapters.

Summary

In this chapter we have discussed communication with special reference to relationships. We have stressed the importance of effective communication as the basis for successful team functioning and highlighted the necessity of effective listening and feedback. Both these skills are underpinned by a climate of openness and trust. In the following chapter, we examine influence and power within the team. The link with communication and promoting healthy working relationships will be demonstrated.

Summary of the Implications for Managers

- Team members' viewpoints and feelings need to be considered if communication is to be effective. Information should be given willingly by all team members and communication should be multidirectional.

- Messages should be simple and clear, and specific examples should be used rather than vague generalisations. Team leaders should encourage their members to consider what they intend to say before actually saying it. Understanding can be checked by asking questions, and this can be supported through active listening, with members displaying a cooperative and searching attitude. People need to be trained to avoid evaluating messages too early, and leaders can enhance understanding by paraphrasing regularly and showing recognition of contributions by providing frequent summaries. Asking questions is indeed an important communication tool, and probing for deeper meaning can be contagious, helping members to eliminate defensive positions.

- Feedback is a valuable part of the communication process. In order to achieve acceptance, it must be given responsibly, showing care and concern for the member. It should also be descriptive rather than evaluative, timed well, and should be valid. Feedback is more likely to be acted on if it concentrates on those behaviours that can be modified and if it focuses on the key areas.

- For coaching to be effective, there must be a clear and realistic definition of desired performance. Goals must be defined, understood and accepted by both the coach and the team member. The skilled coach should be able to detect errors in performance and show the individual how to correct them. This means determining what is important and what is not, thereby prioritising deficiencies. If improvement is to take place, the coach must also provide accurate and supportive feedback.

- Trust and openness are two vital value orientations in teamwork and development. These inevitably lead to cooperation, which means sharing resources, giving and receiving help, and dividing work. Trust should exist at both the team level and between individuals, since this is likely to lead to supportive behaviours for the good of team goals. Such behaviours are characterised by openness, honesty, respect and the absence of defensive barriers. Such a state ensures that team members are open to constructive influence. In such conditions, members can share information, thoughts, feelings, and their reactions to issues. They can become receptive to newcomers and new ideas. They can also share professional problems, challenges and frustrations.

- Communication can become difficult if members do not attempt to account for possible cultural differences among team colleagues.

12

INFLUENCE

CURRENT MANAGEMENT THINKING has seen a move away from leadership based on a hierarchical position of authority to one based on influence and power. "Because of the increasing diversity of the goals and values of employees and their increasing interdependence, the effectiveness of formal authority is diminishing. It must be replaced by influence" (Keys and Case, 1990: 38). In this chapter we acknowledge the importance of influencing in a team setting and support the move away from traditional authority. This is because we believe simply telling a team member to do something through the power of authority is unlikely to build trust and openness, or promote creativity and positive confrontation. Additionally, influencing tactics will become increasingly important in what have been labelled 'leaderless' teams, where no one has vested formal authority. Following an introduction to and explanation of influencing, we describe various influencing strategies, appropriate strategy selection and provide advice on successful influencing.

Power and Influence in the Team Setting

"Influence entails actually securing the consent of others to work with you in accomplishing an objective" (Whetten and Cameron, 1984: 266).

In this sense, influencing can be seen as the act of determining the behaviour of others, a definition that is shared with that of 'power'. Ends and Page (1977: 53), however, suggest it should involve not only affecting the behaviour, but also thinking, attitudes and feelings. From this point of view, influencing becomes a vital skill. Indeed, the same authors equate power and influence: "The ability to influence others in this way is the basis of power in any organization. In fact, *power* and *the ability to influence the behavior of others* are interchangeable terms."

Keys and Case (1990: 38), however, contrast power with influence: "It (influence) can be contrasted with power which is a personal or positional attribute that enables one to influence others and can be thought of as 'continuing or sustained' influence." Other authors also separate authoritative or 'formal' power (the power conferred by status and position) and influence, which is generally defined as 'informal' power. Bacharach and Lawler (1980), for example, identify several distinctions between the two aspects of power. Authority is static, organisationally sanctioned, implies involuntary submission, flows in a downward direction, has a structural source, and is clearly delimited: influence is the opposite of these. From this perspective, there seems to be little other way of working in teams other than using the informal sources of power available. If such sources are to be employed effectively, however, they need to be used skilfully, and in this chapter, we examine what skill might mean in terms of the appropriate use of influencing strategies in the team context.

An important notion in relation to power in teams is that of 'reciprocity'. The team leader can exert only as much power as he allows the team to exert on him. The implication of this is clear: "When a leader is willing to consider the opinions and needs of team members to arrive at a decision or plan a course of action affecting the whole group, they will respond with strong commitment and involvement in carrying out the decision or the plan effectively" (Ends and Page, 1977: 61). This may apply equally to the interactions and flow of influence between team members themselves. This raises an important point: by a person allowing himself to be influenced, it does not result in a reduction in that person's influence over others. In short, influence is more an interactive and reciprocal method for getting things done than simply 'ordering'.

In terms of the methods of influence used, there seems to be a view amongst some individuals that there is only one way to influence people and they use that way whether it brings them success or not. It is quite common, for example, to believe that providing rational justifications for everything will ensure people comply with someone's wishes. In this case, the individual is an advocate of sound reasoning and will often use that strategy in any influencing situation. It is true that a strategy such as this may be successful for a good deal of the time, but it seems unlikely that it can be effective in every influencing situation. There is another issue and it is that of compliance. Whether compliance is synonymous with success is a debatable point, but it may be argued that an effective influencing episode is one in which compliance and *commitment* are obtained.

Influencing is a vital factor of individual behaviour in teams. People want to gain things, persuade colleagues to help them, give them more work, get them to change their minds about certain issues and a host of other outcomes. Influencing is taking place all the time. The fact is, however, that some seem to be better at it than others. Regardless of whether they have formal authority or not, they have the knack of getting what they want. They have developed a highly valued skill: that of determining others' behaviour.

Those who are less successful probably choose the wrong strategies. Kipnis *et al.* (1984) attribute this in part to habit, lack of forethought, or a wrong understanding of whether the other person is willing to comply. They also believe that people can learn to choose appropriate strategies through training and self-examination. People who are effective influencers are flexible and are able to select the optimum strategy for any situation. Even for those who have the formal power to give people orders, the ability to exercise a variety of influencing strategies seems to have greater potential for gaining cooperation and commitment from subordinate colleagues. If they choose to ignore the opinions and needs of team members, and rely on fearful obedience, the result is usually lack of commitment and involvement. It is more difficult to get people involved in activities they have no opportunity to influence.

Generally speaking, the reasons for using influence fall into five categories:

1. To obtain help with the job.
2 . To give people work to do.
3. To get something from someone.

4. To improve performance.
5. To initiate change.

The purpose for which influence is needed will in part determine the appropriate strategy. Another important factor is that of status: the position of the 'target' person in relation to the influencer. This is significant when it comes to the team leader influencing a team member (downward influence) or to a member or group of members influencing the leader (upward influence). It may also apply where people in the team are of different status and there is the acceptance that it has to be acknowledged. Such a multidirectional nature of influence is supported in the literature (Bacharach and Lawler, 1980). In many teams, however, members are generally seen as equals or peers, and the influence direction may be described as predominantly 'horizontal'. Despite this, status differences may be important considerations, because some circumstances dictate that the direction of influence determines which strategies are productive and which are ill-advised.

There are some strategies, of course, which may be effective irrespective of status. For instance, an individual may explain the reasons for wanting something to any team colleague – superior, subordinate or peer – and that is generally an acceptable influencing strategy. At the same time, it has to be recognised that single strategies are unlikely to be effective in every situation.

Kipnis et al. (1980) demonstrated through their research that specific tactics or strategies may be associated with combinations of the reason for using influence, the target of influence, and the amount of resistance shown. They showed that influence is more complex than simply choosing a strategy you like and then using it for all situations. Along similar lines, Leavitt (1978) identified the factors of self, the other person and the interaction as the key considerations.

The questionnaire 'Preferred Styles' with its accompanying scoring chart (Figures 12.1 and 12.2) is designed to give some indication of preferred behaviours, and thus helps to provide a picture of strategy preferences and influencing style.

An explanation is provided of just one framework of influencing strategies and their associated behaviours. The relative advantages and disadvantages are also explained. For this framework, we have drawn primarily on the work of Kipnis et al. (1980, 1984). The strategies are arranged in seven categories, namely: friendliness, bargaining, reasoning,

Figure 12.1   Preferred Styles

For each statement below, you are asked to indicate the extent to which it is true of you. Try to give answers which truly represent your typical behaviour rather than how you think you should behave. Circle the appropriate number for each statement. You can imagine yourself either in the team setting or in the normal work situation. It does not matter. Where the words 'team members' are used, for example, you can substitute 'colleagues' or 'subordinates', etc.

Key
0   This never applies to me.
1   This rarely applies to me.
2   This applies to me very occasionally.
3   This applies to me some of the time.
5   This applies to me most of the time.
6   This applies to me all the time.

1. If I want something doing where I cannot force the issue,   0 1 2 3 5 6
    I try to make my colleague team member feel important.

2. I like to check up on my team members with surprise visits.   0 1 2 3 5 6

3. If I am trying to introduce a change, I write a well-reasoned   0 1 2 3 5 6
    justification.

4. Before meetings, I like to make sure I have some support   0 1 2 3 5 6
    for my ideas.

5. I am prepared to take away one of the team member's   0 1 2 3 5 6
    preferred duties to get what I want.

6. I like to be able to give something in return when a team   0 1 2 3 5 6
    member is asked to do something extra.

7. If I do not get my way with team colleagues, I take the   0 1 2 3 5 6
    matter to the boss.

8. I give people orders wherever possible: it makes life simpler. 0 1 2 3 5 6

9. I like to be seen as a friendly person and I try to get what I 0 1 2 3 5 6
    want by being friendly and acting humbly.

10. I believe that sound logical arguments should win the day.   0 1 2 3 5 6

11. I like to use meetings to raise matters formally.   0 1 2 3 5 6

12. If people don't comply with my wishes, I will make life   0 1 2 3 5 6
    difficult for them.

13. I will remind colleagues of things I have done for them when   0 1 2 3 5 6
    I want something doing now.

14. I hint that the boss supports my stance when I want a team   0 1 2 3 5 6
    colleague to comply with my wishes.

15. I give strict time deadlines when I ask for a colleague team   0 1 2 3 5 6
    member's cooperation.

16. I say something complimentary to a colleague before   0 1 2 3 5 6
    requesting something.

17. I make sure I assemble all relevant facts and information   0 1 2 3 5 6
    before trying to persuade others to do things.

18. I like to have a word with team colleagues who I know are   0 1 2 3 5 6
    on my side before raising an issue at a meeting.

19. I am prepared to put the word around about a team member   0 1 2 3 5 6
    who is uncooperative.

20. I am prepared to make personal sacrifices if someone will   0 1 2 3 5 6
    comply with my wishes.

21. If a colleague will not 'toe the line', I will ask the team   0 1 2 3 5 6
    leader or boss to step in.

22. I keep nagging colleagues until they do what I want.   0 1 2 3 5 6

23. I wait for the right time before approaching someone about   0 1 2 3 5 6
    something.

24. Before asking a colleague for help, I explain the reasons   0 1 2 3 5 6
    carefully.

25. I like to mention that others are in agreement with me   0 1 2 3 5 6
    when I make a request.

26. If I do not get my way, I threaten my non-cooperation in   0 1 2 3 5 6
    the future.

27. If a colleague will agree to do something, I offer to provide   0 1 2 3 5 6
    adequate support and training.

28. I will ask the team leader or boss to have a quiet word with   0 1 2 3 5 6
    a colleague if necessary.

29. I get a few people to support me if I am asking the team   0 1 2 3 5 6
    leader for something.

30. If I want people to do things, I mention their experience   0 1 2 3 5 6
    and abilities, and generally make them feel important.

31. I write a detailed rationale for my boss if I want to   0 1 2 3 5 6
    implement a plan.

32. I am prepared to ask my boss for a response to a request   0 1 2 3 5 6
    by a particular date.

33. I will offer to do something extra for the team leader or   0 1 2 3 5 6
    boss if he or she will meet my demands.

34. I threaten to speak to someone higher if I fail to achieve my 0 1 2 3 5 6
    objective.

35. I am prepared to go over my team leader or even boss's   0 1 2 3 5 6
    head.

36. I make myself a nuisance by continually pestering until I get 0 1 2 3 5 6
    what I want.

37. I request that the team leader or my boss takes a matter   0 1 2 3 5 6
    higher if he or she is unable to deal with it.

38. I sympathise with the difficulties which my request will   0 1 2 3 5 6
    cause the person I am asking.

39. I use unemotional language and straightforward logic   0 1 2 3 5 6
    to support my case.

40. I ask colleagues if they will support my requests.   0 1 2 3 5 6

41. I will offer to help with other work if colleagues will do   0 1 2 3 5 6
    what I want.

42. If a colleague will not comply and if I have the power, I may 0 1 2 3 5 6
    hint at possible loss of promotion or career prospects.

---

assertiveness, upward referral, coalition and sanctions. Similar strategies
are identified by other authors: for example, Margerison (1973: 23) refers
to rewards and punishment, expertise, friendly persuasion, threat and
coercion, bargaining, and involvement and recognition. These are to
be found within the following descriptions. In providing some examples

Preferred Styles Scoring Chart

Enter your scores for each statement on the grid below.

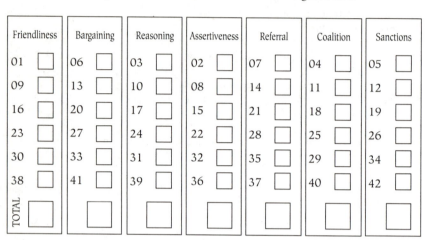

Friendliness	Bargaining	Reasoning	Assertiveness	Referral	Coalition	Sanctions
01 ☐	06 ☐	03 ☐	02 ☐	07 ☐	04 ☐	05 ☐
09 ☐	13 ☐	10 ☐	08 ☐	14 ☐	11 ☐	12 ☐
16 ☐	20 ☐	17 ☐	15 ☐	21 ☐	18 ☐	19 ☐
23 ☐	27 ☐	24 ☐	22 ☐	28 ☐	25 ☐	26 ☐
30 ☐	33 ☐	31 ☐	32 ☐	35 ☐	29 ☐	34 ☐
38 ☐	41 ☐	39 ☐	36 ☐	37 ☐	40 ☐	42 ☐
TOTAL ☐	☐	☐	☐	☐	☐	☐

Figure 12.2   Preferred Styles Scoring Chart

of related behaviours, it should be noted that these are behaviours that might be observed in any given influencing situation: they are not necessarily recommended behaviours.

Influencing Team Members: Strategies

Friendliness

The intention behind this strategy is for the influencer to be seen in a favourable light. It may involve displaying a friendly attitude, smiling, or waiting until the time is right to raise a matter. For example, if a team member senses that the other person has got something on his mind or is pressed for time, he may wait until he knows he can make his request with more confidence of success. Interpersonal skills and sensitivity to others' moods and feelings are critical. These may be demonstrated by using sympathetic comments and generally empathising with the target person.

Another way of deploying this strategy is to make the job sound important or acknowledge the other person's skills or abilities, and perhaps make him feel invaluable. This can be highly productive, especially where the recipient seeks recognition.

If overused, people become suspicious of motives, and the strategy is often seen as distasteful if used excessively with superiors. Simple, supportive remarks probably have the most impact in the strategy. It should be noted, however, that even the seemingly innocuous comment or behaviour can be taken the wrong way: "Cheerful exuberance may be interpreted as overbearing; congratulation may be construed as being unctuous; an attempt not to embarrass may be regarded as coldness" (Torrington *et al.*, 1989: 259).

Bargaining

This strategy, referred to as 'reciprocity' in the Whetten and Cameron (1984) framework, is about negotiation: "If you will do this, I may be able to provide this." It is based on exchange principles and deals. Concessions and compromises may be made, and people may be reminded of past favours.

Trades can be made with such items as time, expertise, effort and resources. For example, in the team setting, members may exchange help with certain parts of tasks, or they may ask to be relieved of a duty at a certain time but agree to make up the time on another occasion. In some circumstances, financial inducements may be offered in return for, say, extra effort to ensure a high-quality outcome to an assignment. In order to retain a team member, responsibilities may be changed to coincide with the individual's career aspirations.

All these examples are based on the principle of giving something away and getting something in return. It is worth noting that one of the central principles in bargaining strategies is the attempt to obtain benefits or concessions which are important, and to give away those things that are not important, but of value possibly to the recipient. For the strategy to be successful, therefore, the influencer must receive at least as much as he concedes.

It seems that political awareness is of benefit in this strategy. The ability to identify opinion leaders in the team and to strike bargains with them can be more productive than attempting to influence those with little impact on the team's thinking and operation. Such opinion leaders may not necessarily be official team leaders.

Like the strategy of friendliness, bargaining demands a degree of empathy: "Managers need to think themselves into the position of the person with whom they are talking, to see the topic as clearly as possible from the other point of view in order to make the most of the exchange" (Torrington *et al.*, 1989: 260).

One of the key problems with the strategy is that team members can become accustomed to exchange – they expect something every time they are asked to help:

> It engenders a highly instrumental view of work. The target person begins to expect that every request is open for negotiation and every completed assignment will generate a reward of equal value. In the extreme form this approach undercuts organizational commitment, as members take on a highly calculative orientation and downplay the value of working together to achieve organizational goals, regardless of personal gain (Whetten and Cameron, 1984: 270).

The same theme is also taken up by Torrington *et al.* (1989: 255) in describing the process of 'accumulating credits', described as

> favours to others, so that there is a scattering of IOUs that can be called in, the bread upon the waters of the Bible. The problems with this type of dealing are first that the 'rewards' offered may have to increase to maintain their value, but also that the exchanges depend on *both* parties being able to reward the other. Offering approval loses its value if approval is not wanted, so that bargaining works best when the parties to the bargain are roughly equal in their power to reward each other.

Greed may also appear and demands may become inflated and, in some cases, this may sour relationships between team members. Another related problem is that some seem to do well out of exchange processes and others invariably end up as 'losers'. This may lead to resentment and a general distrust of the strategy.

Although the strategy seems relatively harmless when compared with more intimidating strategies (such as meting out punishment), the above problems suggest it should be used with discretion. There may be many occasions when a straightforward request would be more appropriate than involvement in striking deals. The user of the strategy, therefore, may have to consider whether bargaining is really necessary in the situation.

Reasoning

A widely used strategy, reasoning is about presenting facts, information and data to support arguments. These are generally thought out in advance and impulsive actions are avoided. The strategy avoids emotional appeals and relies on objective information. Ideas must be well planned and counter-arguments anticipated. It is not a productive strategy, therefore, if there is inadequate preparation.

It is attractive to many people, since it is believed that acceptance by the target person can lead to an internalised commitment. But acceptance does not necessarily follow a winning argument and, in such situations, the target person may be perceived as unreasonable or obstructive for being unwilling to comply. However, the problem may lie with the influencer, since the reasoning strategy may not be the right one for the circumstances. Indeed, an outright reliance on sound reason and logic may be over-optimistic.

In this regard, there are two major considerations. The reason for using influence may itself not be reasonable. There may be motives other than purely 'rational' ones. For example, the 'benefit' or desired change may be difficult to defend in rational terms, and the supporting arguments may be stretched or contrived. The second consideration relates to the target person. An individual who relies almost exclusively on the strategy may make a false assumption that everyone is rational. People do not always respond to logical arguments. In these situations, the reasoning strategy is almost certainly the wrong one to use.

On the same theme, Whetten and Cameron (1984) draw attention to the need to be politically aware, to the fact that people's motives are not always rationally based and that the objective merits of arguments are not always supported. There needs to be an awareness of political undercurrents and a skill to handle them successfully.

Despite the drawbacks, the reasoning strategy seems to have high potential for success across a range of situations, and team members may be advised to develop competence in preparing facts and information to support their influencing attempts. To be successful, however, it may have to be used in conjunction with other strategies. It is also worth noting that the team member who uses rational argument well is generally seen as a 'thinking' individual, one who carefully considers the consequences of actions before attempting to influence people's behaviour.

Assertiveness

The expression 'assertiveness' may be an inadequate one in the context of influencing strategies, since it is usually associated with being 'pushy' and, in some cases, aggressive. As a strategy, it encompasses a range of behaviours, some of which might include those usually associated with the term. Essentially, the key feature of assertiveness is a direct approach and this may manifest itself in various ways.

On some occasions, it may be reflected in firmness, or in the influencer referring to rules and regulations. A direct order to do something would also fall into this category, but in the team context, it may be neither acceptable nor productive to adopt such an approach. Resistance from the target person may impel the influencer to resort to citing rules and regulations. Where a time deadline is added, the strategy becomes even firmer.

Another way in which assertiveness is used to influence the behaviour of other team members is by checking up to see that tasks are being carried out correctly. This may be accompanied by persistent reminders of agreements and commitments (a process which is familiarly known as 'nagging'). It can be productive with the right people and in the right situation; it can also be a source of considerable irritation.

The behaviours mentioned above are generally acceptable at the right times. If there is a good case and if it does not cause antagonism, then the strategy is probably appropriate. Some assertiveness behaviours are best avoided or, at least, used with caution. Raising the voice and displaying anger may demonstrate loss of self-control and may be highly injurious to relationships.

Generally, the team member who uses assertiveness as a strategy is very determined and may be prepared to compromise working relationships. This is the strategy's weakness. Token compliance may be obtained but it may be more difficult to win commitment.

Upward Referral

This strategy simply involves going higher up the chain of command to obtain support for a position. In the team context, it may mean referring a matter to the team leader when members cannot agree something among themselves. In this sense, its main use is as a secondary strategy when compliance cannot be obtained.

The consequences of using such behaviours have to be weighed up. Used frequently, they can undermine relationships. Team members are unlikely to let these referrals pass without comment, and the strategy seems to be even more dangerous if used with the leader. For example, if a team member goes over the leader's head to exert influence, it can result in retributive action. If it is used by the leader as a form of influence on team members, he may be seen as an ineffectual leader by both members and those higher up the organisation. Whilst the strategy can generate useful support if used informally, it should be employed discriminately.

Coalition

This strategy is one that is used widely in teams. It involves using other team members for support. It is a political strategy which needs time, effort and skill to develop. Some people are very adept at it and understand the political dynamics involved. They know which team members are worth forming an alliance with and which are not. It is important, therefore, to identify those in the best position to offer support. Much effort can be wasted in attempting to gain support from those who carry little weight.

One of the most effective settings for the strategy is in team meetings where matters are formally recorded. By raising an issue (sometimes without warning or under another guise), the leader's power may be reduced if it receives strong support from other members, who may have been approached informally in advance. If decisions are then arrived at, it can be difficult for the leader to overturn them.

There is a very obvious danger. It may be seen as conspiracy or 'ganging up'. Again it is necessary to consider the sort of working relationship that is required. An example serves to illustrate this point. A middle manager was very clever at political 'mapping'. He knew the opinion leaders and he always made sure he arrived for lunch at precisely the same time as the boss. He would mention informally his ideas and would generally gain support. He would also interact socially with the key resource allocators. In meetings, he would often say: "I know that the boss would support me in proposing this course of action ..." This, of course, was undoubtedly true, but he compromised his relationship with other managers in the process.

This is a very powerful strategy and can put the influencer in a strong position if the support of the right people is won. The 'right' people are those members who help to create and maintain opinions. The key danger, as we have seen, is that it may damage relationships. Like several of the strategies mentioned so far, it is one to use with discretion.

Sanctions

This strategy may be used by team members against one another or by the leader. Members, for example, may talk about others behind their backs, whilst the leader may withdraw responsibilities that individuals enjoy. The team leader may also monitor someone's work more closely than usual and this is a form of sanction.

There are situations in which the strategy is used in an upward direction. Members may indicate, for example, that the leader may not enjoy the same level of cooperation in the future, and hints may be made about referring the matter to people higher up the organisation.

Such punitive forms of influence fall in the category of 'fear of retribution' (Whetten and Cameron, 1984: 268) and may be open, as in personal threats, or indirect, as in intimidation or implied threat. Examples which the authors give include criticising a report written by a colleague, systematically ignoring someone during a meeting, and giving people impossible tasks.

There are immense dangers in this strategy. While the user may achieve his desired outcome, it almost always has adverse consequences in terms of personal relationships and future levels of cooperation. It can be seen from this list of behaviours that the word 'threaten' is used or implied several times, which may make this a strategy to use only sparingly. In fact, Whetten and Cameron (1984: 269) draw attention to this very problem:

> Threatened sanctions must be sufficiently severe that disobedience is unthinkable. When it is used repeatedly, this approach produces resentment and alienation that frequently generate overt or covert opposition. Consequently, it should be used extensively only when the ongoing commitment of the target person is not critical, opposition is acceptable (the other can be replaced if necessary), and extensive surveillance is possible. Because these conditions tend to stifle initiative and innovative behavior, even when individual compliance is obtained, organizational performance will likely suffer because affected individuals have little incentive to bring emerging problems resulting from changing conditions to the attention of their supervisors.

Appropriate Strategy Selection

The questions that might be asked in determining whether an influencing strategy is appropriately selected and employed are:

1. Was the target person(s) willing to comply?
2. Was there a willing commitment to compliance?
3. Is a good relationship maintained between the influencer and the target person?

Compliance is of little use on its own: it needs to be accompanied by commitment. The third question is an important one. Team members can often be intimidated or coerced into actions they would rather resist, but the effects on relationships may be damaging. In the team context, that is obviously a serious consideration.

Strategy Preferences

The analysis chart mentioned earlier gives a picture of the dominant strategies an individual prefers to employ. Most people have one or two preferred strategies and these are reflected in the higher scores. There is probably little wrong with having dominant strategies that are used skilfully, but an over-reliance on them may be ineffective. There are occasions when less preferred strategies may be appropriate, and some skill in these, therefore, may have to be acquired.

Whetten and Cameron (1984: 270) identify some of the reactions that might occur if a particular type of strategy is being over used:

> Managers frequently get into a rut and habitually use only their favourite or most convenient influence strategy and implement it insensitively. When this occurs, a predictable pattern of employee complaints emerges. If these complaints focus on the violation of rights or the apparent insecurity of the manager, coercion or intimidation are probably being overused. If they focus on unfairness, dashed expectations, or the boss's shifting moods, the problem generally stems from the excessive or ineffective use of bargaining and ingratiation. If the subordinates' complaints center on differences of opinion and conflicting perceptions or priorities, the manager is probably using the rational approach excessively or inappropriately.

The need for sensitive implementation is an interesting point and confirms that influencing is more complicated than mere strategy selection. Success may also depend on the manner in which the strategy is presented and other people that are involved. A study conducted by Dosier *et al.* (1988: 30) found that the manner in which an attempt to influence was presented or communicated appeared to predict the success or failure of the event as much or even more than the tactic utilised or the content of the influence approach. Additionally, the researchers found that tactics used for successful influence attempts did not differ significantly from those used in unsuccessful attempts. They found that "managers who wield influential behaviour do so in a very complex fashion and may select and use a combination of methods, manners of presentation, and supporting people to influence others" (p. 31). This final point requires some clarification. The researchers found that when managers attempted to influence a peer or a superior, they were more likely to be successful if they enlisted the assistance of other members. If they were attempting to influence a subordinate, however, they were more successful if they did it on a one-to-one basis.

Despite all this, some strategies are probably more widely applicable than others. They can be used successfully on a regular basis, especially if a high level of skill in using them is developed. For example, friendliness, reasoning and bargaining all seem to have potential for success. Some of the others have to be used sparingly. Issuing threats and applying some of the assertive-type behaviours, such as raising the voice, may undermine relationships and cause resentment.

The types of strategies used may also be affected by the organisation's (or even team's) environment or culture. Torrington *et al.* (1989: 252), for example, indicate that competition in the climate may militate against some strategies and favour instead political-type strategies. Some settings support the strategies of friendliness and reason, whilst others support bargaining-types of strategies. Yet another work environment may sustain intimidation-type strategies, including aspects of sanctions and assertiveness.

A disturbing effect of such a repressive environment is that openness and the free flow of ideas may be discouraged, and this may lead to team members becoming inert or 'bystanders' (the term is explained later). The team may be easy for the leader to control, but it is unlikely that it will produce work of any quality.

Successful Influencing

Kipnis *et al.* (1984), referring particularly to managers, identified three types of people. These types are just as relevant to the types of members in teams:

- Shotguns
- Tacticians
- Bystanders

Shotguns

These people use strategies indiscriminately and are often unsuccessful in achieving desired outcomes. They are usually inexperienced and with high expectations. Generally they do not consider the impact of their influencing attempts on the target people and, as a result, their personal relationships with other team members are shaky. They may be very ambitious and fail to see the need to establish strong working relationships and extended commitment. Their thinking, therefore, is short term.

Tacticians

Tacticians rely very much on reason and are very deliberate. They do their homework, thinking carefully about their arguments in advance, and they tend to be effective in getting their way. The key to their influencing success is that they are *flexible* in their use of strategies.

Bystanders

Bystanders, in contrast, only see the helplessness of their situation and seldom try to influence other team members, either for personal or team objectives. They express their dissatisfaction with their ability to work effectively.

Flexible, Selective and Rational

Why do people often choose the wrong strategies? First, preferred strategies tend to become habitual, even if inappropriate. Second, they may fail to think things through before attempting to influence. Third, they may misjudge whether someone is willing to comply.

It is likely to be productive in most team settings to follow the example of the 'tactician' and learn to be:

- flexible in the use of strategies;
- selective in the right one for the situation;
- strong on rational strategy.

It is probably true that, in teams, the strategies with the most potential for success are friendliness, reasoning, bargaining and assertiveness. The first two can be used widely and the last one can probably be used in those situations where entirely reasonable and legitimate requests are being made. Getting benefits from people, improving performance and initiating change, apart from the preferred strategies mentioned above, may all require a mix of strategies depending on other factors. Effective team members who need to influence for these reasons are more likely to use a variety of strategies, whereas unsuccessful influencers rigidly adhere to single strategies.

It seems important for team members to recognise their dominant and preferred strategies, and to be able to identify the situations in which they are appropriate. Skill may have to be acquired in implementing other strategies, and this may mean developing the ability to minimise the chances of resistance and resentment to the influencing attempt. Furthermore, some ability may be required in influencing on a one-to-one basis as well as amongst groups of team members: both forms are applicable to team settings.

Influencing in a team presents a distinctly different set of problems to those that arise from individual interactions. First, it is more problematic to respond to the verbal and non-verbal signals of a group of team members than it is to one person. Second, the comments that are made may be interpreted in a variety of ways and will usually be concerned with the effects on team members themselves. Third, there is a feeling of power amongst team members in a group that does not exist to the same extent in a one-to-one interaction. All these have an impact on the influencer and the influencing attempt (Ends and Page, 1977: 60).

Influence has to be seen as a complex multidimensional construct. This has been explained in terms of the various directions in which influence might flow within the team. There is one further consideration. It appears necessary for the leader, at least, to be able to exert influence outside the team with both superiors and peers.

It is even suggested by Ends and Page (1977: 62) that a leader's influence within the team may be in part a function of his influence outside:

> Team members rightfully feel that in return for commitment, involvement, and extra effort their leader should be able to influence the organization enough so that they get their share of recognition, their share of rewards, and the help and cooperation they need from other elements of the organization in order to do a bang-up job. If the leader fails to use the superior work the team is performing to exert influence on the organization, the team will reduce the amount of influence on their behavior that they have allowed.

Sustaining Influence

It may be fair to say that influencing team members now and again is not difficult. What is difficult is being able to sustain that influence over longer periods of time and across various situations. This is an important point. Dosier *et al.* (1988: 22) found that "the immediate success of any short-term attempt appears to be related to the development of long-term, sustained influence built up over time. Conversely, a poor influence record developed from unsuccessful influence attempts may erode managerial influence and manager-subordinate relationships".

Keys and Case (1990: 43–8) suggest that there are five key steps that can be employed to establish sustained influence and which have value to the team context.

1. "Develop a reputation as a knowledgeable team member." Members who possess knowledge and continually build upon that knowledge seem to be in a better position to continually influence others.

2. "Balance the time spent in each critical relationship according to the needs of the work rather than on the basis of habit or social preference." Members should spend time in the relationships which are closely tied to their job and not allocate excessive time to the same or non-productive areas. In short, members need to interact with all levels from superior to subordinates and across teams, departments and organisations. This tends to offer a wider base for successful influencing.

3. "Develop a network of resource persons who can be called upon for assistance." Many influence attempts involve others. This may be especially so when a team is attempting to break into a network or market outside its organisation. The more people in a network, and the more influential these people are, the greater the chance of successful influencing across situations.

4. "Choose the correct combination of influence tactics for the objective and the target to be influenced." As mentioned previously, no single tactic or combination of tactics will work in all situations. Team members must consider the event and person to be influenced very carefully.

5. "Implement influence tactics with sensitivity, flexibility, and adequate levels of communication." How one communicates an attempted influence strategy can be vital. Presentation and approach can be as important as the tactic itself. For example: "Managers who choose rational ideas based on the needs of the target, wrap them with a blanket of humour or anecdotes, and cast them in the language of the person to be influenced, are much more likely to see their influence objective achieved" (Keys and Case, 1990: 48). This draws attention to the need to understand the target person, a view supported by Adams (1990: 31).

Influence then is not manipulation, and for it to be successful on an ongoing basis, both within and outside the team, strategies, objectives and the actors involved need to be carefully considered.

Summary

In summary, there are several considerations in influence strategy selection: the other person's status in relation to the influencer, the personality of the individual involved, the reason for using influence, and whether any resistance is expected. The success of an influencing attempt may be evaluated by the target person's willingness to comply, his commitment to the agreement and whether intended outcomes have been achieved without impairing personal relationships. Friendliness and reason are probably the most effective strategies overall in securing commitment that is willingly given by the target person.

Other strategies may be successful in certain situations, but some may only erode trust and lead to a compliance which has no accompanying commitment. The effects of such strategies on relationships can be harmful. The most dangerous behaviours are those where coercion and intimidation are present, and these might include sanctions, upward referral, coalition, and elements of assertiveness. Team cultures that support and promote these strategies may be problematic, especially if the free flow of ideas is required in a dynamic setting. The 'tactician's' example seems to be the most effective to follow, since this profile exemplifies a flexible approach, the ability to select appropriate strategies for any given situation, and considerable skill in the most widely used and successful strategy of reasoning.

In this chapter we have discussed seven influencing strategies. To become successful influencers, team members must develop skills in a range of these strategies. Successful influencers become adept at selecting the right strategy at the right time in the right situation. We have also made some suggestions as to how influence might be sustained over a period of time. In the next chapter we examine conflict within and between teams.

Summary of the Implications for Managers

- Effective influence means compliance *and* commitment, and is best achieved through a flexible approach, using the best strategy for the situation. In order to determine the success of an influencing episode, three questions need to be asked:

  1. Was there compliance?
  2. Was there commitment?
  3. Were good relationships maintained?

- It is quite acceptable to use dominant strategies, but it is best if they are not overused and not applied to the wrong situations. Generally, friendliness, reasoning and bargaining are relatively safe strategies and carry potential for success. Friendliness is often used to obtain benefits, while reasoning is used to change things and promote ideas. It is advisable to avoid dangerous strategies such as sanctions, upward referral and the more questionable behaviours which fall in the assertiveness category.

- The tactician, a worthy example to follow, uses reasoning skilfully; he plans his influencing and thinks out arguments in advance. He is flexible and selects the appropriate strategy for the circumstances.

- Leaders and team members need to learn to influence both individuals and the team as a whole. The leader in particular must also learn how to exert influence outside the team.

- Team members need to sustain their influence. This can be done by:

  1. developing a reputation as an expert;
  2. balancing time with each critical relationship;
  3. developing a network of resource persons;
  4. selecting the correct combination of influence strategies;
  5. communicating influence strategies effectively.

13

TEAM CONFLICT

CONFLICT IS and needs to be an inevitable fact of team, as well as organisational and personal life (Lindelow and Scott, 1989: 338). The reason for its prevalence in team settings may be attributed largely to the heterogeneity of membership: "The group may be more conflict-laden and less expedient as diverse positions are introduced and assimilated, but the evidence generally supports the conclusion that heterogeneous groups perform more effectively than do those that are homogeneous" (Robbins, 1991: 294). Such a characteristic, there-fore, is at once the team's strength as well as its potential weakness.

Attempting to get rid of conflict altogether may be both an un-realistic and unproductive strategy. There is general agreement in the literature that conflict, if positively utilised, is indeed beneficial to teams. As we have seen in earlier chapters, confrontation and conflict are very necessary for high-performance teams. However, for it to be a positive force, conflict has to be transformed from a potentially de-structive to a constructive experience. If this transformation can be achieved, there is no need to avoid or suppress conflict.

In this chapter, the positive (functional) and the negative (dys-functional) outcomes of conflict will be outlined, and the different types of conflict to be found in teams will be discussed. Some of the sources of conflict will be identified, followed by strategies for dealing with the condition effectively.

Conflict

When most people think of conflict, it conjures up negative images of fights, arguments and unpleasant exchanges. We would be foolish to totally disregard these perceptions. Much of the conflict as it presently occurs *is* destructive and, if allowed to continue unabated, can damage a team's unity and effectiveness. There are, however, two sides to conflict: the unhealthy, destructive side, and the healthy, constructive side. An important role of the team or team leader is to actively work towards skilfully accentuating healthy conflict while devaluing unhealthy conflict.

Robbins (1991: 450) states: "Most behavioral scientists and an increasing number of practitioners now accept that the goal of effective management is not to eliminate conflict. Rather, it is to create the right intensity so as to reap its functional benefits." He continues to list how stimulated, controlled conflict can benefit the organisation:

- Conflict is a means by which to bring about radical change.
- Conflict facilitates group cohesiveness.
- Conflict improves group and organisational effectiveness.
- Conflict brings about a slightly higher, more constructive level of tension.

All four points have obvious interest to those involved in teams. Writing specifically about teams, Wynn and Guditus (1984: 145) dwell also on the positive:

> The presence of conflict in a group can increase the frequency of high-quality solutions to problems. Groups experiencing conflict more frequently employ creative alternatives than groups without it. Groups in crisis show more effective decision-making performance than groups free of conflict. The greater the conflict aroused by a crisis, the greater the consensus once the decision is reached.

These are bold words indeed, but they signal the attitude that may be needed to reach positive outcomes.

The potential outcomes of conflict may be described as falling into four categories:

Lose-lose: Both parties feel they have lost out in resolving the conflict. Animosity often results.

Lose-win: One party is unassertive and lets the other win despite the cost to himself.

Win-lose: One party forces a solution on another, leaving one party feeling defeated and dejected.

Win-win: Both parties feel they have won. This can result from a compromise, but is even more likely from collaboration.

The first three outcomes may lead to conditions in which conflict is destructive. It is unproductive, therefore, when it:

1. prevents the team reaching important goals;
2. stands in the way of cooperation;
3. creates dissatisfaction amongst team members;
4. emphasizes differences of opinion and disagreements;
5. demotivates and demoralises people;
6. causes irresponsible behaviour;
7. interferes with the decision-making process;
8. produces distrust, suspicion and ill will.

On the other hand, conflict can be constructive when it:

1. encourages trust;
2. produces creative solutions;
3. opens discussions;
4. aids individual and team development;
5. increases self-esteem;
6. improves communication;
7. increases involvement and interest in a problem;
8. causes re-evaluation of outdated procedures;
9. allows 'built-up' negative emotions to surface;
10. reduces the chances of groupthink.

In simple terms, too much or the wrong type of conflict produces negative feelings between individuals in the team which can result in destructive consequences. Too little conflict, on the other hand, can inhibit open, innovative discussion of a problem and result in mediocre performance by the team. Robbins (1991: 438–40) notes that conflict not only relates to improved decisions but has also been related positively to productivity. He recounts an example: "An investigation of twenty-two teams of systems analysts found that the more incompatible groups were likely to be more productive. Research and development scientists have been found to be most productive where there is a certain amount of conflict."

Conflict, therefore, may best be seen as a vital source of team energy but it has to be harnessed for the team's benefit. Using the right strategies can transform it into a positive force. From this perspective, the role of the team leader and his capacity to manage conflict behaviours are important (Yukl, 1989: 134). To be able to handle the transformational process adequately, both the leader and members of the team need to have a basic awareness of the types and causes of conflict.

Types of Conflict

Various writers recognise different types of conflict. These are generally called: goal conflict (where people disagree on desired outcomes), cognitive conflict (where thoughts or ideas are seen as incompatible), affective conflict (where people become angry or simply do not like one another) and behavioural conflict (where actions are incompatible).

For our purposes here we have categorised three main types:

- Self-conflicts
- People conflicts
- Team conflicts

Self-conflicts

A useful description of self-conflict (intrapersonal) is given in Sashkin and Morris (1984) and refers to conflicts which occur within an individual. For example, a person may know something would be good for the team, but sees it as counterproductive from a career perspective. Our discussion here, however, is confined to looking at the work of organisational teams and with conflicts between people and those between teams.

People Conflicts

People or interpersonal conflicts can be the most destructive to the team and can come from a number of sources. If not dealt with effectively, they may get out of hand. These types of conflicts *must* be dealt with.

Team Conflicts

There are two types of team conflicts. These can be labelled 'in-team' (intra-group) conflicts and the 'between-team' (inter-group) conflicts. The first type is virtually the same as people conflicts and relates to interpersonal difficulties. 'Between-team' or intergroup conflicts refer to conflict between different work teams, whether permanent or temporary; we shall deal with this later in the chapter. This type of conflict can also be very destructive to the organisation. We begin, however, by examining the possible causes of conflicts.

Causes of Conflict

The causes of conflict give us some fundamental clues about the actions teams can take to convert them into positive forces for improvement. In general terms, conflict can emerge from the team's structure or processes (or even from the larger organisation) or from individuals. The causes of conflict, therefore, might be grouped under team- and people-initiated conflicts.

Team-initiated Conflict

This heading might also include the type of conflict caused by in- adequacies in organisational conditions, namely, structure, environment, size, technology, coordination, competition, communication, and ill- defined goals or role definitions and interdependencies. In the team context though, it might be argued that such obstacles can arise also from the team itself. We now look at some of these in more detail.

Unclear roles and interdependencies

If task roles and expectations in the team are inadequately defined or ambiguous, conflict often results. For example, if a team member is chastised for not completing a task which he did not know he was responsible for, negative feelings will result. Conflict can also result if a group of team members dependent on one another are unsure of their respective commitments, especially if they discover they are duplicating one another's work. Similarly, when the interdependent nature of the task necessitates members relying on one another for task completion, the chances of conflict multiply.

Coordination and control

Conflict can also result from unnecessarily complex coordination or control mechanisms. For example, if these become more important than the task itself, they can lead to the all too common battle for control. Teams may sometimes have to consider loosening administrative constraints, especially where these interfere with task progress.

Limited resources

Yukl (1989: 135) identifies rewards, status and resources as having the potential to give rise to conflict through competition. When resources are limited, both individuals in teams and the teams themselves are often forced to compete for what is available. If this is not dealt with reasonably, conflict is likely to result, as individuals and groups identify inequities in allocation and purport to take retributive action.

Adair (1986: 82) indeed sees an over-emphasis on competition as a major cause of inter-team conflict. It leads to hostility, suspicion, misunderstanding, lack of trust, and stopping of all communication.

Latitude and decision making

How much latitude team members are granted in completing a task and how much they are involved in decision making can also affect the level of conflict. If employees are given freedom to pursue their tasks and subtasks as they see fit, conflict is probably more likely to eventuate. The tradeoff is that more freedom and less structure can often lead to greater creativity: constructive conflict. The degree of flexibility is governed to a certain extent by the nature of the team's assignment or tasks. It is worth noting, however, that in the team setting in modern organisations, flexibility may be essential to stay in touch with advances.

How often and how much team members are involved in decision making also affects the level of conflict. Robbins (1991) found that the rate of conflict multiplied as participation in decision making increased. He also pointed out however that, although the number of conflicts increased, the number of major incidents of conflict actually went down. Apparently the opportunity to discuss and express dissatisfaction in an open forum prevented minor conflicts from expanding. It may also have been due to team members' access to more information and their capacity to tolerate divergent views, both functions, in part, of participative approaches. The view that conflict may become more evident in such conditions is endorsed by Wynn and Guditus (1984: 146): "Participative decision making, rather than suppressing conflict, brings it into the open and energizes forces that can resolve conflict and leave the organization stronger or, in some cases, exacerbate it. But without group problem solving, conflict may not be addressed openly, only to erupt later in greater intensity."

Communication

Lack of successful communication between team members or between the leader and team members can also lead to conflict. Unclear goals, unstated expectations, lack of trust and hidden agendas can all initiate unrest and division within the team. At a broader level, inadequate organisational communication mechanisms can lead to over-competitiveness among teams or a duplication of work.

Inter-team conflict can also be caused by what Daft (1992: 434) calls 'operative goal incompatibility' where the operative goals one team is working towards interferes with those of other organisational groups. In addition to the causes mentioned above, Daft also mentions differentiation, power distribution, uncertainty and the reward system of the organisation as possible sources of inter-departmental conflict.

People-initiated Conflict

Team-initiated causes of conflict can often be controlled by the team's leaders or the wider organisation; people or human conflicts are more difficult to control. Various causes have been identified in the literature. For example, Koehler (1989: 16) mentions differences of opinions, power struggles among competing team leaders, and simple personality clashes. Schmidt and Tannenbaum (1972) look at the issue more broadly and believe that four types of issues commonly cause conflicts:

1. **Disagreement over facts**: where people are aware of the facts but interpret them in different ways.
2. **Disagreement over goals**: where employees disagree over the direction of the team's efforts and the more specific targets they are expected to achieve.
3. **Disagreement over methods**: where members fail to agree on the 'how' of the task.
4. **Disagreement over values**: where there are fundamental differences about what is right and wrong.

Similar material is presented in a model by Maddux (1988: 58) where differences are emphasized as the fundamental causes:

- Differences in needs, objectives and values.
- Differences in perceiving motives, words, actions and situations.
- Differing expectations of outcomes – favourable versus un-favourable.
- Unwillingness to work through issues, collaborate or com-promise.

We have grouped the major causes of people conflicts some-what differently, but our categories encompass the general causes listed above. We examine them under the headings of misunder-standings, emotions, viewpoints and values.

Misunderstandings

Many conflicts arise from misunderstanding between two or more people. Conflict results when a person misunderstands what is expected. This usually comes about through a lack of adequate communication. The team leader or members may assume their colleagues know what is expected but may fail to fully delineate responsibilities and requirements.

Misunderstandings can also arise from the inappropriate choice of words: an unintentional word or comment to someone who is sensitive can easily lead to a conflict situation. The same situation can result between two team members who simply misunderstand each other, either in a personal or work sense.

Emotions

An event or issue is not necessarily needed to give rise to conflict. Emotional conflicts, for example, can be caused by people's personal feelings about others. Emotions tend to last longer than any particular conflict-initiating event. Such conflicts are common in teams and can be insidious. People may refuse to talk to one another or to work together, and the conflict may continue for long after the original cause of the relationship breakdown. It should also be noted that conflict for other reasons sometimes causes emotions to get out of hand. It is perhaps more likely that emotions will become focal in interpersonal conflicts rather than in 'between-team' conflicts.

Viewpoints

These conflicts arise out of a divergence in viewpoints between team members. They may be relatively unimportant or vital to team harmony. Such conflicts may be about goals. For example, one team member may believe that stock levels should be kept high in order to service customers rapidly, whereas another member may see that as a waste of resources and wish to keep costs down by maintaining stock levels to the minimum.

Values

Closely related to the viewpoints issue is that of differences in values or fundamental beliefs. People's values are reflections of their personality and what they believe and, as such, they are difficult, if not impossible in some cases, to change. Sometimes, values are really the root cause of conflict situations which may appear to have other causal factors. As Yukl (1989: 134) observes: "Differences in values and beliefs are likely to cause suspicion, misunderstanding, and hostility." The issue of individual values is discussed separately and in greater detail later.

Dealing with People-initiated Conflicts

There are probably measures that can be taken to minimise the chances of conflict occurring. Such preventive actions might include the leader recognising symptoms of conflict in their early stages and not letting them get out of hand, encouraging shared and collective decisions, and building a climate in which team members feel able to discuss their differences and feelings openly.

While 'prevention is better than cure' is a useful maxim to apply, it is unlikely that all potentially damaging conflict situations can be prevented. Strategies are needed, therefore, to deal with conflicts as they arise.

A person's response to a conflict situation will generally fall into one of five general categories: competing, accommodating, avoiding, compromising and collaborating (Thomas, 1976: 900). Thomas places these responses on two dimensions, reflecting varying degrees of assertiveness and cooperativeness. An assertive response to conflict refers to the extent to which someone tries to satisfy his own concerns. Cooperativeness refers to the extent to which an individual attempts to satisfy the other person's concerns. This is best illustrated on the grid shown in Figure 13.1.

Members of teams may be placed in situations at different times which will require them to utilise all of the five strategies in one form or another.

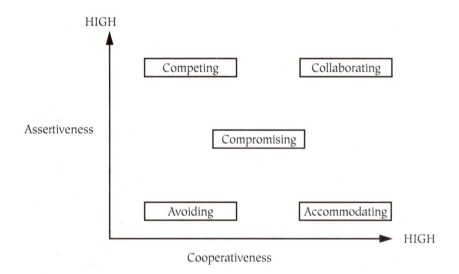

Figure 13.1   Responding to Conflict Situations
(**Source:** Adapted from Thomas, 1976: 900)

Avoiding

The most natural response to a conflict situation for many is to avoid it in some way. Not many people enjoy unpleasantness and tension.

There are times when avoidance is an effective short-term strategy. There are also many instances, however, when it can lead to more serious conflicts. There are a number of ways that it can be avoided.

Postpone

Dealing with the conflict can be postponed until a later date. This can be done to give time to acquire more facts and information. Launching into inappropriate reactive strategies may indeed be counterproductive.

Ignore

Where an individual seeks to initiate or broaden conflict for his own purposes, a useful strategy may be to ignore it.

Isolate

Another avoidance strategy is to isolate the conflicting parties so that they do not have to interact. This is virtually impossible in the team setting and the only isolating action may be to move one or both parties out of the team.

Withhold

When two conflicting parties cannot reconcile their differences, a less drastic option is for them to withhold their feelings from each other: to control themselves.

The last two avoidance responses are probably advisable only in extreme situations. In fact, avoidance strategies are best considered carefully before they are applied. As Petrock (1990: 9) notes: "Leaders who try to suppress conflict by becoming authoritarian will only worsen it. And groups that try to deal with conflict by smoothing things over won't solve problems." If conflict is regularly avoided, ill-feeling can fester below the surface. For this reason, avoidance strategies seem to have most potential as temporary or survival measures, such as when the costs of disagreeing with someone outweigh the benefits.

Accommodating

Accommodating involves one party in attempting to satisfy another party's concerns while neglecting his own. The philosophy behind this strategy is self-sacrifice or keeping the other party happy at all costs.

The approach can be useful in some situations, but is probably unhelpful if it is used too frequently. Constantly giving in to those who are powerful or persuasive can lead to outcomes that are less than ideal. Individuals may wish to maintain cordial relationships, but these may be at the expense of team members' self-respect and result in their being taken advantage of far too often. Accommodation can be a good means of escape for a team member who finds out that he is wrong about something.

Competing

Competing or forcing is the opposite response to accommodating. The individual considers only his own concerns and ignores those of the other party. This is sometimes done through coercive power (if it exists) and being insistent. The team member (or leader) who responds to conflict situations in this way undoubtedly sees them as win-lose events, and he must be on the winning end.

Team members who prefer such approaches are often manipulative and may secure the support of team colleagues who share their views. The approach, if used too frequently, may promote acrimonious challenges or suppressed animosity. Maddux (1988: 58) also suggests communication may break down, trust and support may deteriorate, and hostilities result. Productivity is likely to diminish and the damage is difficult to repair.

Despite the dangers, the use of force does have a place in conflict resolution. It is a quick way of settling disputes and may be necessary where, say, two team members are diametrically opposed on the basis of values, interests or personalities. If conflicting parties will not budge from their positions, forcing them into a solution may be the only alternative. Competition is also useful when crises arise and there is little time for discussion or disagreement.

Compromising

Compromising, which can include arbitration, negotiation and bargaining is an attempt to provide both conflicting parties with at least a reasonably satisfactory result. Both parties are asked to make certain sacrifices in exchange for some concessions from the other – for the good of the team. Each party wins some things and loses others. In the team context, this is a widely used and highly effective strategy. Compromising is really a search for a middle ground and is useful when the conflicting parties "have mutually exclusive goals and relatively equal power" (Roberts and Hunt, 1991: 209).

Compromise can be achieved through a problem-solving process or through the use of a third-party arbitrator. Compromise can also involve negotiation, where the aim is to reconcile differences and to reach agreement with which both parties are happy (Stott and Walker, 1992). Team leaders often find themselves taking the role of the mediator: facilitating and clarifying communication between the two conflicting parties; or of the arbitrator: making a decision after familiarising themselves with both sides of the argument. In some cases, where the team leader is one of the conflicting parties, someone else may be needed to arbitrate.

Since arbitration is often used in the team setting, it is useful to understand what is involved. A system, adapted in part from Torrington (1982), is explained in detail in Stott and Walker (1982: 453). Broadly, it involves:

- anticipating expectations;
- preparing thoroughly by gathering sufficient information about the dispute;
- considering desirable outcome targets;
- planning appropriate physical arrangements for the meeting.

Although various forms of compromise are often used in teams, they do entail risks. Used too frequently, for example, the leader may be seen as someone who is more interested in simply keeping everyone happy rather than in solving problems. Compromise for the sake of compromise should not be the aim.

Collaboration

Wynn and Guditus (1984: 146) are critical of 'bargaining' approaches and prefer to look at 'gaining'. They maintain that, since the former tends to be a problem-solving process that is conducted with the parties essentially isolated, the seeds of disagreement remain deeply rooted in opposition. The gaining process, in contrast, looks at individuals and groups in 'apposition' to one another rather than 'opposition'. They describe the process as one of

> consensus building that begins with the first step and continues throughout. Communication is open and intensive, allowing each group to perceive the

other more accurately. Better communication generates better understanding, but not always agreement. Each begins to get into the appreciative mass of the other, and good things generally happen.

What they are describing is effective collaboration. Collaboration views conflicts as problem-solving situations. It is a process in which conflicting parties confront the situation and attempt to resolve it through collaborative or creative problem solving. This, as Wynn and Guditus clearly indicate, is a powerful strategy for turning destructive conflict into constructive outcomes.

The process encourages conflicting team members to channel their energies into a creative problem-solving process, rather than into fighting with one another. Both or all parties play a constructive role. As Maddux (1988: 58) notes: "Conflict is healthy when it causes the parties to explore new ideas, test their position and beliefs, and stretch their imagination. When conflict is dealt with constructively, people can be stimulated to greater creativity, which will lead to a wider choice of action and better results." Such benefits are, therefore, for both the team and its members.

The steps shown in Figure 13.2 may be used as a guide to collaborative

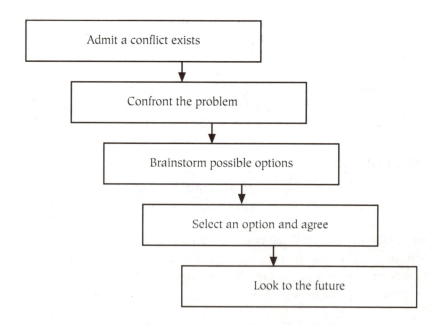

Figure 13.2   A Collaborative Problem-solving Outline

problem solving. They do not cover excessive detail but provide a flexible and workable outline scheme.

Admit a conflict exists

The first step is for those involved to recognise the problem and bring it into the open. The step also involves agreeing where and when it should be discussed.

Confront the problem

This stage involves exploring the issue, the participants' positions and their feelings. It involves a great deal of listening, but the discussion should be confined to the relevant issues rather than the personalities. The issues should be discussed specifically and incrementally.

The key result at this stage is for those involved to attempt to understand the other's point of view. This may be the only way of reaching a mutually satisfying outcome.

Brainstorm possible options

This step involves the generation of alternatives and the search for solutions that are mutually acceptable. It represents an opportunity to use the combined creative powers of the parties involved.

Select an option

It may be desirable to base the selection of the appropriate option on objective and agreed criteria. Such criteria might include the degree of fairness to both parties, the effects on others in the team, the advantages to the team as a whole, and the solution's practicality and potential for permanence.

Look to the future

The final stage is an opportunity to capitalise on any positive feelings that accrued from the collaborative process. Agreement can be reached about implementation and contingencies. Discussion can also take place about avoiding similar conflict episodes in the future and about sustaining good relationships.

Collaboration, despite its obvious advantages, is not always the best strategy. For example, if a conflict is based on divergent values, collaboration can actually polarise differences and is highly unlikely to alter basic beliefs. As Petrock (1990: 9) notes: "Conflicts because of differences in information, perceptions and roles are easier to resolve than conflicts arising from differences in values." Forcing two people with vastly different value systems to collaborate risks deepening the differences and perhaps even intensifying the conflict (Robbins, 1991).

Collaborative strategies nevertheless offer the most productive promise for conflict situations. "Only problem solving is clearly related to positive outcomes in a wide range of (conflict) circumstances" (Sashkin and Morris, 1984: 327). It is also the most effective strategy for transforming destructive conflict into constructive, creative outcomes. We now move on to examine briefly the sort of conflict that might occur between teams.

Inter-group Conflict

Conflict occurs not only between individuals within teams; it occurs also between teams. Daft (1991: 429–31) describes inter-group conflict as being either horizontal: between teams of approximately equal status and power, or vertical: conflict between teams at different hierarchical levels. Inter-group conflict can have a number of effects. Again, these can be positive or negative. Adair (1986: 77) lists some of the responses within the team:

- **Cohesiveness**: Loyalty increases as the other team is seen as the enemy.
- **Perceptions**: The team perceives itself as good and can see only the worst in the other team. Perceptions are therefore distorted.
- **Territorial imperative**: The team protects its physical territory or its area of responsibility.
- **Conformity**: The team demands conformity and accepts more central direction.
- **Atmosphere**: Efforts are directed at team maintenance and this can mean a lower concern on the task.
- **Structure**: Structure is heightened and may represent powerful subgroup interests.

Adair also identifies some of the effects of inter-group conflict between the groups concerned. Team members may become hostile to the other team and this can result in aggressive talk or behaviour. Communication between the teams decreases and listening is selective. Members may attack views advanced by the rival team, although such views may have been accepted within their own camp. Mutual understanding diminishes and there is mistrust, with an emphasis on the politics rather than the problem in question.

The outcome of a conflict that has escalated to a great extent is that one may ultimately win and the other lose. The effects are not really healthy for either team, and that is why such conflicts are best described as highly destructive. The winner becomes more cohesive, more self-congratulatory, less productive and more complacent. The loser may fragment, find scapegoats, indulge in recrimination, and become depressed about the failure. The big loser, of course, is the organisation within which and for which the teams operate. On a positive note, some teams may be able to treat such episodes as learning experiences and consider radical change that may not have been approached in other circumstances.

A collaborative problem-solving approach may alleviate some of the difficulties caused by conflict between teams. Such an approach may necessitate conflicting teams resolving to work together in an attempt to, first, understand the feeling and position of the other team and, second, move towards a solution that is acceptable to the teams involved. This may mean finding a common goal, one that is essential to attain and which can be pursued collaboratively. Adair (1986: 82) suggests it is more likely to be a long-term aim rather than a short-term and specific objective. He goes on to suggest a systematic way of looking at the relationships between teams. It involves defining boundaries and critical interdependencies, identifying the expectations amongst teams of others, defining the nature of the work relationship between teams, taking an audit of the current situation with regard to these issues, and planning the work that needs to be done to put things on a sounder footing.

An episode of inter-team conflict demonstrates how this process might be used with successful results:

In a large multinational manufacturing company, the marketing group was in conflict with the production supervisors' team. Essentially, the marketing people wanted plenty of sales, and to achieve this, they wanted to satisfy customer demands by producing the goods cheaply, with extras, and with fast delivery. Production, on the other hand, felt that the marketing function was working in the realm of the impossible. The production supervisors were more concerned with the right employees and materials, and with producing quality goods. They would not take any shortcuts. "You must deliver," said the marketing team. "We can't," was production's reply.

Fortunately, it was possible to bring the two groups together and to discuss each other's problems. Marketing began to understand why production was concerned with quality, and the latter team began to understand how the company's reward system worked for the marketing people. It was decided that it would be helpful for production to get to know the customers better and to develop a stronger customer-orientation amongst production supervisors and operatives.

It was arranged, therefore, for customers to have a plant tour and to meet the people who made their products. It was taken a step further when the company decided that, if a customer had a complaint about a product once it was installed, the production supervisor concerned would be flown out to the customer to deal with it. This meant a strong relationship forming between the producer and the user.

Despite the immense benefits of making production more marketing-oriented, the marketing team was still largely ignorant about the production process and the difficulties that could arise from day to day. This was largely due to the physical separation of the two functions. The marketing unit was located several miles away in a separate building and they seldom met either professionally or socially. The company decided that bringing them together physically would be a priority strategy.

In looking at root causes of conflict earlier, it was noted that some were initiated by the team's organisation and structure. We now examine briefly some simple strategies for dealing with these causes, many of which can exacerbate people conflict.

Dealing with Team-initiated Conflict

Role definition can help to avoid many of the team-induced problems. Apart from defining team members' respective contributions, the relationships and interdependencies between roles may be similarly clarified and defined. Sashkin and Morris (1984) take up the issue of interdependencies and suggest that a decrease in this type of conflict may be reduced by increasing or decreasing such interdependencies.

A vital component in reducing the likelihood of team-induced conflict is to ensure that channels of communication are open. Members and team leader alike probably need to be aware of expectations and what is happening. This ensures that leaders can identify and intercept conflicts in their early stages, and also that discussion of problems and conflicts can take place in a collaborative environment. If conflicts are particularly intense another method of managing the disagreement may be to limit communication to focused areas, such as a specific goal.

Finally, conflict is a normal part of any environment, and teams certainly experience their fair share of it. It is clear from the above discussion that 'sweeping it under the carpet' is unlikely to be a productive long-term strategy and that positive actions may be needed to at least reduce the potentially damaging effects.

Summary

In summary, it can be argued that conflict can be channelled in many cases into constructive outcomes that lead to increased adaptability, creativity and ultimately, improved productivity. To do this, an awareness of the types and fundamental causes of conflict is necessary and the ability to employ appropriate conflict resolution strategies. The most positive option is probably the collaborative approach, where people work together to gain a greater level of understanding and to search for outcomes that are of mutual benefit and satisfaction. This last sentence, in fact, comes very close to describing a team and its purposes. The development of teams in organisations is in itself a very positive organisational approach to conflict management. By encouraging individuals to work together closely as a team, and to relate openly and honestly with one another, the organisation is promoting constructive conflict and its positive outcomes. This is, of course, if functional conflict becomes part of the organisational culture. Robbins (1991: 439) provides some excellent advice gleaned from organisations who have purposefully built cultures which encourage and value functional conflict:

1. Hewlett-Packard rewards dissenters by recognising people who stick to their ideas and beliefs even if they are rejected by management.

2. Herman Miller Inc. has a formal system where workers can appraise and criticise their boss.

3. IBM also has a formal system where workers can question their superiors with impunity.

4. Companies such as General Electric build 'devil's advocates' into their decision process.

5. When Anheuser-Busch is considering getting into or out of a business, they assign teams the task of making a case for or against the move.

Sad to say, those examples are all too uncommon. The more usual picture is one of organisations suppressing or punishing such shows of conflict.

That is not the end of the conflict story. As we shall see in the next chapter, which looks at how teams might go about making decisions, dissent may be a necessary accompaniment to the process if it is to be effective. If it is handled badly, damaging conflict may occur. The intention is, of course, to make productive use of contrast and ultimately transpose it into unity.

Summary of the Implications for Managers

- It is probably most productive to develop a collaborative approach to conflict resolution. This can be done by bringing the problem into the open, by clarifying and exploring the issues involved and by looking at feelings and understanding different views. Options and solutions can be searched for and then selected according to agreed criteria. It is also helpful to discuss how similar episodes can be avoided in the future. While collaboration can be highly successful, other approaches may have to be considered where there are deep-seated differences in values.

- Conflicts between teams can be intensely problematic. Teams may have to work together to, first, understand the feelings and position of the other team and, second, to move to a mutually acceptable solution which represents the common good.

- Establishing role clarity may help avoid unnecessary conflicts, and this can be done by defining expected contributions, relationships and interdependencies.

14

TEAM PROBLEMS AND DECISIONS

DECISIONS and decision making are central to organisational life and success. "The quality of organizational life is largely a function of the quality of decisions, and the quality of administration is largely a function of the quality of the organization's decision-making capability" (Wynn and Guditus, 1984: 93).

Teams are inevitably involved in solving problems and making decisions. Complexity, in terms of technology, markets and rapid change, when combined with increasing moves towards decentralisation and team structures, necessitate such involvement. The quality of team decisions, as the assertion above so clearly states, can have a considerable impact on both the work of the team and also the larger organisation. It is essential, therefore, that decision-making ability is maximised if teams are to perform effectively.

In this chapter, we use the expressions 'problem solving' and 'decision making' frequently. Although in some texts they are used interchangeably to describe the complete process, it will be helpful to make a distinction. Problem solving is the process of deliberately attempting to overcome barriers which are in the way of an intended outcome or goal. There may be several ways of dealing with such barriers. These can be called options, and decision making is selecting from these options. From this perspective, decision making may best be seen as part of a wider problem-solving process, but most texts choose to take decision making as the fundamental activity.

There can be no doubt as to the importance of decision making. Drummond (1992: 1) cites evidence that managers spend, at minimum, half their time dealing with the outcomes and consequences of poor decision making. She highlights the case of Total Quality Management proponents, who adhere to the belief that it is far cheaper in many ways to do the job properly the first time. "What is the point of organizations seeking to produce quality goods and services if the underlying managerial decision processes are shot through with incompetence?" (p. 1). Teams are coming under increasing pressure to make 'good' decisions and indeed their very formation may have resulted from a quest for quality decision making and decisions.

In Chapter 8 we presented a scheme for optimising team-task performance. In this scheme we highlighted the need to make incisive decisions after analysing problems fully and generating alternative courses of action. We shall now look at the area of team problem solving and decision making in greater detail. The complexity and importance of the topic necessitates comprehensive coverage.

Types of Decision

Not all decisions are of equal importance. However, it may reasonably be assumed that if a decision is to be made by a team, it must be an important one. That assumption may be inaccurate in some situations where teams or their leaders have failed to distinguish between genuinely important decisions and those that are more trivial. Questions need asking, therefore: Is the problem unique? Has a workable solution been found previously? Is it an old problem for which an effective solution has not been found?

It is worth looking at this stage at a typology of decisions in an attempt to formulate some criteria for allocating decision making to teams. Drucker (1966) proposed a framework involving two types of decisions: 'generic' and 'unique'. The former are based on principles, regulations, rules and policies. In other words, the decisions can be made by simply applying the appropriate policy or regulation. Unique decisions, in contrast, are not governed by any predetermined procedures. They are, in essence, creative decisions, since the team can explore all ideas with relevance to the problem.

Likewise, Simon (1980: 316) refers to 'programmed' and 'non-programmed' decisions. He differentiates between the two types. "Decisions are programmed to the extent that they are repetitive and routine, to the extent that a definite procedure has been worked out for handling them ... Decisions are nonprogrammed to the extent that they are novel, unstructured and consequential." 'Programmed' decisions then are similar to generic or routine decisions, whilst 'nonprogrammed' equate with unique decisions, being novel, important and unstructured. Simon (1971: 14) sees types of decisions as being on a continuum rather than as discrete categories.

The framework below is similar to those noted, but breaks the 'generic' decisions into two categories in order to account for those decisions that are made under extreme time pressures and for which a ready-made solution is not necessarily available. There are three broad categories:

- Standard decisions
- Crisis decisions
- Deep decisions

Standard Decisions

Standard decisions include everyday routine decisions. The solutions to them are normally governed by set procedures, rules and policies. They are relatively simple because of their routine nature, and can often be dealt with in a rational and logical manner, or by referring to set procedures. In fact, problems can arise if the decisions are not arrived at by reference to set rules.

There are also standard-type decisions that are not directly covered by organisational procedures. They can still be dealt with almost automatically, and problems may emerge only if the timing goes wrong or if the decision maker is insensitive.

Crisis Decisions

Crisis decisions are those that require quick, precise action and need to be made almost immediately. They are likely to appear without any clear warning and may demand immediate and undivided attention. These decisions allow little planning time and it is not usually feasible or realistic to involve others. As Peterson (1991: 171) notes:

"Obviously, when the missiles start flying, you can't call together a discussion group, but you'll be in a lot better shape if everything is working right and all your people are used to working as a close-knit team."

Deep Decisions

Deep decisions are usually not straightforward and require concentrated planning, discussion and reflection. These are the types of decisions that often involve setting direction or implementing change. They are also the decisions which involve the most debate, disagreement and conflict. Deep decisions often involve substantial time and specialised input. They may require the generation of alternatives from which to choose in reaching a good decision.

Deep decisions can involve selective, adaptive and creative or innovative processes (Woodcock and Francis, 1982). The selective process necessitates finding the best fit between the decision to be made and a number of 'field-tested' solutions. The team's effectiveness in this case depends on its choosing the decision which will be the most acceptable, productive and effective.

Adaptive processes involve the team in combining 'field-tested' solutions with new, more creative answers. The team, therefore, must be able to control and draw on past experience of what works and combine this with a touch of innovation.

Innovative processes involve the team in complex and creative insights into decision making. The team needs to use these skills in important, often poorly understood, unpredictable situations that require novel solutions. There is a danger in treating a complex problem as one that can be cured simply by applying old procedures.

The Decision-making Process

Although all types of decisions are important, little training is required for standard decisions and experience and networks may be the best teacher for crisis decisions. In a team setting, it is quite apparent that 'deep' decisions are the most relevant, and much of the reference to decisions in this section relates to this type of decision. The discussion on problems and decisions has to first set them in context. In simple terms, a problem is presented to the team to solve. This leads to a decision about how to solve it. The decision is then implemented and the results are evaluated. There are many frameworks available to make the process coherent and to explain the activities that must take place at each stage. The 7D Scheme, explained separately, describes a series of seven stages.

In our discussion on problems and decisions, we shall be concentrating on the part of the process that starts with the initial presentation of the problem, and which goes up to the point at which a decision is made. The activities involved in the subsequent implementation, and evaluation and review are explained in our description of the 7D Scheme. We shall address in detail, therefore, the following steps:

1. Identifying and understanding the problem and its causes.
2. Isolating the details of the problem and further defining understanding and desired outcome criteria.
3. Investigating various possible solutions and then evaluating these alternatives for decision applicability.
4. Making a decision.

Usually, these steps are handled by the team responsible for the decision. It is worth noting here, however, that some responsibilities can be delegated to other groups in an effort to make involvement more appropriate and economic. For example, a senior management team comprising twelve people may have the responsibility to reach a decision on implementing a scheme for grievance procedures. The team may delegate the tasks of collecting information and forming an understanding of the problem to a smaller project team. The senior management team may then define the ideal outcome criteria, but leave it to another small project team to investigate possible options and to evaluate them. This information can then be fed back to the management team, which makes the decision.

Decision-making Conditions

Any discussion of the decision-making process must account for the conditions under which decisions are made. Three conditions are generally stated: certainty, risk and uncertainty (Gibson and Hodgetts, 1986: 283).

Certainty is present when the team knows precisely what the outcome of any decision option will be. Such a condition is not very frequent and, in any event, a decision situation such as this is unlikely to attract a team's attention.

Many team decisions are made in conditions of risk. The team may have information, but the consequences are still unpredictable. There are ways, of course, of estimating the probability of some events occurring. These estimates are often based on experience. In considering possible financial outcomes, for example, it is possible to give each option a 'conditional value', the amount to be gained if the option is successful; a 'probability', which is the estimated likelihood of success; and the 'expected value', which is the product of the first two measures. Some decision situations lend themselves to such an approach; others, of course, do not.

Whyte (1991: 25) suggests that decisions are often made depending on how the decision makers *frame* the problem. Decisions are often framed in terms of losses or gains. He provides the following example:

> You are an administrator whose policies have recently resulted in losses of $2 million. You must now decide which of two projects to pursue. One project provides a certain return of $1 million; the other offers an even chance of a $2 million return or nothing. If you have been slow to adapt to your losses, you are likely to frame the decision as a choice between a sure loss of $1 million and an even chance to eliminate all losses, rather than as a choice between a sure gain of $1 million and an even chance to earn $2 million. The former choice is a choice between losses.

How the decision maker frames the decision provides the basis for its 'riskiness'. Such framing, usually seen as a choice between losses, often results in disastrous decisions, and, more often than not, increased losses.

The third condition is that of uncertainty. The probability process described above is not possible because the team is unable to estimate the likely outcome of alternatives. Nevertheless, an approach designed to reduce the uncertainty may still be employed. One such approach is the 'pessimism criterion' which states that the decision makers should ascertain the worst conditions for each option or strategy. The option that offers the best return under such conditions is the one that is accepted. At the opposite end of the scale, another approach is the 'criterion of optimism' in which the most favourable outcomes of each option are considered and assigned a probability figure.

The Delphi technique uses both a qualitative and a quantitative approach to forecasting. It pools the views of 'experts' and demands:

1. an anonymous prediction of important events in the area in question, from each expert in a group, in the form of brief statements;
2. a clarification of these statements by the investigator;
3. the successive, individual requestioning of the experts, combined with feedback supplied from the other experts via the investigator (Gibson and Hodgetts, 1986: 295).

Despite the lack of rigour inherent in the approach, it has been used widely and successfully. The problem with all these attempts at prediction, and thereby reducing uncertainty, is that they are incomplete. They are unable to account for all the social, political, micro-political, economic and technical factors. Teams, therefore, have to scan on an informal basis and be alert to the variables that can affect predictions and outcomes.

Decision-making Models

It is worth noting at this point that such systematic processes often assume rationality and comprehensiveness. They often imply clear, unconflicting objectives, a perfect knowledge of the decision situation and the ability to gather all relevant information, to circumscribe all possible alternatives, and to predict all consequences. This is unlikely to be an accurate picture of what really takes place. As Anderson (1984: 145) notes, information about the problem may be unavailable or too expensive to acquire; the problem may not be recognised; there may be pressures of speed, of higher management preferences, and competitors' actions; and the only alternatives that may be considered are those with which members are familiar or which they know will work. Drummond (1992: 2–4) claims that most organisations con-centrate too much on solutions in search of problems and suggests a number of reasons why decision making is generally handled badly:

- **Not so intelligent guesswork**: Decision makers do not think things through carefully enough; they often exacerbate pro-blems through failing to anticipate consequences and by using inadequate communication. They may also become more interested in trying to attribute blame rather than solving anything.

- **Learned helplessness**: When decision makers have experienced a number of failures they tend to give up.
- **Creating incompetence**: Overly bureaucratic 'checking' mechanisms often detract from innovative decisions and a culture of 'trying new things'.
- **Macho managers**: Perhaps the greatest factor leading to bad decisions is the stereotype of good leaders. They are supposed to be resolute and decisive. Reflection and consideration do not appear to be valued.

Rationality

Classical decision-making theory approached the process as a purely rational one. It assumed that decision makers think and act completely objectively. It also assumed that decision makers know all the alternatives and possible consequences of a situation. In the 1950s several scholars began to challenge this notion and developed so called 'limited rational models'. Perhaps the most famous of these was Herbert Simon (1951) who proposed the concept of 'bounded rationality'. He suggested that decisions were made through a 'satisficing' rather than an 'optimising' mode. In simple terms, Simon believed that decision makers usually settle for the best available decision under the circumstances they face. Rationality, it was claimed, is limited in the case of complex decisions for several reasons: there are simply too many options to think of and it is impossible to consider them all; second, the consequences of decisions cannot be predicted accurately because the future itself is complex; third, managers have habits, values and interpretations of purpose that may be at variance with organisational goals, and these in turn may impede rationality.

Incrementalism

Lindblom (1959) maintained that decisions were made on an incremental basis, generally known as 'the science of muddling through'. It was argued that this decision-making method is the only realistic approach when the problem issues are complex and when uncertainty and conflict are prevalent. Lindblom characterised the decision process as a method of successive limited comparisons, proposing that decisions were made in 'fits and starts' and 'bits and pieces', rather than by any great design (Jones, 1970). Goal setting and option generation were not seen as separate phases. Rather, courses of action emerge as options and consequences are investigated.

Another feature of the model is that only those options that are similar to the current situation are considered. Similarly, the method looks at deviations between the present state and intended outcomes, and takes no account of outcomes that are not directly related to the problem in question. These strategies are aimed at reducing the complexity in the decision-making process. Lindblom argued that by restricting the discussion to the small discrepancies or variations from the present situation, it would be possible to maximise the use of available information.

Adaptive Decision Making

Etzioni (1989) proposed a model of 'adaptive decision making' or 'mixed scanning'. It involves choices about team (or organisational) policy and direction, followed by incremental decisions to move the team in the way prescribed by such policy selection. The model is essentially a hybrid, combining the rationality of classical models with the flexibility of the incremental model. The main benefit is outlined by Hoy and Miskel (1991: 316): "Mixed scanning seeks to use partial information to make satisfactory decisions without either getting bogged down in an attempt to examine all the information or proceeding blindly with little or no information." A few of the activities characteristic of the approach are trial and error, procrastinating, hedging bets, and making reversible decisions.

The incremental model, previously discussed, has received criticism for being too narrow, especially in conditions of complexity and unpredictability. The incremental decisions may often lead to drifting without any clear focus. This is where the mixed scanning model claims to have an advantage. As Hoy and Miskel (1991: 319) advise, the model "is recommended to deal with impossibly complex decisions. Mixed scanning combines the best of both the satisficing and the incremental models. Here, a strategy of satisficing is used in combination with incremental decisions guided by broad policy. Full scanning is replaced by partial scanning of a set of satisfactory options, and tentative and reversible decisions are emphasized in an incremental process that calls for caution as well as a clear sense of destination."

Choices

Based on the above models, it is possible to observe types of choice behaviour that reflect them. Some people try to 'maximise' or make the best possible decision. This, as we have seen, may not be realistic, but the critics may view such attempts from the point of view of reality rather than intent. Trying to make the best decision – under the circumstances – is a reasonable ideal. Others stop searching when they have found a satisfactory solution to the problem: in other words, they 'satisfice'. Yet others 'muddle through', making small incremental decisions rather than the major one. This is certainly not typical of entrepreneurial behaviour, and that is why teams and individuals who 'increment' may lose out to those who take the big risks. Finally, there are those who behave in an 'adaptive' way. They develop the capacity to make decisions so that they can respond quickly (Anderson, 1984: 143).

Garbage Can

Two further models deserve attention. The 'garbage-can' model, developed by Cohen *et al.* in 1972, is largely descriptive and points to the ambiguity evident in the decision-making process. The model explains the difficulty in establishing cause and effect relationships, that different people are involved in decisions and that time is limited. The essential feature of the model is that decisions emerge from largely independent streams of events. Four such streams, namely, problems, solutions, participants and choice opportunities, are explained by Hoy and Miskel (1991: 320). Within the streams, decision making is haphazard and random. Sometimes, decisions may even appear before problems. For example, if someone comes up with a useful idea, a problem may be sought to match it with. The most apt description of the model is understandably from Cohen *et al.* (1972: 2) who state that organisations are "a collection of choices looking for problems, issues and feelings looking for decision situations in which they might be aired, solutions looking for issues to which they might be answers, and decision makers looking for work."

The model is useful in aiding our understanding of why some things happen as they do in teams and organisations, but it seems unlikely that it is truly typical of all organisations. It does help in raising the awareness, however, that an outright reliance on rational behaviour may be over-optimistic and that many factors may be involved in the decision-making process. On this latter point, in-depth analyses over the years have revealed that decision making is probably influenced by several important factors, and these include political considerations, organisational constraints, ideological beliefs and market forces.

Vigilance

Janis and Mann (1977) developed a model that addressed the issue of stress in decision making. One of the reasons for poor decisions, it was claimed, is the way in which people try to overcome stress when they are faced with difficult decisions. Some reactions hinder the effectiveness of the decision-making process and may be called dysfunctional. What Janis (1985) called 'vigilance' is a relatively effective pattern of coping with psychological stress and likely to lead to better decisions. Vigilance necessitates surveying options, analysing targets to be achieved, assessing the risks of the option choice, looking for new information through which to further evaluate options, meticulous evaluation of new information, re-examination of both good and bad consequences of options, and plans of action for implementation along with appropriate contingency plans (Hoy and Miskel, 1991: 323).

A Structure for Decision Making

The decision-making framework we presented earlier is not dissimilar to the above. It is true that it assumes a certain degree of rationality, but it has to be recognised that care must be exercised in defining precise outcomes. These may be impossible to predict in the light of the above discussion with any certainty. Similarly, it may be equally unrealistic to collect all relevant and impacting information. Despite the constraints, it seems necessary to have a structure with which to approach decision making. Such a structure is relevant to most forms of decision making, including the development of strategic plans, medium-range plans, operational plans and the solving of simple job problems. The structure, therefore, provides a coherent framework for approaching decision making.

We now take several of the stages from that framework and examine them in detail. First we look at the process of problem identification and analysis.

Problem Identification

It isn't that they can't see the solution. It is that they can't see the problem.

G.K. Chesterton, *The Scandal of Father Brown*

Probably the first stage in any decision-making process is to recognise that a problem exists and to attempt to understand it. In the case of problems presented to teams, it is usually a requirement that they deal with them. There may be instances, however, when the problem may not fall strictly within a particular team's domain and, under those circumstances, it may be wise to relocate the problem-solving process.

Identifying and understanding the problem is a critical part of the whole process and one which is not always handled effectively in organisations. There is a tendency to take short cuts and to treat 'symptoms' rather than causes. As Peter Drucker, the eminent management writer, is reported to have said: "There're a few things as useless – if not as dangerous – as the right answer to the wrong question." The key in this first stage then is deciding: 'What is the problem?'

Margerison (1973: 37) too notes that, if problem definition is wrong, subsequent planning and action are likely to be wasted. Indeed, the solution that emerges can be inappropriate and irrelevant if the problem has been incorrectly defined in the first place. An example of this occurred in a manufacturing company:

> In the packaging process, the machine that encased delicate components in bubble packs was constantly breaking down, causing serious hold-ups in the distribution chain. Team members at first simply said the machine was getting overheated because it was in a hot environment and the solution would be to buy a powerful fan to cool it. Although it worked for a short while, the fault soon reappeared. The problem, of course, was nothing to do with the environment (although it was a foundry), but was caused by a faulty heating element. The solution was to replace the element and set up a preventive maintenance schedule whereby the element would be changed on a regular basis.

A related and frequent difficulty encountered in everyday life is that most people are typically solution-centred rather than problem-centred. 'We don't have problems, only answers' is a frequently heard and totally insensitive response by many managers to questions about difficulties. Decision making is often *ad hoc* and does not differentiate between the decision and the decision-making process (Drummond, 1992: 5). As Hoy and Miskel (1991: 306) note, the likelihood of chaos in the long run under such conditions is inevitable. They go on to advise that the way a problem is conceptualised is vital to subsequent analysis and solution.

Problems are seldom as they appear on the surface and considerable effort may have to be expended in getting behind the symptoms to search for genuine causes. Sometimes, the definition of the problem may be as complex as the problem itself because of the diffuse elements. In such cases, the problem may have to be broken into sub-problems, and each of these put through the decision-making process. What is most important is that the 'real' problem is addressed. Teams, therefore, need skills of problem identification and analysis in order to be able to attack the fundamental, rather than some perceived, problem.

Several strategies are available to negotiate the problem identification process:

1. Discrepancies may be sought between what might be considered typical and what actually exists.
2. Cause-effect relationships can be examined.
3. Consultation can take place with those in a position to offer insights or different perspectives into a decision situation.
4. The situation can be examined from different angles.
5. The team can be open to all data that might emerge, with members being prepared to accept that they themselves may be a part of the problem.
6. Recurring problems can be spotted. They have not usually been understood adequately in the first place.

In terms of the discussion process, Maier's (1963) advice in his book *Problem Solving Discussions and Conferences* provides useful practical guidance. The problem should be stated without implying any preferred solution (this would inevitably limit discussion). Team members should be encouraged not to make statements but to ask questions in an attempt to seek detailed information about the problem.

Apart from these attempts to identify 'real' problems and their causes, other actions may support the process and facilitate identification. These include listening to and observing team members (and others outside the team). In particular, their concerns and feelings might be noted, especially where dissatisfaction becomes evident. Another strategy may be to watch out for unusual or inconsistent behaviour, since this may point to an underlying problem. It is also worth examining what has been tried for solving the problem before (Snyder, 1988: 216).

A useful procedure for defining problems has been developed by Kepner and Tregoe (1965). It involves finding differences between where symptoms of problems occur and where they do not, when they occur and when they do not, what they are and what they are not, and the changes that might have led to the problem (Anderson, 1984: 130). The causes can thus be narrowed down to what is actually happening. By the end of this stage the team should know what the problem is and what decisions need to be made.

Moving On

At this stage in the process, the decision making starts. The team has identified the 'real' problem and defined the situation. It may have developed some understanding of the causes. Now it must decide whether to:

- do nothing (a decision not to make a decision is a positive decision);
- place the problem on hold but under observation, and return to it at a later date;
- attempt to control the problem;
- move ahead to find a solution and make more decisions.

Probably one of the key steps in the problem analysis process, and one that tends to be neglected, is the defining of criteria of an acceptable solution. What are the minimum goals? What are the necessities and what are the desirables? What is satisfactory (as opposed to perfect)? It is also possible for the team to determine the outcomes that would lead to an extremely satisfying solution and those that would lead to a marginally satisfying solution. Anderson (1984: 133) refers to 'must' criteria and 'want' criteria. Teams have to exercise caution in setting 'must' criteria, since they can eliminate an option with possibilities. 'Must' criteria, therefore, are best re-evaluated on a regular basis in the process. 'Want' criteria are not so critical, but serve to force the team into thinking through the characteristics of the ideal solution. Taking the case of an interviewing panel's problem of whom to hire for a new job, such criteria may be used in the job description. A candidate, for example, 'must' have an honours degree for the job in question; on careful analysis, however, it may be found that the class of degree has little bearing on the job, and the criterion is better relegated to that of a 'want'.

The initial identification and understanding of the problem should determine the course of action to follow. Assuming that a solution must be found and decisions made, it may be necessary to isolate further details and decisions within decisions.

Isolating Details

This part of the process largely corresponds with the 'draw' phase of the 7D Scheme and represents an attempt to define the problem with even more clarity by considering other relevant details. In particular, it involves:

- acquiring situational details;
- defining the problem's scope;
- determining consequences;
- considering constraints.

Situational details

Looking at situational details may partly involve separating facts and opinions. This is particularly true in problems involving personal disputes, since opinions can be severely affected by emotions. Data may need to be collected and organised. It is not realistic to gather all the relevant information, so priorities may have to be set so that the most relevant data is acquired.

Problem scope

The team should consider the extent of the problem. In particular, it might ask questions about the potential impact – can it affect many or just a few? – and about its nature – is it about interpersonal difficulties or about the system? The answers to such questions may determine the resources allocated to the search for solutions. For example, if the problem threatens the competitiveness of the organisation and has detrimental financial consequences, considerable resources may have to be committed to finding a solution. It is worth noting that the types of problems often faced by teams are characterised by complexity and broad scope, and the resource issue is an important one.

Problem consequences

The question of consequences is closely related to scope. The team may need to discuss the likely severity of the problem if it is not tackled effectively. Again, if the impact is damaging, this may determine the extent of resource commitment required (Lewis and Kelly, 1986).

Constraints

Some of the factors that may stand in the way of effective problem solutions may be difficult to detect. They often stem from political sources. Whatever the constraints, part of this 'isolation' process involves identifying constraints and determining their potency. It may be decided that nothing can be done about some constraints, whilst others may present only marginal obstacles.

Criteria for Team Involvement

There is a general acceptance that it is good to involve teams in problem solving and decision making. Collaboration in the process, it is claimed, leads to support for decisions and commitment to implementation. People feel a deeper obligation to support and sustain those decisions they have helped to make. This, it is also widely claimed, can be a powerful force behind organisational success. Byrt (1980: 67) presents a number of arguments in favour of team involvement in decision making:

- The opportunity for deliberation and judgement
- The damping-down of the autocratic use of authority
- The representation of various points of view
- The use of groups to facilitate communication
- Involvement resulting in greater motivation of group members
- The provision of a means of defusing conflict

Part of the success of Japanese companies may be attributed to the focus on commitment and the strategies that support the path to acceptance. It is interesting to note some of the differences between Japan and the United States, for example, in terms of defining the problem and selecting options. In Japan, the emphasis is on a universal understanding of the problem and the underlying issues, whereas problem definition in American organisations (and those of other western countries) is sometimes sadly neglected. The Japanese go for extended debate leading to consensus and bring out areas of dissent; they also evaluate options. In many other cultures, however, involvement is limited, with decisions being made at the top and 'announced'; decision making also tends to be fast, with a search for the one 'right' answer. In short, the processes employed by Japanese companies may, it is claimed, lead to a heightened sense of commitment.

Sometimes, however, teams may be involved in these processes when their involvement is not really necessary. For example, where a decision area clearly involves a single area of competence, it is more likely that only an individual is needed. It may also be possible to determine needed involvement from the nature of the problem. If it is easily defined, has clear boundaries, has fixed criteria for an acceptable solution, contains unambiguous information, and depends on facts rather than values, it is probably best to rely on the expertise of an individual (Wynn and Guditus, 1984: 97).

Indeed, difficulties may emerge from over-involvement. There is now a realisation in some quarters that, although participative decision making is valuable in many situations, in others it can actually be counterproductive. As the above authors (p. 95) observe, it is neither desirable nor feasible to refer all decisions to groups, and that there should be critical determination of which decisions should be undertaken by teams. Byrt (1980: 67) presents a list of some criticisms of too much involvement:

- The unnecessary cost in time and money
- The tendency to compromise
- The danger of domination of groups by demagogues, manipulators or formers of coalitions
- The conformity resulting from group pressure
- The development of factionalism in groups
- Inertia – group members relying on others to think for them

Many of the criticisms of group or team decision making may stem from a lack of awareness in organisations about the correct location for problems and decisions. Indeed, our research showed that senior managers used intuition rather than set criteria when determining which decisions should be handled by their senior management teams (Walker and Stott, 1992). It seems necessary, therefore, to examine a set of criteria that will provide a guide to effective and appropriate involvement of teams in problem solving and decision making.

As a starting point, Wynn and Guditus (1984: 112) point to three conditions under which decisions made by teams are likely to be superior to those made by individuals:

1. The problem is difficult to conceptualise.
2. The problem needs to be reasoned out in related stages.
3. The problem requires coordination and interaction amongst relevant individuals for effective implementation.

Despite the rationale behind such conditions, it is worth noting that "although there is no best way to allocate decision-making responsibility in all circumstances, there are identifiable variables that can dictate who should decide under specific contingencies" (p. 95). Some of these variables and contingencies include those already identified, in particular, the nature of the problem or decision. Other criteria are explained below.

Expertise and Relevance

One of the considerations might be whether expertise is required and the relevance of the decision situation to people's work. In the latter case, it may not be only the relevance to team members themselves, but perhaps to the people they represent. Therefore, when a chief executive decides whether to refer a problem to the senior management team, one consideration may be the relevance of the problem and resulting decision to the workforce they represent.

Relevance, however, has to be seen from a relative perspective. It would be too simplistic to say a decision either affects people's working lives or it doesn't. In fact, it might be argued that all decisions affect people in some way or other. The question is one of degree. The more relevance a decision area has to the members of the team, the greater the need for team involvement.

In terms of expertise and relevance, Bridges (1967) developed what he called the 'Zone of Acceptance'. This refers to an invisible area of decision acceptance perceived by people. If they are likely to accept a decision without involvement, it is inside their zone of acceptance. Conversely, if they are unlikely to accept the decision, it is outside their zone of acceptance.

There are two tests to identify the location of decisions:

1. **The 'test of relevance'**: Do people have a personal stake in the decision outcome?
2. **The 'test of expertise'**: Do people have any expertise which could assist in making a quality decision?

In terms of relevance, it may need to be asked whether team participation is justified in order to achieve ownership, commitment and allegiance to the decision. A recurring theme in the literature is that decisions arrived at in a consensual mode strengthen the team's resolve to make them work.

Sometimes, the decision areas are not necessarily complex, but support is needed to make the decision work. In this case, team involvement may be justified. For example, if the managing director wishes to implement an appraisal system with his senior colleagues, he could simply import an established model or bring in a consultant to design it. However, he would be well advised to involve his management team in such a decision, since the members' understanding and support would be crucial to success. In this case, a performance evaluation system could be controversial and the quality of the outcome could be affected by the behaviour of the participants in the process. Wynn and Guditus (1984: 163) reinforce this point: "If ... group acceptance of the solution is important, then the efficiency inherent in limiting involvement in the resolution of the problem may not be enough to override the benefits of group participation. The absence of broader involvement can, and frequently does, jeopardize successful implementation of even a highly appropriate solution."

The team leader's role, where the lowering of resistance is sought, may be to explain the reasoning behind an intended course of action. Team members are then asked to consider the risks and dangers that might occur if a particular option is implemented. They then have the opportunity to vent their anxieties before action is taken. This, of course, helps to gauge potential resistance, but it also provides a useful opportunity to disseminate important and useful information to team members to enhance the chances of gaining acceptance and, possibly, commitment.

The issue of expertise is also important. Those who have the relevant knowledge and information should not only be involved but also take the lead. From this perspective, power may be more associated with competence than with rank and title. George (1977: 79) suggests it should be the intent "for the individual who comes up with the best solution or who can penetrate a complex problem to carry the day in the decision-making process, not the person with the highest rank."

Using these criteria, it is plain that decision situations need to be outside the zone of acceptance to necessitate team involvement. These criteria do not stand alone, however, and have to be seen in conjunction with several other sets of criteria.

Quality and Acceptance

Two important considerations concern the quality of the decision and its acceptance. Using these dimensions, Maier (1963) produced four 'either / or' situations to guide team and group involvement in decision making. These are shown in Figure 14.1.

Time

Time pressures can also influence the intensity of involvement in decision making. There are two major considerations:

1. How much time is available and required to reach a decision?
2. How much time is needed to develop an understanding of the decision outcome by those expected to implement the decision?

Faced with severe time restrictions, it is difficult to involve teams in decision making. However, it may not take long for one person to make an important and far-reaching decision, but it may take much longer to explain, gain people's commitment and implement. Conversely, if the team is involved, it may take longer to reach a satisfactory decision outcome, but it will almost certainly be easier and quicker to implement and commitment will be more forth-coming. This is shown graphically in Figure 14.2.

Peterson (1991: 58) interestingly disputes the fact that decisions in teams take longer. He advocates fixing set times for decisions and claims that decisions become more solid, that they stick more

CONDITION 1	Neither quality nor acceptance is important.
INVOLVEMENT	No involvement is required.

CONDITION 2	Acceptance is important; quality is not.
INVOLVEMENT	Involvement is appropriate and necessary. This type of situation usually involves decisions that affect people.

CONDITION 3	Quality is important; acceptance is not.
INVOLVEMENT	Although involvement of team members is not vital for acceptance, it may be wise to draw on expertise.

CONDITION 4	Both quality and acceptance are important.
INVOLVEMENT	This situation demands participative processes.

Figure 14.1   Quality and Acceptance

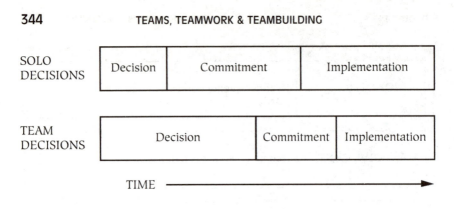

Figure 14.2   Time Taken to Implement Decisions

easily because of the involvement, and that they are actually made faster.

Peterson's view may reflect reality in a few organisations, but a more pragmatic view is that decisions reached through a genuine consensus approach take time, and the question has to be asked about the value of the investment. Time taken on this activity is simply not available for others, so time usage is an issue to be considered seriously.

Need for Interdependencies

Team decision making may be needed in some cases to ensure smooth implementation, not because of the political or potentially controversial elements involved, but because of the coordination difficulties. If the decision centres on the need for specialised units to coordinate their efforts, it may be essential to have their involvement.

A useful model for considering involvement is what Wynn and Guditus (1984: 109) call 'a contingency model for decision-making modes'. We have adapted it and show in Figure 14.3 some general modes of decision making and a list of possible situational variables. The black dots indicate the appropriate decision-making mode. It should be noted, however, that this is merely an example of a model that can be used. Teams would have to devise modes that are applicable to their circumstances, list the situational variables that are most relevant to them, and discuss where the dots should be inserted in their particular contexts for operation.

An appropriate way of using the model is to look at the situational variables that relate to a particular problem and then spot the modes

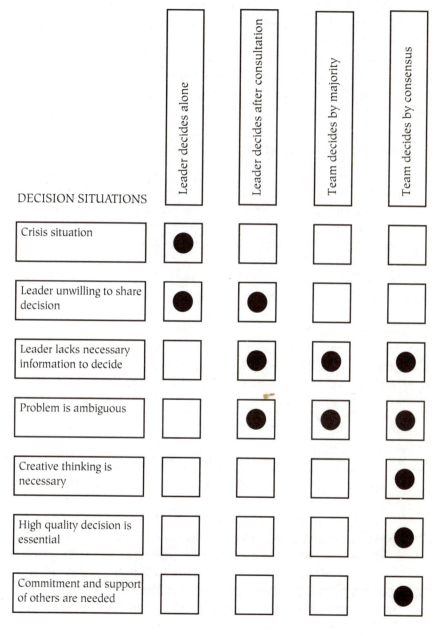

Figure 14.3   Decision-making Situations and Modes

that appear against either the largest number of variables checked or alternatively the most important ones. This is a useful approach for those in charge of agendas to decide whether matters should be referred to teams or not.

Byrt (1980: 68) believes the issue of involvement to be largely academic and the real question lies with the degree or extent of involvement. This appropriately leads our discussion into considering briefly how much involvement might be given to team members.

Extent of Involvement

Vroom and Yetton's (1973) contingency approach suggested that the extent of involvement should be related to the nature of the problem and the problem situation. Their model is based on two sets of rules, the first concerned with quality, and the second with acceptance. They explain, with supporting rationale, the conditions under which group decisions are necessary.

The same authors also showed that there are a number of decision-making style possibilities that reflect the extent of involvement given to the team. For example, it is possible for team members to be simply consulted but to have no impact on the final outcome. On the other hand, the leader may hand over total responsibility to the team for the final decision. These represent almost completely opposite ends of the involvement spectrum. Another related issue is whether to have team member involvement at just one stage of the problem-solving process or throughout the entire operation.

Team leaders, as we can see, have a range of options from which to select when involving team members in decisions. One way of explaining these is on a continuum ranging from 'autocratic' to 'consensus', and a brief description of these possible approaches is provided below:

- **Autocratic:** A decision is made by the leader and announced to the team. Discussion and challenge are not invited. Adair (1986: 67) calls decisions made in this way 'self-authorised decisions'.
- **Final say:** Discussion-generated solutions are permitted. The leader may take them into account when making the final decision or may ignore them.
- **Elite group:** Only selected members of the team are involved in making the decision with the leader. They discuss, make the decision, and then present it to the rest of the team. In some

cases, this process may take place in the presence of other team members.

- **Consultancy**: The leader makes an initial, tentative decision, and then presents it to the team for discussion and the input of its ideas. The team members' opinions are considered openly before a decision is reached. The leader has an open mind and allows refinement of initial decisions, and can tolerate dissenting views and suggestions. After all this, however, the decision is still made by the leader.

- **Majority rules**: All team members are involved in the decision process by having an equal vote. After discussion, the successful decision is the one that receives the most votes. This is sometimes called the 'parliamentarian' arrangement. It can lead to difficulties if the winning majority alienates the minority. The leader has to give those in a minority the opportunity to be heard before arriving at a decision.

- **Consensus**: A decision cannot be reached until all team members agree on a specific decision. Voting is not allowed. This method can produce high quality decisions because of the intense and varied input, but can be very time consuming. Consensus is a decision method for making full use of available human resources, and for resolving conflicts and major problems creatively.

Consensus style obviously has a vast impact on the extent of involvement in decision making that is given to team members. Our attention, therefore, is now turned to this important topic.

Consensus

Consensus may be defined as 'agreement to make a decision on the part of all members of the team after full and open discussion'. We shall see below that it is not the same as unanimous accord. Consensus is largely concerned with agreement to implement a decision that appears to be the most acceptable to the team as a whole. It is important to distinguish between true and false consensus. Adair (1986: 68) states that, in the latter, people may appear to agree, but when it comes to implementation, they seem to have different ideas and, in some cases, have even reserved the right not to implement the decision. In contrast, true consensus means that all team members are prepared to act as if the decision were their own preferred outcome.

There are very persuasive arguments in the literature for achieving consensus. The resultant quality of decisions is a particularly powerful rationale. The reason for this is that the more reliance there is on the team to solve problems, the greater the consideration of alternative outcomes. Another significant advantage is that there are no perceived winners and losers. Other processes may lead to battles where some go away as the triumphant winners and others leave frustrated and determined not to give their commitment to implementation. This is a strong case for achieving decisions on a consensual basis where everyone can gain (Margerison, 1973: 47).

> Consensus, however, is difficult to reach, as all team members must agree on the final decision. Complete unanimity is not the goal as it is rarely achieved, but team members should be able to accept the group ranking on the basis of logic and feasibility. It is unlikely that every detail will meet with everyone's complete approval, but members must be convinced, as individuals, that the decision is the right one and agree to go along with it. Consensus means giving each person an equal chance to influence the outcome. It need not – and rarely does it – mean a unanimous decision. Often a consensus is achieved in the face of strong opposition when the opponents have had their say, feel heard and supported, and agree at last to support the course of action most people want to take (Weisbord, 1985: 29).

Wynn and Guditus (1984: 133) give guidelines on the statements that should be able to be made if the process has produced a genuinely consensual decision:

1. I believe you understand my position.
2. I believe I understand your position.
3. I can support the team's decision because it was reached fairly.

Consensus is only possible in the right interpersonal climate. The team's interpersonal development, therefore, is a necessary adjunct to the decision-making processes. The climate must be characterised by openness, trust and authenticity in interpersonal communication (Anantaraman, 1984a: 156). The same author also specifies three pre-conditions that must be perceived to exist by team members:

> (1) perceived freedom to express one's views in the group;
> (2) perceived freedom to express opposition to views expressed by others in the group; and

(3) a feeling that he has been listened to and understood whenever he expresses his views or opposes the views expressed by others.

Similar, but even broader, conditions are expressed by Wynn and
Guditus (1984: 43) in the form of a protocol. They refer to consensus
as both a mode and mood of decision making, and it is this protocol
that gives rise to the mood:

1 Those who will be significantly affected by a decision participate in
   making it, directly or through representatives.
2 All who have valid and relevant information are fully heard.
3 Everyone is free to express dissent and welcomes the expression of
   others' dissent.
4 Everyone strives hard for openmindedness and understanding of others'
   views.
5 Everyone strives to avoid categorical 'aye' and 'nay' choices, in favour
   of integrative decisions that accommodate the expectations of all.
6 Everyone feels some obligation toward voluntary deference toward
   consensus in the interests of group accord without surrender of his
   advocacy of a minority view.
7 The minority accepts the position of 'loyal opposition,' while pledging
   support of the consensus.
8 The group accepts the right of the chief executive, or small executive
   committee, to substitute a decision for the group's decision when (a)
   consensus is unattainable or (b) sufficient time is unavailable to reach
   consensus.
9 The loyal opposition maintains the right to have the decision re-evaluated
   after a trial period and subject to later reconsideration.

Consensus involves a different approach to problems and issues and
requires a certain degree of skill. One of the processes that is useful
is derived from the negotiation context and is called 'bridging' (Pruitt,
1983). It involves the rephrasing of questions in searching for solutions.
It also applies where there are strongly contrasting views on the action
that should be taken or on priorities. For example, a school management team was discussing the provision of extracurricular activities
for the following year. There were obviously two strong and apparently
irreconcilable views evident. Some felt there should be as many activities
as resources would permit in order to give the children as much choice
as possible; others felt that the school's reputation was suffering
because it never did very well in competitions at district or national levels.
They felt a narrower range on offer would help to focus attention on
activities in which the school could excel and thereby improve its
performance in competition. The obvious question, and the one that

would produce the most difficulties from a consensus perspective, would be: Which view shall we accept? Using a 'bridging' approach, however, the question could be reformulated: How can we solve this problem in such a way that the children enjoy a range of activity options and that the school is able to improve its performance in competitions? This approach is 'integrative', in that it attempts to accommodate different perspectives. There is no cast-iron guarantee that it will work on every occasion, but it helps to refocus thinking and is a useful aid in moving towards consensus.

One of the problems with such consensus approaches is that they may be wrongly associated with chaos, where everyone does his own thing. Democratic approaches to team decision making need the same tight control that any well organised system requires, but the definition becomes more complex in the team setting. Another problem is that simply too many decisions may be put through the process. This may result in overloading team members, increased stress levels, diverting of attention away from more important responsibilities, and too little time for discussion of important issues.

Another problem, which was outlined earlier, is that consensus may take time, and the benefits, therefore, have to be considered. There can be considerable costs involved. The point must be re-inforced that staff time is expensive, and the involvement in consensual approach team meetings must be worth the cost involved. The criteria for referring decisions to teams must be clear and sustainable. Consensus may be a powerful procedure when used successfully, but in some situations it is unrealistic, and it is best applied only to those situations where complete agreement is absolutely essential.

One further problem is that consensus can easily fail. It is comparatively easy to achieve with a small, tightly-knit group, and in fact the opposite problem of 'groupthink' is likely to occur, where consensus decisions are reached with considerable ease. With larger teams, however, consensus is often more difficult. The problem is further exacerbated in the presence of complex problem issues or those that involve risk. Consensus can also fail through delay. This may be caused by a general unwillingness to reach the point of decision or by leaders who prolong the process by trying to achieve 'perfect' outcomes.

The leader's role in a consensus approach is different from that adopted in others. He guides the discussion and uses conflicting viewpoints to draw out and highlight the similarities. He focuses on advantages of proposals in an attempt to integrate the good points of each and then finds options that incorporate such features. The leader has to take a neutral stance, acting as a facilitator so that team members can concentrate on the issues of the problem situation.

Consensus-type approaches have implications for the nature of team member involvement. Participation cannot be peripheral. Members need to have at least as great an understanding of the problem as the leader or those who feed the problem into the team. Members are the ones who have to make the solution work, so they need all the relevant information. The worst thing senior administrators can do is to present teams with problems to solve and then to withhold information that could have an important bearing on the decisions.

Another implication worth noting is the acceptance of, and commitment to, consensus. Leaders may be reluctant to 'let go' totally and reserve the right to veto decisions. In some circumstances and some decision situations, this seems reasonable, but there are considerable dangers in overturning team decisions too often. Used capriciously, the veto compromises the credibility of the consensus approach.

Dissent and Criticism

In discussing consensus, we mentioned the need for dissent. Unfortunately, many teams which perform poorly establish norms that discourage all forms of disagreement, and encourage conformity to the norm of obedient compliance with superiors' views. The absence of dissent and criticism, however, can have a severe and adverse impact on the work of the team.

Margerison and McCann (1989: 17) go so far as to say that the key function of the team meeting is to encourage the expression of different views, and reinforce the view that this is the only way of evaluating strengths and weaknesses of arguments. Dissent, however, has to be handled positively, and this may be achieved by focusing on facts and opinions about task issues rather than the personalities involved. On a practical level, the team leader may need to ask for specific facts to support opinions, and to request opinions from those who offer facts.

How can dissent be encouraged, especially in those settings which have become used to universal agreement and accord? First, time can be set aside in team meetings for tough-minded criticism and to refinement of ideas. Also, the team leader can invite dissent by removing all elements of personal threat. For example, the leader might say, "The other side may not be quite so happy about this course of action. Could someone present the other side's case?" This is a clear invitation to present an opposing view. When an individual responds, the leader can express appreciation and invite others to contribute. Dissent is therefore welcome and even rewarded with a supportive comment. Another strategy, as we saw when we looked at the Monitor Evaluator role, is to have someone in the team who is specifically requested to play the role of devil's advocate and to provide a dissenting voice to all ideas. In particular, the role involves voicing contrary opinions, identifying misinterpretations, and spotting the things that could go wrong with a plan of action. This can be done on a rotating basis.

Generating Options and Selecting

This part of the decision-making process involves the generation of options, their evaluation or analysis, and the selection of the best option: a decision. In short, teams need to decide what is involved if they take a certain route and then decide if they can actually do it. This is the part in which creativity is arguably essential.

The conditions for creating options need to be right, and these typically include:

1. a willingness to make fewer black-and-white distinctions.
2. the use of divergent and creative thinking patterns.
3. time to develop as many reasonable alternatives as possible (Hoy and Miskel, 1991: 310).

Problems usually give rise to several possible solutions. If there were no choice of alternatives, there would be no decision to be made. The team's role is to identify alternatives. Some of the literature advises the consideration of all alternatives alongside all their possible consequences. This seems unrealistic in the context of modern team management. It also seems impractical without the aid of a crystal ball. The sensible approach may be to consider available alternatives and then to decide which offers the most appropriate solution. This is likely to be the one that is consistent with predetermined goals and targets, and which accounts for the identified constraints.

Going along this path towards successful decision outcomes involves two processes: creative thinking and analytical thinking. We now turn our attention to the first of these.

Creativity in Decision Making

Perhaps the strongest argument favouring team decision making lies in the concept of the 'risky shift' (Byrt, 1980: 67). Put simply, the concept indicates that decisions made by teams are usually "more risky, adventurous, innovating than decisions on the same subject made by the members of the group as individuals" (p. 68). Byrt provides reasons given for risky shift:

> The diffusion of responsibility among a number of persons.
>
> The influence of adventurous, vocal members of groups.
>
> The fact that members of groups favouring risky or innovatory decisions are likely to be more committed to their decisions than those favouring safe courses of action are likely to be *theirs*. Consequently, the former may exert more pressure and influence.
>
> The support of others tends to make a person more adventurous.
>
> In many organisations, lip-service at least is paid to the importance of adventurousness – an acceptable value in western countries. Accordingly, overt group pressure is likely to be in favour of more, not less, risk. Nobody wishes to be classed as being unadventurous.

Convergent thinking is analytical, narrowing down to small ideas that can be further analysed and implemented. It is the sort of thinking that produces the solutions to problems. Divergent thinking is creative, providing ideas and possible answers to problems. It is easy to see how these two forms of thinking go together.

We saw earlier how, traditionally, convergent thinkers have carried the day. This is because norms have tended to support logical behaviour. In such an environment, team members are more likely to stick to obvious and safe solutions, even if they are not very effective. In fact, some of them could be described as mediocre or simplistic, and totally inappropriate responses to complex problems. Indeed, convergent thinking on its own can be problematic, because it can act as a self-imposed barrier that gets in the way of new ideas and novel ways of tackling established activities.

To move away from this, and towards developing individuals' capacities for divergent thinking, support is needed for an environment that fosters innovative ways of thinking as the norm. As Woodcock

(1979) observes: "Creativity is a delicate flower which only flourishes in the right conditions, mainly conditions of personal freedom and support; freedom to experiment, try out ideas and concepts and support from those who listen, evaluate and offer help." This obviously means providing the right environment. Adair (1986: 155) suggests teams are capable of providing a context in which creativity might flourish: "Atmosphere, communication, standards, leadership, morale; all contribute to a positive climate which stimulates, triggers, encourages and develops the exploratory thinking of individuals."

This should not mean that team members have to be left alone to be creative. On the contrary, some innovative organisations have found it is advantageous to establish a solid framework within which to develop creative ideas. Such organisations set goals and targets, give rewards, and coordinate the work amongst teams.

> One organisation set the right context for creative ideas by forming problem-solving teams and supporting them with recognition and resources. One of these teams faced a problem of a machine getting oil leaks, and the first response was to use pans and trays to catch the oil and then pour it away. This actually worked, but it was laborious. The problem was associated with the machine's bearings and gaskets, and although some maintenance worked, it was expensive and meant the machine being shut down for lengthy periods. One seemingly silly idea emerged from one member, but this was built on by others, and it resulted in a simple hose being connected to the problem area and the leaking oil was channelled straight back into the machine.

In this team, the conditions for creativity were supportive. In contrast, Anderson (1984: 166) draws on the work of selected studies and examines some of the characteristics of organisations that set conditions for low creativity. It is easy to transpose these observations to the team setting: Such organisations "require employees to adhere to a rigid chain of command, use close supervision, tend to avoid conflict (new and conflicting ideas), and use rewards based on meeting goals established at the top of the organization rather than on giving employees challenging jobs. These organizations create a culture in which the way to succeed is to stick to tried-and-true methods. Challenging authority with ideas and suggestions is not permissible."

Many of these conditions may be familiar to the team setting and it hardly seems surprising that the ideas which emerge are neither novel nor stunning. Anderson goes on to list the characteristics of creative organisations:

> Rules tend to be deemphasized in creative organizations, especially rules about sticking to the formal hierarchy. Many creative organizations encourage ideas from any level. Rules about failure build an attitude that it is permissible to fail if attempts are being made to innovate, although failure is not desirable. The emphasis is on building interest in improving the job and the product. This comes by providing recognition for innovation and 'having fun' on the job while adhering to some deadlines and profit goals. Finally, creative organizations use a management style that deemphasizes the power and status differences between levels in the hierarchy and instead supports team efforts, especially across departments.

Creativity may give rise to ideas capable of being processed into powerful solutions to difficult problems. The fundamental differences between the traditional approach to problem solving and a creative approach which, it is claimed, presents a better alternative to solving problems in the long term, are identified by Snyder (1988: 212):

Typical	Creative
Order	Speculation
Correctness	Options
Control	Building
Certainty	Playfulness
Unidirectionality	Deviations
Fixed classifications	Alterations
Judgements	Richness
Expected answer	Irrelevancy
Detail	
Precision	

The questionnaire entitled 'Creativity' (Figure 14.4) provides a starting point for understanding the creativity of individuals in teams. It may be completed by each individual in the team and used as an approximate measure of innovatory capacity.

Looking at the modern context for decision making, why has creativity become such a prominent feature of the problem-solving

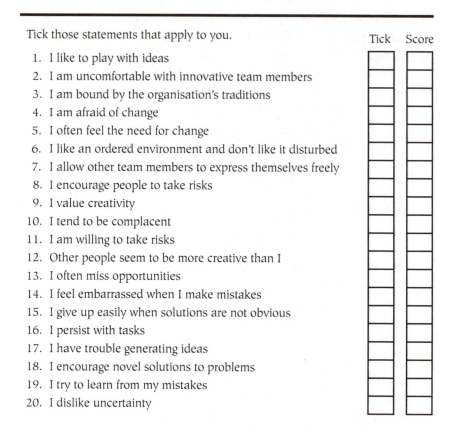

Tick those statements that apply to you.   Tick   Score

1. I like to play with ideas
2. I am uncomfortable with innovative team members
3. I am bound by the organisation's traditions
4. I am afraid of change
5. I often feel the need for change
6. I like an ordered environment and don't like it disturbed
7. I allow other team members to express themselves freely
8. I encourage people to take risks
9. I value creativity
10. I tend to be complacent
11. I am willing to take risks
12. Other people seem to be more creative than I
13. I often miss opportunities
14. I feel embarrassed when I make mistakes
15. I give up easily when solutions are not obvious
16. I persist with tasks
17. I have trouble generating ideas
18. I encourage novel solutions to problems
19. I try to learn from my mistakes
20. I dislike uncertainty

Give yourself 5 points for each statement if you ticked numbers 1, 4, 5, 7, 8, 9, 11, 16, 18, and 19. Place your scores in the score boxes. Then total the scores and enter on the graph below.

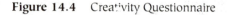

0   10   20   30   40   50

A score in excess of 35 indicates high creativity. The lower the score, the lower the level of creativity.

Figure 14.4   Creativity Questionnaire

process? Generally, the emphasis in decision making has been on finding *the* correct answer or acceptable solutions based on past experiences. This relies very much on convergent thinking, and this has been a skill traditionally cherished in organisations. This presents a barrier to creativity, because once the answer has been found, there may be a reluctance to try other answers. Many teams and organisations support this limitation.

The scene, however, is fast changing, as Wynn and Guditus (1984: 163) observe:

> Increasingly the problems confronting contemporary organizations are not amenable to the more obvious solutions from the past. This may be true for several reasons. The problem may be quite unlike anything that the individual or the organization has previously experienced. Or it may be a recurring concern, but the conditions that now exist make the solutions of the past less desirable or even unacceptable.

A major problem of convergent thinking is that it tends to lead to 'satisficing' as opposed to 'optimising'. Satisficing, as we saw earlier in this chapter, involves finding a solution that is satisfactory under the circumstances, whereas optimising means taking the best course of action (March and Simon, 1958).

In modern conditions, the need is not so much for 'convergent' thinking skill but 'divergent' thinking. This, of course, provides a sound rationale for the involvement of teams in problem solving, since they will usually increase the generation of alternative solutions. Peterson (1991: 37) picks up this very point:

> Working in teams is far better than trying to dream up ideas by yourself. A mental synergism starts occurring, and ideas rapidly bounce off one another. When a lot of disparate knowledge comes together, one person can pick up on what another says and add his or her insights; as a result, you get ideas and solutions that people working in isolation would never come up with on their own.

Each team member usually has the ability to be creative. In the first place, intelligence does not seem to be a prerequisite for creativity. Also, it does not necessarily involve dreaming up new ideas or always making unique inputs. Quite often, it involves combining a number of ideas already tried in an imaginative fashion. Margerison (1973: 43) indeed suggests that useful ideas are often passed over: "In many cases people are looking for the 'perfect' solution, rather than building upon those that are available.

They thus reject the available and relatively good idea for the potentially available theoretically best idea."

Anderson (1984: 137) provides some useful guidelines for improving individuals' creativity:

1. Make sure the problem is well defined, but not too narrowly. Define all its elements.
2. Approach the problem from different angles. Don't jump to conclusions too quickly. Produce *several* alternatives and critically evaluate each one. Try to remove perceptual blocks.
3. Don't worry about being practical (e.g., about costs) too early in the process. This may eliminate ideas prematurely.
4. Focus on the critical attributes of the problem. What is the most important detail that must be solved?
5. Avoid conformity. Be willing to question all ideas and standards if they have drawbacks.
6. Be alert for good solutions for which there currently aren't problems. Store them away for future use. Teflon was discovered this way.
7. Talk to outside experts. Many times they have different, unique perspectives.
8. Take breaks. Getting away from the problem allows time for illumination.

There are moves in some fields to make people more creative by teaching them how to use both sides of the brain. It is claimed that 'left brain' people are less imaginative than their 'right brain' counterparts, and that they need 'whole brain' training to heighten their creative senses. Similarly, those who are naturally innovative need to learn how to approach problems with more awareness of logic and procedure.

One technique designed to help individuals think creatively is called 'inside-out thinking'. Some of the activities that are part of this development tool are as follows:

1. *Thinking about the problem from the opposite end.* A team of car designers was looking at car security, and they concentrated their attention on becoming car 'thieves' by finding ways of breaking into cars. This helped them to design devices that would make things more difficult for thieves.

2. *Assuming all information is inaccurate.* Everything has to be checked out again. Quite often, assumptions become matters of fact over time, making stubborn problems even more difficult to solve.

3. *Looking at the wider problem context.* The marketing staff often failed to get enquiries through to the production planning unit within the prescribed time limit. The management team focused, not on the marketing people's inadequacies, but on their operating environment. They were far removed from production planning (for no obvious reason) and the amount of paperwork they were required to complete when an enquiry came in was unrealistically demanding.

4. *Wearing someone else's shoes.* This involves viewing the problem from a different perspective. It can be quite revealing to understand the situation from the other person's side. For example, the problem may indeed be that the buyer is not providing costings for a project within twenty four hours, but it may be helpful to attempt to 'sit in his seat' and understand why there is a delay.

Criteria for Creativity

Regardless of the techniques used, if teams are to promote creativity amongst their members, four criteria need to be met:

- Members must have open minds.
- They must be willing to take risks.
- They must test out their ideas.
- They must resist making judgements.

Open mind

Problems must be treated as new and different ones, and existing solutions must be assumed temporarily to be inappropriate. Different ideas must be listened to seriously, however bizarre. Indeed, some of the most powerful ideas have emerged from such seeds. The leader may have an important part to play in setting an environment that encourages speculation and imagination, and that avoids immediate acceptance of the one 'obvious' answer.

There must also be a recognition that wisdom is not necessarily synonymous with rank and title. In other words, productive ideas can spring from individuals who are comparatively junior in status, and the team needs to provide the opportunity for these to make open contributions to discussion. There are many instances of teams where ideas are automatically rejected if they stem from a junior member or from someone outside the team.

Taking risks

No one likes to feel foolish and that often prevents them from speaking out in team meetings. The problem can be further exacerbated by colleagues who ridicule suggestions. Teams may need risk-takers in the sense that ideas that have never been tried before may need exploring. They may fail. Successful teams nevertheless are more likely to treat these as learning experiences and continue to support risk-taking.

One of the interesting phenomena amongst teams practising consensual approaches to decision making is that they are more likely to opt for riskier decisions than individuals (Byrt, 1980: 68; Wallach and Kogan, 1965).

Testing ideas

It is easy to get too close to problems and ideas, and this may limit thinking. It may be useful to test out ideas by discussing them with friends and colleagues not involved in the particular decision-making scene. They provide a perspective which can be very different.

Resisting judgements

Margerison (1973: 43) notes: "There is a tendency in most groups to look for weaknesses in the ideas put forward, rather than strengths. There are always some who wish to puncture an idea before it has been tried." What Margerison means by 'tried' is that it should be discussed and its strong points should be identified. When seeking ideas from the team, it is advisable to encourage as many alternatives as possible to solving a problem before evaluating their worth. If judgements are made too soon, open contributions may be discouraged and there is a risk that truly creative decisions will be missed.

The Creative Process

The creative process can be thought of in four stages: preparation, incubation, illumination and verification. The first stage is largely concerned with setting the scene by gathering appropriate information. It has been found that creative solutions and ideas often emerge after a period of inactivity, and incubation, therefore, means allowing the subconscious to work on the data before moving to the third stage, where the individual realises what is the best decision in the circumstances. Sometimes, this occurs quickly, and at others, it takes some time for the right course of action to emerge. The final stage is where modifications are made to the solution and fine tuning takes place.

A slightly different scheme is presented by Anderson (1984: 136) who identifies six steps. The first, 'motivation', is concerned with people's desire to work on a problem. The second stage is 'saturation' and involves team members becoming familiar with the problem. This contradicts those who believe that creative ideas appear like a flash of lightning. The notion of saturation suggests that considerable hard work is involved in coming up with worthwhile ideas. The 'deliberation' stage entails questioning assumptions and looking at old problems in new ways. The next stage, 'incubation', is the same as that in the above framework, where time is allowed for the problem to sink in. 'Illumination' is when the right idea emerges, and the final stage, 'accommodation', is the process of matching the solution to the problem and establishing if it works. It may involve testing out ideas on others and making modifications where necessary.

Generating options

Most forms of creativity, by definition, necessitate the generation of a large number of ideas. Often the best germs of ideas come from those team members who are somewhat unconventional. They may not be the easiest people to work with, and there are many cases of alienation and relationship breakdowns. Some team leaders seem to be incapable of handling those who break easily with convention and who promote their sometimes odd ideas. As we saw when looking at the roles people play in teams, however, these people can be of enormous benefit to teams and their creative instincts perhaps need to be nurtured carefully. Generating options is not a process to be limited to the few talented individuals. It can be undertaken by all team members, and one of the most well-known techniques is that of brainstorming.

Brainstorming

Brainstorming demands that ideas should be stated freely before they are evaluated. In fact, it is best conceptualised in two discrete stages: idea generation and idea evaluation. It demands in the first instance, therefore, that team members stay open-minded, willing to take risks, and that they suspend judgement. They need to develop a 'we wish we could' environment, which helps to break through perceived constraints and to imagine a new world of possibilities (Snyder, 1988: 201). Idea generation and evaluation are two essential processes, but they must be clearly separated so that members can focus on one at a time. We now explain the basic ingredients of the technique.

Nine rules for brainstorming (Sashkin and Morris, 1984: 194):

1. Ask each team member to contribute an idea.
2. List every idea mentioned, even if it is identical to a previous suggestion.
3. Record ideas making them visible to everyone. Usually a flipchart or whiteboard is used.
4. Constantly encourage team members to contribute more ideas when they seem to run dry.
5. Ensure that, before stopping, all ideas have been posted.
6. Encourage silly, amusing and even apparently crazy ideas. It has been found that these can often lead to the most effective solutions. Brainstorming is at the same time a serious and a fun activity.
7. The leader should also contribute as a way of energising the team, especially when ideas are slow in emerging.
8. Encourage team members to expand and add to ideas already posted. This should not involve discussing or judging the ideas in any way.
9. No one may evaluate ideas during the brainstorming period. If this happens in either a negative or a positive way, the individual concerned should be asked for another idea, thereby channelling participation into a contribution.

Snyder (1988: 213) gives more specific guidelines on the process that might be followed. In brief, it involves generating ideas at speed, asking the team (or smaller groups of team members) to decide on their priority ideas, clustering or linking ideas in order to arrive at coherent groupings which should then be labelled, and finally, selecting solution areas. The third stage may be called 'cross-fertilisation' (Rawlinson, 1986: 39) and allows for ideas to be picked up, exchanged and developed in the search for an effective solution.

Related Techniques

Another approach to brainstorming is the 'Gordon' technique, and this is usually applied to technical problems. The team members are not told about the whole problem. A stimulus is given, usually in terms of a word or phrase, and team members are then asked for their ideas. Only the leader, therefore, knows what the problem is exactly, and a process of free association is used.

Earlier, we mentioned the 'Delphi' technique in connection with trying to reduce uncertainty. In effect, the method can be thought of as a modified version of brainstorming, with the participants physically separated. Both brainstorming and Delphi attempt to consider fairly and adequately competing ideas and alternatives. This is particularly important in conditions of decision uncertainty, where a focus on single options can lead to poor or even disastrous decisions.

An attempt was made to combine the respective advantages of brainstorming and Delphi with the introduction of NGT, the 'Nominal Group Technique'. It is a highly structured meeting, with team members forming ideas individually and in writing. Ideas are presented one at a time and the leader (or coordinator) records them so that everyone can see. Discussion then takes place about the relative advantages and disadvantages of each set of ideas. An initial rank ordering is then made, with everyone getting an equal vote. When all ideas have been discussed, the option is selected by a final vote from all team members.

Other Option-generating Techniques

There are other techniques of creating options. Snyder (1988: 217), for example, describes a process of amplifying and redefining the problem in terms of wishes. Team members are encouraged to dream up bizarre, unrealistic and even illegal solutions, and they can do this by prefacing ideas with the words 'I wish that ...'.

Another related technique is that of using 'excursions' to help remove the barriers to creative thinking. It involves transferring the problem to another context and exploring its effects in that setting. Such excursions may involve the use of metaphors, imaging, and the exploration of absurd solutions. A description of the technique can be found in Snyder (p. 217).

Other techniques which are closely related to the above include 'brain-writing', which is a kind of brainstorming on paper, 'confrontation' or the juxtaposition of ideas not usually linked, and 'guided fantasies', the dreaming up of scenarios. 'Synectics', is yet another problem-solving and idea-generating technique (DuBrin et al., 1989: 108). The group comprises a leader, a client, and about six team members.

The process involves short bursts of creative and analytical thinking, with the aim of producing an acceptable solution for the client. After problem analysis and restatement, the client indicates ideas that interest him and the further help he needs. The main stage of the process includes idea generation, paraphrasing and itemised response, a way of involving the client in determining the next steps. The final stage demands a commitment from the client to the possible solution. The main advantage of the process is that it can be completed in about forty-five minutes.

'Forced relationships' takes objects or ideas, and asks team members what could be the resulting product if they were combined. They can be quite unrelated and this is likely to add to the novelty. For example, a pen that contains a digital clock represents a new product combined from two older ones.

'Morphological analysis' takes the variables of a problem and tries to assemble them in new ways. Some may be impossible, while others provide the basis for development. Take the following example from a marketing group meeting in an educational institution:

Studying: college, home, while travelling, abroad.
Student: young, mature.
Employment: unemployed, employed part-time, employed
   full-time.
Activities: Reading, writing, listening, talking.

This list is by no means exhaustive, but it yields nine-six study combinations. For instance, if one puts the following variables together: abroad, mature, full-time, and listening, it is possible to look at providing programmes for busy overseas students by making use of cassette tapes. A useful technique is to arrange the variables on sets of coloured cards, shuffle them and ask team members to come up with ideas from the combinations dealt. It provides a useful tool for stimulating thinking.

One of the acknowledged leaders in the field of creativity is Edward de Bono, and he uses a six-hat method to stimulate creativity. The hats are in different colours, and each one represents one aspect of the thought process: objectivity (white), feeling (red), negativism (black), positivism (yellow), creativity (green), and putting it all together (blue). By wearing one hat at a time, people are able to separate these processes, creativity from objectivity, and so forth (*Straits Times*, 7 April 1992).

Finally, 'check lists' can be used to stimulate or question ideas. Osborn's (1957) generalised check list gives a number of questions that can be applied to ideas or objects:

Put to other uses?	Substitute?
Adapt?	Rearrange?
Modify?	Reverse?
Magnify?	Combine?
Minify?	

The ability to generate alternatives is just as important as selecting the correct alternative. From the above processes, it is apparent that many of the options may be impractical and incapable of being evaluated. Nevertheless, they should be accepted as valid contributions. At some point, however, the team has to become tough-minded and reach some conclusions about the workability of the suggestions. It does this by selecting the most promising ideas and then refining them until they take the shape of an acceptable solution. The initial ideas may have been raw and seemingly impractical, but many suggestions may contain an idea that is worth incorporating in the final solution.

One final point is worth noting. Generating options can be time consuming, and we have already explained that the problem should be sufficiently important to demand a team's attention and the accompanying time commitment. If it is important, it is erroneous to commit team resources to an issue and then expect a problem to be resolved by a 'this or that' decision. We now turn our attention to the next stage in the decision-making process, that of evaluating the alternatives that have been generated.

Evaluating and Analysing Alternatives

There are several ways of evaluating suggestions, alternatives or ideas. The elimination process can start with a consideration of the following questions:

1. Do the organisation's physical facilities make the option impractical?

2. Does the cost of the option make it impossible for the team or organisation to accept?
3. Is it an option that has already been vetoed by senior managers?

Asking these questions will often eliminate a number of alternatives. The brainstorming process, however, usually ensures that there are some remaining. The team's job is then to refine these. It is unlikely that any will be close to ideal at this stage in the process, so the idea-building process must begin. Team members identify the strengths of ideas and their concerns (Snyder, 1988: 210).

Evaluation involves the precarious process of attempting to predict likely outcomes. Whilst it seems impossible to do this with total accuracy, careful thought and analysis can often help to pick up the important points and to avoid the more serious consequences. This is where a team might be at an advantage, since the combined critical judgement of members can be far more effective than a single individual's analysis. Even for teams, however, trying to anticipate the reactions of people and groups of people is frought with difficulties.

Despite the drawbacks, this anticipation process seems essential. It is sometimes referred to as 'reverse brainstorming'. This process tries to account for the various ways in which an idea might fail. Team members are encouraged to play the role of 'devil's advocate'. Answers are thought out to the difficult questions and major obstacles identified.

Drucker (1955) recommends four timeless criteria for evaluating possible alternatives:

1. The risk in relation to the expected outcome
2. The effort required
3. The desired rate of change
4. The availability of resources (human and material)

There are, of course, many other ways of evaluating possible courses of action and reaching decisions through systematic analyses, and reference can be made to the specialist decision making literature, which explains such techniques as 'critical path planning' and 'decision tree analysis'. The latter one is well known and widely used. Alternatives are weighed by first, identifying possible courses of action; second, listing events that might occur; third, giving probability estimates to the events connected with the options; and finally, assessing the outcomes for each act-event. There are variations on this procedure. It is a good way of displaying the various parts of a decision and is particularly useful when the team is dealing with an issue that is characterised by uncertainty. The overall picture of choices, risks and likely outcomes provides a degree of clarity for the team and identifies those areas about which more information is necessary.

A useful way of relating the decision to original intent is by weighting outcome criteria and using a 'decision matrix' to visualise the relative advantages of options. Each criterion is given a weighting either before the problem-solving process begins or at an early stage. For example, a senior management team may wish to interview candidates for a senior post. Before advertising, receiving applications or interviewing, the team may have identified several criteria that are desirable. Some of these will be more important than others. The matrix reflects the various weightings. The team may have decided, for instance, that experience of large-scale employee relations disputes is a major criterion, followed by an ability to handle discipline and grievance procedures effectively. Other criteria may be the ability to use relevant computer applications, to manage department staff, and to write concise management reports. The team may then end up with a matrix which looks like that in Figure 14.5.

By then totalling each candidate's score, the extent to which they meet the predefined criteria can be gauged. A refinement of this process is to award each candidate a score out of, say, ten according to the extent to which he or she measures up to the criterion. For example, the first candidate may have substantial experience in managing disputes and may score eight. His experience of managing staff, however, is limited and he may score only two. These scores are then multiplied by the criterion weightings to produce a more accurate reflection of how each individual matches up to the predefined criteria.

The process can be applied to many team decision situations at the option evaluation stage. It is useful because it forces the team to think through what it really wants and how well the options meet the objectives. It would be foolish, however, to believe that decisions as important as the one in the above example should be based entirely on such an analysis. Other factors may appear that should rightly influence the outcome. Furthermore, it involves a considerable amount of work, and for that reason, it should be used sparingly and

The figures in the upper boxes are those given by the selection team to indicate the extent to which candidates meet the criteria. They are out of 10. That score is then multiplied by the weighting and shown in the lower box.

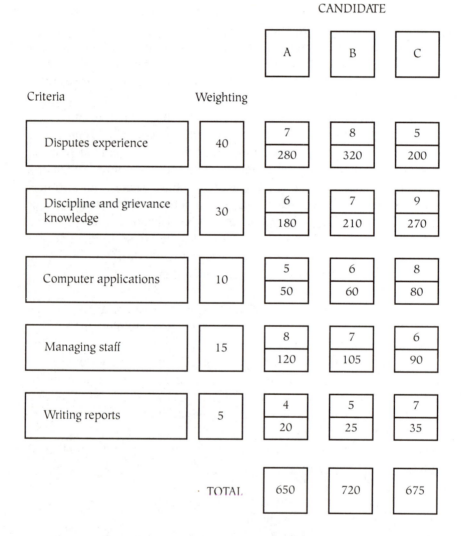

Criteria	Weighting	CANDIDATE A	CANDIDATE B	CANDIDATE C
Disputes experience	40	7 / 280	8 / 320	5 / 200
Discipline and grievance knowledge	30	6 / 180	7 / 210	9 / 270
Computer applications	10	5 / 50	6 / 60	8 / 80
Managing staff	15	8 / 120	7 / 105	6 / 90
Writing reports	5	4 / 20	5 / 25	7 / 35
TOTAL		650	720	675

Figure 14.5 Weighted Decision Matrix

for the more important decisions. Nevertheless, an analysis based on criteria can enable teams to avoid making tacit assumptions and to plot alternatives against specified criteria.

Two further points about the process of idea evaluation, which are noted by Rawlinson (1986: 72), deserve attention. First, there should be a delay between idea generation and evaluation, since they require different types of thinking processes. Furthermore, additional ideas may emerge. Second, after a brainstorming session, evaluation should not take place in the presence of the whole group, since participants may wish to defend their own ideas, and the process is too time consuming for total involvement. Whether one accepts this view or not depends largely on the situation and the participants. Rawlinson, in fact, suggests a procedure for allowing all team members to evaluate by examining lists of ideas on an individual basis and then selecting those considered worthwhile. An alternative to this is to have a small team of three or four people who are deeply involved with the problem and who go through a systematic evaluation process.

The following case was reported in Stott and Walker (1992) and we repeat it here, since it provides a useful example of a team attempting to cope with a very real and critical business problem in a creative way.

John was the owner and managing director of a small company marketing fitness equipment to health clubs and hotels throughout Southeast Asia. Business had been expanding to almost unmanageable proportions and his order books were full. Meeting the orders for equipment was not a problem. He was unable, however, to provide staff to install and service the equipment, or to train the client's instructors in its use. This was serious since the service angle was central to his marketing strategy. Failing to meet his commitments would have had an adverse impact on his reputation and ultimately his profitability.

John assembled his senior management team and went through a brainstorming session. The following options were arrived at:

Alternatives (A):

A1 Cancel orders to small or less important customers.

A2 Train extra employees to service the extra equipment.

A3 Just give basic service and hope nothing major goes wrong.

A4 Contract companies in the clients' own countries to provide the service.

A5 Slow down or stagger delivery, so service commitments will not be needed at the same time.

A6 Merge with a rival company to draw on its resources.

The management team then began to analyse the various alternatives and their possible consequences:

A1 The small companies were still important to John, since they had been a valuable source of support during the earlier period of development. If he cancelled their orders, he could possibly lose not only a source of steady profit but also a group of clients who had become good friends.

A2 The training of new employees had to be conducted some 7,000 miles away in the UK and was quite expensive. The company could afford to train no more than three people. This would not relieve the situation significantly for some time.

A3 To do very basic service might help in some ways, but this would incur a considerable risk that major breakdowns might occur, a very real and potentially damaging risk. To begin with, misuse could damage equipment, but the company would still be responsible under the terms of warranties. Personal injuries occurring as a result of inadequate servicing could cost the company dearly.

A4 There were companies in the various countries that could meet the technical requirements of the servicing, but many of these were unreliable.

A5 Staggered delivery could be arranged, but since the company did not get paid until delivery, this could lead to a serious cash flow problem, which would result in serious financial difficulties in view of the large order book.

A6 There were two rival companies able to help with the servicing, but their business ethics were questionable, and it was not in the company's interest to be associated with them in any way.

In considering the consequences of the various courses of action, the management team was conducting what has been labelled 'marginal analysis'. This is concerned with the additional output that can be achieved by adding an extra input unit. The most commonly used forms of such analyses are 'cost effectiveness analysis' and 'cost benefit analysis'. These deal with alternatives that are difficult to measure in simple financial terms. Cost effectiveness analysis is a technique for selecting the best alternative when objectives are not specifically related to sales costs or profits. It focuses on the results of a programme, helping to weigh the potential benefits of each alternative against their potential cost, and then compares the alternatives in terms of overall advantage (Koontz and Weihrich, 1988: 139).

A type of cost effectiveness analysis was conducted in considering Alternative One. Financial costs were considered alongside the human factors of friendship and loyalty. The team had to weigh the possible benefits of new contracts to the company against the costs (financial and human).

Evaluation or analysis of alternatives, as we have seen, can be a time consuming process, but it must be thorough and systematic. In the above case, it could be seen that some of the options had different possible outcomes. Analysing these helps to narrow down the options. At the end of this process, the best available option is selected and a decision made.

Making the Decision

Having reduced the number of alternatives, a decision can be made that is usually described as the best in the circumstances. It is unlikely to be perfect, since the information available is often imperfect and some of the likely consequences unpredictable. There are also other impacting factors, some of them political, over which teams may have little control.

Earlier, we looked at some models of decision making. In reality, complex decisions are rarely taken using only a given model. Judgements are invariably used, and these are determined by individuals' values, ethics and the politics of the organisation or team (Anderson, 1984: 144). Judgements are also made about whether particular courses of action will be accepted by people, because without their support, implementation can be a precarious process. A word of caution should be entered here, however. Judgement can be clouded by previous experiences, false perceptions, personal likes (that may or may not be shared), or rigid views. Judgement, in such cases, is likely to lead to poor decision making. It is wise, therefore, for teams to examine the factors that contribute to their judgements.

To make the decision, the costs and consequences have to be weighed, and some creativity may be needed. On this note, it is worth looking at the decision that the senior management team in the above case made. Its solution included a combination of two of the possible alternatives.

John and his team drew on their experience to make the decision. They knew some firms had a bad reputation and that equipment was prone to breakdown if not serviced properly. Alternatives could have been tried out, but these often represented an expensive option and would be worth the investment only if the decision was of vital importance. Both methods were useful, but neither was a substitute for sound and rigorous systematic analysis.

John's team conducted such an analysis in reaching its decision. Members considered the potential positive and negative outcomes of each decision, and considered possible costs and benefits. They also drew on their research about such items as the cost of training, cost of contracts, reputation of companies and the time needed. They may also have used a form such as the Alternative to, Consequences for Decision Form (ACD) shown in Figure 14.6.

Sometimes, teams find it almost impossible to reach a decision with which they are satisfied. A question worth asking on these occasions is whether a decision is absolutely necessary. This is not an excuse

ALTERNATIVE: Give basic service and hope nothing goes wrong

POSSIBLE CONSEQUENCES	Positive	Negative
Basic service could meet need	+	
Risk of breakdown (bad for reputation)		–
Risk of breakdown (cost of repair)		–
Personal injury from equipment (legal)		–

Decision on outcome: TOO RISKY

Figure 14.6   ACD Form: John's Team's Decision

for evading responsibilities. It may be possible to delay or even abandon a decision if it is going to be unsatisfactory.

One choice available to the team is the installation of a temporary decision, one that does not solve the problem in question immediately, but which gives time for further consideration. Indeed it can often be a good decision to decide not to make a decision. In such cases, other machinery may come into play. For example, it can be delayed pending the acquisition of more information, it can be made by the leader, or it can be referred to a small group or a relevant individual.

One of the issues a team may have to face is that it contains some members who are not adept at reaching the final decision. Some people are very good at solving complex problems that have intricate patterns of information, but they may lack the ability to make decisions. Similarly, some good decision makers lack the analytical skills to be excellent problem solvers. It is at this point where those who are skilful and incisive in decision making may need to take the lead.

When the decision has been made, it is imperative to stick to it, and this point was emphasized in the systematic model discussed previously. The next part of the process is to make it work.

Clarity about Decision Responsibilities

Finally we turn our attention to the question of who or which team should handle particular decisions. There is much confusion evident over this issue, which is neither helpful to manager nor team. We have already outlined a set of criteria that might be used to determine whether a decision area should fall within the team's domain. Having accepted relevant criteria and applied them to the organisation's prevalent decisions areas, it should be possible to draw up a 'responsibility matrix' that displays clearly where the locus of responsibility for decisions lies. This seems necessary, since the critics of team approaches and participatory styles of management often cite the problem of loss of responsibility control. They claim that accountability is so dispersed that it becomes virtually ineffective. For this reason, instruments of control, such as responsibility matrices and task descriptions, may become even more important.

In the responsibility matrix, the individual decision makers and teams can appear on the vertical axis and the list of decision areas should be on the horizontal axis. In the grid, it can be indicated with the use of symbols whether any unit has the right to inform, amend, or advise. The extent of power may also be indicated. Such a matrix is shown in Figure 14.7. Again using symbols, it could be made clear who can decide without reference to other individuals or teams, who can decide but also inform, and who can decide but seek approval before implementation.

This form of systematic approach has several advantages: it avoids the need to consider involvement for each decision area as it emerges;

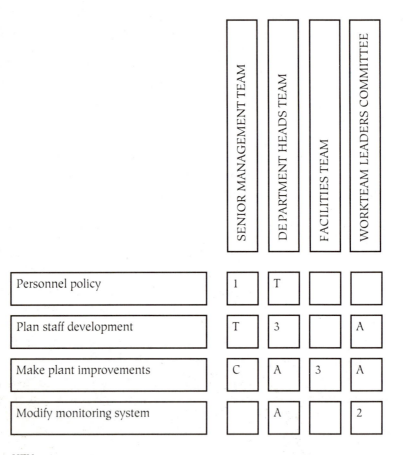

KEY

T	To be informed	1	Power to decide alone
C	Can change	2	Power to decide: should inform
A	Advise	3	Power to decide: should seek advice

Figure 14.7   Team Responsibility Matrix

it shows where responsibility and accountability lie; it reduces ambiguity and role conflict; and it ensures consistency.

Summary

In summary, teams are faced with mostly 'deep' decisions and a coherent approach to problem solving and decision making is needed if the process is to be optimised. In view of the complexity of many of these decision situations, it is becoming essential that an element of creativity is required in the search for effective solutions. The generation of options is an important ingredient in the process, followed by careful evaluation and analysis of the implications of the options. The importance of many of the decisions that teams in modern organisations face suggests that the process has to be followed conscientiously if quality teams are to produce quality decisions.

For the most part, what we have discussed in this chapter inevitably takes place in meetings. It is appropriate, therefore, that we now turn our attention in the next chapter to such meetings and consider how their effectiveness might be optimised.

Summary of the Implications for Managers

- The real problem, not some imagined one, needs to be identified and understood. It should be stated without implying preferred solutions. With this in mind, team leaders should encourage members to ask questions rather than make statements, and detailed information relating to the problem should be sought. In order to understand the actual cause, it is necessary to get beyond the symptoms. This process can be facilitated by:

  - looking for discrepancies between typical and actual;
  - consulting those who can offer multiple perspective insights;
  - looking at the problem from different angles;
  - being open to all data.

- The problem can be investigated further by obtaining situational details, by evaluating its scope, by considering the possible consequences and their seriousness, and by assessing the constraints in the way of certain solution possibilities.

- A decision must be made about whether to:

    1. do nothing;
    2. place the problem on hold;
    3. control it in some way;
    4. find a solution.

- Criteria can be set for solving the problem, and these can be separated into 'must' criteria and 'want' criteria. The former become the characteristics of a successful outcome.

- Then it is necessary to consider whether to involve the team. This can be done by deciding whether members have the expertise and whether they have a stake in the problem. Other criteria for involvement may include the quality of outcome sought, whether members would accept a solution without participating in it, the amount of time available, and whether there is any need for interdependencies.

- Consensus involves the freedom to express ideas and opposition to ideas. It involves team members in listening to and understanding one another. One powerful strategy in achieving consensus is that of finding integrative solutions rather than compromises. These represent solutions that integrate the needs and wishes of various perspectives. If teams are to reach consensual decisions, they need all relevant information, and the leader's role, therefore, becomes facilitative and integrative rather than directive. With this in mind, using the power of veto can be highly damaging if a consensus-type team operation is sought.

- Dissent is necessary for good decisions. The leader should set aside meeting time for tough minded criticism and refinement of ideas. Elements of personal threat should be removed and appreciation should be expressed for dissenting views. Useful strategies to promote dissent are to encourage members to play devil's advocate, to identify weaknesses, to spot what could go wrong, and to pick up misinterpretations.

- In generating options, leaders need to encourage creative and divergent thinking patterns. The right conditions have to be set. This involves considering how goals and rewards are distributed, deemphasizing rules and hierarchy, accepting failure, and re-cognising innovation. Leaders may be well advised not to worry about the question of idea practicality too early in the process, and to focus on critical attributes and the questioning of every-thing.

- Creative techniques, such as brainstorming and 'inside-out thinking', may be usefully employed. Open-mindedness should also be encouraged, and this means opening up speculation and imagination. It is well to remember that the best ideas do not always emerge from senior members, and that less-experienced personnel are often able to contribute creative and potentially useful ideas. There has to be an element of risk-taking if the team is to come up with new ways of approaching problems, but this can be offset to some extent by testing out ideas thoroughly within the team and with people outside the team. It is important in any creative phase to resist the temptation to make judgements, and leaders should probably concentrate on obtaining ideas from all members before allowing evaluation to take place. One way of establishing an innovative atmosphere is by stimulating a 'we wish we could' environment, and this often gives rise to new insights into decision options.

- Evaluation, as we have seen, comes after any creative phase. Considerations might include physical constraints, costs and senior managers' directives. During evaluation, likely outcomes can be predicted and account can be taken of the ways in which ideas might fail. Experience and judgement can be used, but it is important to question the validity of judgement.

- It is also important to consider whether a decision is really necessary. In some instances, it may be prudent to delay making a decision in order to obtain more information, or to refer it to either another body or a sub-group of the team. Assuming that a decision has to be made, however, it should be incisive and there should be a commitment to stick with it.

15

TEAM MEETINGS

Meetings provide opportunity to interrupt a speaker to get clarification, to challenge the accuracy of information or perceptions, to get feedback, to compare values, to resolve conflict, to reach consensus, to achieve coordination of effort in carrying out actions, and to engage in group maintenance behaviors – all of which are more difficult, in some cases impossible, through written communications or one-to-one interaction (Wynn and Guditus, 1984: 212).

THAT REPRESENTS a highly positive view of such events. Yet meetings, it may be argued, represent the greatest source of misused and, sometimes, abused time in organisations. Let us look at this brief episode reported by Miller and Phillips (1986: 54):

As critical path activities fell behind schedule, project status meetings became lengthy and embattled. These meetings were peppered with scapegoating, put-downs and finger pointing. Decisions were being delayed and vital information was being withheld.

Not a very positive way to approach meetings and maybe a scene with which many may be familiar. It is apparent that, in some team environments, such scenes have become accepted as almost a necessary evil. We would argue, however, that it is a major responsibility and

379

challenge for team leaders to ensure that meetings are worth the time investment.

After a brief look at the all too familiar shortcomings of meetings, we examine some guidelines for conducting effective and productive team meetings. In particular, we consider what you should do before, during and after the event. Good preparation and appropriate follow-up action are essential, as is both leader and team member behaviour during the meeting itself. We then look at some matters related to setting up the right conditions, including the issues of membership and the physical setting.

Meetings

What characterises effective meetings? Wynn and Guditus (1984: 212) summarise the features identified by Douglas McGregor:

1. The atmosphere is comfortable. There is no tension or boredom.
2. The discussion involves all members and is relevant to the task at hand.
3. Members understand the team's goals and there is commitment to them.
4. Effective listening takes place and all ideas are considered seriously.
5. Disagreements are aired and there is no ill-feeling when members disagree.
6. Consensus is sought and vote-taking is avoided.
7. Criticism is constructive and freely given.
8. Feelings are expressed as well as ideas.
9. Clear assignments are made and agreed.
10. The leader does not dominate and there is no undue deference to the leader.

These points are worth noting. Teams can display either high levels of productive interaction or severe dysfunction. It is also important to remember that "meetings are a group phenomena [sic], and that people come with more than just information about the topic. They bring their fears, habits, needs, and all the rest of their humanness" (Roberts and Hunt, 1991: 179). Even though we discuss team meetings mainly from an 'efficiency' perspective, it is wise to remember that they are a human activity and, as such, need to take people-related elements into account.

Types of Meetings

Team meetings take many shapes and forms. Any single organisation may have board meetings, production meetings, daily, weekly or monthly meetings, sales meetings, staff meetings, advisory meetings and special project meetings, not to mention committees and, in some organisations, quality circles. The list is seemingly endless.

Scannell (1992: 70), while acknowledging there are no clear lines separating different types of meetings, believes that whether meetings involve the whole staff, a committee, training personnel or only board members, they fall roughly into four categories: Information, Action, Problem Solving and Brainstorming. As with other categorisations, it is likely that any single meeting slot will involve a number of these types to different degrees. Team leaders need to be aware of this and, if necessary, may even consider dividing the agenda along such lines.

Margerison (1973: 22) advances an interesting typology of work-group meetings, separating them according to their relationship to the dimensions of attendance, authority and accountability. The 'command' meeting is for the leader to give instructions. The 'negotiation' meeting, as the name implies, is for bargaining. The 'consultative' meeting is for the giving of advice, and it may involve the leader in giving team members advice or the other way round. The 'committee' meeting, a familiar vehicle in most organisations, is for making decisions that affect the larger community of which the committee is a part. Finally, the 'colleague' meeting is for the sharing of knowledge and skill to solve problems. It is this last type that forms much of the subject of this discussion, although the main points relate to other types of meeting also. The 'consultative' meeting, later described as an 'advisory' meeting in Margerison and McCann (1989: 13), can be used as a prelude to more serious discussion. For example, it can be used by the team to raise questions and gather data before meeting later in a 'colleague' type of meeting to reach agreement on appropriate decisions.

Closely linked to the type of meeting is the purpose for which it is used.

Purposes

While much of the preceding discussion has dwelt on problem analysis and creative decision making, not all team meetings are about

decisions. They may be arranged for such purposes as to give information or to maintain team spirit. Indeed many viable reasons are often
cited for holding meetings. A question that may need to be addressed,
however, is whether some meetings are necessary or whether matters
could be dealt with in a more economical way. Johnson and Johnson
(1991: 447) take a different stance and appear to advocate frequent
meetings: "A good team meets regularly so members can discuss their
work with each other, identify and solve problems blocking success,
and give and receive help and assistance." Implied in their advice, however, is a need for purpose, although we would suggest the purpose
needs to precede the decision to meet. Such purposes might include
the following:

- *Testing out the quality of decisions.* They can be excellent
  vehicles for testing out ideas and developing creative solutions
  to problems. By encouraging members to engage in constructive criticism, only quality ideas will survive and teams may
  avoid the disappointments caused by failing to put decisions to
  the test of critical scrutiny.

- *Disseminating information to team members.* Meetings are
  also suitable for giving information, but they should be used
  for this purpose only sparingly. Such meetings can disrupt
  work unnecessarily. On the other hand, if the information is
  sufficiently important, a meeting is probably the best way to
  disseminate it.

- *Building up team cohesion.* Getting team members together
  in a meeting may contribute to increased cohesion and
  team spirit, but this can be done on an informal basis and
  sometimes away from the workplace. Meetings undoubtedly have
  an effect on the way members interact, but such meetings need
  to be run well.

Poor Team Meetings

There is much criticism in organisations about the quality of meetings,
and, planned badly, they may do little to improve the way teams
perform. Scannell (1992: 70) cites a recent study of senior executives
that identified failure to adhere to the purpose, lack of agenda and
goals, and consuming too much time as the three main reasons for

meeting failures. He adds to these lack of planning, lack of direction, inclusion of the wrong people and conducting the meeting at the wrong place and the wrong time. Below, in summary form, are the more common reasons given for meetings failing to achieve very much:

- *There is no clear reason for bringing the team together.* There seems to be little point in holding team meetings if there is nothing to discuss. If they are intended to improve *esprit de corps*, this has to be clearly stated.

- *They complicate simple matters.* Serious questions need to be asked about the issues involved. Do the issues really need the participation of team members? Are they sufficiently simple to be capable of being handled by one person?

- *They last too long.* With inadequate planning and poor leadership, meetings can use up a disproportionate amount of time. Important matters often receive insufficient attention, while more trivial affairs get extended treatment.

- *They limit involvement.* Team meetings are intended to involve team members, but sometimes only the select or vociferous few are involved. Woodcock (1979: 5) identifies this very dysfunction, leading to a situation where skills are inadequately utilised. He also mentions that some leaders use team meetings to lay down rules rather than use the combined resources of the team. Skill needs to be exercised in ensuring that all members are given the opportunity to contribute to discussion. A real problem is where the leader is unable to limit his own contribution. and that can be inhibiting to less experienced or junior team members.

- *The team avoids making decisions.* If the purpose of a team meeting is to reach a decision, then that objective should be fulfilled before the end of the meeting. Decisions often tend to be avoided because the issues become complicated. The leader has a responsibility, however, to coordinate members' contributions and draw the discussion together in such a way that the issue remains clear. In that way, it becomes easier to arrive at a decision.

- *The meeting is an end in itself.* There are many occasions when members should leave with something to *do*. There should be plans of action. It is not sufficient to hold team meetings for the sake of meeting.

The other side of the coin is that meetings can have a beneficial impact on the work of the team if run well, and they may indeed be seen as essential. In the following pages, we shall look at ways in which an effective meeting might be planned, how team members might engage in purposeful discussion, and how the team might arrive at clear decisions and action plans.

Effective Team Meetings

Preparation

Having decided that a meeting is really necessary, the next step is to clarify the purpose. Is it to obtain reports on progress from individual members, to generate some ideas, or to make a decision? From this purpose, the criteria of success can be defined. If the meeting is intended to discuss an issue thoroughly and then reach a decision, the criterion of effectiveness will be whether a decision is made based on relevant discussion and the weighing up of options.

It is necessary to inform team members in advance what the purpose of the meeting is. This is probably best done in a short sentence with a few lines of explanation. Preparing in this way also presents an opportunity for the team leader to inform team members about what is expected of them. For example, they may be required to confer with their colleagues to gather views, to read certain documents before the meeting, or to think through the issue to be discussed.

The Agenda

It is not necessary to have a formal agenda for most team meetings, but it is essential to have some plans about the items to be discussed. Obviously, thought will be given to which topics should receive attention, but there should also be some consideration about the order of items. Some things must come before others, because they determine the limitations of those other items. It is also advisable to include as few items as is realistically possible, so that the important team issues receive adequate discussion. There are many occasions where the team may be called together to discuss only one item.

It is usually up to the team leader to set the agenda and priorities, although in some work settings, prioritisation can be dealt with at the beginning of the meeting amongst those present. A useful idea is to set a certain amount of time for each item and stick to it. Put the urgent items first and give them little time. Then allot sufficient time to the really important things.

Conducting the Team Meeting

Purpose
It is advisable to state the purpose at the beginning of the meeting and include it as a simple statement at the top of the agenda. Of course there may be more than one major purpose and, if so, this should be made clear. In this way, each member knows why he is there and what the meeting is expected to achieve. Normally this type of information should be disseminated before the meeting, but it certainly will not hurt to reinforce the purpose at the beginning of the meeting.

Interaction
The meeting is a time for interaction and exchange and not, as was indicated above, a vehicle for solo contributions or closed discussions between the team leader and one or more members. The active meeting is about "a crossflow of discussion and debate, with the Chairman occasionally guiding, mediating, probing, stimulating and summarising, but mostly letting the others thrash out ideas" (Video Arts Ltd, 1984: 59).

Many complaints about meetings stem from one or two extroverted or aggressive members monopolising the discussion. To avoid this, skilled team leadership is essential to ensure that everybody who wants to contribute is given the opportunity to do so.

The leader
We have already looked in some detail at the role of the team leader generally, but a few points which relate specifically to the leader role in team meetings are worth reinforcing.

Skills have to be exercised in even the most informal settings. Strategies need to be employed to ensure member involvement, and these might include using names to elicit comments and opinions, and asking those of junior status to make their views known first, so that they are not intimidated by the contrasting views of senior personnel.

The team leader's role, as we saw earlier, is not an easy one, and there are times when great self-restraint has to be shown in withholding views, some of which may be held very strongly. As the Video Arts (1984: 60) presentation notes, the leader is best seen as

> the servant of the group, rather than as its master. His role then becomes that of assisting the group toward the best conclusion or decision in the most efficient manner possible: to interpret and clarify; to move the discussion forward; and to bring it to a resolution that everyone understands and accepts as being the will of the meeting, even if the individuals do not necessarily agree with it.

The leader, therefore, encourages participation, ensures that the discussion stays on line, and tries to stem personal disputes. He also has to deal tactfully, but firmly, with vociferous individuals, those who try to hide away, those who pretend to know it all, those who live in the past and the faultfinders.

Margerison and McCann (1989: 15) suggest it may not be appropriate for the team leader to always lead meetings, since strong opinions may result in pushing ideas through without adequate discussion. It is possible, they suggest, for other team members to handle the 'process' side of the meeting so that everyone is able to contribute fairly. It is also a useful developmental tool to rotate the chairmanship of meetings, and this strategy has worked successfully in many settings. It is also possible that different team members will assume leadership depending on the issues being discussed or information being disseminated.

Tack (1986: 150) identifies seven types of team member who, without skilful team leadership, are unlikely to do much to improve the quality of meetings. He calls them: the compulsive talker, the silent listener, the reminiscent member, the team bigot, the timid member, the overbearing member and the blamer. The leader has to focus their contributions and bring them into the discussion at the appropriate moment. For example, the reminiscer can be very negative, dwelling on the 'good old days'. At the same time, he has experience which can be drawn on and so long as he is pointed in the direction of the future, he can make a useful contribution.

Another potential problem to team meeting effectiveness is the member who becomes the 'digressor', the one who meanders away from the subject with consummate ease. It is imperative in this situation that the leader is determined in his efforts to 'stay on line' but without squashing the self-esteem of the wayward member.

Still on the subject of problems, Margerison (1973: 45) identifies the difficulties that might arise when any team member confuses facts and beliefs. Decisions essentially need to be based on facts, and skill has to be exercised in separating them from beliefs which arise when the discussion attempts to delve into complex issues.

The same author (p. 47) also highlights the difficulties that occur if meetings are allowed to develop into win-lose battles "where the victors go away congratulating themselves on the correctness of their case, and the losers go away frustrated and resolved not to support the decision in the action stage". He advocates that all members should feel they have gained as a result of decisions taken. While this may represent an optimistic goal, there is obvious merit in avoiding the consequences of situations where members feel defeated and disadvantaged. Chapter 13 on team conflict provides useful advice in this area.

Regular summaries

The use of regular summaries by the team leader is an invaluable aid to team meeting effectiveness. Such summaries reinforce the essential points, increase understanding (both for the leader and members), and help to simplify what may be complex ideas. In order to arrive at an accurate summary, clarification may have to be sought from those who fail to articulate their ideas, views and comments clearly.

Discussion stages in problem-solving meetings

Margerison (1974: 148), in looking at the way 'problem solving' business meetings might be managed, identifies six main stages and draws attention to the important problem of people working at different stages at the same time. For example, one person may be proposing a course of action, another weighing up options, and yet another trying to identify the real problem. Indeed, three separate discussions may be taking place.

The implications for the team leader are clear: "The essential thing is to know how to recognize when people are talking at different stages of the problem, and when members are mentally distant from one another. The manager must be able to do this and be able to guide people to concentrate on one area at a time." Margerison (p. 148) then gives the guideline: "When people are discussing at different stages, seek to return the conversation to the stage at which the difference first emerged."

Keeping to time

It was suggested earlier that a set time should be allocated to items based on their relative importance. It is advisable to adhere to these limits, otherwise the remaining items may be unduly neglected. Scannell (1992: 71), while not attempting to devalue the importance of in-depth discussion, states that 60 percent of the members of any group make up their minds on a decision within sixty seconds. Whereas it would be dangerous to accept these figures at face value, it does acknowledge that excessive time spent on often minor items can be counterproductive in achieving team outcomes. Of course, there are occasions when it is right to be flexible because of the nature of the discussion, and the team may decide, therefore, that it would be more productive to stay with a particular issue and defer other items. Such a decision should be a conscious one and not one that arises out of poor management of the meeting.

Reinforcing main points and decisions

At appropriate points during the meeting, in addition to the regular clarifications and summaries, the main points may be repeated, and the decisions and conclusions reached may be reinforced. It is also useful to repeat agreed actions, to name the members responsible for carrying them out, and to specify the deadlines involved.

At the end of the meeting, it is advisable to reinforce the main points one more time. This acts as a summary of the shorter summaries that have taken place during the meeting, and it might also form the basis for the recording of the minutes.

Recording in writing

Recording the main points of the meeting in writing ensures there is no ambiguity, either about what took place or the events that should follow. For team meetings, and especially the more informal ones, there is little point in going into lengthy detail. It is probably quite sufficient to list the significant points, with consequent actions, and to note personnel and timescales.

At the end of the meeting

Before finishing, it is important to check that the purpose for which the team meeting was called has been achieved. The purpose of the next team meeting can also be stated and when it is to be. It is helpful to show how it is related to the present meeting.

After the Meeting

Informing others

Although we are concerned primarily with teams in this book and their successful operation and development, we have to recognise that others are interested in and affected by their work. A team can alienate itself if it completely excludes other interested parties. That is why it may be advisable to keep others informed about the issues discussed. They can receive brief notes about the team's progress and what took place at the meeting, instead of being given the rather daunting looking sets of minutes which are prevalent in many organisations. It is best to summarise the key points, highlighting the decisions taken and stating briefly the implications. The main arguments can also be outlined, but excessive and irrelevant detail is best avoided.

Monitoring

The team leader's job is also concerned with monitoring the actions that might have been agreed during the meeting. Such monitoring need not be invasive, but simply a means of checking that plans are on course and that members have all the necessary information. A watchful eye assures team members of the leader's interest and concern, and there may be occasions where problems can be intercepted through effective monitoring.

Setting the Right Conditions

The time of day

The time at which the team meets can have a considerable impact on the meeting's quality. There are problems if the meeting is held very early or very late. People being inconvenienced can make concentration difficult. This is particularly true of meetings held after work or near to the close of the day when people are anxious to leave and are relatively tired.

Under these circumstances, it is hardly surprising that hasty and poor quality decisions are made.

The duration of the meeting

The length of a meeting can have a similar effect. People begin to get irritated, easily distracted and intensely bored. It is best to set a time limit in order to maintain concentration. If the business is unfinished, then it may be wise to reconvene on another occasion.

The use of frequent breaks is a useful strategy. Far from interrupting the concentration, it actually intensifies it, as team members have time to reflect on the information and get things into perspective. They feel refreshed after a drinks break and the work is likely to be considerably sharper.

Breaks enable people to physically move, which in itself can relieve anxiety and indifference. Where an extended break is just not possible, the simple act of standing up for a few minutes can have a beneficial impact.

In team meetings, where everyone knows everyone else fairly well, members can easily pick up the signals that show concentration is waning. If the issue under discussion is important, it is unlikely to be productive to continue.

Location

It is unwise to underestimate the effect that the choice of location has on a meeting. If it is held away from the workplace in a pleasant environment, this gives a very strong message to participants about their importance and the importance of the task. Another benefit is the absence of interruptions, which are often unavoidable if the meeting is held on organisation territory. Noise, telephones and well-meaning visitors only serve to make the effective conduct of the meeting difficult.

Being realistic, it is unlikely that meetings can be held away from the workplace on a regular basis. Whatever the choice of location, however, the area should be well lit with adequate ventilation. There should be no physical distractions and the seating should be comfortable.

Seating arrangements

Seating arrangements affect the flow of communication between people. For teams, it is important to facilitate interaction and this might best be achieved by having a circular arrangement of chairs without tables. If writing is involved, then the same arrangement but with tables serves the purpose well. It is unwise to have senior members of the team sitting together because, even in an informal arrangement of furniture like this, it can be quite threatening for less experienced colleagues.

Very small teams might have just one table round which all members sit and with this in mind, research has shown that round tables have a beneficial and considerable impact on the flow of communication.

Before concluding this section, one further point demands attention. In the same way that meetings are used to develop the work of teams, meetings themselves may be subject to development, and one way to effect this is through the use of a 'process observer' (Snyder, 1988: 209). The role can be adopted by a team member or an outsider who observes the team in action and gives feedback on communication and interaction patterns. Snyder notes that learning in this way may help the team to eliminate dysfunctional practices and develop more effective patterns of working.

Summary

This chapter has attempted to address some of the key factors in running effective team meetings. Since teams are forced to spend considerable periods together in meetings or meeting-type situations, it is imperative that they hold effective and productive sessions. Preparation is central to ensuring success and at least as much time should be spent on this phase as the meeting itself. The time and effort spent in preparing the agenda, prioritising items and allocating time, and in preparing relevant materials, will help to ensure that the event fulfils its purpose. Similarly, conducting the meeting in such a way that discussion is focused and that members are actively encouraged to contribute, will support efficiency and member involvement. Actions taken after the meeting are also important in making sure that others are kept informed and that agreed actions are actually going according to plan. Finally, setting the right conditions for meetings should not be overlooked. The impact of noise, interruptions, discomfort and inappropriate furniture arrangement can reduce the potential effectiveness. In the next chapter we examine a number of other issues related to teams and their effective deployment.

Summary of the Implications for Managers

- The purpose of the team meeting should be clarified and members informed with a simple purpose statement and a few lines of explanation. They need to be informed about what is expected of them in terms of preparation.

- The items to be discussed should be prioritised and the agenda should be limited to those items that are important and that need to be dealt with by the team. Time can be allocated to each item, with the most time being given to important matters.

- In the meeting, it is advisable to encourage junior colleagues to contribute before the views of senior personnel are heard. The leader should exercise restraint in airing strongly held views. Participation should be encouraged, discussions should be kept on line, and the more vociferous individuals should be dealt with tactfully but firmly.

- Regular summaries by the leader can help to reinforce important points, increase understanding, and simplify complex ideas. The leader should also reinforce details about major decisions, the people involved and the deadlines that must be met.

- After the meeting, others can be informed about what took place. The key points should be summarised, decisions highlighted, implications stated and the main arguments outlined.

- Meetings should be kept realistically short and held at times when concentration can be maintained. For necessarily longer meetings, breaks should be taken. The location and seating arrangements should be suitable for productive and uninterrupted discussion.

- To help the team develop, it is worth considering using a 'process observer' who can observe a team meeting and give feedback which might improve the quality of meetings.

16

OTHER ISSUES

In this chapter, we examine the meaning and relevance of several concepts which we have referred to in other sections of the book or which are part of the general vocabulary of teamwork and development. We therefore look at responsibility, both at team and individual level, and at the four C's – coordination, cooperation, competition and cohesiveness. These concepts have received considerable attention in the literature in relation to team effectiveness. We then examine the importance of norms and values, and yet another 'C', that of conformity, which càn be either a force for success or an evil to be avoided. This is followed by a look at team size and the advice the literature gives about optimising interaction and outcomes. Finally, we examine the issue of membership and consider some of the factors that might have to be accounted for in determining team selection.

Responsibility

Much of what has been written in recent years about workteams indicates the advantages of high degrees of autonomy for the team. This may have come about partly because responsibility is one of the most confusing issues in present-day organisations (Tolle, 1988: 283) and has been allowed to drift higher and higher up the organisational chain to create insufferable overloads. It is not surprising that capable teams with the freedom to act are seen as vehicles for easing the burden of management and improving performance. Autonomy however, by definition, demands responsibility and accountability, and more responsibility almost inevitably means more control by the team itself. From this point of view, too much inspection and supervision from external sources may be detrimental to team success.

Referring to 'self-managed teams', Jessup (1990: 79) clarifies that this trend does not mean diluted accountability. On the contrary, such teams are responsible for the traditional measures of performance, such as service quality, meeting schedules, productivity and cost controls. Such accountabilities carry a considerable commitment on the part of the team. Whether they can be successfully negotiated in the absence of formal team leadership is an interesting point for debate.

Barry (1991: 34) rejects the power of existing leadership approaches to fully account for what he calls 'Bossless Teams': "teams which have no formal or organisationally recognised individual leader". He is of the view that Self-managed Teams are necessary in today's market-place and that the lack of a formally appointed leader does not reduce the need for leadership. Instead, he suggests a distributed leadership model:

> At its heart is the notion that leadership is a collection of roles and behaviors that can be split apart, shared, rotated and used sequentially and concomitantly. This in turn means that at any one time multiple leaders can exist in a team, with each leader assuming a complementary leadership role.

His approach does not reject the need for a leader but promotes the view of leadership being shared by each member depending on specialisations and the needs of the team. In fact, Barry believes leadership in such teams is more important than in more traditionally structured groups. In terms of responsibility in the Bossless team, then, it would seem to be a shared commitment amongst the team as a whole and that would include responsibility for task achievement, team morale and a range of other factors connected with the team's operation.

Regardless of the structure of the team, it is necessary at the outset of a team's operation to clarify the issues of responsibility and accountability. Generally speaking, in a more conventional setting, the team leader or manager may be accountable for the group's decisions, actions and performance. If things go wrong, the leader is usually the one to suffer. Where does the leader stand, however, in a situation where he has committed the team to a consensus mode of decision making? In effect, he may still be accountable, but Wynn and Guditus (1984: 168) suggest the team has a collective moral responsibility. Where greater levels of autonomy are conferred on teams, the account- ability may fall in the domain of the team itself, and this needs to be made clear, since it may impact on what can and cannot take place.

The true nature of responsibility is aptly expressed by Schutz (1989: 8). At an individual level, he states that it is not good enough to blame others and for someone to explain that he was following orders. In real teamwork, all members are responsible for their actions and they are considered to have colluded to bring about the events and relationships that happen.

It has to be recognised that some teams are ready for heavy responsibilities and some are not. Nevertheless, if teams are to be used well, they have to develop a capacity to assume responsibility for their efforts. This can be done by giving them small projects or problems first and letting them enjoy success with those. They can then build up from there. On this point, Jessup (1990: 79) explains some of the duties that teams might assume on an incremental basis, and these include member selection, schedules, dealing with stock and setting goals.

George (1977: 79) too talks about establishing the concept of shared responsibility, where both the team and the individual members are jointly accountable for the outcomes. Practical responsibility may be for subtasks but nevertheless, there should a feeling of duty to reach a successful completion on the part of the team. Such a view is likely to demand a high degree of coordinated interaction.

Coordination

Margerison and McCann (1985: 56) state that a sports team can win only if it uses its members in a coordinated effort. The same is true of workteams. Project teams, for example, rely considerably on coordination, since various tasks must be integrated across func- tional lines (Thamhain, 1990: 15). Effective coordination ensures that individual strengths are put together in the right way and that there is a clear understanding of roles. Without this coordination, work is often duplicated.

Teams not only need to coordinate their own work but also need to ensure that what they are doing is integrated with the overall organisation's mission. If what teams do is not tied to and perceived widely as being beneficial to the organisation, they may not survive. Jessup (1992: 65) makes this very point: "Critical management support erodes quickly when teams don't have a positive effect on the whole organization." Without this wider coordination, different organisational teams run the risk of duplicating the work of others, misdirecting their efforts and wasting organisational resources.

Coordination should not be confused with cooperation, however. Coordination is one step on. It represents a willingness of members to combine their efforts in the pursuit of common goals. It provides, therefore, for productivity, an assurance not guaranteed through cooperation alone (Wynn and Guditus, 1984: 141), although other writers suggest that high levels of structured cooperation may be closely associated with productivity and commitment (e.g. Johnson and Johnson, 1991: 444).

Cooperation

While we have tried to differentiate between coordination and co-operation, they are, of course, closely linked. For example, the efforts of different functional units may have to be coordinated, but there also has to be cooperation. They have to see one another as customers (Arajs, 1991: 76). Teams too have to see other organisational teams in the same light. There are occasions where teams may see their goals as mutually exclusive and may enter into competition for scarce resources. Within organisations, it is generally more productive to seek inter-team cooperation, and this would suggest organisations may need to look at their processes for supporting integrated effort, such as those involving rewards.

Graham (1991: 39) describes cooperation as the essence of all successful group working. Relations between members in the team and inter-group relations must be based on cooperation. She has no delusions, however, about the nature of cooperation:

> Cooperation does not mean always the pleasant spectacle of the parties walking peacefully hand in hand all the way. Over time, individual interests change. There can be many different views on how best to deal with new situations, but differences or conflict in the healthy group, when they arise, will be resolved in the main on the basis of mutual accommodation.

The onus may be on the leader to establish a cooperative climate. The sharing of knowledge and experience has to be encouraged in order to promote high-quality work. Those who are guarded and unwilling to share produce a confused and insecure climate, which usually leads to individuals going their own ways. Members may work in isolation and may refuse to give assistance to or receive help from their team colleagues. This condition is unlikely to support team performance.

Like several other writers, Harris (1986: 29) draws attention to the need to provide the right conditions to elevate team performance. He refers to a team culture that promotes team spirit and cooperation amongst both team members and organisational teams, a view supported by Huszczo (1990: 38) who sees effective teams as those that work to improve levels of cooperation with other organisational work units.

How is cooperation achieved? Part of the answer comes from Johnson and Johnson (1991: 443) who state that it just does not happen by chance. Cooperation has to be carefully structured amongst team members. They give the example of sales teams, which may be structured competitively, individualistically or cooperatively. In the cooperative mode, they work together to maximise their sales as a team and the structure, therefore, encourages them to help one another for the mutual good, rather than fight against one another. If someone has too much work, he may give information to someone else who can use it in order to lift sales. Seen from this viewpoint, reward systems and related processes need to be congruent with cooperative effort. Johnson and Johnson claim that "teams structured cooperatively will be more productive than teams structured competitively or individualistically". High levels of cooperation lead to productivity, commitment and social competence. Competition, in contrast, may not be quite so effective.

Competition

It would be too simplistic, however, to focus on the drawbacks of a structure that encourages competition, for, as Graham (1991: 43) notes, it is possible to combine it appropriately and proportionately with cooperation. Adair (1986: 85) too points out that competition is not antithetically opposed to cooperation. Competition can be positively associated with quality improvements and maintenance of standards. One can indeed have competition between organisational teams but within a supportive framework. "Competition here, within that framework, is invaluable in providing challenges, leading to finding the better alternative, the better product or service that satisfies more fully certain needs and wants."

Teams have to exercise caution, however, in letting perceptions become destructive. Competition between teams can lead to mistrust and hostility unless the situation is skilfully managed. Cooperation is easier to manage, in that openness and trust, supported by frequent displays of good faith, will evoke similar responses from cooperating parties (p. 48). In contrast, "competing groups mistrust each other and, through the process of mounting reciprocity, the relationship becomes embedded in mistrust".

On a positive note, however, Adair (1986: 86) suggests that "within groups or organisations competition should be regarded much as a game, but a game with a serious object: to raise the standards of all concerned towards a common level of excellence". It is evident that team standards can slip over time. Indifference and complacency can set in. This is a serious matter if the team's environment is changing and the team is failing to keep up with new demands and expectations. Performance that was considered high last year may be marginal this year. Competition in this context can be healthy because it is likely to lead to raised standards.

Whereas competition may not be thought of as a universally desired pursuit in teams, the next concept, cohesiveness, has nothing but the most positive overtones and it is often cited as one of the key effectiveness indicators.

Cohesiveness

Anantaraman (1984a: 150) defines a cohesive team as "one that provides satisfaction for its members or one that has a high probability of doing so", while Ends and Page (1977: 146) provide a definition which emphasizes the bond that forms between members in a closely knit team: "If they like to be together and work together as a group, and resist any effort to divide them into several distinct groups, then we say the team is cohesive." The same focus – member commitment and attraction to the group – is echoed by Johnson and Johnson (1991: 462) and Robbins (1991: 298).

Cohesiveness should be separated from morale, although it can be seen how they are linked. Adair (1986: 21) explains how morale describes the team's condition "in relation to confidence, discipline and sense of common purpose. It covers the condition of people's attitudes to the task, their loyalty to one another and their self-respect."

For several authors, cohesiveness seems to have been limited to a discussion to one of these features of morale – unity of purpose (Tolle, 1988: 280) – but the concept is more wide-ranging. Anantaraman, for instance, lists a number of factors that contribute to group cohesion, and these include: proximity, size, shared values and interests, complementary personalities, homogeneity in terms of race, religion or community, rank, supervision, and external threats.

He also identifies the characteristics of cohesive teams:

> A strongly felt need to maintain the identity and integrity of the group; a minimal level of divisive friction with the accompanying confidence that it can be sorted out; an adaptability to change through interpersonal readjustments; a strong in-group feeling; a shared consensus of goals and values; open interpersonal communication; and the pride of belonging to the elite group.

Such characteristics can give rise to both advantages and disadvantages. Adair (1986: 20) lists some of these:

Advantages	Disadvantages
More cooperation	Difficult for new members
Good communication	New ideas restricted
Resistance to frustration	Changes resisted
Reduced turnover	Seen as awkward
Low tolerance of slackers	Low cooperation with other teams

Johnson and Johnson (1991: 463) also provide a list of factors that might determine the outcomes expected from membership, and these include the nature of goals, goal and procedures clarity, the likelihood of goal attainment, past success, levels of cooperation, conflict management, similarity of attitudes, and the comparative attractions of membership in other teams. It is easy to see from this that a whole range of issues enter the cohesion equation.

The matter becomes even more complex when one considers that the degree of cohesion is likely to be constantly changing, since different team members will have different levels of attraction to the team and their attraction will vary over time.

The reason cohesiveness develops is through mutual need satis-faction. If members are gaining in terms of esteem and other higher order needs, and they see interdependence as contributing to needs satisfaction, they will continue to work together in order to prolong the benefits (Ends and Page, 1977: 147). Johnson and Johnson (1991: 464) raise several points in relation to such needs. For them, cohesive teams are a source of security for members, serving to reduce anxiety. They also provide acceptance and approval, important in terms of psychological health, and this may lead to participation. They also allow for expressions of hostility and conflict, important in the sense that holding back such feelings may have damaging effects on attitudes and behaviours, and lead to poor communication between members. "Regardless of how angry members of a cohesive group may become with one another, they are more apt to continue communication, which enables the group to resolve conflicts and capitalize upon controversies, both of which increase its productivity."

How does the leader decide how cohesive the group is? This is not an easy question to answer but the same authors (p. 463) provide a useful, if slightly simplistic, list of indicators that can contribute to conclusions about group cohesion:

- Whether team members are punctual for team meetings
- Whether they attend
- Whether there is trust and support
- Whether individuality is accepted
- Whether they have fun together

Determining the level of cohesiveness may be interesting from an academic viewpoint, but what relevance does it have for the team leader? It appears it may have a significant impact on goal achieve-ment by being linked to:

- retention of members;
- participation;
- conformity.

Johnson and Johnson (1991: 463) refer to research in the field which demonstrates that as cohesiveness increases, the team is able to hold on to its members more easily, and the longer it can do this, the more likely it is to achieve goals. So retention is an important attribute of a cohesive group. Increased participation is another attribute, which obviously increases the team's resources to complete tasks. The final feature is that of conformity. In cohesive units, team members are willing to conform to team norms, and where these are consistent with productivity orientations, people will work harder.

They go on to provide some invaluable observations on the features of cohesiveness. Cohesive teams are invariably:

- structuring cooperation and encouraging cooperative interaction;
- successfully meeting the personal needs of team members;
- maintaining and supporting high levels of trust;
- establishing team norms that encourage individuality, trusting and trustworthy behaviour, and concern and affection between the team members.

Some of the earlier points about what determines cohesiveness are elaborated on by Robbins (1991: 298) and his explanations serve also as a useful guide in elevating cohesiveness levels:

1. Plenty of time should be spent together and it is best if members are placed in close proximity.
2. It should be reasonably difficult to get into the team. Robbins calls this 'severity of initiation', and indicates that rites such as applications, interviews and so forth may contribute to cohesiveness.
3. The team should be kept manageably small to allow adequate interaction and avoid clique formation. Robbins refers to some interesting evidence, however, that suggests small teams are more cohesive if they comprise members of the same sex. In mixed gender teams, larger groups appear to be more cohesive.
4. A team that deals with external threats well and builds up a portfolio of successes in goal achievement will become attractive. It is important, therefore, to record successes and make them known.

Highly cohesive teams are generally thought to be more effective than teams with low levels of cohesiveness. Effectiveness in terms of performance, however, may not be simply the consequence of cohesiveness but also the *cause*. As we have seen above, achievement may increase attraction and thereby cohesiveness, so while it is necessary to consider the factors that might improve cohesiveness, it cannot be seen in isolation from the effects of successful achievement and performance.

There is one more factor to consider. Robbins (1991: 301) draws attention to the importance of performance norms, which affect the relationship between cohesiveness and productivity: "If performance-related norms are high (for example, high output, quality work, cooperation with individuals outside the group), a cohesive group will be more productive than a less cohesive group. But if cohesiveness is high and performance norms are low, productivity will be low." This appropriately illustrates the importance of establishing the right norms.

Norms

Personal work values and understanding what is expected in terms of behaviour are developed through the team's system of norms and values. "The influence of the group over an individual member is quite substantial, and a team, like its individual members, develops its own unique and distinctive sense of identity or group self concept" (Jacobs and Everett, 1988: 12). "A norm is a sentiment shared by members of a group concerning what should or should not be done " (Mukhi et al., 1988: 276). Norms, therefore, help to form behaviour, but they do this without drawing on external controls.

Johnson and Johnson (1991: 452) explain that team norms must be established that promote conformity in terms of interactive behaviours amongst team members and that support the distribution of power in such a way as to maintain harmony amongst those members. From this, it is clear that norms represent a particularly important considera-tion to the work of any team. Indeed, as Petrock (1990: 9) notes, a team does not become productive until sound norms are in place. Norms appear in matters of consequence to a team. As Johnson and Johnson (1991: 452) observe, norms are concerned primarily with behaviour that affects task goal attainment and the ability of the team to survive in a healthy condition. Robbins (1991: 291) actually defines what makes a norm important. It is significant:

- if it helps the team to survive;
- if it increases the predictability of team members' behaviours;
- if it prevents as much interpersonal discomfort as possible;
- if it allows people to express the central values of the team and be clear about the team's distinctive identity.

Norms serve to define appropriate behaviour by team members in relation to:

1. outsiders;
2. the team's own members;
3. the task;
4. non-work activities (Anantaraman, 1984a: 147).

From this list, it is possible to derive significant matters over which norms may be formed. They include effectiveness and productivity, relationships with the team leader and others in authority, interpersonal relationships with fellow team members, and social interaction. These are in general terms. At a more practical level, Kirkpatrick and Smith (1991: 5) explain how norms in relation to seven important characteristics were examined during a teambuilding intervention: the characteristics were openness, conformity, support, confronting difficulties, risk-taking, shared values, and energy. Similarly, Petrock (1990: 9) talks about norms for productivity and excellence as a team develops in competence.

A slightly different framework of norms is explained by Robbins (1991: 290). There are four classes: performance-related processes, appearance factors, informal social arrangements and allocation of resources.

- **Performance-related processes:** This is concerned with norms about how hard people should work, their productivity and how they communicate. They are extremely powerful and can significantly affect performance.
- **Appearance factors:** This category includes appropriate standards of dress, personal appearance, and when it is acceptable to, say, arrive late or leave early.
- **Informal social arrangements:** This includes whether meals are taken together, who pays, special social occasions and actions to be taken when someone is in hospital.
- **Allocation of resources:** Norms related to this category can originate in the team as well as the organisation. They include task assignment, allocation of new equipment, who gets what type of computer and so forth. The impact of these norms should not be underestimated, as they can affect team member satisfaction and thereby the performance of the team.

Certain behaviours are deemed to be acceptable and within the confines of the norm limits. This may be thought of as conformity. Non-conformity is where the behaviour exceeds the limits of tolerable behaviour. What are these limits? The answer is somewhat complex, because they tend to vary according to several factors. Two of these factors are the importance of the team task and the individual's position in the team. To compound the difficulties, the range of acceptable behaviour can vary in its extent, specificity, and permissiveness. Anantaraman (1984a: 147) takes up the two major factors and explains how the range of acceptable behaviour might vary:

> In matters crucial to the group such as identity of the group, major goals of the group and the continued existence of the group, the range of tolerable behaviour is proportionately narrow ... The leader is subject to a narrower range of tolerable behaviour than the other members in matters of consequence to the group.

For those who have worked in teams, the power of norms will have been felt. But where does this power come from? Johnson and Johnson (1991: 455) explain that norms constitute some of the personal power given up by team members so that, as individuals, they allow themselves to be influenced by these norms or 'moral obligations'. They carry sufficient weight to require members to conform if they (the members) wish to continue as members of the team. Feldman (1984), as cited in Roberts and Hunt (1991: 182), believes norms can develop in a number of ways:

(1) as explicit statements by supervisors or coworkers;
(2) as critical events in the group's history;
(3) in terms of primacy, or by virtue of their introduction early in the group's history; and
(4) as carry over behaviors from past situations.

At a practical level, Johnson and Johnson (1991: 456) provide some useful guidelines for team leaders in establishing and maintaining support for team norms:

1. Members must be made aware of team norms and it must be clear that every member accepts and practises them.
2. It must be demonstrated that the norms facilitate task accomplishment.
3. It helps if team members can be part of the process of setting up norms.

4. Enforcement should be immediate and consistent.
5. Helpful cultural norms that support task accomplishment and good relationships amongst members should be brought into the team.
6. Norms should be flexible enough to be changed when they are not helpful to team effectiveness.

Values

Norms are best seen as part of a wider value system. Such a system refers to the aspects of team life that are important to the members. Goals and targets, therefore, if perceived as being of importance, represent a type of value. Attitudes, political preferences and religious affiliations may also be part of the values fabric. Each individual team member brings certain values with him to the workplace but these can be altered by the culture of the team or organisation. "While people obviously enter organizations with established values, these values and the new ones formed by experience in the organization are constantly tested and shaped by situations that play out in the organizational environment" (McCall et al., 1988: 8).

Values, as we have seen in looking at the particular case of norms, are powerful determinants of acceptable behaviour. It is important that teams are built on memberships with similar values patterns, otherwise dysfunctions may occur. Organisations or teams aim for a shared value system. As Blunt (1990: 5) states in discussing organisational cultures: "Shared values, what people genuinely believe to be good or bad, desirable or undesirable, acceptable or unacceptable, are the essence of organisational culture. The more clearly articulated and more widely shared these values, the more robust, effective and lasting the culture." Obviously then the more 'shared' the culture, the better.

One of the more frequent examples of non-shared values is that of conflicting orientations towards quality or quantity. Some members of the team may have strong preferences for high-quantity output at the expense of quality, while others may be perceived as working slowly when they focus on quality and settle for lower levels of production. It makes sense to base selection decisions, in part, on values appropriate to the team. If successful performance hinges on attention to detail, team members should be selected who place a high value on careful and high quality work. More general advice is offered by George (1977: 79) who lists examples of the types of values that most members should agree on. Such values include giving customer satisfaction, keeping to schedules and commitments, providing good value, and recognising the contributions of other team members.

It is not always possible to have the ideal of completely shared values. Even in teams that are carefully selected, there will be individual value differences. For example, some members may value highly the expression of dissonant views, but others may value much more the feeling of harmony and accord. The fact that people have strong feelings about these orientations shows the power of values. It may be tempting to force personal values onto others, but this is an unwise strategy and it may be better to respect others' values. While it may seem from this that there is little chance of reconciling such vastly different values, there probably is hope. Echoing the thoughts earlier of McCall *et al.*, it might be argued that where there are high levels of interdependence, and people derive prestige and satisfaction from their team membership, there is less chance that team members will hold out for values and behaviours that are too far removed from the team's values.

Conformity

In discussing values and norms at various points in this book, conformity is mentioned frequently. It refers to the individual's changes in behaviour as a result of the team's influences. It is seen as desirable that members conform to the team's norms and values.

Roberts and Hunt (1991: 183) list four variables which influence conformity to the team's norms. They are: personality characteristics of team members (intelligence, age, self-blame and authoritarianism); stimuli that evoke conformity (aspects of the situation related to the norm the individual member is conforming to); situational factors (group size, unanimity of the majority and group structure); and inter-group relations (composition of the group, past success, personal identification with the group.)

Jacobs and Everett (1988: 11), however, point to the dangers of over-conformity. Members may be held in low regard if, for various reasons, they fail to comply with norms, and this may result in a 'natural conservatism', where feelings are not shared and values not made explicit. We have also seen how it may be disadvantageous to the team to isolate those with considerable innovatory skills but who may find it difficult to conform in the same way that more conventional members are able to comply with behavioural expectations.

We have also discussed the dangers of excluding any conflict from team settings.

In relation to the problem of whether or not to conform, people are vulnerable, since their desire for acceptance is likely to override any resistance they might have toward norms of behaviour. Conformity, despite the more positive picture presented in our discussion of team norms, generally has negative connotations. "Many people think of conformity as a blind, unreasoning, spineless, weak, slavish adherence to the demands of the majority of peers or of authority figures" (Johnson and Johnson, 1991: 452). It may, in fact, be good or bad. Conformity to team norms, where those norms strongly violate individual values and principles, may not enhance the work of the team. There was an instance of a business school course team staff member who had strong religious views and would not work on Sundays. The workteam believed residential programmes were important and could only be operated over weekends. The team coerced the individual to sacrifice his personal values, but he felt guilty about his involvement and his heart was not really in the job. The converse may also be true. Conformity may also support values and beliefs, and it may improve the team's operation without compromising individual principles and values.

One issue about which there appears to be little conformity of opinion is that of how many members a team should have to operate effectively. We now turn our attention, therefore, to a topic that has fascinated a number of experts for some time, that of ideal team size.

Team Size

There is some variation in the literature about the ideal size of a team. Francis and Young (1979), for example, suggest that nine is the outside limit, but qualify this by indicating that teamwork characteristics can be cultivated in larger groups. As we have seen, this may be particularly true in those teams where there is mixed gender membership.

Nine, in fact, seems somewhat on the large side when compared with the ideas of other authors. Johnson and Johnson (1991: 447), for instance, give a range of between two and six members, and this is to ensure that there is meaningful face-to-face interaction. They suggest that the smaller the team, the clearer it becomes to individual team members that their contributions and efforts are needed.

There are obvious disadvantages, however, with a team being too small in number. It can limit the range of ideas and the roles to be enacted. For example, the fewer members there are, the less chance there may be of having someone with innovatory skills or with strong analytical abilities. Peterson (1991: 43) makes this point and suggests a membership of between six and twelve persons. "If you have fewer than six, you might not get a broad range of opinions, and a few personalities could wind up dominating the group. More than twelve members becomes too unwieldy, not to mention that it's often hard to get a word in edgewise." Referring to productivity or new product teams in excellent companies, equally moderate figures are suggested by Peters and Waterman (1982: 127): between five and ten, with an ideal figure of around seven. They noted that the task forces observed in their research invariably had less than ten members.

Robbins (1991: 292) points to the evidence that small teams are quicker at task completion than their larger counterparts. He also notes that the nature of their activities is a major moderating variable. If they are involved in problem solving, larger teams do better than smaller ones. Larger groups (say, more than twelve) are good at acquiring the necessary data and providing diverse inputs, but smaller teams are able to work better at processing the input. He suggests that teams of seven tend to be more effective, therefore, for taking action.

Again, drawing on the research, Robbins raises some interesting points in relation to the size issue. One relates to individual performance in the team:

> Increases in group size are inversely related to individual performance. More may be better in the sense that the total productivity of a group of four is greater than one or two, but the individual productivity of each group member declines. This may be attributable to either believing in fairness of effort ("I will do only as much as others") or to the dispersion of responsibility.

The practical message for managers and leaders is to ensure that, even in the team setting, individual efforts can be identified.

Overall, it seems that small groups are manageable and still allow for diverse input. Large groups may provide the conditions in which a few team members can dominate discussion, subgroups can spring up, members can hide and decisions can take an inordinate amount of time to be reached. Taking the advice from the literature generally, the average figure for preferred membership size works out to about seven. Interestingly, this is the group size advocated by Belbin in our discussion of team roles. It is probably unwise to look at team size in isolation; it should be seen in conjunction with the issue of team membership.

Membership

> Heraclitus said: 'Nature desires eagerly opposites and, out of them, it completes its harmony, not out of similars.' Managers would do well to ponder upon this (Graham, 1991: 52).

Our discussion of team size above also drew attention to the issue of membership, the implication being that diversity is more to be desired than homogeneity. This is a common problem in teams, and we mentioned briefly in examining the relevance of team roles that many teams may comprise mainly 'Implementors', people of the same type with similar behavioural patterns. Buhler and McCann (1989: 14) make this point in looking at selection. They suggest it is a critical mistake for team leaders to select mirror images – individuals with the same strengths and personality characteristics as the leader. Adair (1986: 157) too calls for balance, but focuses on the mental skills (which he sets aside from personality, experience and knowledge considerations) that are needed in the team. These are: analysing, reasoning, synthesising, holistic thinking, valuing, intuition, memory, creativity, and numeracy or literacy. An explanation of these mental attributes is given in Adair.

Timmons (1979: 202) takes up this very point, drawing attention to the need for complementary experience and capabilities rather than similarities. He gives the case of a high-technology venture team comprising members with the same skills, of roughly the same age, with the same training, and having had similar working experience. They had a high level of expertise, but lacked skill in other areas and failed to understand crucial human resource, marketing and financial implications. The team, like many others, failed to survive. The aim, as Harris (1986: 29) notes, should be to find members who, as a team, provide all the necessary skills.

Failing to provide the required skills, knowledge and experience can indeed have serious consequences, as the following case shows:

> A multinational company deployed its facilities engineer and his assistant to link up with a commissioned architect to travel to a proposed site abroad to design a new plant. This small team talked with relevant locals and produced appropriate plans. Unfortunately,

because of the limited involvement, all the considerations were from the engineering point of view, and at the senior management meeting, the human resources manager pointed out that rest rooms and recreation facilities had not been built into the design. There were further imperfections. The canteen provision was inadequate and the female employees refused point blank to travel to the plant if there was only a unisex toilet which the team had designed. Much of the work had to be re-done and this cost the company a considerable sum of money in another visit and architect's fees.

Having the appropriate skills may mean hard decisions having to be made. Sometimes, it may be appropriate to encourage individuals to 'retire' when their contributions are no longer relevant. At the very least, teams have to be flexible in their membership arrangements. They should be able to draft in new members when they recognise there are certain deficiencies (Huszczo, 1990: 40), although they must avoid the danger of overcompensating for weaknesses (Buhler and McCann, 1989: 14). Nevertheless, there should be provision to bring in resources for crucial action.

There are other hard decisions with regard to membership. There are occasions when people expect to be part of the team by virtue of precedent or position. But membership needs to be determined by the ability to contribute to the solving of problems (Kazemak and Albert, 1988: 108). In other words, access to important information and the possession of essential skills are more important contributory considerations than rank.

Crouch and Yetton (1987: 123) examined the issue of changes in team membership and its effect on team functioning. They found that team performance can decline when a vital member leaves. They suggest that the simplest way to maintain a successful team, if the team leader leaves, is "to promote a manager who has had task experiences similar to those of the previous manager". Similarly, they see the leaving of less effective personnel as an opportunity to revitalise an ailing team by introducing high-performing individuals.

Robbins (1991: 294) looks at the interesting issue of 'group demography', defined as the degree to which team members share a common demographic characteristic. In relation to turnover, it appears that the age of team members or the date they join a workteam can affect the turnover rate. It is suggested that those with dissimilar experiences will have a higher turnover rate, because communication is not so easy, and conflict and power struggles make team membership less attractive. "People who enter together or at approximately the same time are more likely to associate with one another, have a similar perspective of the group or organization, and thus are more likely to stay." Where membership retention is an issue, therefore, demography is an important consideration.

Probably the two key considerations in determining membership revolve around technical or professional competence, and the role contributions that can be made. Individual attributes may also be taken into consideration, however. Adair (1986: 132) provides a list of desirable attributes, and these include the ability to listen to others and to build on their contributions, flexibility of mind, the ability to give and inspire trust, and the likeable qualities of a person. He includes this last characteristic because it is apparent that people work better with those they like. It must be emphasized that these are not essential attributes and they would certainly not assume precedence over more important membership selection factors.

Summary

In this chapter we have discussed a number of general concepts touched upon in other sections of the book. We examined responsibility, coordination, cooperation, competition and cohesiveness, conformity and the norms and values in relation to teams. We also looked at team size and membership. The next section emphasizes the organisational dimension, so vital to total team development.

Summary of the Implications for Managers

- In real teamwork, all members are responsible for their actions and they work together to bring about events. Responsibility has to be given in increasing doses. Inexperienced teams can at first be given smaller projects and problems to deal with, and as they gain in confidence, they can take on larger responsibilities.

- Integrated effort needs to be supported in the team's processes, such as in the way rewards are distributed. This is important if there is to be effective coordination and cooperation. On this count, leaders should establish a cooperative climate, where members see one another as 'customers', and should not support excessive individualism. A team that is structured cooperatively is likely to be more productive than one structured individualistically or competitively.

- Competition can be combined with cooperation and lead to quality improvements or the maintenance of standards. Competition, in this sense, is between teams but within a supportive framework, and may involve finding better alternatives, products and services. All teams within an organisation can then enjoy the rewards of such a process.

- As cohesiveness increases, major benefits accrue. First, the team finds it easier to keep members and thereby achieve goals. Second, there is more participation, and therefore more resources to complete tasks. Third, there is more conformity to team norms. If these norms match productivity orientations, people will work harder. The performance norms, however, must be high, otherwise a cohesive group will have low productivity.

- Cohesiveness can be increased by:
    - structuring cooperation and encouraging cooperative interaction;
    - meeting team members' personal needs;
    - supporting high levels of trust;
    - Having norms that support trusting behaviour and concern.

- Other ways in which cohesiveness might be increased include team members spending plenty of time together, making it possible for them to work in close proximity, making entry to the team prestigious and difficult, keeping the team small, and recording successes and making them known to outsiders.

- There are several important considerations for leaders in relation to norms:
    - They should be made clear to members.
    - It should be shown that they make task accomplishment easier.
    - They should be formulated in part by members themselves.
    - Their enforcement should be immediate and consistent.
    - Norms that support task achievement and healthy relationships should be imported.
    - They should be flexible – changed when they are no longer helpful.

- Smaller teams are likely to lead to effective interaction and faster task completion. It is often found that individual productivity may decrease, even in seemingly effective teams, and it may be advisable to find ways of considering individual inputs.

- In looking at team membership, complementary experience and abilities are more important factors than similarity. There should be flexibility in membership, with the facility to draft in new members when required and to 'retire' others. Membership of the team is best determined by the ability to contribute to problem solving, and this implies the need to consider the individual's access to information or the possession of essential skills rather than his rank or status in the organisation.

Section 5

The Organisation

17

ORGANISATIONAL SUPPORT FOR TEAMS

IN SOME WAYS, it could be argued that this section of the book should really appear at the beginning, since much of what we say about teams and their development can only be realistic if there is support from the organisation in which they operate. Indeed, some experts believe that team development must start at the top: that conditions in which teams can thrive have to be established by the chief decision makers. This is a view that makes good sense. An organisation that wishes to draw on the immense benefits that teams can provide must show a commitment to their work and employ a structural system that supplies strong support to teams.

Structure and Integration

The structure of an organisation may have a significant bearing on team effectiveness. Various structures can be employed which can either encourage or discourage effective team actions. As we have indicated frequently throughout the book, teams do not operate in a vacuum. They are part of a wider organisational structure and culture and, as such, need to interact and relate with other organisational teams and actors.

One such possible structure is based on Likert's linking-pin device, in which the leader of one team is a member of the next team up in the organisational chain. This effects an integration between teams at all levels and ensures no team is working in isolation. The precise nature of the structure does not matter. What is important is that roles and relationships are congruent with teamwork demands. Chance (1989: 25) notes that teambuilding is of little value if a conducive teamwork environment does not exist: "This means more than a kind word for the group's efforts from the chief executive. It means making structural changes." And Peterson (1991: 38) is adamant that it is the responsibility of management to put the right structural framework in place so that involvement is facilitated, a point confirmed by Thamhain (1990: 16) in stating that it is a critical responsibility of senior management to provide the right environment for innovative teams.

Another structure that has received much attention is a holistic one, described by Lau (1988: 14):

> The radial teamwork structure is composed of various group clusters, each having equal power and importance within the organization. Each group is linked to each other via an appointed leader. In addition, all the groups revolve around the top leader in the organisation. This structure greatly enhances communication and accessibility to both the chief leader and to all areas of the organization.

A hint of things to come is provided by Huszczo (1990: 37), although at this stage it appears to be more of an ideal than a realistic, widely accepted possibility. He refers to turning the organisational hierarchy upside down. "Work teams that are actually involved in the production of goods and the delivery of services are being seen as the top of the organization. The rest of the hierarchy is the support staff to make sure that those teams are effective." Despite any criticism, the idea draws attention to where the important and productive organisational activities might be.

While an overlapping structure may not always be appropriate, it seems important that the team is linked to significant points higher up the organisation. This can be done through the manager or co-ordinator, the one who is seen as responsible for the team. This person's job may be to provide adequate resources to the team, to communicate relevant information and to hold responsibility for tasks not yet delegated to the team (Jessup, 1990: 81). Similarly, linkages that enable the right information to be delivered to the right locations as quickly as possible have to be established. Another solid organisation strategy for ensuring coordination is to clearly, accurately and widely communicate company plans. If all teams are familiar with the overall direction and strategy of the organisation they may develop a feeling of 'pulling together', furthering positive intergroup relations. If various team representatives are involved in the planning, all the better.

The greater the degree of autonomy the team enjoys, the more important it is to show the relationships amongst the various organisational components. This is because, traditionally, charts have shown lines between individual positions, but the relationships between teams has been unclear. This is an important consideration where teams become responsible for significant decisions. There needs to be clarity about the linkages between permanent teams and projects teams, and between teams and senior management. This has obvious implications for the way in which organisational charts are drawn.

This problem is particularly evident in those organisations that demand a team approach amongst top managers, but the structure shows them as separate individuals each reporting independently to the chief executive. It may be difficult under such conditions to expect them to work collaboratively. There are many cases of production managers failing to plan appropriate schedules because contact with marketing and other related functions is minimal. An associated problem may be the type of career structures promoted by the organisation. If progression 'up the ladder' is predominantly based on individual achievement, the structure is not supporting teamwork.

It may also be important to examine ways in which cross-functional linkages can be established. What is more important than the mechanisms, however, is systemic compatibility: a commitment throughout the organisation to support participation and the work of teams. This is particularly so in those organisations that seek to make widespread use of team approaches.

Organisational support may also mean providing roles that enhance team operation. Jessup (1990: 82) looks in particular at self-managed teams and explains three roles that support the work of the team. They must be provided by the organisation. These roles – administrator, coach, and advisor – are not organisational titles, but roles that relevant individuals can play at appropriate times. They also apply to the leader. Indeed, Blanchard (1988: 8) advises the manager to withdraw from the leadership role and allow others to assume the responsibility for leading the team. This inevitably frees him to become more of a coach and advisor, and also a link with the larger organisation. For the organisation to encourage individuals to adopt such support-giving roles demands a highly supportive organisational climate.

Climate

We have seen how the basic ingredients of teamwork relate to the fundamental values of openness, trust and participation. The values of the organisation have to be consistent with these if team development is allowed to take place. For example, it would be pointless to make team development efforts in an organisation that fostered secrecy and suspicion. "The question of personal risks involved for members in practising openness in the context of organizational politics and the consequent fear of retribution will loom large in the minds of the participants and make the team-building effort worthless and futile" (Anantaraman, 1984b: 221).

The point is reinforced by Jacobs and Everett (1988: 10). They insist an environment of sharing, openness and mutual support must be provided if people are to take risks, and to make tentative and specula-tive suggestions. Without the right environment, the tendency is for people to play things safe and to advocate low-risk strategies.

This leads us on to a brief discussion of an important factor of the organisational support system, that of climate. We have already examined the relevance of values and attitudes to the work of teams and these, together with the imperatives of tradition, combine to produce a climate that is either conducive or a hindrance to team effectiveness.

The importance of climate is amply illustrated by Ends and Page (1977: 92):

> It affects the amount of work workers are willing to do. It affects the amount of initiative and ingenuity they are willing to display. It affects their willing-ness to commit themselves to high-performance goals. It affects their attitudes toward taking risks. It also affects their attitudes toward supervisors, peers, subordinates, and even toward themselves.

The same authors identify five major determinants of climate, namely, the value system, patterns of power and authority, team morale and cohesiveness, openness in communications, and relationships with other groups (p. 93). We have touched on several of these already. It is worth mentioning, however, the importance of teams being able to collaborate and the impact this might have on the organisational climate. An absence of interdependence and high levels of animosity between teams may have an adverse effect on overall organisational performance, and also impair the team's operation, since the scope for support is decreased.

The reason that this may happen can often be attributed to the 'parochial' management problem. This occurs where managers (and maybe team leaders) protect their 'territory' and see themselves as being in competition with other managers and teams. George (1977: 72) mentions that they may take a narrow view of their roles and fail to see the overall needs of the business. This indicates a need for individuals in the higher echelons of organisations to team up with their counterparts instead of competing in the typical political turf wars (Huszczo, 1990: 37).

While we have focused on the fostering of trust as a function of the team so far, it is worth noting that the organisation may take the lead in this regard. An organisation that trusts its members and teams is likely to create a far more supportive climate than one that employs strategies which gives signals about suspicion. In the *Straits Times* of Singapore, 9 March 1992, a story was reported about Neptune Orient Lines in which sterner measures were to be imposed on managers and executives who were late for work. While that would be difficult to criticise, the company used a time clock system, which may arguably have been a clear indication of the company's lack of trust. In the same report, a spokesman for IBM explained that, in contrast to NOL's 'clocking-in' practice, his company's policy was based on trust and respect for the individual. It is hard to imagine how real teamwork can be fostered in a climate of suspicion and mistrust. Indeed, the episode resulted in more than one executive speaking out critically about the company, hardly a way of establishing supportive organisational relationships.

For teams to operate effectively, the wider organisation needs to emphasize cooperation rather than competition among groups. Although we have discussed the advantages and disadvantages of intergroup competition elsewhere, they are worth reinforcing here in relation to the issue of climate. Hellriegel *et al.* (1989: 247) summarise the attitudinal and behavioural consequences of organisations creating climates based on competition rather than cooperation.

> In extremely competitive relationships, groups tend to be distrustful and unresponsive, to emphasize self interests, to interact only when required to do so, to resist influence or control from each other, and so on. On the other hand, a highly cooperative relationship tends to be characterized by trust,

responsiveness, emphasis on mutual interests, easy and frequent communication, acceptance of mutual influence or control.

Quite obviously, organisations which support cooperative environments are more likely to produce effective teams than those which allow or encourage excessively competitive climates.

The role of the organisation, therefore, is an important one. Thamhain (1990: 12), looking at organisational conditions for innovative workteams, concluded that "successful organizations and their managers pay attention to human factors. They appear effective in fostering a work environment conducive to innovative work, that is, where people find challenging assignments that lead to recognition and professional growth. Such a professionally stimulating environment seems to lower communication barriers and conflict and enhances the desire of personnel to succeed. Also, it seems to enhance organizational awareness of greater environmental trends and the ability to prepare and respond to these challenges effectively."

Climate is sometimes confused with atmosphere and it is admittedly difficult to separate the two concepts, but the more enduring nature of climate needs to be emphasized. Usually, people will talk about the group atmosphere as warm and relaxed or as cold, hostile and tense. "Atmosphere affects how members feel about a group and the degree of spontaneity in their participation. Atmosphere may be temporary; climate implies a prevailing condition" (Adair, 1986: 22). Seen in this light, climate is a feature that organisations would be advised to neglect at their cost.

Finally, it is worth consolidating an earlier contention that supportive organisational infrastructures have an enormous impact on team operations. As Tolle (1988: 285) says: "Harmonious, trusting, and cooperative management team relationships are usually effects of solid successful management systems – not *causes*".

Overall Organisational Support

George (1977: 80) puts together several of these climate and cultural factors to specify the conditions needed in the organisation for a genuine task-team approach to succeed:

1. An atmosphere of openness and trust
2. A willingness of members (of whatever status) to interact on an equal basis

3. Acceptance of change
4. Willingness of subunits to subordinate their interests
5. Individuals who like to work in teams
6. A good organisation development programme
7. A sense of growth

The organisation, therefore, has to do its part. This may necessitate radically new ways of thinking. For example, the way that performance is monitored and recognised may have to be viewed differently. Up to now, we have tended to think in terms of the individual, but this may be totally inappropriate if the team concept is being promoted. For example, it would be foolish to reward the individual members of a sports team differently according to their performance if the club were trying to promote collective responsibility. Belzer (1989: 13) indeed suggests that it is important to praise a team's effort without singling out individuals.

Performance appraisal systems similarly may need to be approached differently. It may be necessary in the future to conduct performance appraisals on teams rather than just individuals. This is not easy because, in some contexts, the need to reward individual effort is not far short of national policy. People look to individual talent, provide incentives based on individual performance and give individuals responsibility. This is not something that can be changed overnight. If teams are to be accepted as a valid organisational progression, however, there have to be changes in the way performance is examined and recognised, and these changes may have to be gradual.

Giving organisational support implies giving teams and their members organisational membership. The fact is that, in many organisations, membership is peripheral. Members are given information only on a 'need to know' basis. There is much secrecy and suspicion. It seems important however that if teams are involved in, say, product development, they should know what the organisation thinks of their work and what customers think of their ideas. They may need to be given sensitive financial data and information about profits in an attempt to rid the organisation of any 'them' and 'us' feeling.

The organisation sets the tone for what goes on in teams. If the atmosphere in the team is sour, it may say a great deal about the organisation's attitude to the team. Good supportive management tends to lead to responsive teams, willing to serve the organisation and its customers. It is true that teams may have one or two genuinely negative thinkers but, as Peterson (1991: 185) points out, these tend to thrive only in a bad environment. On the other hand, if the environment is really supportive of team efforts, Peterson (p. 182) claims that people will operate in a 'team way' without being conscious about it. They will brainstorm ideas; managers will push responsibility down the organisation; there will be a free flow of information; and people will try to help one another.

We mentioned earlier the importance of creativity in teams and their decision making. It is unlikely to grow unless the organisation supports and nurtures the creative process. While we focused on ways in which creativity might be developed at an individual level, Professor Dougherty at the University of Pennsylvania explains that the problem is not really with individual creativity, but with organisational structures (and processes) that squash creativity (*Straits Times*, 7 April 1992). Organisational support, therefore, is a major consideration if innovation is to be encouraged.

In essence, what we are describing is a performance-based work culture, aptly described by Todryk (1990: 18). In order to expand such a culture, top management must support team members who are willing to learn new skills, methods and procedures and who are willing to modify attitudes so that the team can increase its effectiveness. Recognition from the top is vital if people are to be motivated to continue adapting skills and attitudes.

We have seen the effects that structure and climate might have on the work of teams and suggested the sorts of conditions that might need to be present for them to operate effectively. There are other important factors at the organisational level. These include strategy, resources, systems and processes, culture and the physical environment.

Strategy has an impact because it will determine what is important to the organisation and thereby the power of certain teams. Important activities tend to win resource support and this will be an important aspect of organisational support for the team. It can generate a feeling of certainty or it may have the potential for considerable conflict between teams. The impact of adequate resource provision must not be underestimated. A team cannot do a good job without the right tools.

The systems and processes that operate in the organisation also have an effect on teams. Rules and regulations, for instance, will to a large extent determine the behaviour of team members. If they are too restrictive, they will impose such considerable constraints that creativity may be completely stifled. Other processes that have an effect include those used in selection – they determine what kinds of people will be in teams – and those used in considering performance. In terms of performance, the behaviours that are rewarded will be reinforced. Culture too has an effect, in that team members have to abide by standards if they are to remain in favour (Robbins, 1991: 281).

Thamhain (1990: 15) also mentions the importance of image building and providing interesting work in relation to new product teams. The former involves giving high priority and visibility to the project, and it may have a unifying effect on the team. It is also suggested that the organisation should accommodate professional interests and wishes of employees, since innovative performance in the team may increase when individuals are professionally interested and stimulated. A similar point is made by Belzer (1989: 13), who advises enhancing a team's identity by advertising the status of a project and the team's achievements. On a practical note, she suggests using company newsletters and department meetings to publicise success, and mentioning each member of the team by name.

The physical work environment has an important effect on team members' behaviour. If they are in close proximity without physical barriers, the opportunity is there to interact frequently. If they are separated by offices, screens or buildings, the chances are that inter-action will be a planned activity. There are other considerations. The sort of work space a team is allocated should reflect the professional level and needs of those involved. Facilities should be given on the basis of needs rather than rank, and there should be adequate equipment and materials (Thamhain, 1990: 15).

There is one more factor which is of critical importance. It has been implied several times already, but it needs reinforcing: the attitude of top management is crucial to success. Effective leadership is needed to demonstrate the sincerity of efforts to give teams greater responsibility. Support has to be provided if teams and their members are to sustain considerable endeavours on behalf of the organisations they serve.

Support for Team Development

Probably the most visible and effective method the organisation has at its disposal for supporting its people is that of development. Organisations willing to commit financial and human resources to improving individuals and teams on an ongoing basis are showing their support in a number of ways. Firstly, they are sending a very clear message to everybody that they value improvement, change and 'better ways of doing things'. Secondly, they are improving the quality, skills and self-esteem of their members by exhibiting their belief in and commitment to them.

This type of support for teams implies support for team development. Whereas it is generally accepted that most organisations are increasing support for individuals in the form of training and development activities, unfortunately, little attention is given to developing the work of teams as units. This may be largely because it is considered too much of an imposition to remove an entire team from the work site or from its day-to-day operations. There is also a prevalent assumption that people need only a cursory knowledge of team dynamics and interpersonal skills for things to work adequately. However, as Huszczo (1990: 39) observes: "Much of the activity involved in team development is the interplay of working through the concepts together. The whole is greater than the sum of the parts; time is needed to examine the fits between the parts."

Support also implies that top managers must become familiar with the essence of teamwork and even the focus of teambuilding efforts. It is not sufficient to send groups of employees on teambuilding programmes without recognising the implications and application in the organisation. Teams must be responsible for implementing what they have learned; trainers need to ensure clarity on the part of participants on how learning can be transposed to the work setting; and management needs to ensure adequate follow-up and accountability. Approached in this way, team development becomes an integrated activity and one that can have a real impact on organisational life.

Much of what has been said earlier about support for teams applies to team development efforts. Woodcock (1979: 18) notes, for example, that over-control will stifle teams, training policy methods and practice need to be resolved, a supportive management philosophy needs to be established, and reward systems need to be linked to effective teamwork. This last point is one that deserves further elaboration.

Rewards

Earlier we touched on the subject of rewards and how they might be used to support team approaches. We suggested that rewarding individuals tends to support individualistic orientations, and a radical rethink of such systems needs to be made. Chance (1989: 25) notes: "Individual incentives, such as piece work, merit pay, and bonuses, are not designed to foster group cooperation. Most experts recommend incentives based upon the performance of the team as a whole. This, they reason, will encourage people to work together, share information, help one another out."

Wynn and Guditus (1984: 114) make the same point, explaining that working with others in teams has the potential for competition or cooperation. Since the latter is more generally desirable, we can encourage it by basing rewards on overall team performance and by deemphasizing individual performance.

Referring specifically to innovation, Galbraith and Kazanjian (1986: 167) reinforce this point and suggest that successful creative efforts are not dependent on individuals working alone: "Recognizing this, a number of firms have also created group reward structures that provide a bonus to all members of the project team if the innovation activity succeeds." This clearly displays a need for organisational systems and processes to be congruent with strategies. If organisations have strategies that demand coordinated team effort, then important processes such as reward systems should match those strategies. Huszczo (1990: 39) believes that those involved in conducting team development episodes have a responsibility to consider to what extent organisational systems recognise and reinforce good teamwork. As he correctly observes, once members realise that rewards are given, not for teamwork, but for individual performance and effort, they will revert to individualised behaviour. Essentially, the organisation should create a mind set where individuals are not concerned about who gets credit for success – that credit should come through the success of the team (Tarkenton, 1986: 31).

Peterson (1991: 82) takes a radical look at evaluation and rewards in relation to supporting the team-driven organisation. Rewards could become the responsibility of teams themselves and they could evaluate both their members and also the work of other teams at the same level.

The same writer also gives some useful practical advice about the way that management can recognise team success. The team can be praised publicly and this represents an excellent way of rewarding the members. Management may also choose to do things like take the team out to dinner and to let everyone know that this is being done and why (p. 106).

Changing the reward system to support effective team operation may, as we have said already, require new ways of thinking. A culture may have to be established in which members refer to 'we' rather than 'I', where they share in the successes, and where they take collective responsibility for failure. This leads us in the next chapter into a discussion of how culture may have a significant bearing on the work and development of organisational teams, and we also examine the important issue of the wider cultural context.

Summary

In this chapter we have emphasized the importance of strong organisational support for teams. Such support includes carefully planned and integrated structures, and the development of an open and collaborative climate. Supporting a team may require organisations to rethink certain issues such as appraisal and reward systems, as well as providing financial and material resources. Perhaps the best way for organisations to support the growth of teams is to aim towards promoting a culture that values individual and group development. In the next chapter we look at this and several other cultural considerations.

Summary of the Implications for Managers

- The organisation's structure should support team operation and that means delineating relationships between teams across the organisation, and between teams and top managers. If teams are to succeed, there needs to be commitment throughout the entire organisation to support participation and collaboration. This necessitates the free flow of information both horizontally and vertically. There should also be a commitment to broad involvement in decision making. In an organisation that supports teamwork, authority is likely to be associated with expertise and organisational purpose.

- In order to develop a climate that is conducive to the team approach, teams must collaborate and top managers must also 'team up'. The organisation must trust teams to work effectively and there must be respect for individuals.

- Such an operation demands radically new ways of thinking, and this may involve senior managers in considering the ways in which performance is monitored and recognised. Thinking has to be more in terms of the team than the individual. Rewards, therefore, should not be for individual effort but should promote collective responsibility. Even performance appraisals, traditionally conducted with individuals, may have to be worked with teams. Such an approach involves giving people real organisational membership and this means opening up information rather than cloaking the organisation in secrecy and suspicion.

- Teams and customers can be linked. The environment can be creative and supportive. Members can brainstorm ideas, responsibility can be pushed well down the organisation, and people can generally help, rather than hinder, one another.

- A performance-based work culture is likely to support the work of teams. In such a culture, management supports people willing to learn new skills, methods and procedures. Resources, however, must also be adequate if high levels of performance are to be achieved.

- Creativity should not be stifled by excessive rules, regulations and behavioural constraints. High status and visibility can be given to teams that operate well and support the organisation's mission. The interests and wishes of members can also be accommodated.

- Top managers need to become familiar with the essence of teamwork and development, and they need to ensure that members implement what they have learnt during development episodes. They need to ensure that there is clarity about how team development relates to the workplace, and there should be management follow-up and accountability.

- We have already indicated that there must be a reorientation of rewards to the team and a deemphasis on the individual. The strategy of the organisation, therefore, must be aligned to the reward system. Teams may also control rewards and have an input into decisions regarding rewards to other teams.

18

CULTURAL CONSIDERATIONS

THROUGHOUT THE TEXT we have referred to the impact of organisational variables on teams and team performance. One of the most powerful of these is the culture of the organisation. Different organisations have different cultures, some weak, some strong. In this chapter, we examine briefly the concept of organisational culture and its place in the team setting. We then discuss an emerging problem in many organisations, that of mixed national or ethnic cultures in teams, and how their work can be affected. In today's shrinking market-place, which is typified by globalisation, mergers, takeovers and 'agreements', it is not uncommon for teams to comprise members drawn from vastly different cultural backgrounds.

Organisational Cultures

Robbins (1991: 572) defines organisational culture "as a system of shared meaning held by members that distinguished the organization from other organisations". Daft (1992: 317) expands the definition: "*Culture* is a set of values, guiding beliefs, understandings, and ways of thinking that is shared by members of an organization and is taught to new members as correct. It represents the unwritten, feeling part of the organisation. The purpose of culture is to provide members with a sense of organizational identity and to generate a commitment to beliefs and values that are larger than themselves."

Corporate or organisational culture then, to a large extent, lays the framework within which teams must operate. The impact of this is obvious, for example, as organisations move increasingly towards decentralisation. Promoting a strong culture has been a constant theme in many influential reports and writings about the future directions of companies (for example see: Barham *et al.*, 1988 in the UK; Dunphy and Stace, 1990 in Australia; Peters and Waterman, 1992 in the US).

It is impractical to look at the work of teams without examining the cultures within which they must operate. Some cultures will obviously encourage teamwork, whereas others will not. Even the most dedicated proponent of teams and teamwork has little chance of building a productive team, for example, if the culture promotes and rewards individual competition as the sole basis for promotion, or if the organisation has a history of mistrust and autocratic control.

A recent study, *Management for the Future*, conducted in the UK, stressed the importance of culture for future corporate success. It is widely felt that, in highly decentralised companies, corporate culture will perform a more integrative role than corporate strategy in holding the organisation together (Barham *et al.*, 1988: 28). The same authors describe a cultural 'ideal' gleaned from studying various successful companies and promote this for future success. Interestingly, many of the constructs described promote team-style operation. The cultures they describe:

- are growth- and results-oriented but also believe work should be fun;
- promote confidence and a belief in the organisation's ability to handle the future;
- welcome change as an opportunity, not a threat;
- believe in providing both challenge and a supportive psychological environment for people to take initiative and responsibility at all levels of the firm;
- foster customer-awareness throughout the firm, and aim for high levels of quality and service;
- stress both teamwork and the ability of each individual to contribute, learn and develop;
- emphasize results rather than process;

- are very open with little emphasis on status, and strong accent on high-quality communication, consultation, and listening;
- believe in integrity and fair-dealing with employees, suppliers and customers;
- are more tolerant of 'unconventional' types of people and encourage creative ways of doing things (p. 29).

Types of Cultures

We have already mentioned that there is no single culture. Different cultures are what make organisations different. Several different cultural typologies have been developed, and a particularly useful one is that devised by Harris (1986). He suggests that organisations are hybrids of four different types of cultures: power, role, achievement and support. Harris believes that the achievement culture is the way of the future. Interestingly, his achievement culture is often found in project teams and high-tech companies which are oriented to 'making a difference' (Barham *et al.*, 1988: 30). Regardless of the categorisation used, all organisational cultures have strengths and weaknesses and few fall within an 'ideal' description. Most are a mixture of various elements. Even within many (especially larger) organisations, teams can develop their own subcultures which are, in effect, organisationally bounded hybrids.

Cultures within Cultures

Whereas many writers describe culture from a whole organisation perspective (there is general agreement that an organisation's culture has certain common properties), there exist in many organisations varying subcultures. What this means is that, although everybody in the organisation adheres to a certain set of core values, different groups or teams can develop subcultures which often take account of specialised problems or situations and unique experiences and expectations. Often, teams tend to form subcultures, especially if they are longer term or permanent teams. It is important to note that teams that develop separate subcultures must still be guided by the core values of the dominant culture. As Robbins (1991: 575) reminds us: "If organisations had no dominant culture and were composed only of subcultures, the value of organizational culture as an independent variable would be significantly lessened, because there would be no uniform interpretation of what represented appropriate behavior".

Teams, then, often develop subcultures of their own to deal with specific tasks.

Organisation culture can have a significant impact on the team's operation and even if teams develop individual subcultures these will still be heavily influenced by the overall organisational culture. Teams communicate their culture to new members through stories, rituals, material symbols and the language they use. If cultures do not value or communicate behaviours such as collaboration, development, risk-taking, openness and trust, it is unlikely these will be present in a team setting. Organisational culture may indeed be a powerful determinant of team success.

Impact of National Cultures

As the business world shrinks in geographical terms and companies develop broader, more global perspectives, cultural differences will make themselves more manifest. While what we have to say is of concern to the industrialised world generally, the Southeast Asian context provides a fascinating case. With many major nations in varying degrees of recession, Southeast Asian economies have been flourishing and attracting interest from both established and infant multi-national concerns. Countries like Singapore, for example, are enjoying steady growth, which is backed up by considerable political stability.

Predictions indicate that, by the beginning of the next century, many of the leading companies will have established corporate headquarters in the region. Accompanying such moves will be difficulties in matching values and cultural norms. For example, an influx of expatriate managers, with established management patterns, behaviours and ways of teamworking, may find their expectations and ways of doing things not very well received by their Asian counterparts. This may lead to confusion and misunderstanding unless there is a real effort to understand such differences. Of course, this may not be easy for those who have been schooled in purely Western-based management theory and practice.

As Blunt and Richards (1993: 3) state:

> The structures and cultures of, for example, successful Japanese, Korean, and overseas Chinese enterprises are significantly different from one another and from most forms of organisation and culture found among western enterprises. Managers everywhere clearly stand to benefit from an improved understanding of their nature and the (national) cultural and institutional settings which give rise to them.

The impact of cultural differences on teams and effective team-work is a complex issue and it would be impossible to do it justice in the context of this discussion. There is an expanding body of literature in this area, especially related to Asia, and a recent compilation of readings by Blunt and Richards (1993) provides an extremely useful resource.

Throughout the book, we have implied that the culture of the team and the organisation has a significant impact on the team's operation. We have acknowledged the powerful effect of organisational cultures and now recognise the impact of societal or national culture on teams. How often have we heard the cry, "It can happen in Japan but not here"? Managers in Southeast Asian cultural contexts may argue that practices that enjoy success in the West are not possible in their own situations. Less dramatic, but similar to a certain extent, are the beliefs that, say, American practices cannot work in the United Kingdom.

These beliefs are important when we examine teamwork. Peterson (1991: 151) is quite controversial in his approach to cultural difficulties. His belief is that teamwork can be practised successfully in any context: "Any manager who says that the ideas behind teamwork and participative management can work in another country but not in his or her own back yard is copping out."

It is true that many do hide behind supposed cultural barriers. It is also true to note that cultures are not static; they do change over time. But whether we can accept Peterson's assertion without question is another matter. Culture is a serious issue if we accept Todryk's (1990: 17) statement that culture, expressed as the ideas, customs, skills, arts and values of a team, impacts team productivity, effectiveness and profitability. It seems, without doubt, that culture has an effect, and it may either facilitate or obstruct team development, in the way that we normally interpret that expression.

Robbins (1991: 587) cited research by Adler (1986: 46–7) suggesting that national culture has a greater impact on employees than organisational cultures: "German employees at an IBM facility in Munich, therefore, will be more influenced by German culture than by IBM's culture." He qualifies this by citing Schneider (1988: 239) who claims that organisations will account for this at the hiring stage. In other words, companies may be more concerned with employing workers who fit better with their corporate culture than for other reasons.

Perhaps the most influential work on cultural differences in management was conducted by Geert Hofstede (1987) who examined international differences in work-related values. As Richards (1991: 9) explains, Hofstede was concerned with differences in 'mental programming' among similar people in different nations, as expressed in the distribution of certain values. Values he defines as "broad preferences for certain states of affairs over others: which are a main part of our acquired mental programming, in other words, of our culture" (Hofstede, 1987: 10). Hofstede, using IBM data, attempted to identify dominant value patterns in various cultures, and found that cultural patterns varied on four dimensions. These were (p. 8):

- Power distance: The extent to which less powerful organisa- tional members and units accept that power is unequally distributed.
- Individualism to collectivism: This dimension describes the degree to which individuals are integrated into groups.
- Masculinity to femininity: The distribution of roles between sexes.
- Uncertainty avoidance: The extent to which a culture pro- grammes its members to feel comfortable or uncomfortable in unstructured situations.

We shall look now in slightly more depth at the special case of culture as a contextual issue. For this, we draw extensively on the work of Rigby (1987: 65) who explored some major differences in values and behaviour in relation to multinational workteams and their effectiveness.

Power Distance and Uncertainty Avoidance

Rigby's work utilised two of Hofstede's major dimensions, each concerned with values and behaviours, and which were likely to create problems: relationship to authority or Power Distance (PDI), and Uncertainty Avoidance (UAI).

Power Distance is concerned with the distance that members of the team maintain between one another. In high PDI cultures, members accept that power is distributed unequally and react to directive and autocratic management favourably. They can accept edicts from authority and are loathe to disagree with the boss or team leader.

This has real implications for team development efforts as they are traditionally organised and practised. Rigby explains the effects (p. 67):

> Team members from high PDI backgrounds often find difficulty fitting into team development activities where participants are temporarily divested of status and all talk to each other as equals. They are shocked at being addressed inappropriately and are often, themselves, unable to address others in the specified open manner, consequently suffering significant stress. Under these circumstances such members often suffer a loss of identity, withdraw psychologically from the group or 'freeze' for the duration of the meeting, and build up considerable resentment against the consultant and fellow participants.

It is easy to see how these people are unlikely to respond to team interaction and development exercises, especially those where openness and frankness are required. They will be reluctant to discuss their own or others' behaviour. They will refuse to be critical of superiors (including the team leader) and will avoid confrontation and honest expressions of opinions and feelings. In contrast, those from low PDI environments will be extremely open and may be confrontational, creating a different set of problems for team development.

Hofstede's study found Asian countries to be characterised by high power distance, low to medium uncertainty avoidance, low individualism, and medium masculinity (Blunt, 1988). From a team perspective, in cultures characterised by high power distance, any type of criticism is considered unacceptable and organisational members are usually unwilling to make decisions without approval from superiors. In such conditions, it is unlikely that teams can be successful when measured against criteria discussed in this book.

The second dimension (UAI) is concerned with how people from different cultures react to situations of uncertainty and ambiguity. Those from high UAI environments need structure, clear instructions, and they respect rules and regulations. They like agreement, find conflict distasteful, and do not like competition within the team.

The implications for team development are clear. If the approach used is unstructured, it can cause confusion, anxiety and resentment. Also, if openness has been forced and feelings about authority exposed, there can be resentment later. Those from low UAI environments may regret having been frank while others have played safe.

It has to be accepted that there are enormous difficulties for those who have to work on development issues with teams that comprise high PDI or high UAI membership. Successful team operation as we normally explain it is highly unlikely in such situations. Nevertheless, there are some things that can be done, and Rigby (p. 69) explains several of the techniques that he has found useful in working with teams with high PDI:

- Use the least confrontational methods.
- Use confidential data-gathering techniques rather than open verbal or visual techniques.
- Break team members into subgroups of similar status.
- Do not suspend normal hierarchical relationships.
- Hold meetings without authority figures present if appropriate.

In working with teams with high UAI, he suggests the following:

- Give clear agendas, goals and explanations.
- Use your own expertise where appropriate rather than adopt a mere process role.
- Answer questions if possible.
- Do not set up situations that lead to failure. These participants are unlikely to learn from failure.

It is wise to be aware of the ways in which members can suffer embarrassment or threat, or even challenges to their values. It may also be advisable to have ways in which members can retreat without loss of face.

Other items of advice when working in difficult situations include the following: Assume low levels of trust amongst team members; over-structure activities and give plenty of detailed information; avoid simulated activities, but stay with real-life events; and monitor members for signs of confusion, withdrawal, resentment or boredom.

There is an increasing problem for many organisations, especially those that operate across continents, that many of their teams will comprise members from different kinds of environments. So while team leaders may be cautious in their day-to-day team operations, and team development experts may be restrained in their efforts in order to account for the presence of those from high PDI or UAI backgrounds, others may become frustrated with the slowness of progress.

In such cases, it may be possible to subgroup according to cultural backgrounds, or it may be possible to employ methods that allow team members to choose their own levels of openness without others feeling pressured to do likewise.

However, there is a further problem worth noting. Putting Power Distance and Uncertainty Avoidance together has an impact on what people think an organisation should be, and this may lead to an inappropriate configuration. As Hofstede (1993: 114) notes: "Larger Power Distances are associated with greater centralisation, while stronger Uncertainty Avoidance is associated with greater formalization."

This important cultural problem is likely to increase in importance in view of expanding internationalisation and even the diversity of cultural mix being found in domestic operations. It is not an easy one to resolve. As Rigby so rightly notes (p. 71): "Although the potential for synergy is tantalisingly apparent in the multicultural work team, the methods for bringing about its realisation are still, to say the least, rudimentary."

That cultural values affect teamwork is undeniable. The important question is what organisations can do to facilitate teamwork in such difficult contexts. While the advice of Rigby above may be useful, caution may need to be exercised in going too far down the road of concession and compromise. The very nature of teamwork is characterised by open relationships, trust, empowerment and risk-taking. If there is total acquiesence to cultural imperatives, and team members have to accept seniors' ideas without question, quality outcomes will be severely compromised. In such circumstances, decision making is likely to be poor and one may question the value of team operation. Interestingly, as an example, Richards (1991) notes that "work-related values in Brunei are not receptive or conducive to effective problem solving and to organisational performance as defined in Western thinking".

In terms of development, it is probably right to tread lightly and not to indulge in high risk activities, but those cultural norms that hinder effective teamwork may need to be tackled. This is not easy. Richards (1991) suggests it may be time in certain countries to "devise more appropriate models and then modify cultural values to fit them". On an optimistic note, he goes on to say that national cultures are complementary and cites the success of the 'Five Dragons' of Asia in exploiting Western developed technology according to Eastern principles.

Summary

Cultures, then, are very important in determining the success or other-wise of team endeavours. If the organisation's culture does not value cooperative effort and open criticism, it is unlikely that teamwork will flourish. In this chapter, we have examined very briefly organisational cultures and how teams may actually develop their own 'subcultures' within the broader organisationally defined cultural boundaries. We also discussed the effect of national or ethnic cultures on teams and their operations. Regardless of team make-up and culture, all teams seem to go through sequential stages of development; the final chapter deals with this issue.

Summary of the Implications for Managers

- Organisational culture has a significant influence on how, and indeed whether, teams operate effectively and productively.

- Different types of organisational cultures exist, not all are conducive to teamwork.

- Teams may develop distinct subcultures, but these must still be guided by the core values of the greater organisation.

- Care should be taken when dealing with cross-national teams, as research seems to indicate that workers may be more influenced by their national culture than by organisational culture.

- If working with teams that are culturally used to a high 'power distance', it is advisable to:
  1. avoid confrontation;
  2. use confidential data-gathering methods;
  3. keep people of similar status together;
  4. avoid, if possible, having authority figures present at team meetings.

- In high 'uncertainty avoidance' environments, it may be prudent to:
  1. set clear goals and expectations;
  2. use the leader's expertise;
  3. set up situations that lead to success.

- The leader needs to be aware of the ways in which individuals might feel embarrassed or threatened. There also needs to be an awareness of differing values. Such individuals need a way of retreating without losing face. Other items of advice that may prove useful in such settings include the following:
  - Assume low trust.
  - Over-structure activities.
  - Stay with real-life events.
  - Watch out for confusion, withdrawal, resentment or boredom.

Team Growth and Development

19

PHASES OF DEVELOPMENT

TEAMS BEGIN as a collection of individuals and, some would argue, without a great deal of concern for the unit's success. Adair (1986: 15) sums up this early state well in explaining how new members may have uncertainties about what is going to happen; how they may be apprehensive or even dread the future; how they may be deeply concerned or indifferent; and how the terms of reference may be so poorly defined that the new team is not sure of its limits. Such is the level of uncertainty teams may face. It is possible, however, for them to progress through a series of stages leading to a high degree of ability. Relationships between members can develop to such an extent that people become friends for life.

A number of frameworks have been developed in an attempt to explain the stages through which groups pass. Tuckman and Jensen (1977) use the expressions 'forming', 'storming', 'norming', 'performing' and 'adjourning'. Others add stages like 'producing' and 'ending', while Zapp (1987: 8) uses a framework which seems to apply to a particular context: 'development', 'focusing', 'performance' and 'leveling'. Francis and Young (1979) use the expressions 'testing', 'infighting', 'getting organized' and 'mature closeness'. In this chapter we present a model of team development which has similarities with many of these frameworks.

Four Growth Stages

We explain the development of teams in four growth stages. As we look at these, it should be noted that not all teams progress at the same pace, and some may not even make it beyond the early immature stages. It is also possible that teams may regress to earlier stages when their members change or when they face new or unfamiliar challenges. The phases are:

- polite niceties,
- politicking,
- achieving,
- competence.

Polite Niceties

It is unlikely in the early days of a team's life that people openly divulge their innermost thoughts or reveal their emotions; they tend to talk about the inconsequential things. At this stage, people are weighing one another up and deciding where they stand in the group. There is a great deal of uncertainty about the team's purpose, structure and leadership. Some members like to display their strength, while others prefer to see how disruptive they can be. Yet others prefer to stay in the background and watch what is going on. The fact is that people are different and respond in vastly different ways to the new setting for their efforts.

Members do not really know one another well and they seem to have little care for one another. They will not reveal their weaknesses and there is little openness. They tend to be extremely polite and this acts as a convenient defence mechanism. In this phase, the team (if it can be called such) is at its most ineffective. Unfortunately, some groups of colleagues in organisations never get past the stage of *polite niceties* and never achieve very much as a consequence.

Koehler (1989: 15) calls this stage 'Orientation' and identifies it as a phase in which members learn the rules. It is also a time when team members are developing an understanding of, and possibly a commitment to, the team's goals. It requires skilful direction and leadership.

Woodcock (1989: 16) refers to a group in this stage as an 'undeveloped' team. The characteristics identified are: feelings are not dealt with; people are scared to suggest changes; leadership is seldom challenged and members may be disheartened; there is a lot of talking and very little listening; personal weaknesses are concealed; mistakes are used as evidence to convict people rather than as opportunities for learning; there is little shared understanding; and people confine themselves to their own defined task areas.

The lack of openness we mentioned earlier is probably a natural phenomenon of this stage, but it may be exacerbated by the cultural context or by the organisation and its support for or discouragement of certain attitudes and behaviours.

It seems important at the beginning to handle the initial stages of a team's life sensitively. This is best done in an orientation programme. As Cohen (1988: 23) maintains: "The well-executed orientation process can increase the rate of development and degree of quality within a team." This, of course, applies equally to the beginning of any teambuilding effort with newly formed teams.

Politicking

Eventually, people get to know one another for what they really are. Positions in the team emerge and there may be an element of conflict as rivals vie for the leadership, each with their band of supporters. This may be due partly to the resistance to the control that the team imposes on individuality (Robbins, 1991: 278). There may be differences of opinion and difficulties may affect relationships. Interest or splinter groups may form and there is a great deal of micropolitical activity. The more complex or dangerous the task, the more the chance of ill-feeling and arguments surfacing.

Todryk (1990: 20) notes that it is during this stage that teams decide how they will operate. It is done by covert communication and the major issues to be explored are concerned with control, including questions about the way in which control is exercised and what happens to delinquents. It is important that these issues are addressed, since successful resolution of the difficulties may determine whether the team is able to progress to a more advanced stage of development.

The ones who are skilled in micropolitical activities tend to be highly active during this phase. They will develop relationships with influential people, while others develop coalitions on the basis that there is strength in numbers. Some will try to make themselves indispensable by choosing those activities and responsibilities that are critical to the team. It is probably true that the organisational underworld becomes more active in this phase, and particularly in more permanent and high-profile teams.

There are also improvements in the way tasks are carried out. There is some experimentation, options may be considered, and there may be debate about values, beliefs and preferences. More risky issues may be opened up and personal relationships may be addressed. A useful advance is that views and problems may be looked at, and there is a greater likelihood that real listening takes place. As Woodcock (1989: 17) notes, however, the team still lacks the capacity to perform in an efficient, cohesive and methodical way.

An interesting point to note is that some research has focused on the problems of mixed gender teams. There is often a great deal of competitiveness, just as there may be in single gender teams, but things are done more subtly. Members are sometimes attracted to a member of the opposite sex and this can produce quite irrational behaviours, which may compromise team effectiveness.

Achieving

Again, many teams in organisations fail to get past the political phase. If individuals can achieve a degree of tolerance and temper their own satisfactions, they can then experiment with new ways of doing things and learn to accommodate other members' strengths and weaknesses.

As the team experiences success, it may be prepared to reduce its insularity and attempt to relate with other teams. People are proud to be members of the team. Relationships are good and people are able to combine their distinctive contributions to work together effectively. They like to spend social time together and their families may even share holidays.

Members may have an amazing knowledge of how one another will behave in any given situation. Some sports teams display this attribute and it results in performance at the highest level. Relationships are deep and people do not have to pretend. Members begin to realise that a great deal can be accomplished through collaborative effort. It is no surprise, therefore, that Koehler (1989: 15) calls this stage 'Realization', one in which they learn to share responsibility for effort and results. It is also not uncommon for many teams to fail to achieve this level of development.

Perhaps one of the more important indicators of this phase is that the team is more methodical in the way it approaches problems and tasks. It can cope with a systematic scheme such as that presented in Chapter 8. There are agreed operating rules, and members are usually committed to them. Woodcock (1989: 18) appropriately calls a team that has reached this stage of development a 'consolidating' team.

Competence

Teams that reach this competence phase can achieve a vast amount and are capable of dealing with tasks that are complex, dangerous or need excessive efforts on the part of members.

Koehler (1989: 15) uses the label 'Production' to describe this phase, one in which there is trust and unity, and where members are proud of their involvement and achievements. Petrock (1990: 10) uses a similar expression, 'Producing', and explains some of the positive characteristics of this phase: "Team members have developed rapport and cohesiveness. The leadership function is shared. Decision-making abilities have been sharply honed. Time is spent on important issues only, and an incredible volume of work gets completed." There is also flexibility, involvement in important matters, and strong commitment to the team.

Problems begin to occur, however, when the team resists any form of challenge and believes that everything it does is right. It may fail to analyse information adequately and avoid engaging appropriate decision-making mechanisms. It may even get rid of people with dissenting views and insulate members from information which represents contrasting opinions.

Discussing the characteristics of what he puts in a separate stage, Petrock goes on to identify the possible occurrence of falling productivity, member anxiety, increased conflict, lessening of team skills, and the denying that changes in the team have really happened (p. 10). The athletics analogy is a useful one in understanding why things change. As Shonk and Shonk (1988: 78) note, "No athletic team has stayed on top for very long: Either its competition got better, the team itself got worse, or both ... Either it no longer does what it originally did to get to the top, or it fails to develop the tactics that are needed to keep it there."

The model we have presented here is for ease of understanding. It does not mean that teams progress neatly from one stage to the next having passed a set of entry criteria. As Adair (1986: 28) rightly observes: "Consistent and identifiable stages of development in all groups probably do not exist. Group growth is a gradual process in which themes and subtleness may intertwine but in which the dramatic quality is the wholeness." He claims there is a danger in oversimplifying and destroying the holistic feature of team growth.

It would also be simplistic to say that teams at advanced stages of development are necessarily more effective than younger teams. For example, where high levels of conflict are desirable, a team in its second phase may be more effective than a mature unit. Robbins (1991: 278) also notes that teams do not always proceed clearly from one stage to the next. In fact, several stages may be going on simultaneously. And, as we mentioned earlier, teams may even regress to a previous stage. Adair (1986: 28) too notes: "It does appear that in some groups change takes a cyclic or spiral form, with movement backwards and forwards. In other groups change seems to happen in sudden leaps and bounds, interspersed with plateau periods where no change occurs." For these reasons, it is important to exercise caution in believing that automatic progression takes place or that advanced phases are always the most effective. The model simply helps us to understand that teams are dynamic, and it draws attention to some of the complications that might occur during the team's life.

In examining the final phase, we drew attention to the problem of the team that sees itself as beyond criticism and challenge. This leads us into a discussion of an unfortunate phenomenon present in many mature teams, that of 'groupthink'.

Groupthink

Teams that work together over a period of time may become complacent. Strong feelings of cohesiveness can also lead to high levels of conformity. Members learn to agree with one another with too much ease and they become arrogant about their decisions. The team is coerced, not consciously, by a feeling of uniformity. It can be quite insidious. Cohesiveness, as we shall see, can be interpreted wrongly and lead to high levels of ineffectiveness:

> The need for cohesiveness is misunderstood, when any expression of difference, be it of interest or of view, is taken as inimical to the well-being of the group as a whole. Uniformity will tend to make the group a closed system, a homogeneous mass of 'yes' people who do become nonentities, incapable or unwilling to assert themselves in any way, leading to general ineffectiveness and impoverishment, to the phenomenon of 'the group-think' (Graham, 1991: 44).

When this condition takes hold, the team will even fail to accept 'new blood' to revitalise the operation. It will engage in a sort of nepotism, choosing people who will toe the line and concur with the team's wishes.

Essentially, teams can either marshall their forces and produce outstanding work, or they can obstruct task accomplishment by reducing autonomy and failing to draw on individual talents. Wynn and Guditus (1984: 117) define groupthink as "a deterioration in mental efficiency, reality testing, and moral judgements as the result of group pressures".

Janis (1971; cited in Wynn and Guditus, 1984: 118) identifies five forces that might lead to groupthink:

1. **Groupy:** The team may condemn dissent through social pressure, regarding it as disloyal behaviour.
2. **1984:** Alternative solutions are not considered, in order that there might be a general feeling of agreement.
3. **Kill:** There is criticism of those who express dissent outside the team. They are seen as evil since they cannot accept the wisdom of the team.
4. **Norms:** Critical thoughts are suppressed so as to avoid disunity.
5. **Stress:** Team decisions are not utilised in conditions which create pressures.

Hoy and Miskel (1991: 338) also identify some factors that encourage concurrence seeking. One of these is the presence of leadership that is strong, charismatic and partial. Members are then likely to try to please the leader. Another factor is the absence of norms that demand systematic analysis. Homogeneity of team members' backgrounds and beliefs may also contribute to likemindedness. Other factors include situational conditions and the team's level of esteem. All these may produce "overestimation of the group, closed-mindedness, and pressure of unanimity. Such behaviour makes for low vigilance in decision making, which ultimately results in defective decision making with a low probability of a successful outcome."

In simple terms, there are signs that teams can observe which give warnings about the presence of groupthink:

1. The team ignores dangers, takes too many risks and assumes that everything will work out perfectly.

2. The team rationalises its decisions so it can ignore outside opportunities.
3. The team regards its decisions as morally correct, regardless of ethical considerations.
4. The team negatively stereotypes rivals outside the team.
5. The team puts pressures on members who disagree and implies disloyalty.
6. Team members fail to express reservations about ideas or advance counter-arguments.
7. The team assumes that silence means agreement.
8. Team members may believe they should protect the team from information that might threaten togetherness (Janis, 1982).

Groupthink tends to occur more in groups that are very cohesive, are isolated from outside contact and lack a tradition of impartial leadership. As Mukhi *et al.* (1988: 284) state: "Under groupthink, the group's zeal for consensus surpasses its zeal for realistic conditions." Groupthink is a real threat to many groups and needs to be avoided or overcome when it is present.

Overcoming Groupthink

Jacobs and Everett (1988: 11) talk about 'loosening up' conformity by raising the consciousness of team members or improving the real communication in the group, and trying to avoid dialogue that simply conforms to team norms. This may be easier said than done, and it seems a more diverse and detailed set of strategies may be needed to untie a group that is bound up in its own superiority. On this score, Wynn and Guditus (1984: 119) produce a useful list of countervailing actions that might neutralise the hazards of groupthink, and we look at just two of the major ones here:

*   *Using outsiders.* One strategy is to utilise resources outside the team. Involving others in the problem-solving process can help to avoid some of the dangers of groupthink. For example, a sub-committee may be set up to examine a particular issue. The team is then drawing on the creative inputs of others while still retaining control of the final decision.

*   *Encouraging divergent views.* First, dissent can be promoted rather than suppressed. We have seen already how leaders

can encourage and reward team members who express contrasting views. Second, those in positions of authority can hold back their views until later in the discussion so that others are not threatened. Third, someone who can play the 'devil's advocate' role can be briefed and given support in carrying it out. The specific behaviours to be encouraged are showing dissent, testing assumptions to determine if they are really accurate, questioning the accuracy and reliability of information, and outlining the more adverse consequences of particular courses of action.

Another way of generating alternative views is to use brainstorming, because this legitimises creative and unusual views. Members can also be encouraged to build on and adapt others' ideas in attempts to arrive at creative solutions.

By asking the team to identify the things that could go wrong with a proposed solution and what contingencies should be available, the team can be exposed to different views.

Even these strategies may not be productive in those teams that operate in cultural contexts that do not support openness. As we saw when we looked at the particular problems of certain cultural settings, members, despite support and encouragement, may still be reluctant to take any actions or express views that could be described as disloyal or critical of leader and colleagues. It may be possible in such circumstances to have anonymous feedback using questionnaire-type instruments, but these should be used with discretion and preferably as a last resort.

Groupthink is less likely to occur where the team is linked and exposed to the views of other teams. Feedback from other units will serve to "introduce divergent thought, widen the knowledge base, question assumptions, and specify the impact of proposed actions upon units in the organization" (p. 120).

Other strategies available include using outside experts to challenge the views of the team and 'second chance' meetings where team members are instructed to express doubts they might have before a final decision is taken.

Team Development at Different Phases

The maturity level of the team is an important consideration when it comes to planning development. Barner (1989: 50) notes that teams require different learning approaches and different facilitator roles according to whether they are newly formed or established. Newly formed teams can benefit from learning approaches that use simulated team challenges in order to build skills and strategies. In contrast, more established teams come to the development setting with a wide range of experiences, and the learning focus may be on resolving performance problems. Barner suggests it may not be advisable to rely on simulated activity with such teams, but rather to explore and master real-life team performance situations.

The role of the facilitator or consultant in team development is also determined to some extent by the degree of team maturity. Younger teams may benefit from instruction and support, whereas established teams may prefer a facilitative and guiding role. In the latter case, an observer role is also appropriate, since behaviours and techniques can be observed, and improvements made only in those areas that need some remedial action.

Useful Strategies

Below are some suggestions about ways in which the development of teams might be facilitated. It should be noted, however, that it may take some considerable time before real changes are noticed.

Phase 1

They should get to know one another in different settings.   One of the problems with teams in the early stages of development is that they meet only in the work situation and, depending on the nature of the task, there may be little opportunity for relationships to develop. The occasional lunch for team members or a party when they can bring their families along can be useful events.

Providing the opportunity to take the team away for a few days in a residential setting is a form of team development which should be looked at very seriously. Failing that, a day trip or spending some time in the same car may help in relationship-building.

At this stage of development (or lack of it) in particular, it is very important to get people together for a more 'intensive' experience than that which is available in the daily work routine. The advantages are considerable. Members can develop self-awareness, a greater understanding of the way in which their behaviour affects other team members, and they may then be able to modify their behavioural patterns if necessary. The leader too may need to develop an increased level of self-awareness in order to improve the way in which leader-member relations develop.

They can have fun together.   Work is often very serious. It is surprising how quickly people can get to know one another when the situation is more relaxed and members can let their hair down. George (1987: 124) notes that fun is essential to both the individual and to the team's strength and health. This can be achieved by organising activities like social events and the occasional outing. George also advocates plenty of laughter in the team, although this may have to be handled sensitively in some contexts. He claims that shared laughter is a sign that bridges are being built between team members and that communication is healthy between people of different status.

Social interaction is a strategy suggested by Belzer (1989: 13). She advocates lunches, dinners and other types of social occasions where people can interact on a personal basis, something that is not really possible during the formal events of work life. By sharing food and drink at all meetings, it is suggested that psychological bonds typical of family life may be formed.

Team members should express how they really feel.   It should be demonstrated at this stage that the team supports open and frank views, so when feelings are expressed, this is welcomed and confirmed.

Being able to express feelings may also lead to increased control of them. For example, feelings of hostility or aggression can become dysfunctional if they are not coped with adequately. Members can learn how to make such feelings known, but with minimal risk to personal relationships.

Members should be asked to state their honest concerns.   It is important for team members to voice their concerns. For example, if they are worried that a particular course of action might affect them personally, they need to bring this into the open, otherwise it may interfere with the work.

Members should be encouraged to reveal their strong points.   In some situations, members may be shy about revealing the skills and experiences they bring with them into the team. They consider it immodest to 'sing their own praises'. It is important, however, to discover the ways in which members might contribute effectively to the team, and there may be strengths not immediately apparent but which have relevance to task performance.

People should be encouraged to share some details of their life away from work. This is just one strategy for making relationships less peripheral. It is useful to demonstrate that the team is interested in members as people and not simply as tools to do the work.

Trust and confidence should be built up. There should be trust and confidence in the integrity of the leader and, of course, in other members also. They should be able to say things to one another face-to-face. Strong disapproval should be shown for talking behind backs. The leader may have an important part to play here. As Petrock (1990: 9) claims: "Successful leaders encourage discussion of how trust is built and foster trust-building behaviors by modeling them."

Phase 2

Openness about feelings should be encouraged. This is something that needs to be progressively developed. The team leader also needs to be open in relationships with the team, since this is likely to lead to higher levels of responsiveness.

Ideas should be discussed seriously. We have already discussed the importance of encouraging and developing ideas. Team members should be made to feel they can contribute freely without being ridiculed. We have seen how the fragments of seemingly impracticable ideas can be converted to something of great use.

Even the smallest successes can be celebrated. It is advantageous for teams to celebrate success because it shows that it is the *team* that has achieved something and it helps to reinforce the cooperative (rather than competitive) effort. George (1987: 126) suggests that ceremonies should be organised to announce the introduction of a new product or to mark a particular effort that was the result of the team's cooperation. He also gives some practical small-scale actions that can be taken to signify effort and team spirit. These include pictures on the wall of past teams and scrapbooks to document the history of a team's life.

Conflicts should be identified and exposed, and attempts should be made to achieve compromise or reconciliation.   There is no greater hindrance to team development than festering conflicts and ill-feeling. Differences need to be exposed and discussed constructively. The focus should be clearly on the problem and not the personalities involved. Conflict, as we discovered earlier, can be highly beneficial. There is a saying which sums it up: "When two men in a business always agree, one of them is unnecessary." But members often fall out because they see things in different ways, and these may turn into personal disputes which can be quite injurious to the team and its effective functioning. Such situations need to be addressed.

Phase 3

Strengths and weaknesses should be analysed.   A team that has reached this level of maturity is a reasonably effective unit, but there is still room for improvement. It is helpful at this stage to consider what the team is good at and where its weaknesses lie. Answers to the second question may indicate where improvement efforts should be directed.

New ways of doing things can be tried out.   It is best for a team to assume that the way in which it goes about tasks can be improved on. It can set some time aside for questioning its procedures and it can positively encourage team members to advance ideas that will effect improvements.

Individual differences should be built on as strengths.   The differences which individual members bring with them to the team can be an enormous asset and can be used in a creative way. But there is a tendency in many situations to try to exercise greater control than that which is necessary and to lay down excessive norms of conformity. This phenomenon has been witnessed in some sports teams which have failed to capitalise on the creative talents of some individuals and opted for a more systematic conformity, which has done little to aid team performance. It may often be conflict that leads to the suppression of different skills and talents, but this reaction is more likely to lead to mediocrity than innovative solutions to complex problems. The management of this aspect of team-work has to be skilful, for it is too easy to achieve compromise by restraining talent. Furthermore, a great deal of individual resentment can build up if individual creative abilities are not used and fostered.

The required individual skills should be developed. Because things tend to be going very well when a team has reached this stage of development, there is now the opportunity to provide for the extension of team members' skills. Such development will bring in new ideas and provide refreshing experiences for the members.

Each individual's role in the task should be clarified. It may be easy to lose sight of the overall task as individuals become involved in their own activities. Roles need to be clarified and responsibilities reassessed.

Link-ups with other teams should be established. One of the dangers of successful teams is that they become very insular and detach themselves from other teams or people doing similar work. The most effective teams always recognise that there is room for improvement and prefer to draw on the successful experiences of other units in order to enhance their own performance.

Team successes should be celebrated. Recognising success is just as vital in this phase as in the previous one. Celebrating does not need to be an extravagant affair: it can be a get-together at coffee time and a few words of encouragement and congratulation from the boss.

The team's operation should be reviewed regularly. Review is a key process in development, so that the information can be used to realign some activities. A constant search for better ways of doing things, by internal evaluation or looking at other teams' performance, can only elevate the chances of team success.

Phase 4

Others can be allowed to assume the leader's role. At this stage of development, the team has reached a high level of competence and it can now afford to look towards the development of individuals in order to support the longer term needs of the team. It may be productive to give others the opportunity to lead various aspects of the work, and this can prove to be of benefit to the individual, team and organisation.

Opposing views should be included and treated seriously. One of the biggest dangers for teams is a belief that they are infallible. They need to be constantly exposed to rival views lest they become insulated from the real world. There are many examples of organisations that employ inappropriate practices, largely because the senior-management team has not exposed itself to the conflicting views of others.

The routine should be changed occasionally.   One way of avoiding staleness is to change the routine. The occasional change of venue for a meeting or bringing in an outsider can help to avoid the stagnation which can depress performance.

Someone from outside the team can be asked to comment on its performance.   It is useful to employ an outsider who can comment on the team's performance without the constraining factor of personal involvement. Some senior management teams obtain the services of consultants to examine their work and this can be useful if the team has been together for a long time and with little change of membership.

Summary

In this concluding chapter, we have presented a four-stage framework of team development. The four phases were: Polite niceties, Politicking, Achieving and Competence. Not all teams progress through these stages at the same pace and some stages may be missed out altogether. We have cautioned against the dangers of allowing complacency to set in and thus allowing a high-performing unit to turn into a relatively ineffective outfit.

Summary of the Implications for Managers

- The early stages of a team's life should be handled sensitively and with a recognition that team members are likely to relate to others in particular ways until they have become established. While it may be difficult to bring some teams out of their early stages of inexperience and low effectiveness, a more complex problem is how to deal with the mature team that has become over-complacent and insulated from outside influence. In order to offset the potential damage of groupthink, it is necessary to loosen up the conformity through such strategies as using outsiders or forming sub-committees to look at certain issues. Divergent views need to be encouraged, and this process can be supported by asking people to express dissent, persuading authority figures to withhold views, and getting some-one to play 'devil's advocate'. This last role involves testing the accuracy of assumptions, questioning the accuracy and reliability of information, and outlining the adverse consequences of a course of action. Other strategies include brainstorming and building on ideas, linking up with other teams, and holding 'second chance' meetings to reconsider decisions.

- Below is a summary of some of the strategies that might be used to help teams develop and mature, according to the level at which they find themselves:

Phase 1
Members can be encouraged to get to know one another socially.
They can have fun together.
They should begin to express their feelings.
They should state their concerns.
They can reveal what they are good at.

Phase 2
The leader can encourage more openness about feelings.
Small successes can be celebrated.
Conflicts can be exposed and dealt with.

Phase 3
The strengths and weaknesses of the team should be analysed.
New ways of doing things should be tried out.
Individual skills can be built on.
Task roles for individuals should be clarified.
Links with other teams can be formed.
The team's performance should be reviewed regularly.

Phase 4
Others can try taking on the leadership role.
Opposing views should be positively encouraged.
Routines can be altered.
An outsider can be used to comment on the team's performance.

CONCLUSION

IN THIS BOOK, we have attempted to examine a whole range of issues relevant to organisational teams, the way they work together, and their development. An understanding of the contribution teams can make to organisational success is invaluable but on its own, an understanding is insufficient. Teams have to grow and develop, and our text has attempted to offer guidelines for managers, team leaders and others responsible for facilitating development. The strategies, behaviours and actions we have outlined need conscious attention. Needs have to be identified and appropriate development efforts applied.

The success of team development, however, as we have emphasized throughout, is not solely dependent on specific interventions, nor on the methods and processes used. Success, for one author, is more likely to be due to effective relationships and people's willingness to learn. The essence of success, therefore, is to be found in people "learning to respect each other as human beings; learning to maturely acknowledge their competencies and their weaknesses; learning to solve problems in an open and trusting environment; making a commitment to become a learning community" (Bradford, 1989: 50).

That, of course, has a ring of truth about it, and the point is worth making that behavioural and learning advances over time are of the utmost importance. Team development interventions may facilitate this

461

process, but they cannot be seen as the answers to all teamwork ills. They have to be approached with discretion. Tolle (1988: 278) makes the point that

> team building is neither the panacea of its optimistic proponents nor the bound to fail, 'fooling around with people's minds', intervention seen by its detractors. It can be a useful intervention at selective points in the evolution of an organization. But, to be successful, team building requires good planning, concrete goals and objectives, and a skilled and resourceful leader. Most important, it must be carefully and selectively applied at the right time to the right set of organizational problems.

This is a point we have tried to reinforce constantly, that development covers a range of issues and that it must be applied selectively.

We have seen how the claims for team organisation are persuasive. In conditions of high growth, for example, George (1977: 80) has shown how task teams might offer a positive climate for decision making and how middle management might be strengthened for even further growth. The team approach in this context is efficient in its resource deployment, effective in the quality of decision making, and highly flexible in coping with environmental and organisational change. We have also identified some of the drawbacks and the things that can go wrong. But, as Chance (1989: 25) claims: "Team organization is certainly one of the grand business experiments of our time".

Experiments are unlikely to succeed without the full support of the organisations within which they are conducted. We have looked at the question of rewards, incentives and other support mechanisms the organisation might provide. But we have also intimated that more radical steps might be needed if organisations are to adopt real and far-ranging team approaches. On this point, it is worth pondering on an extract from Robbins (1991: 304) who adapts some material from Harold Leavitt's writings:

> Operationally, how would an organization that was designed around groups function? One answer to this question is merely to take the things that organizations do with individuals and apply them to groups. The idea would be to raise the level from the atom to the molecule and *select* groups rather than individuals, *train* groups rather than individuals, *pay* groups rather than individuals, *promote* groups rather than individuals, *fire* groups rather than individuals, and so on down the list of activities that organizations have traditionally carried on in order to use human beings in organizations.

In the past, the human group has been primarily used for patching and mending organizations that were built around the individual. The time is rapidly approaching, and it may already be here, for management to begin redesigning organizations around groups.

Such radical propositions, as eminently sensible as they might sound, do not succeed overnight. Even the smaller, simpler changes often take an inordinate amount of time to effect. It would be the height of optimism, therefore, to expect organisations to change from autocratic operations to team-driven dynamos at the stroke of a pen. Generating a participative culture takes time, but for those organisations that have been prepared to invest time and effort in establishing, developing and supporting team approaches, the investment has proved worthwhile.

The word 'change' is an important one. It suggests that teams and the people in them do not remain static for long. As Adair (1986: 27) notes: "Groups are alive; they do not stand still in time and space. The analytical approach needs to be complemented by a holistic view of the moving, living, dynamic whole." This 'organic' view implies that everything affects everything else. A change in a norm will affect atmosphere, and this may affect involvement, which in turn will affect cohesion. It is unwise, therefore, to view any of the elements we have discussed in isolation.

Finally, it looks as if teams are going to be with us for some considerable time. Not all situations, admittedly, are right for teamwork,

but the growth of technology and competitiveness in most industries means that teams will be used more in the future than they have in the past. Right now, many organizations are in the transition stage, moving toward a team structure. They are moving toward increased flexibility in meeting market demands and toward using human resources in diverse ways rather than in just one function. All of this is exciting (Anderson, 1984: 584).

We share the excitement. Organisations at last seem to have realised that liberating their most precious resources and guiding them in the organisation's direction will bear fruit, both for the organisation in pursuit of its mission and for the members in terms of satisfaction, fulfilment and a genuine desire to make a worthwhile contribution to success.

BIBLIOGRAPHY

Ackoff, R. (1986) *Management in Small Doses*, Wiley: New York.

Adair, J. (1973) *Action Centred Leadership*, Gower: Aldershot, England.

Adair, J. (1985) *Management Decision Making*, Gower: Aldershot, England.

Adair, J. (1986) *Effective Teambuilding*, Gower: Aldershot, England.

Adair, J. (1988) *Effective Leadership*, Gower: Aldershot, England.

Adams, J. (1990) 'Essentials of effective influence', *Training and Development Journal*, **44**(1), 31–3.

Adler, N. (1986) *International Dimensions of Organizational Behavior*, Kent: Boston.

Anantaraman, V. (1984a) 'Group Dynamics and the Human Relations Organizational Model' in Anantaraman, V., Chong, L., Richardson, S. and Tan, C. (eds) *Human Resource Management: Concepts and Perspectives*, Singapore University Press: Singapore.

Anantaraman, V. (1984b) 'Teambuilding' in Anantaraman, V., Chong, L., Richardson, S. and Tan, C. (eds) *Human Resource Management: Concepts and Perspectives*, Singapore University Press: Singapore.

Anderson, C. (1984) *Management: Skills, Functions, and Organization Performance*, Brown: Dubuque, Iowa.

Arajs, B. (1991) 'Testing the teamwork theory', *Graphic Arts Monthly*, **63**(6), 76.

Avolio, B. and Bass, B. (1988) 'Transformational Leadership and Beyond' in Hunt, J., Baliga, B., Dachler, H. and Schriesheim, C. (eds) *Emerging Leadership Vistas*, Lexington: Massachusetts.

Bacharach, S. and Lawler, E. (1980) *Power and Politics in Organizations*, Jossey-Bass: San Francisco.

Barham, K., Fraser, J. and Heath, L. (1988) *Management for the Future*, Ashridge Management Research Group and Foundation for Management Education: Berkhamstead, England.

Barner, R. (1989) 'The right tool for the job', *Training and Development Journal*, **43**(7), 46–51.

Barrett, J. (1970) *Individual Goals and Organizational Objectives*, Center for Research on Utilization of Scientific Knowledge, University of Michigan: Ann Arbor, Michigan.

Barry, D. (1991) 'Managing the bossless team: Lessons in distributed leadership', *Organizational Dynamics*, Summer, 31–47.

Bechtel, D. (1980) 'Dhabi fehru: An MBO Activity' in Pfeiffer, J. and Jones, E. (eds) *A Handbook of Structured Experiences for Human Relations Training* (Volume VII), University Associates: San Diego, California.

Beer, M. (1976) 'The Technology of Organization Development' in Dunnette, M. (ed.) *Handbook of Industrial and Organizational Psychology*, Rand McNally: Chicago, Illinois.

Beer, M. (1980) *Organization Change and Development: A Systems View*, Goodyear: Pacific Palisades, California.

Belbin, R. (1981) *Management Teams: Why They Succeed or Fail*, Heinemann: London.

Belzer, E. (1989) 'Twelve ways to better team building', *Working Woman*, **14**(8), 12, 14.

Berelson, B. and Steiner, G. (1964) *Human Behavior: An Inventory of Scientific Finding*, Harcourt Brace Jovanovich: New York.

Berger, M. (1991) 'Breaking down barriers. Part II: Interdepartmental team-building', *Industrial and Commercial Training*, **23**(2), 7–11.

Betof, E. and Harwood, F. (1992) 'Raising personal empowerment', *Training and Development*, **46**(9), 31–4.

Blake, R. and Mouton, J. (1964) *The Managerial Grid* , Gulf: Houston, Texas.

Blanchard, K. (1988) 'Shaping team synergy', *Today's Office*, **22**(9), 6–11.

Blunt, P. (1988) 'Cultural consequences for organisational change in a Southeast Asian state: Brunei', *The Academy of Management Executive*, **11**(3), 235–40.

Blunt, P. (1990) 'Organisational Culture and Development', invited paper to the European Community Management Institute Seminar, 29 June, Beijing, People's Republic of China.

Blunt, P. and Richards, D. (eds) (1993) *Readings in Management, Organisation and Culture in South and Southeast Asia*, NTU Press: Darwin.

Boss, R. (1991) 'Team building in health care', *Journal of Management Development*, **10**(4), 38–44.

Boud, D. (1987) 'A Facilitators View of Adult Learning', in Boud, D. and Griffin, V. (eds) *Appreciating Adults Learning: From the Learners' Perspective*, Kogan Page: London.

Bradford, J. (1990) 'Getting together: a composite case study in team building', *Optimum*, **20**(2), 38–51.

Brandt, R. (1992) 'Are we committed to quality?' *Educational Leadership*, **50**(3), 3.

Bridges, E. (1967) 'A model for shared decision making in the school principal-ship', *Educational Administration Quarterly*, **3**, 49–61.

Brookfield, S. (1986) *Understanding and Facilitating Adult Learning: A Comprehensive Analysis of Principles and Effective Practices*, Open University Press: Milton Keynes, England.

Brownell, J. (1986) *Building Active Listening Skills*, Prentice Hall: Englewood Cliffs, New Jersey.

Brunt, M. (1987) 'Marketing Schools' in Craig, I. (ed.) *Primary School Management in Acton*, Longman: Harlow, England.

Buhler, P. and McCann, M. (1989) 'Building your management team (Part I)', *Supervision*, **50**(9), 14–15, 26.

Buller, P. (1986) 'The team building – task performance relation: some conceptual and methodological refinements', *Group and Organization Studies*, **11**(3), 147.

Buller, P. and Bell, C. (1986) 'Effects of team building and goal setting on productivity: A field experiment', *Academy of Management Journal*, **29**, 306–28.

Burdett, J. (1989) 'Teambuilding: a manager's construction guide', *Canadian Manager*, **14**(4), 16–19.

Byrt, W. (1980) *The Human Variable*, McGraw-Hill: Sydney.

Cacioppe, R., Warren-Langford, P. and Bell, L. (1990) 'Trends in human resource development and training', *Asia Pacific Human Resource Management*, **28**(2), 55–72.

Carr, C. (1989) *The New Manager's Survival Manual: All the Skills You Need for Success*, Wiley: New York.

Chance, P. (1989) 'Great experiments in team chemistry', *Across the Board*, **26**(5), 18–25.

Cohen, D., March, J. and Olsen, J. (1972) 'A garbage can model of organizational choice', *Administrative Science Quarterly*, **17**, 1–25.

Cohen, M. (1988) 'Orientation: The first step in team building', *Training and Development Journal*, **42** (January), 20.

Crosby, P. (1986) *Quality Without Tears*, McGraw-Hill: Singapore.

Crouch, A. and Yetton, J. (1987) 'The Management Team: An Equilibrium Model of Management Performance and Behavior' in Hunt, J., Baliga, B., Dachler, H. and Schriesheim, C. (eds) *Emerging Leadership Vistas*, Lexington: Massachusetts.

Daft, R. (1992) *Organization Theory and Design* (Fourth Edition), West: St. Paul, Minnesota.

Davidson, J. (1985) 'A task-focused approach to team building', *Personnel*, **3** (March), 16–18.

De Meuse, K. and Liebowitz, S. (1981) 'An empirical analysis of team-building research', *Group and Organization Studies*, **6**(3), 357–78.

Dingley, J. (1986) 'Recent developments in the area of motivation', *IMDS*, July/August, 21–4.

Dosier, L., Case, T. and Keys, B. (1988) 'How managers influence subordinates: An empirical study of downward influence tactics', *Leadership and Organization Development Journal*, **9**(5), 22–31.

Drucker, P. (1954) *The Practice of Management*, Harper and Row: New York.

Drucker, P. (1955) *The Practice of Management*, Heinemann: London.

Drucker, P. (1966) *The Effective Executive*, Harper and Row: New York.

Drummond, H. (1992) 'Another fine mess: Time for quality decision making', *Journal of General Management*, 18(1), 1–14.

DuBrin, A., Ireland, R. and Williams, J. (1989) *Management and Organization*, South-Western Publishing: Cincinnati, Ohio.

Dunphy, D. (1989) *Organisational Change by Choice*, McGraw-Hill: Sydney.

Dunphy, D. and Stace, D. (1990) *Under New Management: Australian Organisations in Transition*, McGraw-Hill: Sydney.

Dyer, W. (1977) *Team Building: Issues and Alternatives*, Addison-Wesley: Reading, Massachusetts.

Dyer, W. (1980) 'Group Behaviour' in Ritchie, J. and Thompson, P. (eds) *Organization and People*, West: St Paul, Minnesota.

Dyer, W. (1985) *Team Building: Issues and Alternatives* (Second Edition), Addison-Wesley: Reading, Massachusetts.

Eden, D. (1985) 'Team development: a true field experiment at three levels of rigour', *Journal of Applied Psychology*, **70**(1), 94–100.

Ends, E. and Page, C. (1977) *Organizational Team Building*, Winthrop: Cambridge, Massachussetts.

Etzioni, A. (1989) 'Humble decision making', *Harvard Business Review*, **67**, 122–6.

Everard, K. and Morris, G. (1985) *Effective School Management*, Harper and Row: London.

Feldman, J. (1984) 'The development and enforcement of group norms', *Academy of Management Review*, **9**, 47–53.

Fiedler, F. and Garcia, J. (1987) *New Approaches to Effective Leadership: Cognitive Resources and Organizational Performance*, Wiley: New York.

Francis, D. and Young, D. (1979) *Improving Work Groups: A Practical Manual for Teambuilding*, University Associates: La Jolla, California.

Frank, M. (1990) *How to Run a Successful Meeting in Half the Time*, Corgi: London.

Galbraith, J. and Kazanjian, R. (1986) *Strategy Implementation: Structure, Systems and Process*, West: St Paul, Minnesota.

George, P. (1987) 'Team building without tears', *Personnel Journal*, **66**(11), 122–9.

George, W. (1977) 'Task teams for rapid growth', *Harvard Business Review*, March/April, 71.

Gibson, J. and Hodgetts, R. (1986) *Organizational Communication: A Managerial Perspective*, Academic Press: Orlando, Florida.

Goldsmith, W. and Clutterbuck, D. (1984) *The Winning Streak*, Penguin: Harmondsworth, England.

Graham, P. (1991) *Integrative Management: Creating Unity from Diversity*, Blackwell: Oxford.

Greco, G. (1988) 'Teams score victories at work', *Nation's Business*, **76**(4), 38–40.

Greenberg, J. and Greenberg, H. (1988) 'Developing a winning team', *Agency Sales Magazine*, **18**(7), 56–60.

Griffin, R. (1984) *Management*, Houghton Mifflin: Boston, Massachusetts.

Handy, C. (1976) *Understanding Organisations*, Penguin: Harmondsworth, London.

Harris, P and Harris, D. (1989) 'High performance team management', *Leadership and Organization Development*, **10**(4), 28–32.

Harris, P. (1985) *Management in Transition*, Jossey-Bass: San Francisco, California.

Harris, P. (1986) 'Building a high performance team', *Training and Development Journal*, **40** (April), 28.

Hastings, C., Bixby, P. and Chaudhry-Lawton, R. (1986) *The Superteam Solution: Successful Teamworking in Organisations*, Gower: Aldershot, England.

Hellriegel, D., Slocum, J. and Woodman, R. (1989) *Organisational Behavior* (Fifth Edition), West: St Paul, Minnesota.

Hemphill, J. (1949) *Situational Factors in Leadership*, Bureau of Business Research, College of Commerce and Administration, Ohio State University: Columbus, Ohio.

Hersey, P. and Blanchard, K. (1977) *Management of Organization Behavior: Utilising Human Resources*, Prentice Hall: Englewood Cliffs, New Jersey.

Herzberg, F., Mausner, B. and Snyderman, B. (1959) *The Motivation to Work*, Wiley: New York.

Hitt, W. (1988) *The Leader-Manager: Guidelines for Action*, Battelle: Columbus, Ohio.

Hofstede, G. (1987) 'The applicability of McGregor's theories in South East Asia', *Journal of Management Development*, **6**(3), 9–18.

Hofstede, G. (1988) 'The Confucius connection: From cultural roots to economic growth', *Organisational Dynamics*, **17**, 4–21.

Holden, L. (1990) 'Teamwork: A delicate balance (Part II)', *Managers Magazine*, **65**(7), 19–21.

Holmes, G. (1992) 'Cooperative staff teams', *The Practising Administrator*, **14**(2), 8–9.

Horak, B., Guarino, J., Knight, C. and Kweder, S. (1991) 'Building a team on the medical floor', *Health Care Management Review*, **16**(2), 65–71.

House, R. and Mitchell, T. (1977) 'Path-Goal Theory of Leadership' in Davis, K. (ed.) *Organizational Behavior*, McGraw-Hill: New York.

Hoy, W. and Forsyth, P. (1986) *Effective Supervision: Theory into Practice*, Random House: New York.

Hoy, W. and Miskel, C. (1991) *Educational Administration*, McGraw-Hill: Singapore.

Hunt, J. (1979) *Managing People at Work*, Pan: London.

Hurst, D., Rush, J. and White, R. (1989) 'Top management teams and organizational renewal', *Strategic Management Journal*, **10** (Summer), 87.

Huse, E. (1980) *Organization Development and Change*, West: St Paul, Minnesota.

Huszczo, G. (1990) 'Training for team building', *Training and Development Journal*, **44**(2), 37–43.

Iacocca, L. with Novak, W. (1984) *Iacocca: An Autobiography*, Bantam: New York.

Jacobs, R. and Everett, J. (1988) 'The importance of team building in a high-tech environment', *Journal of European Industrial Training*, **12**(4), 10–16.

Janis, I. (1971) 'Groupthink', *Psychology Today*, November, 43–6.

Janis, I. (1982) *Groupthink: Psychological Studies of Policy Decisions*, Houghton Mifflin: Boston, Massachusetts.

Janis, I. (1985) 'Sources of Error in Strategic Decision Making' in Pennings, J. (ed.) *Organizational Strategy and Change*, Jossey-Bass: San Francisco, California.

Janis, I. and Mann, L. (1977) *Decision Making: A Psychological Analysis of Conflict, Choice, and Commitment*, Free Press: New York.

Jessup, H. (1990) 'New roles in team leadership', *Training and Development Journal*, **44**(11), 79–83.

Jessup, H. (1992) 'The road to results for teams', *Training and Development Journal*, **46**(9), 65–8.

Jewell, L. and Reitz, H. (1981) *Group Effectiveness in Organizations*, Scott Foresman: Glenview, Illinois.

Johnson, C. (1986) 'An outline for team building: cooperation, collaboration and communication are the ingredients of an effective team', *Training: The Magazine of Human Resources Development*, **23** (January), 48.

Johnson, D. and Johnson, F. (1991) *Joining Together: Group Theory and Group Skills*, Prentice Hall: Englewood Cliffs, New Jersey.

Jones, C. (1970) *An Introduction to the Study of Public Policy*, Duxbury Press: Belmont, California.

Kanter, R. (1983) *The Change Masters*, Random House: New York.

Kaplan, R., Lombardo, M. and Mazique, M. (1985) 'A mirror for managers: Using simulation to develop management teams', *Journal of Applied Behavioural Science*, **21**(3), 241–53.

Karp, K. (1987) 'The Lost Art of Feedback' in Pfeiffer, J. (ed.) *The 1987 Annual: Developing Human Resources*, University Associates: San Diego, California.

Kazemek, E. (1991) 'Ten criteria for effective team building', *Healthcare Financial Management*, **45**(9), 15.

Kazemek, E. and Albert, B. (1988) 'Learning the secret to teamwork', *Healthcare Financial Management*, **42**(9), 108–10.

Keidel, R. (1985) *Game Plans. Sports Strategies for Business*, Dutton: New York.

Kepner, C. and Tregoe, B. (1965) *The Rational Manager*, McGraw-Hill: New York.

Keys, B. and Case, T. (1990) 'How to become an influential manager', *Academy of Management Executive*, **4**(4), 38–51.

Kezsbom, D. (1990) 'Are you really ready to build a project team?', *Industrial Engineering*, **22**(10), 50–5.

Kidder, T. (1981) *The Soul of a New Machine*, Little, Brown: New York.

Kipnis, D., Schmidt, S. and Wilkinson, I. (1980) 'Intraorganizational influence tactics: Explorations in getting one's way', *Journal of Applied Psychology*, **65**(4), 440–52.

Kipnis, D., Schmidt, S., Swaffin-Smith, C. and Wilkinson, I. (1984) 'Patterns of managerial influence: shotgun managers, tacticians and bystanders', *Organizational Dynamics*, Winter, 58–67.

Kirkpatrick, T. and Smith, B. (1991) 'Team development for real', *Industrial and Commercial Training*, **23**(4), 3–8.

Kizilos, T. and Heinisch, R. (1986) 'How a management team selects managers', *Harvard Business Review*, September/October, 6.

Koehler, K. (1989) 'Effective team management', *Small Business Reports*, **14**(7), 14–6.

Koontz, H. and Weihrich, H. (1988) *Management* (Ninth Edition), McGraw-Hill: Singapore.

Kotter, J. (1982) *The General Managers*, Free Press: New York.

Kotter, J. (1990) *A Force for Change: How Leadership Differs from Management*, Free Press: New York.

Laabs, J. (1991) 'Team training goes outdoors', *Personnel Journal*, **70**(6), 56–63.

Lanza, P. (1985) 'Team appraisals', *Personnel Journal*, **64** (March), 47.

Larson, P. (1989) 'Winning strategies', *Canadian Business Review*, **16** (Summer), 40.

Lau, B. (1988) 'Reducing job stress through team building and positive management, part II', *Management Quarterly*, **29** (Winter), 13.

Lawler, E. and Mohrman, S. (1987) 'Quality circles: After the honeymoon', *Organizational Dynamics*, Spring, 42–54.

Le Due, A. (1980) 'Motivation of programmers', *Data Base*, Summer, 4–12.

Leavitt, H. (1978) *Managerial Psychology*, University of Chicago Press: Chicago, Illinois.

Leavitt, H. and Bahrami, H. (1988) *Managerial Psychology: Managing Behavior in Organizations* (Fifth Edition), University of Chicago Press: Chicago, Illinois.

Leithwood, K. (1992) 'The move towards transformational leadership', *Educational Leadership*, **49**(5), 8–12.

Leong, W. (1990) 'Problem Solving Simulation' in Low, G., Chong, K., Leong, W. and Walker, A. (eds) *Developing Executive Skills*, Longman: Singapore.

Lewin, K. (1951) *Field Theory in Social Science*, Harper and Row: New York.

Lewis, M. and Kelly, G. (1986) *20 Activities for Developing Managerial Effectiveness*, Gower: Aldershot, England.

Limerick, D., Cunnington, B. and Trevor-Roberts, B. (1985) *Frontiers of Excellence*, Australian Institute of Management: Queensland.

Lindblom, C. (1959) 'The science of muddling through', *Public Administrative Review*, **19**, 79–99.

Lindelow, J. and Scott, J. (1989) 'Managing Conflict' in Smith, S. and Piele, P. (eds) *School Leadership: Handbook for Excellence*, ERIC: Oregon.

Looram, J. (1985) 'The transition meeting: taking over a new management team', *Supervisory Management*, **30**(9), 29–36.

Loton, B. (1991) 'Reflections: Good management beyond the nineties', *The Practising Manager*, **11**(2), 27–31.

Low, G. (1990) 'Conflict Management Simulation' in Low, G., Chong, C., Leong, W. and Walker, A. (eds) *Developing Executive Skills*, Longman: Singapore.

Lussier, R. (1990) *Human Relations in Organizations*, Irwin: Homewood, Illinois.

Maddux, R. (1988) *Teambuilding: An Exercise in Leadership*, Crisp: Los Altos, California.

Maier, N. (1963) *Problem Solving Discussions and Conferences*, McGraw-Hill: New York.

March, J. and Simon, H. (1958) *Organizations*, Wiley: New York.

Margerison, C. (1973) *Effective Work Groups*, McGraw-Hill: England.

Margerison, C. (1974) *Managerial Problem Solving*, McGraw-Hill: England.

Margerison, C., McCann, D. and Davies, R. (1988) 'Air-crew team management development', *Journal of Management Development*, **7**(4), 41–54.

Margerison, M. and McCann, D. (1985) *How to Lead a Winning Team*, MCB University Press: Bradford, England.

Margerison, M. and McCann, D. (1989) 'How to improve team management', *Leadership and Organization Development Journal*, **10**(5), 4–42.

Maslow, A. (1954) *Motivation and Personality*, Harper and Row: New York.

Maxwell, J. (1990) 'Managing human resources in the 1990s: International perspectives', *The Practising Manager*, **10**(2), 9–14.

McCall, M., Lombardo, M. and Morrison, A. (1988) *The Lessons of Experience: How Successful Executives Develop on the Job*, Lexington: Massachusetts.

McCann, D. and Margerison, C. (1989) 'Managing high performance teams', *Training and Development Journal*, **43** (November), 52.

McClelland, D. (1961) *The Achieving Society*, Van Nostrand: Princeton, New Jersey.

McClenahen, J. (1990) 'Not fun in the sun', *Industry Week*, Issue 239, 20, 22–4.

McLagan, P. (1989) 'Models for HRD practice', *Training and Development Journal*, September, 49–59.

Meyer, G. (1991) 'Analyzing a team's dynamics before hiring the team', *Information Strategy: The Executive's Journal*, **7**(3), 40–3.

Miller, B. and Phillips, R. (1986) 'Team building on a deadline', *Training and Development Journal*, **40** (March), 54.

Miller, J. and Longair, R. (1985) *New Directions in Middle Management – A Dilemma*, Australian Institute of Management: Victoria, Australia.

Mintzberg, H. (1973) *The Nature of Managerial Work*, Harper and Row: New York.

Mondy, R. and Noe, R. (1990) *Human Resource Management* (Fourth Edition), Allyn and Bacon: Boston.

Moore, J. (1988) 'Guidelines concerning adult learning', *Journal of Staff Development*, **9**(3), 2–5.

Morris, W. and Sashkin, M. (1976) *Organization Behavior in Action: Skill-Building Experiences*, West: St Paul, Minnesota.

Mossman, A. (1982) 'Management Training for Real', unpublished address to the 1982 Conference of The Institute of Personnel Management, Harrogate, England.

Mossman, A. (1983) 'Making choices about the use of the outdoors in manager and management development', *Management Education and Development*, **14**(3), 182–96.

Mossop, M. (1988) 'Total teamwork: How to be a leader, how to be a member', *Management Solutions*, **33** (August), 3.

Mukhi, S., Hampton, D. and Barnwell, N. (1988) *Australian Management*, McGraw-Hill: Sydney.

Mullins, L. (1985) *Managing Organizational Behavior*, Pitman: London.

Nadler, D. and Lawler, E. (1983) 'Motivation: A Diagnostic Approach' in Hackman, R., Lawler, E. and Porter, L. (eds) *Perspectives on Behaviour in Organisations* (Second Edition), McGraw-Hill: New York.

Naisbitt, J. (1982) *Ten New Directions Transforming Our Lives: Megatrends*, Futura: London.

Newsom, W. (1990) 'Motivate now', *Personnel Journal*, February, 51–5.

Noone, L. (1984) *The Social Manager*, HRA: London.

O'Mahoney, T. (1984) 'Human Motivation: A Review of Theories and an Attempted Integration', unpublished paper, Luton College of Higher Education: Luton, England.

Osborn, A. (1957) *Applied Imagination*, Scribner: New York.

Ouchi, W. (1981). *Theory Z: How American Business Can Meet the Japanese Challenge*, Addison-Wesley: Boston.

Owens, R. (1987) *Organizational Behaviour in Education*, Prentice Hall: Englewood Cliffs, New Jersey.

Owens, T. (1989) 'Business teams', *Small Business Reports*, 14(1), 52–8.

Peters, T. and Waterman, R. (1982) *In Search of Excellence*, Harper and Row: New York.

Peterson, D. (1991) *Teamwork: New Management Ideas for the Nineties*, Victor Gollancz: London.

Petrock, F. (1990) 'Five stages of team development', *Executive Excellence*, 7(6), 9–10.

Petrock, F. (1991) 'Ford's teamwork training gets employees involved', *Human Resources Professional*, 3(3), 30–2.

Porter, L. and Lawler, E. (1968) *Managerial Attitudes and Performance*, Dorsey Press: Homewood, Illinois.

Pruitt, D. (1983) 'Achieving integrative agreements' in Bazerman, M. and Lewicki, R. (eds) *Negotiating in Organizations*, Sage: Beverly Hills, California.

Ramsay, L., Samson, D. and Sokal, A. (1991) 'Quality Management Practices in Australian Industry' in *TQMI Conference 91*, Monash University Printing Services: Melbourne, 5–20.

Rawlinson, J. (1986) *Creative Thinking and Brainstorming*, Wildwood House: Aldershot, England.

Reddin, W. (1967) 'The 3-D management style theory: A typology based on task and relationships-orientation', *Training and Development Journal*, 21 (April).

Rees, W. (1988) *The Skills of Management* (Second Edition), Routledge: London.

Richards, D. (1991) 'Flying against the wind? Culture and management development in Southeast Asia', *Journal of Management Development*, 10(6), 7–21.

Rigby, J. (1987) 'The challenge of multinational team development', *Journal of Management Development*, 6(3), 65–72.

Robbins, S. (1974) *Managing Organizational Conflict: A Nontraditional Approach*, Prentice Hall: Englewood Cliffs, New Jersey.

Robbins, S. (1991) *Organizational Behavior: Concepts, Controversies and Applications*, Prentice Hall: Englewood Cliffs, New Jersey.

Roberts, K. and Hunt, D. (1991) *Organizational Behavior*, PWS-Kent: Boston.

Robinson, D. (1990) 'Blueprint for human resource development', *World Executive Digest*, January, 37, 40.

Sashkin, M. and Morris, W. (1984) *Organizational Behavior: Concepts and Experiences*, Reston Publishing: Reston, Virginia.

Scannell, E. (1992) 'We've got to stop meeting like this', *Training and Development Journal*, **46**(1), 70–1.

Schermerhorn, J., Hunt, J. and Osborn, R. (1991) *Managing Organizational Behavior*, Wiley: New York.

Schmidt, W. and Tannenbaum, R. (1972) 'Management of Differences' in Burke, W. and Hornstein, H. (eds) *The Social Technology of Organization Development*, University Associates: La Jolla, California.

Schneider, S. (1988) 'National vs corporate culture: Implications for human resource management', *Human Resource Management*, Summer.

Schriesheim, C. and Neider, L. (1989) 'Leadership theory and development', *Leadership and Organization Development Journal*, **10**(6), 17–25.

Schutz, W. (1989) 'Real teamwork', *Executive Excellence*, **6**(10), 7–9.

Seiler, R. and Said, K. (1983) 'Problems encountered in operationalising a company's strategic plans', *Managerial Planning*, **31**(4), 16–20.

Senge, P. (1990) *The Fifth Dimension: The Art and Practice of the Learning Organization*, Doubleday: New York.

Sergiovanni, T. (1990) *Value Added Leadership*, Harcourt Brace Jovanovich: New York.

Shonk, W. and Shonk, J. (1988) 'What business teams can learn from athletic teams', *Personnel*, **65**(6), 76–80.

Simon, H. (1951) *Administrative Behaviour*, Macmillan: New York.

Simon, H. (1971) 'The New Science of Management Decisions' in Welch, L. and Cyert, R. (eds) *Management and Decision Making*, Penguin: Harmondsworth, England.

Simon, H. (1980) 'Decision Making and Organisational Design' in Connor, P. (ed) *Organizations: Theory and Design*, SCA: Chicago, Illinois.

Simpson, W. (no date) *The Manager's Guide to Target Setting*, Donald: London.

Snyder, K. (1988) *Competency Training for Managing Productive Schools*, Harcourt Brace Jovanovich: San Diego, California.

Staff, A. (1990) 'Take me to your leader', *The Economist*, 2 June, 67.

Stewart, R. (1986) *The Reality of Management*, Pan: London.

Stogdill, R. (1948) 'Personal factors associated with leadership: A survey of the literature', *Journal of Psychology*, **25**, 35–71.

Stott, K. and Walker, A. (1991) 'Effective task completion: The 7D model of planning', *The Practising Administrator*, **13**(1), 45–8.

Stott, K. and Walker, A. (1992a) *Making Management Work: A Practical Approach*, Prentice Hall: Singapore.

Stott, K. and Walker, A. (1992b) 'Ruining or developing team-work – Take your choice', *The Practisng Manager*, **13**(1), 25–7.

Straits Times (1992) 'NOL to punish persistently late executives', 9 March.

Straits Times (1992) 'Power to the staff', 9 April.

Straits Times (1992) 'QCC', 6 August.

Tack, A. (1986) *The High Quality Manager*, Gower: Aldershot, England.

Tannenbaum, R. and Schmidt, W. (1958) 'How to choose a leadership pattern', *Harvard Business Review* , **36** (March/April), 95–101.

Tarkenton, F. (1986) 'Tarkenton on teambuilding', *Management Solutions,* **31** (October), 30.

Teire, J. (1982) 'Working together: A practical look at teambuilding', *Industrial and Commercial Training,* **14**(6), 201–6.

Thamhain, H. (1990) 'Managing technologically innovative team efforts toward new product success', *Journal of Product Information Management,* **7**(1), 5–18.

Thomas, K. (1976) 'Conflict and Conflict Management' in Dunnette, M. (ed.) *The Handbook of Industrial and Organisational Psychology*, Rand McNally: Chicago, Illinois.

Tichy, N. and Devanna, M. (1986) *The Transformational Leader*, Wiley: New York.

Timmons, J. (1979) 'Careful self-analysis and team assessment can aid entrepreneurs', *Harvard Business Review*, November/December, 198.

Todryk, L. (1990) 'The project manager as team builder: Creating an effective team', *Project Management Journal*, **21**(4), 17–22.

Tolle, E. (1988) 'Management team building: Yes but!', *Engineering Management International*, **4**(4), 277–85.

Torrington, D. (1982) *Face to Face in Management*, Prentice Hall: London.

Torrington, D., Weightman, J. and Johns, K. (1989) *Effective Management: People and Organisation*, Prentice Hall: Hemel Hempstead, England.

Tuckman, B. and Jensen, M. (1977) 'Stages of small-group development revisited', *Group and Organizational Studies*, 419–27.

Video Arts Ltd (1984) *So You Think You Can Manage?*, Methuen: London.

Vroom, V. and Yetton, P. (1973) *Leadership and Decisionmaking*, University of Pittsburgh Press: Pittsburgh, Pennsylvania.

Walker, A. and Stott, K. (1992) 'The Use of Senior Management Teams in Educational Institutions', unpublished paper presented at Educational Research Association Conference, Singapore, September.

Walker, W. (1991) 'Tight Ship to Tight Flotilla: The First Century of Scholarship in Educational Administration', invited address to the American Educational Research Association, April, Chicago, Illinois.

Wallach, M. and Kogan, N. (1965) 'The roles of information, discussion, and consensus in group risk taking', *Journal of Experimental Social Psychology*, **1**, 1–19.

Watkins, P. (1989) 'Leadership, Power and Symbols in Educational Administration' in Smyth, J. (ed.) *Critical Perspectives on Educational Leadership*, Falmer: New York.

Watson, C. (1981) *Results-Oriented Management: The Key to Effective Performance*, Addison-Wesley: Reading, Massachusetts.

Watts, B. (1988) *Creating the Hands-On Manager*, Mercury: London.

Weisbord, M. (1985) 'Team effectiveness theory', *Training and Development Journal*, **39**(1), 27–9.

Welsh, A. (1980) *The Skills of Management*, Gower: Aldershot, England.

Westcott, J. (1988) 'Humor and the Effective Workgroup' in Pfeiffer, J. (ed.) *The 1988 Annual: Developing Human Resources*, University Associates: San Diego, California.

Whetten, D. and Cameron, K. (1984) *Developing Management Skills*, Scott Foresman: Glenview, Illinois.

Whyte, G. (1991) 'Decision failures: Why they occur and how to prevent them', *Academy of Management Executive*, 5(3), 23–31.

Whyte, W. (1956) *The Organization Man*, Simon & Schuster: New York.

Wolff, M. (1988) 'Before you try team building', *Research Technology Management*, 31(1), 6–8.

Woodcock, M. (1979) *Team Development Manual*, Gower: Aldershot, England.

Woodcock, M. (1989) *Team Development Manual* (Second Edition), Gower: Brookfield, Vermont.

Woodcock, M. and Francis, D. (1982) *The Unblocked Manager*, Gower: Aldershot, England.

Woods, M. and Thomas, E. (1990) 'The practical application of Interplace II', *Industrial and Commercial Training (UK)*, 22(5), 17–23.

Wynn, R. and Guditus, C. (1984) *Team Management: Leadership by Consensus*, Charles E Merrill: Columbus, Ohio.

Yukl, G. (1981) *Leadership in Organizations*, Prentice Hall: Englewood Cliffs, New Jersey.

Yukl, G. (1989) *Leadership in Organizations*, Prentice Hall: Englewood Cliffs, New Jersey.

Zapp, T. (1987) 'How to build a winning team: Here's a refresher course in good old-fashioned teamwork', *Managers Magazine*, 62 (June), 7.

Zenger, J. and Miller, D. (1974) 'Building effective teams', *Personnel*, 51(2), 20–9.

INDEX

THE AUTHORS

KENNETH STOTT is a university lecturer with wide experience of leading development programmes for managers from both public and private sectors. Currently based in the UK at Middlesex University, he has also worked in university education in Southeast Asia. His publications with Allan Walker include *Making Management Work: A Practical Approach* and *The Fabulous Manager*, both of which have received wide acclaim from students and teachers of management and from practising managers. He has written widely for the international management literature and is a regular contributor to international conferences. His work in the area of team development is highly regarded and he has worked successfully with organisations seeking to improve the quality of their teamwork. His background also includes experience of working with teams on the international sporting scene.

ALLAN WALKER is a university lecturer with broad experience in developing, coordinating and teaching management development courses for senior educational managers in Australia and the Asia-Pacific region. He has experience working in universities in the USA, Singapore and Australia and is currently working at the Northern Territory University in Darwin, Australia. He has coauthored three books with Kenneth Stott, edited a number of other volumes and is a regular contributor to scholarly and practitioner journals. He has acted as consultant for various educational bodies in Australia and Southeast Asia. His current interests include issues related to teams, organisational change, strategic planning and practical management skills.